Concise Guide to

Critical Thinking

Concise Guide to

Critical Thinking

Lewis Vaughn

New York Oxford
OXFORD UNIVERSITY PRESS

Oxford University Press is a department of the University of Oxford. It furthers the University's objective of excellence in research, scholarship, and education by publishing worldwide. Oxford is a registered trade mark of Oxford University Press in the UK and certain other countries.

Published in the United States of America by Oxford University Press
198 Madison Avenue, New York, NY 10016, United States of America.

Library of Congress Cataloging-in-Publication Data
Names: Vaughn, Lewis, author.
Title: Concise guide to critical thinking / by Lewis Vaughn.
Description: New York : Oxford University Press, 2017. | Includes index.
Identifiers: LCCN 2017008092 | ISBN 9780190692896 (student edition)
Subjects: LCSH: Critical thinking.
Classification: LCC BC177 .V379 2017 | DDC 160--dc23 LC record available at https://lccn.loc.gov/2017008092

9 8 7 6 5 4 3
Printed by LSC Communications, United States of America

Contents

Preface

MANY INSTRUCTORS TEACHING CRITICAL THINKING WANT A LARGE TEXTBOOK THAT covers most or all of the traditional ground—the fundamentals of argument, categorical and propositional logic, inductive logic, scientific reasoning, evidence and experts, and argumentative writing. My own *Power of Critical Thinking*, 5th edition, is in this category, and like many other such texts it is over five hundred pages long, has four-color graphics, and features a wide range of pedagogical aids—examples, exercises, text boxes, writing prompts, chapter objectives, and more. But there are many teachers who favor a smaller, less rigorous text that nonetheless provides students with the basics of critical thinking and argumentative writing. Some who teach critical thinking do not want to cover all the material found in the larger texts, and some who teach introductory philosophy courses want a smaller supplemental textbook that helps prepare students for philosophical thinking and writing.

Now for those who prefer a more compact text, there is the *Concise Guide to Critical Thinking*. It's a shorter, less expensive textbook that covers all the fundamentals of critical thinking and writing and does so as clearly and directly as possible. For instructors it's more manageable than the larger books but more substantial than many of the smaller critical thinking handbooks.

The *Concise Guide* includes the following:

- **Six chapters on identifying, evaluating, and devising deductive and inductive arguments**. There's substantial coverage of common deductive argument patterns, inductive arguments and statistics (including enumerative induction, argument by analogy, and opinion polls), causal arguments, moral and legal arguments, and long and complex arguments.
- **Comprehensive coverage of inference to the best explanation.** This textbook devotes two chapters to inference to the best explanation because (1) it is probably the type of inference that students use most, (2) it can be especially fertile ground for diverse cases and examples that students are likely to find intriguing, and (3) it implies a framework for thinking about claims and theories as well as a method for assessing their worth. Step-by-step instructions and plentiful examples show students how to use this

kind of inference to assess theories and claims in science, pseudoscience, ethics, medicine, the media, and popular culture.

- **A chapter on obstacles to critical thinking.** Chapter 2 contains a review of many of the factors that may impede critical thinking—bias, habit, tradition, emotion, skewed perceptions, rationalizations, and certain philosophical outlooks. Along with explanations of how these factors affect thinking are suggestions on how to avoid or minimize them.

- **Extensive treatment of scientific reasoning.** The book offers a chapter each on inductive reasoning, causal arguments, scientific theories and inference, and scientific method and theory evaluation. Extended examples show how scientific reasoning applies to an array of questions in many scientific fields, everyday life, and even the realm of extraordinary phenomena.

- **Emphasis on evaluation of evidence, authority, and credibility.** Throughout this text (and especially in chapter 6), considerable ink is expended to show students how to assess the evidence and claims proffered by scientists and other experts, the news media, advertising, and everyday experience. In each case, the relevant principles or procedures are explained and illustrated. The chapter even provides a reasoned response to the so-called posttruth media environment and the plague of "fake news."

- **A chapter on fallacies and rhetorical persuaders**, covering an extensive list of fallacies of irrelevant premises, fallacies of unacceptable premises, and rhetorical techniques of persuasion.

- **A substantial chapter on writing argumentative essays.** It covers the steps involved in planning, researching, writing, and revising a paper as well as material on style and content. Topics include essay structure, thesis, outlining, revising drafts, and more. An annotated sample paper is included.

- **Plenty of exercises**, with selected answers in the back of the book. These include review questions, exercises for applying critical thinking skills, writing assignments and prompts, and self-assessment quizzes—end-of-chapter tests (with answers) that allow students to gauge their understanding of the material.

Acknowledgments

MANY REVIEWERS HELPED MAKE THIS BOOK BETTER THAN IT WOULD HAVE BEEN otherwise. I'm happy to thank the following for all their judicious criticism and insightful ideas:

Carlos A. Colombetti, Skyline College
Sharon Crasnow, Riverside Community College, Norco
Susie Crowson, Del Mar College
Jeffrey Fry, Ball State University
Marianna Bergamaschi Ganapini, Johns Hopkins University
Cynthia Gobatie, Riverside City College
Chris Kramer, Rock Valley College
John M. Ludes, University of Nevada, Las Vegas
Marlisa Moschella, University of Nevada, Las Vegas
Gregory Salmieri, Lecturer at Rutgers University
Eldar Sarajlic, Assistant Professor at CUNY BMCC
Nicholas Ryan Smith, Assistant Professor at BMCC, CUNY
Karl Stocker, Professor at ECSU
Ted Stryk, Roane State Community College
Corine Sutherland, Cerritos Community College
Johnnie Terry, Sierra College
Beverly J. Whelton, Wheeling Jesuit University

CHAPTER

1

Critical Thinking, Facts, and Feelings

YOU CAME INTO THIS WORLD WITHOUT OPINIONS OR JUDGMENTS OR VALUES OR viewpoints—and now your head is brimming with them. If you tried to write them all down, you would be busy for the rest of your life (and would probably win an award for being the world's biggest bore). They help you make your way through the world. They guide you to both failure and success, ignorance and understanding, good and bad, paralysis and empowerment. Some of your beliefs truly inform you, and some blind you. Some are true; some are not. But the question is, *which ones are which*? This kind of question—a question about the *quality* of your beliefs—is the fundamental concern of **critical thinking**.

Determining the quality or value of your beliefs is a function of thinking, and the kind of thinking that does this job best is critical thinking—a skill that higher education seeks to foster. This means that critical thinking is not about *what* you think, but *how* you think.

Notice also that the question about the quality of beliefs is not about what factors *caused* you to have the beliefs that you do. A sociologist might tell you how society has influenced some of your moral choices. A psychologist might describe how your emotions cause you to cling to certain opinions. Your best friend might allege that you have unconsciously absorbed most of your beliefs directly from your parents. But none of these speculations have much to do with the central task of critical thinking.

Critical thinking focuses not on what *causes* a belief, but on *whether it is worth believing*. A belief is worth believing, or accepting, if we have *good reasons* to accept it. The better the reasons for acceptance, the more likely the belief is to be true. Critical thinking offers us a set of standards embodied in techniques, attitudes, and principles that we can use to assess beliefs and determine if they are supported by good reasons. After all, we want our beliefs to be true, to be good

1

guides for dealing with the world—and critical thinking is the best tool we have for achieving this goal.

Here's one way to wrap up these points in a concise definition:

> **CRITICAL THINKING:** The systematic evaluation or formulation of beliefs, or statements, by rational standards.

Critical thinking is *systematic* because it involves distinct procedures and methods. It entails *evaluation* and *formulation* because it's used to both assess existing beliefs (yours or someone else's) and devise new ones. And it operates according to *rational standards* in that beliefs are judged by how well they are supported by reasons.

Critical thinking, of course, involves **logic**. Logic is the study of good reasoning, or inference, and the rules that govern it. Critical thinking is broader than logic because it involves not only logic but also the truth or falsity of statements, the evaluation of arguments and evidence, the use of analysis and investigation, and the application of many other skills that help us decide what to believe or do.

Ultimately, what critical thinking leads you to is knowledge, understanding, and—if you put these to work—empowerment. In addition, as you're guided by your instructor through this text, you will come to appreciate some other benefits that cannot be fully explored now: Critical thinking enables problem solving, active learning, and intelligent self-improvement.

Why It Matters

In large measure, our lives are defined by our actions and choices, and our actions and choices are guided by our thinking—so our thinking had better be good. Almost every day we are hit by a blizzard of assertions, opinions, arguments, and pronouncements from all directions. They all implore us to believe, to agree, to accept, to follow, to submit. If we care whether our choices are right and our beliefs true, if we want to rise above blind acceptance and arbitrary choices, we must use the tools provided by critical thinking.

We, of course, always have the option of taking the easy way out. We can simply glom onto whatever beliefs or statements come blowing by in the wind, adopting viewpoints because they are favored by others or because they make us feel good. But then we forfeit control over our lives and let the wind take us wherever it will, as if we had no more say in the outcome than a leaf in a storm.

A consequence, then, of going with the wind is a loss of personal freedom. If you passively accept beliefs that have been handed to you by your parents, your culture, or your teachers, then those beliefs are *not really yours*. You just happened to be in a certain place and time when they were handed out. If they are not really yours, and you let them guide your choices and actions, then they—not you—are in charge of your life. Your beliefs are yours only if you critically examine them for yourself to see if they are supported by good reasons.

To examine your beliefs in this way is to examine your life, for your beliefs in large measure define your life. To forgo such scrutiny is to abandon your chance of making your life deliberately and authentically meaningful. The great philosopher Socrates says it best: "The unexamined life is not worth living."

Thus, in the most profound sense, critical thinking is not only enlightening but also empowering. This empowerment can take several forms:

Skills for learning and exploring. Some species of critical thinking is essential in every intellectual endeavor, every profession, and every college course. Economics, literature, philosophy, ethics, science, medicine, law—these and many other fields require you to understand and use argument, evaluation, analysis, logic, and evidence. Critical thinking is the common language of many worlds, and practicing it will help you make your way in them.

Defense against error, manipulation, and prejudice. For lack of good critical thinking, many intelligent people have been taken in by clever marketers, dubious "experts," fake news, self-serving politicians, charming demagogues, skillful propagandists, dishonest bloggers, wooly conspiracy theorists, misguided gurus, knee-jerk partisans, and alarmist xenophobes. For want of a little logic and careful reflection, you can easily choose the wrong career, wrong friends, wrong spouse, wrong investments, wrong religion, and wrong leaders. Without some skill in moral reasoning (critical thinking applied to ethics), you risk making bad decisions about right and wrong, about good and bad. Critical thinking is no guarantee against any of these errors, but it does provide your best possible defense.

Tools for self-discovery. A central goal of higher education is to enable students to think critically and carefully for themselves, to confront issues and problems and then devise their own warranted, defensible answers. This means you must be able not only to critically examine the arguments and assertions of others but also to apply these critical powers to your own ideas. To discover what to believe—that is, to find out which claims are worthy of belief—you must weigh them in the balance of critical reasoning. A central question of a mature intellect is, "What should I believe?" This is the fundamental query at the heart of all your conscious life choices. Only you can answer it, and ultimately only critical thinking can guide you to justified answers.

Critical thinking applies not just to some of your individual beliefs but to all of them together. It applies to your worldview, the vast web of fundamental ideas that help you make sense of the world, what some people call a philosophy

In January 2017, Reuters news service published a pair of photos showing the relative size of the crowds attending Donald Trump's presidential inauguration and Barack Obama's January 2009 inauguration. The Obama crowds appeared much larger than Trump's. President Trump quickly berated the "dishonest media" for making the attendance at his inauguration seem small by comparison, and his new White House spokesman Sean Spicer asserted that some in the media were guilty of "deliberately false reporting." Who was right? What critical thinking skills would you have used to determine the facts?

of life. We all have a worldview, and most of us want the beliefs that constitute it to be true and coherent (to fit together without internal contradictions). Devising a coherent worldview is the work of a lifetime—and can only be done with the help of critical thinking.

Our choice whether to apply critical thinking skills is not an all-or-nothing decision. All of us use critical thinking to some degree in our lives. We often evaluate reasons for (and against) believing that someone has committed a crime, that an earnest celebrity is deluded, that one candidate in an election is better than another, that gun control laws should be strengthened or weakened, that we should buy a car, that the legendary Bigfoot does not exist, that a friend is trustworthy, that one university is superior to another, that the bill being considered in Congress would be bad for the environment, that Elvis is living the good life in a witness-protection program. But the more urgent consideration is not just whether we sometimes use critical thinking, but how well we use it.

Many people, however, will have none of this—and perhaps you are one of them. They believe that critical thinking—or what they take to be critical thinking—makes one excessively critical or cynical, emotionally cold, and creatively constrained.

For example, there are some who view anything that smacks of logic and rationality as a negative enterprise designed to attack someone else's thinking and score points by putting people in their place. A few of these take the word *critical* here to mean "fault-finding" or "carping."

Now, no doubt some people try to use critical thinking primarily for offensive purposes, but this approach goes against critical thinking principles. The *critical* in critical thinking is used in the sense of "exercising or involving careful judgment or judicious evaluation." Critical thinking is about determining what we are justified in believing, and that involves an openness to other points of view, a tolerance for opposing perspectives, a focus on the issue at hand, and fair assessments of arguments and evidence. To paraphrase a bumper-sticker slogan: Good critical thinking does not make cynics—people make cynics.

Some people fear that if they apply critical thinking to their lives, they will become cold and unemotional—just like a computer abuzz with logic and rote functions. But this is a confused notion. Critical thinking and feelings actually complement one another. Certainly part of thinking critically is ensuring that we don't let our emotions distort our judgments. But critical thinking can also help us clarify our feelings and deal with them more effectively. Our emotions often need the guidance of reason. Likewise, our reasoning needs our emotions. It is our feelings that motivate us to action, and without motivation our reasoning would never get off the ground.

Then there's this dubious assumption: Critical thinking is the enemy of creativity. To some people, critical thinking is a sterile and rigid mode of thought that constrains the imagination, hobbles artistic vision, and prevents "thinking outside the box." But critical thinking and creative thinking are not opposed to one another. Good critical thinkers can let their imaginations run free just like anyone else. They can create and enjoy poetry, music, art, literature, movies, social media, and plain old fun in the same way and to the same degree as the rest of the world. Critical thinking can complement creative thinking because it is needed to assess and enhance the creation. Scientists, for example, often dream up some very fanciful theories (which are an important part of doing science). These theories pop into their heads in the same sort of ways that the ideas for a great work of art appear in the mind of its creator. But then scientists use all of their critical thinking skills to evaluate what they have produced (as artists sometimes do)—and this critical examination enables them to select the most promising theories and to weed out those that are unworkable. Critical thinking perfects the creation.

In a very important sense, critical thinking is thinking outside the box. When we passively absorb the ideas we encounter, when we refuse to consider any alternative explanations or theories, when we conform our ideas to the wishes of the group, when we let our thinking be controlled by bias and stereotypes and superstition and wishful thinking—we are deep, deep in the box. But we rise above all that when we have the courage to think critically. When we are willing to let our beliefs be tried in the court of critical reason, we open ourselves to new possibilities, the dormant seeds of creativity.

Critical thinking covers a lot of territory. It is used across the board in all disciplines, all areas of public life, all the sciences, all sectors of business, and all vocations. It has played a major role in all the great endeavors of humankind—scientific discoveries, technological innovations, philosophical insights, social and political movements, literary creation and criticism, judicial and legal reasoning, democratic nation building, and more. The *lack* of critical thinking has also left its mark. The great tragedies of history—the wars, massacres, holocausts, tyrannies, bigotries, epidemics, and witch hunts—grew out of famines of the mind where clear, careful thinking was much too scarce.

Claims and Reasons

Critical thinking is a rational, systematic process that we apply to beliefs of all kinds. As we use the term here, *belief* is just another word for statement, or claim. A **statement** is an assertion that something is or is not the case. The following are statements:

- A triangle has three sides.
- I am cold.
- You are a liar.
- You are not a liar.
- I see blue spots before my eyes.
- $7 + 5 = 12$
- You should never hit your mother with a shovel.
- The best explanation for his behavior is that he was in a trance.
- Rap music is better than punk rock.
- There are black holes in space.

So statements, or claims, are the kinds of things that are either true or false. They assert that some state of affairs is or is not actual. You may know that a specific statement is true, or you may not. There may be no way to find out at the time if the statement is true or false. There may be no one who believes the statement. But it would be a statement nonetheless.

Some sentences, though, do *not* express statements:

- Does a triangle have three sides?
- Is God all-powerful?
- Turn that music off.

- Stop telling lies.
- Hey, dude.
- Great balls of fire!

The first two sentences are questions. The second two are commands or requests. The fifth sentence is a greeting. The sixth one is an exclamation. None asserts that something is or is not the case.

When you're engaged in critical thinking, you're mostly either evaluating statements or formulating them. In both cases your primary task is to figure out how strongly to believe them. The strength of your belief should depend on the quality of the reasons in favor of the statements. Statements backed by good reasons are worthy of strong acceptance. Statements that fall short of this standard deserve weaker acceptance.

Sometimes you may not be able to assign any substantial weight at all to the reasons for or against a statement. There simply may not be enough evidence to decide rationally. Generally when that happens, good critical thinkers don't arbitrarily choose to accept or reject a statement. They suspend judgment until there is enough evidence to make an intelligent decision.

 QUICK REVIEW

Why Critical Thinking Matters
- Our thinking guides our actions, so it should be of high quality.
- If you have never critically examined your beliefs, they are not truly yours.
- To examine your beliefs is to examine your life. Socrates: "The unexamined life is not worth living."
- Critical thinking involves determining what we're justified in believing, being open to new perspectives, and fairly assessing the views of others and ourselves.
- Critical thinking provides skills for learning and exploring; defense against error, manipulation, and prejudice; and tools for self-discovery.
- Critical thinking complements both our emotions and our creativity.
- Critical thinking is thinking outside the box.

Reasons and Arguments

Reasons provide support for a statement. That is, they provide us with grounds for believing that a statement is true. Reasons are themselves expressed as statements. So a statement expressing a reason or reasons is used to show that another statement is true or likely to be true. This combination of statements—a statement (or statements) supposedly providing reasons for accepting another statement—is known as an **argument**. Arguments are the main focus of critical thinking. They are the most important tool we have for evaluating the truth of statements (our own and those of others) and for formulating statements that are worthy of acceptance. Arguments are therefore essential for the advancement of knowledge in all fields.

Often people use the word *argument* to indicate a quarrel or heated exchange. In critical thinking, however, *argument* refers to the assertion of reasons in support of a statement.

The statements (reasons) given in support of another statement are called the **premises**. The statement that the premises are intended to support is called the **conclusion**. We can define an argument, then, like this:

> **ARGUMENT:** A group of statements in which some of them (the premises) are intended to support another of them (the conclusion).

The following are some simple arguments:
1. Because banning assault rifles violates a constitutional right, the U.S. government should not ban assault rifles.
2. The *Wall Street Journal* says that people should invest heavily in stocks. Therefore, investing in stocks is a smart move.
3. When Judy drives her car, she's always late. Since she's driving her car now, she will be late.
4. Listen, any movie with clowns in it cannot be a good movie. Last night's movie had at least a dozen clowns in it. Consequently it was awful.
5. The war on terrorism must include a massive military strike on nation X because without this intervention, terrorists cannot be defeated. They will always be able to find safe haven and support in the X regime. Even if terrorists are scattered around the world, support from nation X will increase their chances of surviving and launching new attacks.
6. No one should buy a beer brewed in Canada. Old Guzzler beer is brewed in Canada, so no one should buy it.

Here are the same arguments with the parts easily identified:
1. [Premise] Because banning assault rifles violates a constitutional right, [Conclusion] the US government should not ban assault rifles.
2. [Premise] The *Wall Street Journal* says that people should invest heavily in stocks. [Conclusion] Therefore, investing in stocks is a smart move.
3. [Premise] When Judy drives her car, she's always late. [Premise] Since she's driving her car now, [Conclusion] she will be late.
4. [Premise] Any movie with clowns in it cannot be a good movie. [Premise] Last night's movie had at least a dozen clowns in it. [Conclusion] Consequently, it was awful.

5. [Premise] Without a military intervention in nation X, terrorists cannot be defeated. [Premise] They will always be able to find safe haven and support in the X regime. [Premise] Even if terrorists are scattered around the world, support from nation X will increase their chances of surviving and launching new attacks. [Conclusion] The war on terrorism must include a massive military strike on nation X.

6. [Premise] No one should buy a beer brewed in Canada. [Premise] Old Guzzler beer is brewed in Canada. [Conclusion] So no one should buy it.

What all of these arguments have in common is that reasons (the premises) are offered to support or prove a claim (the conclusion). This logical link between premises and conclusion is what distinguishes arguments from all other kinds of discourse. This process of reasoning from a premise or premises to a conclusion based on those premises is called **inference**. Being able to identify arguments, to pick them out of a block of nonargumentative prose if need be, is an important skill on which many other critical thinking skills are based.

Now consider this passage:

The cost of the new XJ fighter plane is $650 million. The cost of three AR21 fighter bombers is $1.2 billion. The administration intends to fund such projects.

Is there an argument here? No. This passage consists of several claims, but no reasons are presented to support any particular claim (conclusion), including the last sentence. This passage can be turned into an argument, though, with some minor editing:

The GAO says that any weapon that costs more than $50 million apiece will actually impair our military readiness. The cost of the new XJ fighter plane is $650 million dollars. The cost of three AR21 fighter bombers is $1.2 billion. We should never impair our readiness. Therefore, the administration should cancel both these projects.

Now we have an argument because reasons are given for accepting a conclusion. Here's another passage:

Allisha went to the bank to get a more recent bank statement of her checking account. The teller told her that the balance was $1,725. Allisha was stunned that it was so low. She called her brother to see if he had been playing one of his twisted pranks. He wasn't. Finally, she concluded that she had been a victim of bank fraud.

Where is the conclusion? Where are the reasons? There are none. This is a little narrative hung on some descriptive claims. But it's not an argument. It could be turned into an argument if, say, some of the claims were restated as reasons for the conclusion that bank fraud had been committed.

Being able to distinguish between passages that do and do not contain arguments is a very basic skill—and an extremely important one. Many people think that if they have clearly stated their beliefs on a subject, they have presented an argument. But a mere declaration of beliefs is not an argument. Often such assertions of opinion are just a jumble of unsupported claims. Search high and low and you will not find an argument anywhere. A writer or speaker of these claims gives the readers or listeners no grounds for believing the claims. In writing courses, the absence of supporting premises is sometimes called "a lack of development."

Here are three more examples of verbiage sans argument:

Attributing alcohol abuse by children too young to buy a drink to lack of parental discipline, intense pressure to succeed, and affluence incorrectly draws attention to proximate causes while ignoring the ultimate cause: a culture that tolerates overt and covert marketing of alcohol, tobacco and sex to these easily manipulated, voracious consumers. [Letter to the editor, *New York Times*]

[A recent column in this newspaper] deals with the living quarters of Bishop William Murphy of the Diocese of Rockville Centre. I am so disgusted with the higher-ups in the church that at times I am embarrassed to say I am Catholic. To know that my parents' hard-earned money went to lawyers and payoffs made me sick. Now I see it has also paid for a high-end kitchen. I am enraged. I will never make a donation again. [Letter to the editor, *Newsday*]

I don't understand what is happening to this country. The citizens of this country are trying to destroy the beliefs of our forefathers with their liberal views. This country was founded on Christian beliefs. This has been and I believe still is the greatest country in the world. But the issue that we cannot have prayer in public places and on public property because there has to be separation of church and state is a farce. [Letter to the editor, *Douglas County Sentinel*]

The passage on alcohol abuse in children is not an argument but an unsupported assertion about the causes of the problem. The passage from the disappointed Catholic is an expression of outrage (which may or may not be justified), but no conclusion is put forth, and no reasons supporting a conclusion are offered. Note the contentious tone in the third passage. This passage smells like an argument. But, alas, there is no argument. Each sentence is a claim presented without support.

Sometimes people also confuse **explanations** with arguments. An argument gives us reasons for believing *that something is the case*—that a claim is true or probably true. An explanation, though, tells us *why or how something is the case.* Arguments have something to prove; explanations do not. Ponder this pair of statements:

1. Adam obviously stole the money, for three people saw him do it.
2. Adam stole the money because he needed it to buy food.

Statement 1 is an argument. Statement 2 is an explanation. Statement 1 tries to show that something is the case—that Adam stole the money. And the reason offered in support of this statement is that three people saw him do it. Statement 2 does not try to prove that something is the case (that Adam stole the money). Instead, it attempts to explain why something is the case (why Adam stole the money). Statement 2 takes for granted that Adam stole the money and then tries to explain why he did it. (Note: Explanations can be used as integral *parts* of arguments. As such they are powerful intellectual and scientific tools that help us understand the world.)

It's not always easy to recognize an argument, to locate both premises and conclusion, but there are a few tricks that can make the job more manageable. For one, there are **indicator words** that frequently accompany arguments and signal that a premise or conclusion is present. For example, in argument 1, cited earlier in this chapter, the indicator word *because* tips us off to the presence of the premise "Because banning assault rifles violates a Constitutional right." In argument 2, *therefore* points to the conclusion "Therefore, investing in stocks is a smart move."

Here are some common premise indicators:

because	due to the fact that	inasmuch as
in view of the fact	being that	as indicated by
given that	since	for
seeing that	assuming that	the reason being
as	for the reason that	

And here are some common conclusion indicators:

therefore	it follows that	it must be that
thus	we can conclude that	as a result
which implies that	so	which means that
consequently	hence	ergo

Using indicator words to spot premises and conclusions, however, is not foolproof. They're just good clues. You will find that some of the words just listed are used when no argument is present. For example,

- I am here *because* you asked me to come.
- I haven't seen you *since* Woodstock.
- He was *so* sleepy he fell off his chair.

Note also that arguments can be put forth without the use of *any* indicator words:

> We must take steps to protect ourselves from criminals. We can't rely on the government—law enforcement is already stretched thin. The police can't be everywhere at once, and they usually get involved only after a crime has been committed.

As you may have noticed from these examples, the basic structure of arguments can have several simple variations. For one thing, arguments can have any number of premises. Arguments 1 and 2 have one premise; arguments 3, 4, and 6, two premises; and argument 5, three premises. In extended arguments that often appear in essays, editorials, reports, and other works, there can be many more premises. Also, the conclusion of an argument may not always appear after the premises. As in argument 5, the conclusion may be presented first.

Occasionally the conclusion of an argument can be disguised as a question—even though we would usually expect a question not to be a claim at all. (For purposes of examining such arguments, we may need to paraphrase the conclusion; in some arguments, we may also need to paraphrase premises.) Most of the time readers have no difficulty discerning what the implicit conclusion is. See for yourself:

> Do you think for one minute that liberal Democrats in Congress will support a bill that makes gun control legislation impossible? They have never voted that way. They have already declared that they will not allow such a bill. And their leadership has given them their marching orders: Don't support this bill.

Probably the best advice for anyone trying to uncover or dissect arguments is this: *Find the conclusion first.* Once you know what claim someone is trying to prove, isolating the premises becomes much easier. Ask yourself, "What claim is this writer or speaker trying to persuade me to believe?" If the writer or speaker is not trying to convince you of anything, there is no argument to examine.

Finally, a fundamental distinction in critical thinking is this: Persuading someone to agree with you is not the same thing as presenting a good argument. You can influence people's opinions by using words to appeal to their ego, gullibility, bigotry, greed, anger, prejudice, and more. You just have to use emotional language, psychological ploys, semantic or syntactic tricks, and outright lies. But having done so, you would not have demonstrated that *any* belief is true or warranted. You would not have shown that a claim is *worthy of acceptance*. This latter task is a matter of logic and argument. The machinations of raw persuasion are not.

Certainly the presentation of a good argument (in the critical thinking sense) can sometimes be psychologically compelling. And there are times when persuasion through psychological or emotional appeals is appropriate, even necessary. You just have to keep these two functions straight in your mind.

Arguments in the Rough

As you've probably guessed by now, in the real world, arguments almost never appear neatly labeled as they are here. As suggested earlier, they usually come imbedded in a thicket of other sentences that serve many other functions besides articulating an argument. They may be long and hard to follow. And sometimes a passage that sounds like an argument is not. Your main challenge is to identify the conclusion and premises without getting lost in all the "background noise."

Ponder this passage:

[1] A. L. Jones used flawed reasoning in his letter yesterday praising this newspaper's decision to publish announcements of same-sex unions. [2] Mr. Jones asserts that same-sex unions are a fact of life and therefore should be acknowledged by the news media as a legitimate variation on social partnerships. [3] But the news media are not in the business of endorsing or validating lifestyles. [4] They're supposed to report on lifestyles, not bless them. [5] In addition, by validating same-sex unions or any other lifestyle, the media abandon their objectivity and become political partisans—which would destroy whatever respect people have for news outlets. [6] All of this shows that the news media—including this newspaper—should never (explicitly or implicitly) endorse lifestyles by announcing those lifestyles to the world.

There's an argument here, but it's surrounded by extraneous material. The conclusion is sentence 6—"All of this shows that the news media—including this newspaper—should never (explicitly or implicitly) endorse lifestyles by announcing those lifestyles to the world." Since we know what the conclusion is, we can identify the premises and separate them from other information. Sentences 1 and 2 are not premises; they're background information about the nature of the dispute. Sentence 3 presents the first premise, and sentence 4 is essentially a restatement of that premise. Sentence 5 is the second premise.

Stripped clean of nonargumentative material, the argument looks like this:

[Premise] But the news media are not in the business of endorsing or validating lifestyles. [Premise] In addition, by validating same-sex unions or any other lifestyle, the media abandon their objectivity and become political partisans—which would destroy whatever respect people have for news outlets. [Conclusion] All of this shows that the news media—including this newspaper—should never (explicitly or implicitly) endorse lifestyles by announcing those lifestyles to the world.

Now see if you can spot the conclusion and premises in this one:

[1] You have already said that you love me and that you can't imagine spending the rest of your life without me. [2] Once, you even tried to propose to me. [3] And now you claim that you need time to think about whether we should be married. [4] Well, everything that you've told me regarding our relationship has been a lie. [5] In some of your letters to a friend you admitted that you were misleading me. [6] You've been telling everyone that we are just friends, not lovers. [7] And worst of all, you've been secretly dating someone else. [8] Why are you doing this? [9] It's all been a farce, and I'm outta here.

And you thought that romantic love had nothing to do with critical thinking! In this passionate paragraph, an argument is alive and well. The conclusion is in sentence 4: "Well, everything that you've told me . . . has been a lie." Sentence 9, the concluding remark, is essentially a repetition of the conclusion. Sentences 1, 2, and 3 are background information on the current conflict. Sentences 5, 6, and 7 are the premises, the reasons that support the conclusion. And sentence 8 is an exasperated query that's not part of the argument.

You will discover that in most extended argumentative passages, premises and conclusions make up only a small portion of the total wordage. A good part of the text is background information and restatements of the premises or conclusion. Most of the rest consists of explanations, digressions, examples or illustrations, and descriptive passages.

Of all these nonargumentative elements, explanations are probably most easily confused with arguments. As we've seen, arguments try to prove or demonstrate that a statement is true. They try to show *that* something is the case. Explanations, however, do not try to prove that a statement is true. They try to show *why* or *how* something is the way it is. Consider these two statements:

- People have a respect for life because they adhere to certain ethical standards.
- People should have a respect for life because their own ethical standards endorse it.

The first statement is an explanation. It's not trying to prove anything, and no statement is in dispute. It's trying to clarify why or how people have respect for life. The second statement, though, is an argument. It's trying to prove, or provide support for, the idea that people should have a respect for life.

You should be able to locate the conclusion and premises of an argument—even when there is a lot of nonargumentative material nearby.

As you can see, learning the principles of critical thinking or logic requires at least some prior knowledge and ability. But, you may wonder (especially if this is your first course in critical or logical reasoning), Where does this prior knowledge and ability come from—and do you have these prerequisites? Fortunately, the answer is yes. Since you are, as Aristotle says, a rational animal, you already have the necessary equipment, namely, a logical sense that helps you reason in everyday life and enables you to begin honing your critical reasoning.

 KEY WORDS

argument	conclusion	critical thinking
explanation	indicator words	inference
logic	premise	statement

 EXERCISES

Exercises marked with * have answers in "Answers to Exercises" (Appendix A).

Exercise 1.1

*1. What is critical thinking?

2. Is critical thinking primarily concerned with *what* you think or *how* you think?

3. Why is critical thinking systematic?

*4. According to the text, what does it mean to say that critical thinking is done according to rational standards?

5. According to the text, how does a lack of critical thinking cause a loss of personal freedom?

*6. What does the term *critical* refer to in critical thinking?

7. In what way can feelings and critical thinking complement each other?

*8. What is a statement?

9. Give an example of a statement. Then give an example of a sentence that is not a statement.

10. According to the text, by what standard should we always proportion our acceptance of a statement?

*11. What is an argument?

12. Give an example of an argument with two premises.

13. What is a premise?

*14. What is a conclusion?

15. Why can't a mere assertion or statement of beliefs constitute an argument?
16. True or false: All disagreements contain an argument.
*17. Does the following passage contain an argument? *Sample passage:* I couldn't disagree more with Olivia. She says that video games provoke young men to violence and other insensitive acts. But that's just not true.
18. Does the following passage contain an argument? *Sample passage:* Alonzo asserts that the government should be able to arrest and imprison anyone if they are suspected of terrorist acts. But that's ridiculous. Doing that would be a violation of basic civil liberties guaranteed in the Bill of Rights.
*19. What are indicator words?
20. List three conclusion indicator words.
21. List three premise indicator words.
22. Give an example of a short argument that uses one or more indicator words.
*23. What is probably the best strategy for trying to find an argument in a complex passage?
24. True or false: You can almost always find an argument in narrative writing.

Exercise 1.2

For each of the following sentences, indicate whether it is or is not a statement.

*1. Now that you're mayor of the city, do you still believe that the city government is a waste of time?
2. Do not allow your emotions to distort your thinking.
3. If someone wants to burn the American flag, they should be able to do it without interference from the police.
*4. Do you think that I'm guilty?
5. Should our religious beliefs be guided by reason, emotion, or faith?
6. Stop driving on the left side of the road!
*7. The Vietnam War was a terrible mistake.
8. The Vietnam War was not a terrible mistake.
9. I shall do my best to do my duty to God and my country.
*10. Are you doing your best for God and country?

Exercise 1.3

For each of the following passages indicate whether it constitutes an argument. For each argument specify what the conclusion is.

*1. René hates Julia, and she always upsets him, so he should avoid her.
2. Do you think the upcoming election will change anything?
3. I pledge allegiance to the flag of the United States of America and to the republic for which it stands, one nation under God, indivisible, with liberty and justice for all.

*4. Why do you think you have the right to park your car anywhere you please?

5. Wait just a minute. Where do you think you're going?

6. If you smoke that cigarette in here, I will leave the room.

*7. The *Titanic* sank, and no one came to save it.

8. Jesus loves me, for the Bible tells me so.

9. Spiderman is a better superhero than Superman because kryptonite can't hurt him, and he doesn't have a Lois Lane around to mess things up.

10. "Whether our argument concerns public affairs or some other subject we must know some, if not all, of the facts about the subject on which we are to speak and argue. Otherwise, we can have no materials out of which to construct arguments." [Aristotle, *Rhetoric*]

*11. If guns are outlawed, then only outlaws will have guns. Don't outlaw guns.

12. If someone says something that offends me, I should have the right to stop that kind of speech. After all, words can assault people just as weapons can.

13. "Citizens who so value their 'independence' that they will not enroll in a political party are really forfeiting independence, because they abandon a share in decision-making at the primary level: the choice of the candidate." [Bruce L. Felknor, *Dirty Politics*]

14. If someone says something that offends me, I cannot and should not try to stop them from speaking. After all, in America, speech—even offensive speech—is protected.

*15. "Piercing car alarms have disturbed my walks, café meals or my sleep at least once during every day I have lived in the city; roughly 3,650 car alarms. Once, only once, was the wail a response to theft . . . Silent car alarms connect immediately to a security company, while the noisy ones are a problem, not a solution. They should be banned, finally." [Letter to the editor, *New York Times*]

16. "If history is a gauge, the U.S. government cannot be trusted when it comes to sending our children to war. It seems that many years after Congress sends our children to war, we find out that the basic premise for the war was an intentional lie." [Letter to the editor, *L.A. Daily News*]

Exercise 1.4

For each of the following passages indicate whether it constitutes an argument. For each argument specify both the conclusion and the premises.

*1. Faster-than-light travel is not possible. It would violate a law of nature.

2. You have neglected your duty on several occasions, and you have been absent from work too many times. Therefore, you are not fit to serve in your current capacity.

3. Racial profiling is not an issue for white people, but it is an issue for African Americans.

*4. The flu epidemic on the East Coast is real. Government health officials say so. And I personally have read at least a dozen news stories that characterize the situation as a "flu epidemic."

5. Communism is bunk. Only naïve, impressionable pinheads believe that stuff.

6. "Current-day Christians use violence to spread their right-to-life message. These Christians, often referred to as the religious right, are well known for violent demonstrations against Planned Parenthood and other abortion clinics. Doctors and other personnel are threatened with death, clinics have been bombed, there have even been cases of doctors being murdered." [Letter to the editor, *Arizona Daily Wildcat*]

*7. "I am writing about the cost of concert tickets. I am outraged at how much ticket prices are increasing every year. A few years ago, one could attend a popular concert for a decent price. Now some musicians are asking as much as $200 to $300." [Letter to the editor, *Buffalo News*]

8. "Homeland security is a cruel charade for unborn children. Some 4,000 per day are killed in their mother's womb by abortion. This American holocaust was legalized by the Supreme Court in an exercise of raw judicial power." [Letter to the editor, *Buffalo News*]

9. Witches are real. They are mentioned in the Bible. There are many people today who claim to be witches. And historical records reveal that there were witches in Salem.

*10. Stretched upon the dark silk night, bracelets of city lights glisten brightly.

11. Vaughn's car is old. It is beat up. It is unsafe to drive. Therefore, Vaughn's car is ready for the junkyard.

Exercise 1.5

For each of the following conclusions, write at least two premises that can support it. Your proposed premises can be entirely imaginary. To concoct the premises, think of what kind of statement (if true) would convince you to believe the conclusion.

EXAMPLE

Conclusion: Pet psychics can diagnose a dog's heartburn 100 percent of the time.

Premise 1: In the past fifty years, in hundreds of scientific tests, pet psychics were able to correctly diagnose heartburn in dogs 100 percent of the time.

Premise 2: Scientists have confirmed the existence of energy waves that can carry information about the health of animals.

1. What this country needs is more family values.
2. All animals—rodents, dogs, apes, whatever—have moral rights, just as people do.
*3. Every woman has the right to abort her fetus if she so chooses.
4. When I looked into your eyes, time stood still.
5. Repent! The end is near.
*6. When it comes to animals, Vaughn doesn't know what he's talking about.
7. Suspicion has arisen regarding the financial dealings of Governor Spendthrift.
8. The Internet is the most dangerous tool that terrorists have in their arsenal.
*9. The Internet is the best tool that law enforcement officials have against terrorists.
10. Pornography is good for society because it educates people about sexuality.
11. Pornography is bad for society because it misleads people about sexuality.
*12. *Stranger Things* is the greatest series Netflix has ever offered.
13. It is the duty of every student to prevent this arbitrary tuition increase.
14. Jill cannot hold her liquor.

Exercise 1.6

For each of the following passages, determine if there is an argument present. If so, identify the premises and the conclusion.

*1. "[T]he Religious Right is *not* 'pro-family'. . . . Concerned parents realize that children are curious about how their bodies work and need accurate, age-appropriate information about the human reproductive system. Yet, thanks to Religious Right pressure, many public schools have replaced sex education with fear-based 'abstinence only' programs that insult young people's intelligence and give them virtually no useful information." [Rob Boston, *Free Inquiry Magazine*]

2. "[Francis Bacon] is the father of experimental philosophy. . . . In a word, there was not a man who had any idea of experimental philosophy before Chancellor Bacon; and of an infinity of experiments which have been made since his time, there is hardly a single one which has not been pointed out in his book. He had even made a good number of them himself." [Voltaire, *On Bacon and Newton*]

*3. "Is there archaeological evidence for the [Biblical] Flood? If a universal Flood occurred between five and six thousand years ago, killing all humans except the eight on board the Ark, it would be abundantly clear in the archaeological record. Human history would be marked by an absolute break. We would see the devastation wrought by the catastrophe in terms of the destroyed physical remains of pre-Flood human settlements. . . . Unfortunately for the Flood enthusiasts, the destruction of all but eight of the world's people left no mark on the archaeology of human cultural evolution." [Kenneth L. Feder, *Frauds, Myths, and Mysteries*]

4. "Subjectivism claims that what makes an action [morally] right is that a person approves of it or believes that it's right. Although subjectivism may seem admirably egalitarian in that it takes everyone's moral judgments to be as good as everyone else's, it has some rather bizarre consequences. For one thing, it implies that each of us is morally infallible. As long as we approve of or believe in what we are doing, we can do no wrong. But this cannot be right. Suppose that Hitler believed that it was right to exterminate the Jews. Then it was right for Hitler to exterminate the Jews. . . . But what . . . Hitler did was wrong, even if [he] believed otherwise." [Theodore Schick, Jr., *Free Inquiry Magazine*]

 ## Self-Assessment Quiz

Answers appear in "Answers to Self-Assessment Quizzes" in Appendix B.

1. What is an argument?
2. Name at least three premise indicators and three conclusion indicators.
3. Select the sentence that is *not* a statement:
   a. When I met you, you didn't know anything about logic.
   b. Read the story and write a complete review of it.
   c. Four score and seven years ago our fathers brought forth on this continent a new nation.
   d. The best pizza in town can be had at Luigi's.

4. From the following list, select the conclusion that is supported by the premises in the following argument:

   When conservative John Wately last spoke on this campus, he was shouted down by several people in the audience who do not approve of his politics. He tried to continue but finally had to give up and walk away. That was unfortunate, but he's not the only one. This kind of treatment has also happened to other unpopular guest speakers. How easily the students at this university forget that free speech is guaranteed by the Bill of Rights. University regulations also support free speech for all students, faculty, and visitors and strictly forbid the harassment of speakers. And this country was founded on the idea that citizens have the right to freely express their views—even when those views are unpopular.

a. John Wately is a fascist.
b. We should never have guest speakers on campus.
c. Campus speakers should be allowed to speak freely without being shouted down.
d. Some guest speakers deserve to have the right of free speech and some don't.

5. Indicate whether the following passage contains an argument. If it does, specify the conclusion.

We live in an incredibly over-reactionary society where the mindless forces of victim demagoguery have unfortunately joined with the child-worship industry. It is obviously tragic that a few twisted kids perpetuated such carnage there in Columbine. [Letter to the editor, Salon.com]

6. Indicate whether the following passage contains an argument. If it does, specify the conclusion.

"War doesn't solve problems; it creates them," said an Oct. 8 letter about Iraq. World War II solved problems called Nazi Germany and militaristic Japan and created alliances with the nations we crushed. . . . The Persian Gulf war solved the problem of the Iraqi invasion of Kuwait. The Civil War solved the problem of slavery. These wars created a better world. War, or the threat of it is the only way to defeat evil enemies who are a threat to us. There is no reasoning with them. There can be no peace with them . . . so it's either us or them. What creates true peace is victory. [Letter to the editor, *New York Times*]

7. Indicate whether the following passage contains an argument. If so, specify the conclusion.

Paul Krugman will always reach the same answer, namely that President Bush is wrong about everything. This time, he asserts that the federal government is "slashing domestic spending." Really? The president's budget request for 2003 would raise domestic spending 6 percent. Even setting aside spending that is related to homeland security, the president's request was for more than 2 percent growth, or nearly $7 billion in new dollars. In total, over the last five years, domestic spending will have skyrocketed by more than 40 percent. [Letter to the editor, *New York Times*]

For questions 8–12, indicate which sentences or sentence fragments are likely to be conclusions and which are likely to be premises.

8. Therefore, the Everglades will be destroyed within three years.
9. Assuming that you will never reach Boston
10. This implies that you are not driving as safely as you should.
11. Given all the hoopla surrounding the football team
12. It follows that sexual harassment should be a crime.

For questions 13–15, write at least two premises for each of the numbered conclusions. You can make up the premises, but you must ensure that they support the conclusion.

13. DNA evidence should be disallowed in cases of capital murder.
14. Computers will never be able to converse with a human being well enough to be indistinguishable from humans.
15. The great prophet Nostradamus (1503–1566) predicted the September 11 terrorist attacks.

Read the following argument. Then in questions 16–20, supply the information requested. Each question asks you to identify by number all the sentences in the argument that fulfill a particular role—conclusion, premise, background information, example or illustration, or reiteration of a premise or the conclusion. Just write down the appropriate sentence numbers.

[1] Is global warming a real threat? [2] Or is it hype propagated by tree-hugging, daft environmentalists? [3] The president apparently thinks that the idea of global climate change is bunk. [4] But recently his own administration gave the lie to his bunk theory. [5] His own administration issued a report on global warming. [6] It gave no support to the idea that global warming doesn't happen and we should all go back to sleep. [7] Instead, it asserted that global warming was definitely real and that it could have catastrophic consequences if ignored. [8] For example, global climate change could cause heat waves, extreme weather, and water shortages right here in the United States. [9] The report is also backed by many other reports, including a very influential one from the United Nations. [10] Yes, global warming is real. [11] It is as real as typhoons and ice storms.

16. Conclusion.
17. Premise or premises.
18. Background information.
19 Example or illustration.
20. Repetition of conclusion or premise.

Writing Assignments

1. Select an issue from the following list and write a three-page paper defending a claim pertaining to the issue. For guidance in writing argumentative essays, see chapter 12.

   • Should there be a constitutional amendment banning the desecration of the American flag?
   • Should a representation of the Ten Commandments be allowed to be displayed in a federal courtroom?
   • Should the legal drinking age be lowered?
   • Should the private ownership of fully automatic machine guns be outlawed?

2. Obtain the "Letters to the Editor" section of any newspaper (including student newspapers and online newspapers). Select a letter that contains at least one argument. Locate the conclusion and each premise. Next go through the letters again to find one that contains no argument at all. Rewrite the letter so that it contains at least one argument. Try to preserve as much of the original letter as possible. Stay on the same topic.

Obstacles to Critical Thinking

CRITICAL THINKING DOES NOT HAPPEN IN A VACUUM BUT IN AN "ENVIRONMENT" that's often hostile to it. It takes place in the real world in the minds of real people who almost always have thoughts, feelings, experiences, and cognitive tendencies that, given half a chance, would sabotage critical reasoning at every turn. The sparkling palace of our mind is grand—except for the demons chained in the basement.

Recall our definition of critical thinking: *The systematic evaluation or formulation of beliefs, or statements, by rational standards.* This means, of course, that several factors must be present for the process of critical thinking to be fully realized. If the process fails to be systematic, or falls short of being a true evaluation or formulation, or ignores rational standards, critical thinking can't happen. Because we are fallible, there are a thousand ways that this failure of reason could come about. And there is no cure for our fallibility.

We should expect then that thinking critically will often be difficult and even unpleasant (as painful truths sometimes are), and indeed it is. But there are ways to (1) detect errors in our thinking (even subtle ones), (2) restrain the attitudes and feelings that can distort our reasoning, and (3) achieve a level of objectivity that makes critical thinking possible.

Doing all this—and doing it consistently—requires *awareness, practice,* and *motivation.* If we are to think critically, we must be *aware* of not only what good critical thinking involves but also what sloppy thinking entails. Then we must *practice* avoiding the pitfalls and using the skills and techniques that critical thinking requires. And we must be *motivated* to do all of this, for it is unlikely that we will use critical thinking very much if we can't appreciate its value and therefore have little motivation to make the extra effort.

We can sort the most common impediments to critical thinking into two main categories: (1) those hindrances that arise because of *how* we think and (2) those that occur because of *what* we think. There is some overlap in these categories; how people think is often a result of what they think and vice versa. But in general, category 1 obstacles are those that come into play because of psychological factors (our fears, attitudes, motivations, desires, and cognitive dispositions), and category 2 impediments are those that arise because of certain philosophical ideas we have (our beliefs about beliefs). For example, a category 1 hindrance is the tendency to conform our opinions to those of our peers. This conformism often grows out of some psychological need that is part of our personality. A common category 2 problem is the belief that objectivity in thinking is impossible or that we really don't know anything or that we don't know what we think we know.

In this chapter we review the most common category 1 and 2 barriers to critical thinking and practice uncovering and neutralizing them. The motivation to learn these lessons well is up to you.

Psychological Obstacles

No one is immune to category 1 obstacles. We are all heir to psychological tendencies and habits that affect our behavior and channel our thinking. They tend to persist or recur, haunting our minds until we have the awareness and the will to break free of them.

Self-Centered Thinking

As humans we spend a great deal of time protecting, maintaining, and comforting our own mental life, our own *selves*—a perfectly natural urge that does no harm until we push our self-serving efforts too far. How far is too far? From the standpoint of critical thinking, we have taken things too far when we accept claims for no good reason—when our thinking is no longer systematic and rational. In the service of our almighty selves, we distort our judgment and raise our risk of error, which is ironically a risk to ourselves.

Self-interested thinking takes several forms. We may decide to accept a claim *solely on the grounds that it advances, or coincides with, our interests.* You may think, "I believe the city should lower the sales tax for convenience stores because I own a convenience store," or, "I am against all forms of gun control because I am a hunter," or, "This university should not raise tuition because I am a student, and I don't want to pay more tuition." There is nothing inherently wrong with accepting a claim that furthers your own interests. The problem arises when you accept a claim *solely because* it furthers your interests. Self-interest alone simply cannot establish the truth of a claim. To base your beliefs on self-interest alone is to abandon critical thinking.

The influence of self on your thinking can take another form. You may be tempted to accept claims *for no other reason than that they help you save face.* We all like to think of ourselves as excelling in various ways. We may believe that we are above average in intelligence, integrity, talent, compassion, physical beauty, sexual prowess, athletic ability, and much more. But we not only like to think such things about ourselves, we want others to think the same about us. The rub comes, however, when we accept or defend claims just to cover up the cracks in our image. You make a mistake, and so you blame it on someone or something else. You behave badly, and you try to justify your behavior. You make a judgment or observation that turns out to be wrong, and you're too embarrassed or proud to admit it.

The consequences of self-centered thinking can be, well, self-destructive. In the realm of critical thinking, this devotion to yourself can prevent careful evaluation of claims, limit critical inquiry, blind you to the facts, provoke self-deception, engender rationalizations, lead you to suppress or ignore evidence, and beget wishful thinking. And these mistakes can decrease your chances of success (however you define success) and hamper your personal growth, maturity, and self-awareness. Such egocentricism can also leave you wide open to propaganda and manipulation by people who appeal to your personal desires and prejudices. How easy would it be for people to control your choices and thoughts if they told you exactly what you wanted to hear?

 IS IT WRONG TO BELIEVE WITHOUT GOOD REASONS?

Some philosophers have asserted that it is morally wrong to believe a proposition without justification or evidence. One of these is the famous biologist Thomas Henry Huxley. Another is mathematician W. K. Clifford (1845–1879). This is how Clifford states his view:

> It is wrong always, everywhere, and for anyone, to believe anything upon insufficient evidence. If a man, holding a belief which he was taught in childhood or persuaded of afterwards, keeps down and pushes away any doubts which arise about it in his mind . . . and regards as impious those questions which cannot easily be asked without disturbing it—the life of that man is one long sin against mankind.[1]

Clifford thinks that belief without evidence is immoral because our actions are guided by our beliefs, and if our beliefs are unfounded, our actions (including morally relevant actions) are likely to be imprudent.

Other people (especially those who know you fairly well) may be amused or puzzled by your stubborn adherence to claims that obviously conflict with the evidence. Or they may think it odd that you cling to ideas or behaviors that you loudly condemn in others.

When examining a claim or making a choice, how can you overcome the excessive influence of your own needs? Sometimes you can do it only with great effort, and sometimes the task is much easier, especially if you remember these three guidelines:

- Watch out when things get very personal.
- Be alert to ways that critical thinking can be undermined.
- Ensure that nothing has been left out.

You are most likely to let your self-interest get in the way of clear thinking when you have a big personal stake in the conclusions you reach. You may be deeply committed to a particular view, dogma, political party, or principle; or you may want desperately for a particular claim to be false or unjustified; or you may be devoted not to particular claims but to *any* claims that contradict those of someone you dislike. Such zeal can wreck any attempt at careful, fair evaluation of a claim.

The twentieth-century philosopher Bertrand Russell asserts that the passionate holding of an opinion is a sure sign of a lack of reasons to support the opinion:

> When there are rational grounds for an opinion, people are content to set them forth and wait for them to operate. In such cases, people do not hold their opinions with passion; they hold them calmly, and set forth their reasons quietly. The opinions that are held with passion are always those for which no good ground exists; indeed the passion is the measure of the holder's lack of rational conviction.[2]

The dead giveaway that you are skewing your thinking is a surge of strong emotions. If your evaluation or defense of a position evokes anger, passion, or fear, your thinking could be prejudiced or clouded. It is possible, of course, to be emotionally engaged in an issue and still think critically and carefully. But most of the time, getting worked up over a claim or conclusion is reason enough to suspect that your thinking is not as clear as it should be.

The rule of thumb is: If you sense a rush of emotions when you deal with a particular issue, stop. Think about what's happening and why. Then continue at a slower pace and with greater attention to the basics of critical reasoning, double-checking to ensure that you are not ignoring or suppressing evidence or getting sloppy in your evaluations.

If you understand the techniques and principles of critical thinking, and you have practiced applying them in a variety of situations, you are more likely than not to detect your own one-sided self-centered thinking when it occurs. An alarm should go off in your head: "Warning—faulty reasoning." When your alarm sounds, double-check your thinking, look for lapses in arguments and claims, and weed them out.

Group-Centered Thinking

In the old television series *Star Trek: The Next Generation*, the crew of the starship *Enterprise* encounters an unusual threat: the Borg. The Borg is a collective of individual minds that have been stripped of individuality and merged into a single group-mind with evil intentions. Much of the Borg storyline (which spans several episodes) is about the dignity and importance of individualism as opposed to the conformism of the Borg hive. The thought of losing one's self in the monolithic Borg is presented as a profound tragedy—a theme that strikes a chord with humans. Individualism, independence, and freedom of thought are what we want, what we must have.

Or so we say. Despite our apparent longings, we humans spend a great deal of our time trying to conform to, or be part of, groups. We want to belong, we want the safety and comfort of numbers, we want the approval of our beloved tribe. All of which is perfectly normal. We are, after all, social creatures. Conformist tendencies are a fact of life. But trouble appears when our conformism hampers—or obliterates—critical thinking.

We all belong to multiple groups—family, employees, gender, church, club, professional society, political party, advocacy group, you name it—and we can be susceptible to pressure from all of them. Much of the time, there is intense pressure to fit into groups and to adopt ideas, attitudes, and goals endorsed by them. Sometimes the influence of the group is subtle but strong and can occur in the most casual, "unofficial" gatherings. The claims and positions adopted by the group can be implicit, never spoken, but well understood. The political blog, the group of Christians or Muslims or Jews who happen to meet on the bus, the collection of peers who support the same political cause—all these can exert a noticeable influence on our beliefs.

PREJUDICE, BIAS, AND RACISM

Group pressure often leads to prejudice, bias, and racism. (To a lesser extent, so does self-interest.) But what do these terms mean?

Prejudice in its broadest sense is a judgment or opinion—whether positive or negative—based on insufficient reasons. But usually the term is

A police sign ordering a "'white only" waiting room at the bus station in Jackson, Mississippi, May 1961.

continues

PREJUDICE, BIAS, AND RACISM

continued

used in a more narrow way to mean a negative, or adverse, belief (most often about people) without sufficient reasons. At the heart of prejudice, then, is a failure of critical thinking. And the use of critical thinking is an important part of eradicating prejudiced views.

Bias is another word for prejudice, both in the general and the narrow sense. Sometimes the word is also used to mean an inclination of temperament or outlook—as in "My bias is in favor of tougher laws."

Racism is a lack of respect for the value and rights of people of different races or geographical origins. Usually this attitude is based on prejudice—specifically an unjustified belief that one group of people is somehow superior to another.

Group pressure to accept a statement or act in a certain way has several overlapping subtypes (some of which we'll cover in more detail in later chapters). When the pressure to conform comes from your peers, it's called—surprise—**peer pressure**. When the pressure comes from the mere popularity of a belief, it's known as—believe it or not—an **appeal to popularity** (also known as an appeal to the masses). When the pressure comes from what groups of people do or how they behave, it's called an **appeal to common practice**. In all cases, the lapse in critical thinking comes from the use of group pressure *alone* to try to support a claim.

There's another kind of group influence that we have all fallen prey to: the pressure that comes from presuming that our own group is the best, the right one, the chosen one, and all other groups are, well, not as good. You can see this kind of ethnocentrism in religions, political parties, generations, social classes, and many other groups. The assumption that your group is better than others is at the heart of prejudice.

This we-are-better pressure is probably the most powerful of all. We all have certain beliefs not because we have thought critically about them but because our parents raised us to believe them or because the conceptual push and pull of our social or political group has instilled them in us. That is, we may believe what we believe—and assume that our beliefs are better than anyone else's—because we were born into a family or society that maintains such views. We may be a Catholic or a Democrat or a racist primarily because we were born into a Catholic or Democratic or racist family or society. Like the influence of the self, this endemic pressure can lead to wishful thinking, rationalization, and self-deception. Group thinking can also easily generate narrow-mindedness, resistance to change, and stereotyping (classifying individuals into groups according to oversimplified or prejudiced attitudes or opinions).

But as comfortable as our inherited beliefs are, when we accept them without good reason, we risk error, failure, and delusion. And as we discussed in chapter 1, if we have certain beliefs solely because they were given to us, they are not really our beliefs. The sign of a maturing intellect is having the will and the courage to gradually prune beliefs that are groundless.

For critical thinkers, the best way to deal with the power of the group is to proportion your belief to the strength of reasons.

After thinking critically about claims favored by groups, you may find that the claims are actually on solid ground, and you really do have good reason to accept them. Or you may find that there is no good reason for believing them, and so you don't accept them. Either way, critical thinking will give you a clearer view of the group and yourself.

Resisting Contrary Evidence

An all-too-human tendency is to try to resist evidence that flies in the face of our cherished beliefs. We may deny evidence, or ignore it, or reinterpret it so it fits better with our prejudices. Resisting evidence may be psychologically comforting (for a while, anyway), but it thwarts any search for knowledge and stunts our understanding.

It's shockingly easy to find examples of the blatant denial of evidence. Scientific research and commonsense experience show that the practice permeates all walks of life. A political activist may refuse to consider evidence that conflicts with his party's principles. A scientist may be so committed to her theory that she refuses to take seriously any data that undermine it. An administrator of a grand program may insist that it is a huge success despite all evidence to the contrary.

Often our resistance to contrary evidence takes a subtle form. If we encounter evidence against our views, we frequently don't reject it outright. We simply apply more critical scrutiny to it than we would to evidence in favor of our views, or we seek out additional confirming information, or we find a way to interpret the data so it doesn't conflict with our expectations.

In one study, proponents and opponents of the death penalty were presented with evidence concerning whether capital punishment deterred crime. Both those opposed to and those in favor of capital punishment were given two types of evidence—(1) some that supported the practice and (2) some that discredited it. Psychologist Thomas Gilovich describes the outcome of the study:

> The results of this experiment were striking. The participants considered the study that provided evidence consistent with their prior beliefs—regardless of what type of study that was—to be a well-conducted piece of research that provided important evidence concerning the effectiveness of capital

punishment. In contrast, they uncovered numerous flaws in the research that contradicted their initial beliefs. . . . Rather than ignoring outright the evidence at variance with their expectations, the participants cognitively transformed it into evidence that was considered relatively uninformative and could be assigned little weight.[3]

There is no cure for our tendency to resist opposing evidence. The only available remedy is to *make a conscious effort to look for opposing evidence*. Don't consider your evaluation of a statement or argument finished until you've carefully considered *all the relevant reasons*. Ask yourself, "What is the evidence or reasons against this statement?" This approach is at the heart of science. A basic principle of scientific work is not to accept a favored theory until competing (alternative) theories are thoroughly examined.

 LEFT-WING/RIGHT-WING BIAS

Is there a left-wing bias in the news media? A right-wing bias? Some swear the *New York Times* and PBS slant the news to the left; others say *Fox News* tilts it to the right. The charge that the news is politically slanted—left or right—regularly starts arguments (the nasty, pointless kind) and usually lacks supporting evidence. Whether the allegation is true is not an issue we can settle here, and fortunately we need not settle it to apply critical thinking to the news media.

Many factors can render news reports unreliable, incomplete, or misleading—even when no political bias is at work. *Critical thinking requires that we not assume without good reason that a report gives us an entirely accurate picture.* The best way to ensure that we get the whole story is to read a variety of newspapers, newsmagazines, opinion journals, and websites.

The worst approach is to rely only on news sources that reinforce our existing political views. People have a natural tendency to seek out only evidence that supports their treasured beliefs and to resist evidence that contradicts them. They want to watch, hear, and read only what is psychologically comforting—and to avoid what disturbs their worldview. But this strategy undermines serious inquiry and reflection, stunts our understanding, and blights independent thinking.

Do you ever read magazines, newspapers, or websites that run counter to your political beliefs? Do you associate only with people who share your political views? Do you ever seriously consider plausible objections to your positions? Do you think the availability of other points of view online helps open up the debate beyond older media biases? Or does it just reinforce what readers of each blog already think they know?

Looking for Confirming Evidence

We often not only resist conflicting evidence but also seek out and use only confirming evidence—a phenomenon known as *confirmation bias*. When we go out of our way to find only confirming evidence, we can end up accepting a claim that's not true, seeing relationships that aren't there, and finding confirmation that isn't genuine.

In scientific research on confirmation bias, when subjects are asked to assess a claim, they often look for confirming evidence only, even though disconfirming evidence may be just as revealing. For example, in one study, a group of subjects was asked to assess whether practicing before a tennis match was linked to winning the match; another group, whether practicing before a match was linked to losing the match. All the subjects were asked to select the kind of evidence (regarding practice and winning or losing matches) that they thought would be the most helpful in answering the relevant question. Not surprisingly, the subjects deciding whether pregame practicing was linked to winning focused on how many times players practiced and then won the match. And subjects assessing whether practicing was associated with losing focused on how many times players practiced and then lost the match.

Sometimes we look for confirming evidence even when disconfirming evidence is more telling. For example, take this claim: All swans are white. You can easily find confirming instances; white swans are plentiful and ubiquitous. But even your seeing thousands of white swans will not conclusively confirm that all swans are white because there may be swans in places where you haven't looked. But all you have to do is find one black swan to conclusively show that the claim is false. (People used to believe that the claim was absolutely true—until black swans were discovered in Australia.) In such cases, confirmation bias can lead us way off course.

The moral to this story is that when we evaluate claims, we should look for disconfirming as well as confirming evidence. Doing so requires a conscious effort to consider not only the information that supports what we want to believe but also the information that conflicts with it. We have to seek out disconfirming evidence just as we keep an eye out for confirming evidence—an approach that goes against our grain. We naturally gravitate to people and policies we agree with, to the books that support our views, to the magazines and newspapers that echo our political outlook. Acquiring a broader, smarter, more critical perspective takes effort—and courage.

Preferring Available Evidence

Another common mistake in evaluating evidence is the *availability error*. We commit this blunder when we rely on evidence not because it's trustworthy but because it's memorable or striking—that is, psychologically available. In such cases, we put stock in evidence that's psychologically impressive or persuasive, not necessarily logically acceptable. You fall for the availability error if you vote to convict a murder suspect because he looks menacing, not because the evidence points to his guilt; or if you decide that a Honda Civic is an unsafe vehicle because you saw one get smashed in a highway accident; or if, just because you watched a TV news report about a mugging in your city, you believe that the risk of being mugged is extremely high.

Being taken in by the availability error can lead to some serious misjudgments about the risks involved in various situations. Some people (are you one of them?) believe that air travel is more dangerous than many other modes of transportation, so they shun travel by airplane in favor of the automobile. Their conclusion is based on nothing more than a few vivid media reports of tragic plane crashes. But research shows that per mile traveled, flying is far safer than automobile travel. Your chances of dying in a plane crash in 2001 were 1 in 310,560, but the odds of your dying in a car accident were only 1 in 19,075. The fact is, there are plenty of less vivid and less memorable (that is, psychologically unavailable) things that are much more dangerous than air travel: falling down stairs, drowning, choking, and accidental poisoning.

The availability error is very likely at work in many controversies regarding environmental hazards. Because the alleged hazard and its effects can be easily and vividly imagined and the scientific data on the issue are not so concrete or memorable, the imagined danger can provoke a public scare even though the fear is completely unwarranted. Brain cancer from the use of cell phones and childhood leukemia from living near power lines—both these putative hazards have provoked fear and public demands for action. But scientific studies have shown these concerns to be groundless. Many environmental hazards are real, of course. But concluding that they exist solely on the basis of scary thoughts is to commit the availability error.

If we're in the habit of basing our judgments on evidence that's merely psychologically available, we will frequently commit the error known as hasty generalization. We're guilty of hasty generalization when we draw a conclusion about a whole group based on an inadequate sample of the group. We fall into this trap when we assert something like this: "Honda Civics are pieces of junk. I owned one for three months, and it gave me nothing but trouble." Our experience with a car is immediate and personal, so for many of us it can be a short step from this psychologically available evidence to a very hasty conclusion. If we give in to the availability error and stick to our guns about lousy Civics in the face of good evidence to the contrary (say, automobile-reliability research done by the Consumer's Union or similar organizations), we should get an F in critical thinking.

Philosophical Obstacles

A worldview is a philosophy of life, a set of fundamental ideas that helps us make sense of a wide range of important issues in life. The ideas are fundamental because they help guide us in the evaluation or acceptance of many other less basic ideas. They are answers to the "big questions" of life, such as, What do

I know? Is knowledge possible? What is real and what is not? How do I know which actions are morally right?

In this section we investigate how some elements of a worldview—certain fundamental but problematic ideas—may undermine critical thinking. These notions can give rise to category 2 obstacles to critical reason, for they may affect our thinking through the content of our beliefs.

Subjective Relativism

Like science, critical thinking may be underpinned by a number of propositions that few people would think to question. Science, for example, is based on the proposition that the world is publicly understandable—that it has a certain structure (independent of what anyone thinks), that we can know the structure, and that this knowledge can be acquired by anyone. Critical thinking is based on similar ideas. Among the most basic is the notion that the truth of a claim does not depend on what a person thinks. That is, your believing that something is true *does not make it true.*

The idea that truth depends on what someone believes is called **subjective relativism**, and if you accept this notion or use it to try to support a claim, you're said to commit the **subjectivist fallacy**. This view says that truth depends not on the way things are but solely on what someone believes. Truth, in other words, is relative to persons. Truth is a matter of what a person believes—not a matter of how the world is. This means that a proposition can be true for one person, but not for another. If you believe that dogs can fly, then it is true (for you) that dogs can fly. If someone else believes that dogs cannot fly, then it is true (for him) that dogs cannot fly.

You've probably encountered subjective relativism more often than you realize. You may have heard someone (maybe even yourself!) say, "This is *my* truth, and that's *your* truth," or, "This statement is true *for me.*"

Many critics of subjective relativism maintain that it can undermine critical thinking in a fundamental way. In large part, critical thinking is about determining whether statements are true or false. But if we can make a statement true just by believing it to be true, then critical thinking would seem to be unnecessary. The subjectivist fallacy, they say, may be an excuse to forgo the tough job of critical inquiry.

Most philosophers see the situation this way: We use critical thinking to find out whether a statement is true or false—*objectively* true or false. Objective truth is about the world, about the way the world is regardless of what we may believe about it. To put it differently, there is a way the world is, and our beliefs do not make it. The world is the way it is, regardless of how we feel about it.

These same philosophers would probably be quick to point out that some objective truths *are* about our subjective states or processes. It might be true, for example, that you're feeling pain right now. But if so, the claim that you are feeling pain right now is an objective truth about your subjective state.

Also, they would readily admit that there are some things about ourselves that obviously *are* relative because they are one way for us and another way for someone else. You may like ice cream, but someone else may not. Your liking ice cream is then relative to you. But the truth about these states of affairs is not relative.

Subjective relativism (as well as other forms of relativism) is controversial, and we needn't spend much time on it here. But you should know at least that many philosophers have (through the use of critical thinking!) uncovered some odd implications that seem to render the view implausible. First, they point out that if we could make a statement true just by believing it to be true, we would be infallible. We could not possibly be in error about anything that we sincerely believed. We could never be mistaken about where we parked the car or what we said about political violence or what some general said about carpet bombing. Personal infallibility is, of course, absurd, and this possibility seems to weigh heavily against subjective relativism.

Subjective relativism (as it applies to morality) also implies an implausible *moral equivalence*. It says that the sincere moral views of any individual are as good or as true as those of any other. If the serial killer and cannibal Jeffrey Dahmer approved of his slaughtering seventeen people, then it is morally right. If you disapprove of the slaughter, then it is morally wrong. By the lights of moral subjectivism, Dahmer's view is no better or worse than yours.

Many critics think that subjective relativism's biggest problem is that it's self-defeating. It defeats itself because its truth implies its falsity. The relativist says, "All truth is relative." If this statement is objectively true, then it refutes itself because if it is objectively true that "All truth is relative," then the statement itself is an example of an objective truth. So if "All truth is relative" is objectively true, it is objectively false.

Prisoners in the concentration camp at Sachsenhausen, Germany, Dec. 19, 1938. Social relativism implies that societies are infallible—even about such horrors as the Nazi's imprisonment and murder of millions of people in World War II.

Social Relativism

To escape the difficulties of subjective relativism, some people posit **social relativism**, the view that truth is relative to societies. The claim is that truth depends not on an individual's beliefs, but on society's beliefs. So a claim can be true for the Chinese but false for Americans, true for college students but false for public officials, true for Baptists but false for atheists. To many, this kind of relativism, like the subjective kind, also seems to render critical thinking superfluous.

Social relativism is attractive to many because it seems to imply an admirable egalitarianism—the notion that the beliefs of different societies are all equal. But a lot of philosophers maintain that it has most of the same defects that subjective relativism has. For example, according to social relativism, individuals aren't infallible, but societies are. The beliefs of whole societies cannot be mistaken. But this notion of societal infallibility is no more plausible than the idea of individual infallibility. Is it plausible that no society has ever been wrong about anything—never been wrong about the causes of disease, the best form of government, the number of planets in our solar system, the burning of witches, the Nazi policy of killing six million Jews?

Equally troubling, social relativism implies that other cultures are beyond moral criticism; we cannot legitimately criticize them because each culture is the maker of its own moral truth. We cannot accuse another culture of immoral behavior because whatever behavior that culture genuinely endorses is moral. To accept this implication of social relativism is to say that if the people of Germany approved of the extermination of millions of Jews in World War II, then the extermination was morally right. But this is implausible. Our moral experience suggests that we can and do condemn other societies for morally heinous acts.

Social relativism also has a difficult time explaining the moral status of social reformers. We tend to believe they are at least sometimes right and society is wrong. When we contemplate social reform, we think of such moral exemplars as Martin Luther King, Jr., Mahatma Gandhi, and Susan B. Anthony, all of whom agitated for justice and moral progress. But one of the consequences of social relativism is that social reformers could *never* be morally right. By definition, what society judges to be morally right is morally right, and since social reformers disagree with society, they could not be right—ever. But surely on occasion it's the reformers who are right and society is wrong.

Critics like to point out that just as subjective relativism is self-defeating, so is social relativism. The claim that "All truth is relative to societies" is self-defeating because if it is objectively true, then it is an example of an objective truth—and that means that the claim is objectively false.

If you accept relativism, you may be tempted to care very little about critical thinking, and that would be your loss. Fortunately, there is no good reason why you should neglect critical thinking in the name of relativism.[4]

Skepticism

If knowledge were impossible, critical thinking—as a way of coming to know the truth or falsity of claims—would seem to be out of a job. Most of us, though, believe that we *can* acquire knowledge. We think that we know a great many things—that we are alive, that our shoes are a certain color, that there is a tree on the lawn, that the Earth is not flat, that rabbits cannot fly, that 2 + 2 = 4. But not everyone would agree. There are some who believe that we know much less than we think we do or nothing at all. This view is known as **philosophical skepticism**, and thinkers who raise doubts about how much we know are known as **philosophical skeptics**.

This is no place to dive into a debate on skepticism, but we can take a quick look at the most important type of philosophical skepticism and see what, if anything, it has to do with critical thinking. This form of skepticism says that knowledge requires certainty—if we are to know anything, we must be certain of it. This means that our knowledge isn't knowledge unless it is beyond any *possibility* of doubt. If knowledge requires certainty, however, there is very little that we know because there are always considerations that can undermine our certainty.

But it seems that our knowledge *does not* require certainty. All of us can cite many situations in which we do seem to have knowledge—even though we do not have absolutely conclusive reasons. We usually would claim to know, for example, that it is raining, that our dog has spots, that we were born, that the moon is not made of green cheese—even though we are not absolutely certain of any of these. These situations suggest that we do know many things. We know them not because they are beyond all *possible* doubt, but because they are beyond all *reasonable* doubt. Doubt is always possible, but it is not always reasonable. Rejecting a reasonable claim to knowledge just because of the bare possibility that you may be wrong is neither reasonable nor necessary.

Critical thinking does have a job to do in our efforts to acquire knowledge. Its task, however, is not to help us find claims that we cannot possibly doubt but to help us evaluate claims that vary in degrees of reasonable doubt—that is, from weak reasons (or no reasons) to very strong reasons.

 KEY WORDS

appeal to common practice	appeal to popularity (or to the masses)	peer pressure
philosophical skepticism	philosophical skeptics	social relativism
stereotyping	subjective relativism	subjectivist fallacy
worldview		

 **EXERCISES**

Exercises marked with * have answers in "Answers to Exercises" (Appendix A).

Exercise 2.1

*1. According to the text's definition of critical thinking, what factors must be present for critical thinking to be realized?
2. What are the two main categories of common obstacles to critical thinking?
3. What did W. K. Clifford say about the morality of believing claims?
4. What is stereotyping?
*5. From the standpoint of critical thinking, what event signals that we have allowed our bias in favor of ourselves to go too far?
6. According to the text, what effect can our urge to save face have on our thinking?
*7. When are you most likely to let your self-interest get in the way of clear thinking?
8. How does subjective relativism imply infallibility?
9. How are subjective and social relativism self-defeating?
10. According to the text, how might selective attention affect your thinking when you are examining evidence for or against a claim?
*11. How might the influence of a group that you belong to affect your attempts to think critically?
12. According to the text, what is the most powerful group pressure of all?
13. What is the appeal to popularity?
*14. What is a worldview?
15. In order to know something, must it be beyond all possible doubt? Why or why not?
16. According to the text, how could subjective relativism make critical thinking unnecessary?
*17. Is critical thinking concerned with the *objective* or the *subjective* truth of claims?
18. What is social relativism?
19. What is philosophical skepticism?
20. Does our knowledge require certainty?
*21. What kind of doubt is involved in the acquisition of knowledge?

Exercise 2.2

For each of the following passages, indicate whether it contains examples of self-interested thinking, face-saving, or group pressure. Some of these are really tough.

*1. Mary: Animals have the same rights as humans.

Jenna: What makes you think that?

Mary: I love animals, and there are so many that are treated horribly all over the world. It's heartbreaking.

2. Jonathan: My essay is better than Julio's.

Betty: Why do you think yours is better than all the others? Do you agree that the content and writing of all the essays are similar?

Jonathan: Well, yes.

Betty: Do you agree that all the other benchmarks of quality are nearly identical?

Jonathan: Yes, but mine is still better.

3. Dear friends, as your state senator I will continue my tireless work on your behalf. I will continue to use my considerable talents to make this district even better. I will continue to let my integrity be the guide for all my actions.

*4. We cannot allow those people to move into this neighborhood. They're not like us.

5. I oppose women becoming members of this club. If I endorsed their claims, every friend I've got in the club would turn his back on me.

6. His statements about the West Bank are all false, of course. He's an Israeli.

*7. Christianity is superior to all other religions. I was raised Christian, and all my relatives are Christians. This is the only religion I've known, and the only one I need.

8. I'm due for tenure next year, so I am in favor of continuing the tradition of tenure at this university.

9. The United States is the greatest nation on the face of the earth. I don't know anything about other countries, and I don't want to know.

*10. If Joan is appointed to the committee, I am guaranteed to have a job for the rest of my life. I wholeheartedly favor Joan's appointment.

11. Free speech should not extend to pornographers. Right now they are allowed to espouse their smut on the Internet and many other places. That's just not how I was raised.

Exercise 2.3

Read each of the following claims. Then select from the list any statements that, if true, would constitute good reasons for accepting the claim. Be careful: In some questions, none of the choices are correct.

*1. John: The newspaper account of the charges of pedophilia lodged against Father J. Miller, a Catholic priest in our town, should never have been printed.

a. The charges are false.

b. John is a Catholic.

      c. Important evidence that would exonerate Father Miller was not mentioned in the newspaper account.

      d. The town is predominantly Catholic.

2. Alice: The speed limit on I-95 should be 70 mph.

      a. Raising the speed limit to 70 mph would result in faster and safer traffic.

      b. The state commission on highways did a study showing that I-95 should have a limit of 70 mph.

      c. Alice travels I-95 every day and needs to drive 70 mph to get to work on time.

      d. Alice drives I-95 every day.

*3. Janette: Women are less violent and less emotional than men.

      a. A study from Harvard shows that women are less violent and less emotional than men.

      b. Janette is a woman.

      c. Janette is a member of a group of women who are fighting for the rights of women.

      d. Janette and all her friends are women.

4. Brie: People should buy stock in IBM, an action that will push the price per share higher.

      a. Brie owns a large proportion of IBM stock.

      b. Brie is chair of the board at IBM.

      c. The stock market is weak.

      d. Brie has a large family to support.

5. Colonel Stockton: The United States should attack the terrorists in Iran, even at the risk of a full-scale war with Arab states.

      a. The terrorists have humiliated Colonel Stockton's forces.

      b. The terrorists have humiliated the United States.

      c. Colonel Stockton is loyal to his troops, all of whom want to attack the terrorists in Iran.

      d. Attacking the terrorists in Iran would cause no casualties and would result in world peace.

*6. Morgan: Capital punishment is always wrong.

      a. All of Morgan's friends agree that capital punishment is wrong.

      b. If Morgan favored capital punishment, her friends would abandon her.

      c. Morgan is president of the Anti–Capital Punishment League.

      d. Morgan has already made her views known and cannot change her mind without seeming to be inconsistent.

7. Angelo: Marijuana should be legalized.
    a. All of Angelo's friends smoke marijuana.
    b. Legalizing marijuana would reduce the consumption of marijuana and save lives, money, and resources.
    c. Angelo has already said on television that marijuana should be legalized.
    d. Angelo likes to smoke marijuana.

Exercise 2.4

Read each of the following passages. Indicate whether it contains examples of the kind of group pressure that encourages people to conform (peer pressure or appeal to popularity) or the type that urges people to think that one's own group is better than others. For each example of group pressure, specify the possible negative consequences. A couple of these are very difficult to classify.

    *1. Ortega is deeply religious, attending church regularly and trying to abide by church law and the Scriptures. He has never considered any other path. He believes that laws should be passed that forbid people to shop on Sunday and that designate Easter as a national holiday.

    2. John goes to a prestigious college where many students use illegal drugs. Nearly everyone in John's frat house uses them. So far, he hasn't tried any, but his frat brothers frequently ask if he wants some. And he has noticed that he is rarely invited to any frat parties.

    *3. A northeast college has invited a famous writer to be a guest speaker in the campus-wide distinguished speaker series. She is an accomplished poet and essayist. She is also a Marxist and favors more socialism in the United States. During her speech she is shouted down by a small group of conservative students and faculty.

    4. Yang Lei is a conservative columnist for one of the best conservative journals in the country. But she yearns for greener pastures—namely, a regular column for a weekly newsmagazine. She gets her dream job, though the magazine does have liberal leanings. The first few columns she writes for the magazine are a shock to her friends. Politically they are middle-of-the-road or even suspiciously liberal.

    5. Alex is a fourth-grade teacher at a suburban elementary school in Tennessee. He is liked by students and teachers alike, and he has superior teaching skills. He is also a homosexual. When a group of fundamentalist Christians learn that Alex is gay, they pressure the school board to fire him.

    6. Sylvia writes a column for the university newspaper. In her last installment, she argues that in a time of national crisis, the US Justice Department should have the power to arrest and detain literally anyone suspected of terrorism. Her arguments are well supported and presented with a tone of tolerance for those who disagree with her. And most students do disagree—vehemently. Hundreds of letters to the editor arrive at the newspaper, each one denouncing Sylvia and calling her a fascist and a few names that could not be published. In Sylvia's next column, she apologizes for her statements, says that she made serious errors, and declares that her statements should be viewed as hypothetical.

*7. Advertisement: When you make the best car in the world, everyone wants it. Audi XK2. A car in demand.

Exercise 2.5

Read each of the following scenarios. Indicate whether it contains examples of self-interested thinking or face-saving and, for each instance, specify the possible negative consequences.

*1. Barbara thinks that she is a superior student with excellent writing and math skills. She frequently says so to her friends and sometimes ridicules other people's grades and test scores. She predicts that her SAT scores will be in the 2100s. When she finally takes the test, she's calm, alert, and eager to get a fantastic score. Afterwards she says that she feels great. Her scores come back in the 1200s. She explains that the test doesn't count because it's obviously scored wrong and, besides, she's not a good test taker.

*2. City assemblyman Jackson is in a position to cast the deciding vote on two proposals for the development of a new city park. Proposal 1 offers a parcel of land near the assemblyman's house, which affords him a beautiful view. Its drawbacks are that it costs twice as much as proposal 2 and cannot be easily accessed by most of the public. Proposal 2 suggests a parcel of land near the center of town. It is convenient to the public, has a more beautiful setting, and will raise property values in the area. Assemblyman Jackson says that the obvious best choice is proposal 1.

3. Antonio is a college student who responds predictably to his scores on tests. If the score is high, he remarks that he hardly studied at all and that his score ranks among the highest in the class. If the scores are low, he says that the instructor grades unfairly, that the test was flawed, and that he intends to protest his grade to the grade-review committee.

4. Sheila is a bright medical scientist. For years she has been working on a series of clinical studies that could establish her favorite medical hypothesis—that high doses of vitamin E can cure skin cancer. Each study in the series has added more evidence suggesting that the hypothesis is probably true. The last study in the series is crucial. It is a much larger study than the others, and it will confirm or invalidate the usefulness of vitamin E for skin cancer. When the study is completed, she examines the data. Instead of confirming her hypothesis, the study suggests not only that her pet idea is unfounded but also that the doses of vitamin E used are toxic, causing terrible side effects in patients. She concludes, though, that the study results do not disconfirm her hypothesis but are merely inconclusive.

5. David and Max are in a heated debate about the theory of biological evolution. David rejects the theory in favor of creationism, which says that life on Earth was created or facilitated by a supreme intelligence. Max rejects creationism in favor of evolution. David marshals an abundance of facts that seem to prove his case. In addition, he alleges that evolution is false because there are huge gaps in the fossil record suggesting that there has never been a smooth, tidy progression of species from earlier forms to later forms. Max has no answer for this fossil-record gap argument and looks exasperated. David is about to declare victory when Max suddenly begins to quote the research findings of reputable biologists showing that there really are no gaps. After the debate some of Max's friends quietly congratulate him for being clever enough to quote research findings that are fictitious.

 ## Self-Assessment Quiz

Answers appear in "Answers to Self-Assessment Quizzes" in Appendix B.

1. According to the definition of critical thinking given in the text, what factors must be present for critical thinking to be realized?
2. From the standpoint of critical thinking, what event signals that we have allowed our bias in favor of ourselves to go too far?
3. According to the text, how might selective attention affect our thinking when we are examining evidence for or against a claim?
4. According to the text, what is probably the most powerful group pressure of all?
5. According to the text, what is a worldview?
6. What kind of doubt is involved in the acquisition of knowledge?
7. According to the text, why is it important to look for opposing evidence when evaluating claims?

Read each of the following scenarios. Indicate whether it contains examples of self-interested thinking, face-saving, or both.

8. Edgar predicts that Horace Windblower will win the 2016 presidential election. In fact, he bets money on it and brags that he always predicts the winners. Windblower loses by the widest margin in US history. At first,

Edgar refuses to pay the bet but finally relents. He claims that the election was rigged from the very beginning.

9. Lois strongly believes in UFO abductions—people being kidnapped by space aliens. She says that she has absolute proof: a small piece of metal that she says is "not of this earth" and a cut on her shin that she says came from alien probes. However, several metallurgists in the area say that the piece of metal is ordinary aluminum. And her daughter reminds her that she got the cut on her shin when she ran into a desk drawer. Lois doesn't say anything else about her "evidence," and she asserts that the real proof is in the skies in the form of alien spacecraft.

10. One day Julie and Jill hear their instructor read a list of arguments for and against abortion. Half the arguments are pro, and half con. Julie is on the pro side, Jill on the con side. Later when they discuss the abortion arguments, they recall the facts differently. Julie remembers that most of the arguments were for abortion rights. Jill remembers only the arguments against abortion and can't recall any pro arguments.

Specify whether the following passages are examples of face-saving, self-serving, or group-pressure thinking, or a combination of these.

11. The world would be better off if everything were run by Republicans.
12. Everyone believes in affirmative action. That fact alone ought to convince you to do the same.
13. Look, every student I know cheats on exams once in a while. So why not you? Why do you have to be such a Boy Scout?
14. People should do whatever makes them happy.
15. Congressman Hornblower: Anyone who doesn't believe in God shouldn't have a say in how this nation is run. I don't think that atheists should even be citizens.
16. Yes, I smoked marijuana in college, but I didn't inhale.
17. In the United States about 75 percent of the population has some kind of religious belief or denominational affiliation. In light of this, how can you say you're an unbeliever? If you're an unbeliever, you're un-American.

Read each of the following statements and indicate whether it is an example of the subjectivist fallacy or social relativism.

18. This may not be your truth, but it's my truth.
19. It's true for me that killing innocent civilians is morally wrong. It may not be true for you.
20. Chinese diplomat: My country cannot be judged by some universal standard. It must be judged by its own unique criteria and norms.

Writing Assignments

Select an issue from the following list and write a three-page paper defending a statement pertaining to the issue. Follow the procedure discussed in chapter 12 for identifying a thesis and an appropriate argument to defend it.

- Are the media biased?
- Should a single corporation be allowed to own as many media outlets (newspapers, radio and TV stations, publishers, etc.) as it wants?
- Should the US government be allowed to arrest and indefinitely imprison without trial any American citizen who is suspected of terrorism?
- Should immigrants to the United States ever be banned simply because of their religion?
- Should racial profiling be used to do security screening of airline passengers?

Identifying and Evaluating Arguments

I N THIS CHAPTER WE RESUME OUR DISCUSSION OF ARGUMENTS BEGUN IN CHAPTER 1, delve deeper into the dynamics and structure of different argument types, and get more practice in identifying and critiquing simple (and not so simple) arguments in their "natural habitat."

Remember, in chapter 1 we defined an argument as a group of statements in which some of them (the premises) are intended to support another of them (the conclusion). An essential skill is the ability to identify arguments in real-life contexts and to distinguish them from nonarguments. To recognize an argument, you must be able to identify the premises and the conclusion. Indicator words such as *because* and *since* often signal the presence of premises, and words such as *therefore* and *thus* can point to a conclusion.

Argument Basics

The point of *devising* an argument is to try to show that a statement, or claim, is worthy of acceptance. The point of *evaluating* an argument is to see whether this task has been successful—whether the argument shows that the statement (the conclusion) really is worthy of acceptance. When the argument shows that the statement is worthy of acceptance, we say that the argument is *good*. When the argument fails to show that the statement is worthy of acceptance, we say that the argument is *bad*. There are different ways, however, that an argument can be good or bad. There are different ways because there are different types of arguments.

Arguments come in two forms—**deductive** and **inductive**. A deductive argument is intended to provide logically *conclusive* support for its conclusion. An inductive argument is intended to provide *probable*—not conclusive—support for its conclusion.

A deductive argument that succeeds in providing such decisive logical support is said to be **valid**; a deductive argument that fails to provide such support is said to be **invalid**. A deductively valid argument is such that if its premises are true, its conclusion *must* be true. That is, if the premises are true, there is *no way* that the conclusion can be false. In logic, *valid* is not a synonym for true. A deductively valid argument simply has the kind of logical structure that *guarantees* the truth of the conclusion *if* the premises are true. "Logical structure" refers not to the content of an argument but to its construction, the way the premises and conclusion fit together. Because of the guarantee of truth in the conclusion, deductively valid arguments are said to be **truth preserving**.

Here's a simple deductively valid argument:

All dogs have fleas.
Bowser is a dog.
So Bowser has fleas.

And here's a golden oldie.

All men are mortal.
Socrates is a man.
Therefore, Socrates is mortal.

And one in regular paragraph form:

[Premise] If abortion is the taking of a human life, then it's murder. [Premise] It is the taking of a human life. [Conclusion] So it necessarily follows that abortion is murder.

In each of these arguments, if the premises are true, the conclusion must be absolutely, positively true. It is impossible for the premises to be true and the conclusions false. The conclusion *logically follows* from the premises. And the order of the premises makes no difference.

A deductively *invalid* version of these arguments might look like this:

All dogs are mammals.
All cows are mammals.
Therefore, all dogs are cows.

If Socrates has horns, he is mortal.
Socrates is mortal.
Therefore, Socrates has horns.

In each of these, the conclusion does *not* logically follow from the premises. Each is an attempt at a deductively valid argument, but the attempt fails. And, again, this would be the case regardless of the order of the premises.

An inductive argument that succeeds in providing very probable—but not conclusive—logical support for its conclusion is said to be **strong**. An inductive argument that fails to provide such support is said to be **weak**. An inductively strong argument is such that if its premises are true, its conclusion is *very likely* to be true. The structure of an inductively strong argument cannot guarantee that the conclusion is true if the premises are true—but the conclusion can be rendered very probable and worthy of acceptance. (Here again, the structure and content of an argument are distinct elements.) Because the truth of the conclusion cannot be guaranteed by the truth of the premises, inductive arguments are not truth preserving.

Let's turn our first two deductively valid arguments into inductively strong arguments:

> *Ninety-five percent of dogs have fleas.*
> *Therefore, Bowser, my dog, very likely has fleas.*

> *Ninety-eight percent of humans are mortal.*
> *Socrates is human.*
> *Therefore, Socrates is very likely to be mortal.*

Notice that in the first argument, it's entirely possible for the premise to be true and the conclusion false. After all, if only 95 percent of dogs have fleas, there is no guarantee that Bowser has fleas. Yet the premise, if true, makes the conclusion very probably true. Likewise, in the second argument it is possible that even if 98 percent of humans are mortal and Socrates is human, the conclusion that Socrates is mortal could be false. But the premises, if true, make it very likely that the conclusion is true.

Here are three more inductive arguments about some everyday concerns:

> *Almost every computer I've purchased at an online store has been a dud.*
> *Therefore, the next computer I purchase at the same online store will likely be a dud.*

> *Maria's car broke down yesterday.*
> *When it broke down, it made the same noise and spewed the same stinky exhaust that it always does when it breaks down.*
> *Maria's car breaks down a lot.*
> *Her mechanic, who does excellent work, always says the same thing: The problem is the carburetor.*
> *Therefore, Maria's car trouble yesterday was probably due to a carburetor problem.*

> *Twenty toddlers out of the twenty-one at the day care center have a cold. Therefore, this toddler (Johnny) very probably has a cold.*

Logical validity or logical strength is an essential characteristic of good arguments. But there is more to good arguments than having the proper structure. Good arguments also have *true premises*. A good argument is one that has the proper structure—*and* true premises. Take a look at this argument:

All pigs can fly.

Vaughn is a pig.

Therefore, Vaughn can fly.

The premises of this argument are false—but the conclusion follows logically from those premises. It's a deductively valid argument with all the parts in the right place—even though the premises are false. But it is not a good argument. A good argument must have true premises, and this argument doesn't. A deductively valid argument that has true premises is said to be **sound**. A sound argument is a good argument, which gives you good reasons for accepting its conclusion.

Note, however, that deductively valid arguments can have true or false premises and true or false conclusions. Specifically, deductively valid arguments can have false premises and a false conclusion, false premises and a true conclusion, and true premises and a true conclusion. A valid argument, though, cannot have true premises and a false conclusion—that's impossible. See for yourself:

False Premises, False Conclusion

All dogs have flippers.

All cats are dogs.

Therefore, all cats have flippers.

False Premises, True Conclusion

My dog Bowser is a cat.

All cats bark.

Therefore, Bowser barks.

True Premises, True Conclusion

Bowser is a dog.

All dogs are mammals.

Therefore, Bowser is a mammal.

A good inductive argument must also have true premises. For example:

Scientific studies show that 99 percent of dogs have three eyes.

So it's likely that the next dog I see will have three eyes.

This is an inductively strong argument, but it's not a good argument because its premise is false. When inductively strong arguments have true premises, they are said to be **cogent**. Good inductive arguments are cogent. Bad inductive arguments are not cogent.

You may have noticed another important difference between deductive and inductive arguments. The kind of support that a deductive argument can give a conclusion is *absolute*. Either the conclusion is shown to be true, or it is not. There is no sliding scale of truth or falsity. The support that an inductive argument can provide a conclusion, however, can vary from weak to extremely strong.

Both deductive and inductive arguments can be manipulated in various ways to yield new insights. For example, let's say that you have formulated a valid deductive argument, and you know that the conclusion is false. From these facts you can infer that at least one of the premises is false. Using this tack, you can demonstrate that a premise is false because in a valid argument it leads to an absurd conclusion. Or let's say that you've fashioned a valid argument, and you know that your premises are true. Then you can infer that the conclusion must be true—even if it's contrary to your expectations. Or maybe you put forth a strong inductive argument, and you know that the premises are questionable. Then you know that the conclusion also can't be trusted.

If you don't already have a sense of the wide-ranging usefulness of deductive and inductive arguments, the coming pages will make the point clear. You will find abundant evidence that the utility of both types of arguments is *universal*. They apply everywhere, work everywhere, and instruct everywhere—in everyday and professional life, in scientific realms, and in moral and philosophical explorations.

 NO ARGUMENTS, JUST FLUFF

Once you get really good at spotting arguments in a variety of passages, you may be shocked to see that a massive amount of persuasive writing contains no arguments at all. Apparently many people—including some very good writers—think that if they clearly express their opinions, then they have given an argument. You could look at this state of affairs as evidence that people are irrational—or you could view it as a time-saver: No need to waste your time on a bunch of unsupported opinions.

Unsupported opinions are everywhere, but they seem to permeate political writing, letters to the editor, and anything that's labeled "spiritual." Sometimes opinions are so weakly supported that they're almost indistinguishable from completely unsupported ones. Here's a taste:

My family and friends have season tickets for the Buffalo Bandits. The disrespect that is shown to America by this team is appalling, particularly in this time of war. As both the Canadian and American

continues

NO ARGUMENTS, JUST FLUFF

continued

national anthems are sung before each game, members of the team are hopping around, tugging at their uniforms, talking and carrying on amongst themselves. The players can't even wait for the national anthem to finish before they run off to their respective field positions. Whether one is for or against the war is irrelevant. Have some respect for America and what it stands for.

[Letter to the editor, *Buffalo News* website]

No argument here, just indignation.

So after a decade of progress, we have our smog problem back (as if it ever left). Another problem overlooked? Couldn't be because of all the giant behemoths (SUVs) on the road, could it? Nah. Or letting all the trucks from south of the border into our country without safety and smog inspections could it? Nah. It couldn't be because of the government, you think? Nah.

[Letter to the editor, *Daily News* (Los Angeles) website]

No argument here either.

Judging Arguments

When it comes to deductive and inductive arguments, the most important skills you can acquire are being able to identify them and determining whether they are good or bad. Much of the rest of this text is devoted to helping you become proficient in these skills. This chapter will serve as your first lesson and give you a chance to practice what you learn.

So the obvious questions here are: When you come face to face with an argument to evaluate, (1) how can you tell whether it's deductive or inductive, and (2) how can you determine whether it gives you good reasons for accepting the conclusion (whether it's sound or cogent)? The following is a suggested four-step procedure for answering these questions, one that will be elaborated on here and in later chapters.

Step 1. Find the argument's conclusion and then its premises. Use the techniques you learned in chapter 1.

Step 2. Ask: Is it the case that if the premises are true the conclusion *must* be true? If the answer is yes, treat the argument as *deductive*, for it is very likely meant to offer conclusive support for its conclusion. The argument, then, is deductively valid, and you should check to see if it's sound. If the answer is no, proceed to the next step.

Step 3. Ask: Is it the case that if the premises are true, its conclusion is *very probably* true? If the answer is yes, treat the argument as *inductive*, for it is very likely meant to offer very probable support for its conclusion. The argument, then, is inductively strong, and you should check to see if it's cogent. If the answer is no, proceed to the next step.

Step 4. Ask: Is the argument intended to offer conclusive or very probable support for its conclusion but *fails* to do so? If you reach this step, you will have already eliminated two possibilities: a valid argument and a strong one. The remaining options are an invalid argument or a weak one. So here you must discover what type of (failed) argument is intended. These two guidelines can help you do that:

> **GUIDELINE 1:** Generally if an argument looks deductive or inductive because of its form, assume that it is intended to be so.

Bad arguments may sometimes look like good arguments because the arrangement of their premises and conclusion—their form—is similar to that found in reliable arguments. Such argument forms are an indication of what kind of argument is intended, and that fact gives you some guidance on determining argument type.

> **GUIDELINE 2:** Generally if an argument looks deductive or inductive because of indicator words (and its form yields no clues), assume that it is intended to be so.

As suggested earlier, arguments are often accompanied by words or phrases that identify them as deductive or inductive. Terms that signal a deductive argument include "It necessarily follows that," "it logically follows that," "absolutely," "necessarily," and "certainly." Words signaling an inductive argument include "likely," "probably," "chances are," "odds are," and "it is plausible that." Such indicator words, though, are not foolproof clues to argument type because they are sometimes used in misleading ways. For example, someone might end an inductively strong argument with a conclusion prefaced with "it necessarily follows that," suggesting that the argument is deductively valid. But argument-type indicators may still be useful, especially when the argument form yields no clues (when Guideline 1 doesn't apply).

In step 4, once you discover which kind of argument is intended, you will know that it is either invalid or weak (because in steps 2 and 3 we eliminated the possibility of a valid or strong argument). The only remaining task is to determine whether the premises are true.

Let's try out the four-step procedure on a few arguments. Consider this one:

[Premise] Unless we do something about the massive AIDS epidemic in Africa, the whole continent will be decimated within six months. [Premise] Unfortunately we won't do anything about the AIDS epidemic in Africa. [Conclusion] It necessarily follows that the whole of Africa will be decimated within six months.

Step 1 is already done for us; the premises and conclusion are clearly labeled. In step 2, we must ask, "Is it the case that if the premises are true, the conclusion must be true?" The answer is yes: If it's true that the AIDS epidemic in Africa will decimate the population in six months unless "we do something," and it's true that "we won't do anything," then the conclusion that Africa will be decimated in six months *must* be true. So this argument is deductively valid. To determine if it's sound, we would need to check to see if the premises are true. In this case, the first premise is false because, under current conditions, it would take longer than six months for the epidemic to decimate the whole continent. The other premise ("we won't do anything") is at least dubious since we can't predict the future. So what we have here is a deductively valid argument that's unsound—a bad argument.

Now let's analyze this one:

[Premise] This week, under pressure from the American Civil Liberties Union, the school board rescinded its policy of allowing school-sponsored public prayers at football games. [Premise] All the school board members agreed with the policy change. [Premise] And a memo from the board was circulated to all students, teachers, and coaches declaring that there will be no more public prayers at football games. [Conclusion] Let's face it, the days of public prayers at our school football games are over.

From step 2 we can see that even if this argument's three premises are all true, the conclusion can still be false. After all, even if everything described in the premises happens, there still could be a public prayer at a football game (perhaps because of some mistake or an act of protest on the part of school-prayer advocates). So the argument can't be deductively valid. But if we go through step 3, we can see that if all the premises are true, the conclusion is very likely to be true, making the argument inductively strong. If the premises *are* true, the argument would be cogent.

See what you think of this one:

[Premise] If you act like Bart Simpson, you will be respected by all your classmates. [Premise] But you don't act like Bart Simpson. [Conclusion] It follows that you will not be respected by all of your classmates.

This argument flunks the tests in steps 2 and 3: It is not deductively valid, and it is not inductively strong. But it does resemble a deductive argument in two ways. First, it displays a pattern of reasoning that can, at first glance, seem deductive. Actually, it uses an argument pattern that is always deductively *invalid* (called denying the antecedent). This alone should be evidence enough that the argument is indeed deductive but invalid. But it also contains an argument indicator phrase ("it follows that") that suggests an attempt at a deductive form.

You'll get more exposure to argument forms and indicator words in the rest of this chapter (and the rest of this text). Ultimately, practice in distinguishing different types of arguments and their relative worth is the only way to gain proficiency (and confidence!) in making these judgments.

So far we've spent most of our time assessing the logical structure of arguments—that is, whether they are valid/invalid or strong/weak. We haven't focused as much attention on evaluating the truth of premises because that's a big issue best considered separately—which is what we do in chapters 5 and 6.

Uncovering Implied Premises

Sometimes arguments not only are faulty but also have a few pieces missing. Premises (and sometimes even conclusions)—material needed to make the argument work—are often left unstated. These implicit premises, or assumptions, are essential to the argument. Of course, certain assumptions are frequently left unsaid for good reason: They are obvious and understood by all parties to the argument, and boredom would set in fast if you actually tried to mention them all. If you wish to prove that "Socrates is mortal," you normally wouldn't need to explain what *mortal* means and that the name Socrates does not refer to a type of garden tool. But many arguments do have unstated premises that are not only necessary to the chain of reasoning but also must be made explicit to fully evaluate the arguments.

For instance:

> The easy availability of assault rifles in the United States has increased the risk of death and injury for society as a whole. Therefore, assault rifles should be banned.

Notice that there is a kind of disconnect between the premise and the conclusion. The conclusion follows from the premise *only* if we assume an additional premise, perhaps something like this: "Anything that increases the risk of death and injury for society as a whole should be banned." With this additional premise, the argument becomes:

> The easy availability of assault rifles in the United States has increased the risk of death and injury for society as a whole. Anything that increases the risk of death and injury for society as a whole should be banned. Therefore, assault rifles should be banned.

Now that all the premises are spelled out, you can evaluate the *full* argument just as you would any other. Not only that, but you can see that the unstated premise is questionable, which is the case with many implicit premises. Not everyone would agree that anything raising the risk of death or injury should be banned, for if that were the case we would have to outlaw automobiles, airplanes, most prescription drugs, most occupations, and who knows how many kitchen appliances! Many unstated premises are like this one: They're controversial and therefore should not be left unexamined.

Here's another one:

> Anyone who craves political power cannot be trusted to serve the public interest. Senator Blowhard can't be trusted to serve the public interest.

As stated, this argument seems like a rush to judgment because the first premise concerns *anyone* who craves power, and suddenly Senator Blowhard is denounced as untrustworthy. Something's missing. What we need is another premise connecting the first premise to the conclusion: "Senator Blowhard craves political power." Now let's plug the implicit premise into the argument:

> Anyone who craves political power cannot be trusted to serve the public interest. Senator Blowhard craves political power. He can't be trusted to serve the public interest.

So exactly when should we try to ferret out an unstated premise? The obvious answer is that we should do so when there appears to be something essential missing—an implied, logical link between premises and conclusion that is not a commonsense, generally accepted assumption. Such implicit premises should never be taken for granted because, among other things, they are often deliberately hidden or downplayed to make the argument seem stronger.

Be aware, though, that many times the problem with an argument is not unstated premises, but invalid or weak structure. Consider this:

> If Tariq works harder, he will pass his calculus course. But he will not work harder, so he will not pass calculus.

This argument is invalid; the conclusion does not follow from the premises. Like most invalid arguments, it can't be salvaged without altering it beyond what is clearly implied. It's just a bad argument. The same goes for weak arguments. They usually can't be fixed up without adding or changing premises gratuitously. Remember, the point of articulating unstated premises is to make explicit what is already implicit. Your job as a critical thinker is *not* to make bad arguments good; that task falls to the one who puts forth the argument in the first place.

To make sure that your investigation of implicit premises is thorough and reasonable, work through the following three-step process.

Step 1. Search for a credible premise that would make the argument *valid*, one that would furnish the needed link between premise (or premises) and conclusion. Choose the supplied premise that

  a. is most plausible
  and
  b. fits best with the author's intent.

The first stipulation (a) means that you should look for premises that are either true or likely to be thought true. The second stipulation (b) means that premises should fit—that is, at least not conflict—with what seems to be the author's point or purpose (which, of course, is sometimes difficult to discern). If the premise you supply is plausible and fitting (with author's intent), use it to fill out the argument. If your supplied premise is either not plausible or not fitting, go to step 2.

Step 2. Search for a credible premise that would make the argument as *strong* as possible. Choose the supplied premise that fulfills stipulations a and b. If the premise you supply is plausible and fitting, use it to fill out the argument. If your supplied premise is either not plausible or not fitting, consider the argument beyond repair and reject it.

Step 3. Evaluate the reconstituted argument. If you're able to identify a credible implicit premise that makes the argument either valid or strong, assess this revised version of the argument, paying particular attention to the plausibility of the other premise or premises.

Now let's apply this procedure to a few arguments:

If the Fed lowers interest rates one more time, there will be a deep recession. I'm telling you there's going to be a deep recession.

The first step is to see if there's a credible premise that would make the argument valid. We can see right away that one premise will do the trick: "The Fed has lowered interest rates again." Adding it to the argument will supply the needed link between the existing premise and the conclusion. We also can see that our new premise is plausible (the Fed has lowered interest rates again) and seems to fit with the point of the argument (to prove that there will be a recession). Our resulting argument, though, is probably not a good one because the premise about the effect of the Fed's lowering interest rates is dubious.

Now examine this one:

Security officer Jones lied on her employment application about whether she had a criminal record. Security officer Jones will do a lousy job of screening passengers for weapons.

The sentence "Security officer Jones will do a lousy job of screening passengers for weapons" is the conclusion here. To try to make this argument valid, we would need a premise like "Any security officer at the airport who has lied on his or her employment application about having a criminal record will do a lousy job of screening passengers for weapons." This premise fits the point of the argument, but it isn't plausible. Surely it cannot be the case that *any* security officer who has lied will do a lousy job of screening. A more plausible premise is "Most security officers at La Guardia airport who have lied on their employment applications about having a criminal record will do a lousy job of screening passengers for weapons." This premise will do, and this is now a good argument—assuming that the other premise is true.

What about this one:

The use of marijuana should be legal because it's an act that brings pleasure to people's lives.

To try to make this argument valid, we might add this premise (or one like it): "Any act that brings pleasure to people's lives should be legal." But this premise is hard to accept since many heinous acts—such as murder and theft—may bring pleasure to some people, yet few of us would think those acts should be legal. To try to make the argument strong, we might change it like this:

Almost any act that brings pleasure to people's lives and doesn't harm others should be legal. Using marijuana brings pleasure to people's lives and doesn't harm others. Therefore, using marijuana should be legal.

By adding the stipulation about not harming others, we've rendered the argument strong.

Assessing Long Arguments

Some arguments are embedded in extended passages, persuasive essays, long reports, even whole books. When you have to evaluate a very long passage, you're almost always faced with three obstacles:

1. Only a small portion of the prose may contain statements that serve as the premises and conclusion. (The rest is background information, reiterations of ideas, descriptions, examples, illustrations, asides, irrelevancies, and more.)
2. The premises or conclusion may be implicit.
3. Many longer works purporting to be filled with arguments contain very few (or no) arguments and no credible evidence.

Fortunately, you can usually overcome these impediments if you're willing to put in some extra effort. The following is a three-step procedure that can help:

Step 1. Study the text until you thoroughly understand it. You can't locate the conclusion or premises until you know what you're looking for—and that requires having a clear idea of what the author is driving at. Don't attempt to find the conclusion or premises until you "get it." This understanding entails having an overview of a great deal of text, a bird's-eye view of the whole work.

Step 2. Find the conclusion. When you evaluate extended arguments, your first task, as in shorter writings, is to find the conclusion. There may be several main conclusions or one primary conclusion with several subconclusions. Or the conclusion may be nowhere explicitly stated but embodied in metaphorical language or implied by large tracts of prose. In any case, your job is to come up with a single conclusion statement for each conclusion—even if you have to paraphrase large sections of text to do it.

Step 3. Identify the premises. Like the hunt for a conclusion, unearthing the premises may involve condensing large sections of text into manageable form— namely, single premise statements. To do this, you need to disregard extraneous material and keep your eye on the "big picture." Just as in shorter arguments, premises in longer pieces may be implicit. At this stage you shouldn't try to incorporate the details of evidence into the premises, though you must take them into account to fully understand the argument.

Let's see how this procedure works on the following selection:

The Case for Discrimination
Edgardo Cureg was about to catch a Continental Airlines flight home on New Year's Eve when he ran into a former professor of his. Cureg lent the professor his cell phone and, once on board, went to the professor's seat to retrieve it. Another passenger saw the two "brown-skinned men" (Cureg is of Filipino descent, the professor Sri Lankan) conferring and became alarmed that they, and another man, were "behaving suspiciously." The three men were taken off the plane and forced to get later flights. The incident is now the subject of a lawsuit by the ACLU.

Several features of Cureg's story are worth noting. First, he was treated unfairly, in that he was embarrassed and inconvenienced because he was wrongly suspected of being a terrorist. Second, he was not treated unfairly, because he was not wrongly suspected. A fellow passenger, taking account of his apparent ethnicity, his sex and age, and his behavior, could reasonably come to the conclusion that he was suspicious. Third, passengers' anxieties, and their inclination to take security matters into their own hands, increase when they have good reason to worry that the authorities are not taking all reasonable steps to look into suspicious characters themselves. . . .

Racial profiling of passengers at check-in is not a panacea. John Walker Lindh could have a ticket; a weapon could be planted on an unwitting 73-year-old nun. But profiling is a way of allocating sufficiently the resources devoted to security. A security system has to, yes, discriminate—among levels of threat.

[*National Review,* July 1, 2002]

In this example, the author has given us a break by alluding to the conclusion in the title: Discrimination by racial profiling is a justified security measure. Notice that this conclusion is not explicitly stated in the text but is implied by various remarks, including "A security system has to, yes, discriminate." Given this conclusion, we can see that the entire first paragraph is background information—specifically, an example of racial profiling. The first premise is implicit. We glean it from the comments in the second paragraph: Racial profiling is a reasonable response in light of our legitimate concerns about security. The second premise is explicit: Profiling is a way of allocating sufficiently the resources devoted to security.

Laid out in neat order, this argument looks like this:

(1) *Racial profiling is a reasonable response in light of our legitimate concerns about security.*

(2) *Profiling is a way of allocating sufficiently the resources devoted to security.*

(3) *Therefore, discrimination by racial profiling is a justified security measure.*

A fact that can further complicate the argument structure of a long passage is that complex arguments can sometimes be made up of simpler arguments (subarguments). For example, the conclusion of a simple argument can serve as a premise in another simple argument, with the resulting chain of arguments constituting a larger complex argument. Such a chain can be long. The complex argument can also be a mix of both deductive and inductive arguments. Fortunately, all you need to successfully analyze these complex arguments is mastery of the elementary skills discussed earlier.

Let's take a look at another long passage:

Contemporary debates about torture usually concern its use in getting information from suspects (often suspected terrorists) regarding future attacks, the identity of the suspects' associates, the operations of terrorist cells, and the like. How effective torture is for this purpose is in dispute, mostly because of a lack of scientific evidence on the question. We are left with a lot of anecdotal accounts, some of which suggest that torture works, and some that it doesn't. People who are tortured often lie, saying anything that will make the torturers stop. On the other hand, in a few instances torture seems to have gleaned from the tortured some intelligence that helped thwart a terrorist attack.

Is torture sometimes the right thing to do? The answer is yes: in rare situations torture is indeed justified. Sometimes torturing a terrorist is the only way to prevent the deaths of hundreds or thousands of people. Consider: In Washington, D.C. a terrorist has planted a bomb set to detonate soon and kill a half million people. FBI agents capture him and realize that the only way to disarm the bomb in time is for the terrorist to tell them where it is, and the only way to get him to talk is to torture him. Is it morally permissible then to stick needles under his fingernails or waterboard him? The consequences of not torturing the terrorist would be a thousand times worse than torturing him. And according to many plausible moral theories, the action resulting in the best consequences for all concerned is the morally correct action. When we weigh the temporary agony of a terrorist against the deaths of thousands of innocents, the ethical answer seems obvious.

The length of this passage might suggest to you that the argument within it is long and tangled. But that's not the case here. The conclusion is this: In rare situations torture is morally justified. The first paragraph just provides background information; the second contains two premises. A paraphrase of the first premise would go something like this: In a ticking-bomb scenario, the consequences of not torturing a terrorist would be far worse than those of torturing him. The second premise says that the morally right action is the one that results in the best consequences for all concerned.

The argument then looks like this:

(1) *In a ticking-bomb scenario, the consequences of not torturing a terrorist would be far worse than those of torturing him.*

(2) *The morally right action is the one that results in the best consequences for all concerned.*

(3) *Therefore, in rare situations torture is morally justified.*

The best way to learn how to assess long passages is to practice, which you can do in the following exercises. Be forewarned, however, that this skill depends heavily on your ability to understand the passage in question. If you do grasp the author's purpose, then you can more easily paraphrase the premises and conclusion and uncover implicit statements. You will also be better at telling extraneous stuff from the real meat of the argument.

 KEY WORDS

cogent argument	deductive argument	inductive argument
invalid argument	sound argument	strong argument
truth preserving	valid argument	weak argument

EXERCISES

Exercises marked with * have answers in "Answers to Exercises" (Appendix A).

Exercise 3.1

1. What is a deductive argument?
2. What is an inductive argument?
3. Are inductive arguments truth preserving? Why or why not?
*4. The terms *valid* and *invalid* apply to what types of arguments?
5. What kind of guarantee does a deductive argument provide when it is valid?
6. Can an inductive argument guarantee the truth of the conclusion if the premises are true? Why or why not?
7. What is the difference between an inductively strong argument and an inductively weak one?
*8. What is the term for valid arguments that have true premises?
9. What is the term for strong arguments that have true premises?
10. Can a valid argument have false premises and a false conclusion? False premises and a true conclusion?
11. What logical conclusion can you draw about an argument that is valid but has a false conclusion?
*12. Is it possible for a valid argument to have true premises and a false conclusion?
13. In what way are conclusions of deductive arguments absolute?

Exercise 3.2

For each of the following arguments, follow the four-step procedure to determine whether it is deductive or inductive, valid or invalid, and strong or weak. Indicate the results of applying each step.

EXAMPLE 1
Colonel Mustard did not commit the murder. Someone who had committed the murder would have dirt on his shoes and blood on his hands. Colonel Mustard has neither.

Step 1: Conclusion: Colonel Mustard did not commit the murder. Premises: Someone who had committed the murder would have dirt on his shoes and blood on his hands. Colonel Mustard has neither.
Step 2: Deductively valid.
Step 3: Does not apply.
Step 4: Does not apply.

EXAMPLE 2

Ninety-five percent of people who smoke pot are irresponsible and forgetful. Looks like you smoke pot all the time. Ergo, you're irresponsible
and forgetful. Can you remember that?

Step 1: Conclusion: Ergo, you're irresponsible and forgetful. Premises:
Ninety-five percent of people who smoke pot are irresponsible
and forgetful. Looks like you smoke pot all the time.

Step 2: Not deductively valid.

Step 3: Inductively strong.

Step 4: Does not apply.

1. Either Jack is lying or he is not. If his ears turn red, he's lying. If they don't
turn red, he's telling the truth. His ears are red. Jack is lying.

*2. Ethel graduated from Yale. If she graduated from Yale, she probably has a
superior intellect. She has a superior intellect.

3. If you go to that party, you're completely nuts. You're going to the party. It
necessarily follows that you're nuts.

4. "Good sense is of all things in the world the most equally distributed,
for everybody thinks himself so abundantly provided with it, that even
those most difficult to please in all other matters do not commonly desire
more of it than they already possess." [René Descartes, *A Discourse on
Method*]

5. All philosophers are absent-minded. All philosophers are teachers. It
necessarily follows that all absent-minded people are teachers.

*6. Every musician has had special training, and everyone with special train-
ing has a college degree. Thus, every musician has a college degree.

7. People with high IQs also have psychic abilities. People with high SAT
scores—which are comparable to high IQ scores—also probably have psychic abilities.

8. If Elvis Presley's name is spelled wrong on his tombstone, there must be
some kind of conspiracy surrounding the death of the King. His name is
spelled wrong. Therefore, there's a conspiracy.

*9. Some actors sing, and some play a musical instrument. So some actors
who sing also play a musical instrument.

10. Anyone who is not a bigot will agree that Chris is a good fellow. Some
people in this neighborhood think that he's anything but a good fellow.
Some people in this neighborhood are bigots.

11. "In the actual living of life there is no logic, for life is superior to logic."
[Daisetz Teitaro Suzuki, *Essays in Zen Buddhism*]

12. A vase was found broken on the floor; some money had been taken out of
the safe; and there were strange scratches on the wall. It therefore follows
that someone obviously burglarized the place.

13. All the evidence in this trial suggests that Lizzy Borden is guilty of murder. Let's face it: She's probably guilty.
14. If everything was all right, there would be no blood on the floor. Of course, there is plenty of blood on the floor. Therefore, everything is not all right.
*15. If minds are identical to brains—that is, if one's mind is nothing but a brain—androids could never have minds because they wouldn't have brains. Clearly, a mind is nothing but a brain, so it's impossible for androids to have minds.
16. "From infancy, almost, the average girl is told that marriage is her ultimate goal; therefore her training and education must be directed towards that end." [Emma Goldman, "Marriage and Love"]
17. If you have scratches on your body that you can't account for, and you feel that you have been visited by space aliens, then you really have been visited by space aliens. You have such scratches, and you have experienced such feelings. Doubtless you have been visited by space aliens.
18. If bombs are falling on London, war has started. The bombs are falling now. War has begun.

Exercise 3.3

For each of the following arguments, indicate whether it is valid or invalid, strong or weak.

1. Joe says that the food in the restaurant is first-rate. So it's first-rate.
2. Social welfare is by definition a handout to people who have not worked for it. But giving people money that they have not earned through labor is not helping anyone. It follows then that social welfare does not help anyone.
*3. If CNN reports that war has started in Syria, then war has started in Syria. CNN has reported exactly that. War must have started.
4. If $r = 12$, then $s = 8$; $r = 12$; therefore, $s = 8$.
5. Any sitcom that tries to imitate *The Big Bang Theory* is probably a piece of trash. All of this season's sitcoms try to ape *The Big Bang Theory*. They've gotta be trash.
6. "Poetry is finer and more philosophical than history; for poetry expresses the universal and history only the particular." [Aristotle, *Poetics*]
7. Either you're lying or you're not telling the whole story. You're obviously not lying, so you're just relating part of the story.
*8. Either your thinking is logical or it is emotional. It's obviously not logical. It's emotional.
9. It is unwise to touch that electrical wire. It might be hot.
10. A recent Gallup poll says that 80 percent of Americans believe in the existence of heaven, but only 40 percent say they believe in hell. People are just too willing to engage in wishful thinking.

11. Many young black men have been shot dead by white police officers. Black people have often been harassed by white policemen. From these facts we can conclude that the recent tragic shooting in Chicago of a black teen by a white police officer was a case of first-degree murder.

12. "We say that a person behaves in a given way because he possesses a philosophy, but we infer the philosophy from the behavior and therefore cannot use it in any satisfactory way as an explanation, at least until it is in turn explained." [B. F. Skinner, *Beyond Freedom and Dignity*]

13. You flunked the last three tests. You didn't show up for the last eight classes. And you haven't written any of the essays. Looks like you don't know the material.

*14. Bachelors are unmarried. George is a bachelor. He has never taken a wife.

15. Bachelors are unmarried, and George acts like he's not married. He's a bachelor for sure.

16. If Alicia is alone on a trip, she will be afraid. She's alone on the latest trip. She is afraid.

17. If the universe had a beginning, then it was caused to begin. We know that the universe did have a beginning in the form of the Big Bang. So it was caused to come into existence. If it was caused to come into existence, that cause must have been God. God caused the universe to come into existence.

*18. If the United States is willing to wage war in the Middle East, it can only be because it wants the oil supplies in the region. Obviously the United States is willing to go to war there. The United States wants that oil.

19. "Someone must have been telling lies about Joseph K., for without having done anything wrong he was arrested one fine morning." [Franz Kafka, *The Trial*]

20. Anyone willing to take the lives of innocent people for a cause is a terrorist. Many Christians, Jews, and Muslims have taken innocent lives in the name of their religious cause. Many Christians, Jews, and Muslims have been terrorists.

21. If he comes back, it's probably because he wants money. There he is. He wants money.

22. If you're eighteen, you're eligible to vote. But you're only seventeen. You're not eligible to vote.

*23. I like geometry. My geometry teacher likes me. Therefore, I will pass my geometry course with flying colors.

Exercise 3.4

I. For each of the following arguments, identify the implicit premises that will make the argument valid.

EXAMPLE

The engine is sputtering. It must be out of gas.

Implicit premise: Whenever the engine sputters, it's out of gas.

*1. Any senator who is caught misusing campaign funds should resign his seat. Senator Greed should resign.

2. Jenna is a highly motivated runner, so she is sure to finish the race.

3. In the first week at the box office, the movie grossed over $30 million. So it's sure to win at least one Oscar.

4. The FBI doesn't have a very serious focus on stopping terrorism. Another major terrorist attack will happen in this country.

*5. The author of the book on interventionist wars is either biased or incompetent as a journalist. So she's biased.

6. The conflict in Indonesia is a genuine war. So it can't possibly be morally justified.

7. The Taliban regime fell because it persecuted women.

8. The US government should limit its activities to the Western Hemisphere because it doesn't have the resources to cover the whole world.

*9. If the engine starts right away, it's because of the tune-up I gave it. Must be because of the tune-up I gave it.

10. Taslima did not criticize US military action in the Gulf War or in the war in Afghanistan. She must be a hawk.

II. To each of the following arguments, change or add a premise that will make the argument strong.

1. The Republicans are more articulate about their policies and more realistic about world events than the Democrats are. They will surely win the next election.

2. Aziz regularly eats at McDonald's, so Aziz is likely to gain a few pounds.

*3. Six out of ten of my teenage friends love rap music. So 60 percent of all teens love rap music.

4. Seventy-one percent of the faculty and staff at Goddard Community College are Democrats. So most of the students are probably Democrats.

5. Miriam was in the library when the books were stolen from the librarian's desk. She was also seen hanging around the desk. So she's probably the one who stole them.

*6. If Assad's fingerprints are on the vase, then he's probably the one who broke it. He's probably the one who broke it.

7. If the president needs more money to balance the federal budget, he will get it from Social Security. Well, he's almost certainly going to get it from Social Security.

8. Ninety percent of students at Boston College graduate with a B.A. degree. Li Fong will probably graduate from Boston College with a B.A. degree.

*9. The murder rates in most large American cities on the East Coast are very high. The murder rates in most large cities in the West and Midwest are very high. So the murder rate in New Orleans must be very high.

10. John has a typical American diet. His fat intake is probably excessively high.

 ## Self-Assessment Quiz

Answers appear in "Answers to Self-Assessment Quizzes" in Appendix B.

1. What is a deductive argument? an inductive argument?
2. What is a valid argument? an invalid one? What is a strong inductive argument?
3. What is a sound argument?

Indicate whether the following arguments are deductive or inductive.

4. If you refuse to surrender, then you will be arrested. You refuse to surrender. Prepare yourself: You will be arrested.
5. There's an 80 percent chance that the hurricane will veer northward tomorrow and hit Tampa. So Tampa will probably feel the force of the hurricane tomorrow.
6. Ethel is reckless. She is going to have an accident sooner or later.
7. Whatever Hillary Clinton says is true. She says that the Republicans are weak. So the Republicans are weak.

In each of the following arguments, identify the implicit premise that will make the argument either valid or strong.

8. Jones has never openly criticized any military action against any Middle Eastern nation. He is a warmonger.
9. Maria failed her driving test three times. She's probably not paying attention.
10. If 60 percent of people believe in astrology or tarot cards, the future of the country does not look bright. Grades in college science courses will probably drop dramatically.

For each of the following exercises, provide an example of the argument pattern indicated.

11. If the job is worth doing, then it's worth doing well. The job is worth doing. Therefore, it's worth doing well.

12. If Austin is happy, then Barb is happy. Barb is not happy. Therefore, Austin is not happy.

13. If Einstein invented the steam engine, then he's a great scientist. Einstein did not invent the steam engine. Therefore, he is not a great scientist.

14. If Buffalo is the capital of New York, then Buffalo is in New York. Buffalo is in New York. Therefore, Buffalo is the capital of New York.

Identify the conclusion in the following arguments.

15. Cole is up to no good. He's been acting suspiciously for days, and he told Rachel that he was going to steal something valuable.

16. The sitcom *Orange Is the New Black* is becoming really lame. The writing is predictable and plodding. The acting is worse than ever.

17. If dolphins have minds comparable to ours, then these creatures are self-conscious, intelligent, and creative. If they are self-conscious, then they should react appropriately when they see their reflections in a mirror. They do react appropriately. If they're intelligent, they should be able to solve complex problems. They can solve such problems. If they're creative, they should be able to create some form of art. In a rudimentary way, they do create art. They are definitely self-conscious, intelligent, and creative.

18. If the dictum to always tell the truth in all circumstances is a valid moral principle, then it should fit well with our considered moral judgments. But it does not fit well with our considered moral judgments because there are times when lying is actually the right thing to do, as when we lie to save a life. So the dictum to always tell the truth is not a valid moral principle.

19. I don't think that I should vote for any independent candidate in the next election. Independents never win, and I want the person I vote for to win. Also, independents have a tendency to be a little wacky. And we definitely don't need any more wacky politicians in power.

20. Creationism is an inadequate theory about the origins of life. It conflicts with science, and it is incapable of predicting any new facts.

Writing Assignments

1. Select an issue from the following list and write a three-page paper defending a claim pertaining to the issue. Follow the procedures discussed in chapter 12 for outlining the essay and identifying a thesis.
   - Should the US government be permitted to kill American citizens overseas who have been identified as terrorists?
   - Should the federal government allow parents to withhold lifesaving medical care from their children on religious grounds?
   - Does pornography lead to violence against women?
   - Should the police or other security officers be permitted to use racial profiling to prevent terrorist attacks?
   - Should doctor-assisted suicide be legalized in all fifty states?
2. Find a 150- to 200-word passage purporting to present an argument for a particular view but actually being devoid of arguments. Look in magazines or newspaper letters to the editor or advocacy or political websites. Then rewrite the passage and include an argument for the original view.
3. Visit a website intended to support a particular view on a social or political issue. Using the information on the website, write a 100-word passage containing an argument for a view that the website might endorse.

Deductive Argument Patterns

ARLIER WE DISCUSSED THE IMPORTANCE OF BEING FAMILIAR WITH ARGUMENT patterns, or forms, the structures on which the content is laid. The point was that knowing some common argument forms makes it easier to determine whether an argument is deductive or inductive. But being familiar with argument forms is also helpful in many other aspects of argument evaluation. Let's take a closer look at some of these forms.

Common Forms

Since argument forms are structures distinct from argument content, we can easily signify different forms by using letters to represent statements in the arguments. Each letter represents a different statement in much the same way that letters are used to represent values in a mathematical equation. Consider this argument:

> *If the job is worth doing, then it's worth doing well.*
>
> *The job is worth doing.*
>
> *Therefore, it's worth doing well.*

We can represent this argument like this:

If *p*, then *q*.

p.

Therefore, *q*.

Notice that the first line in the argument is a compound statement—it's composed of at least two constituent statements, which are represented in this case by *p* and *q*. So we have three statements in this argument that are arranged into an argument form, one that is both very common and always valid. We can plug any statements we want into this form, and we will still get a valid argument. The premises may be true or false, but the form will be valid.

Some of the more common argument patterns that you encounter are like this pattern—they're deductive, and they contain one or more **conditional**, or if-then, premises. The first statement in a conditional premise (the *if* part) is known as the **antecedent**. The second statement (the *then* part) is known as the **consequent**.

The pattern shown here is called **affirming the antecedent** or, to use the Latin term, **modus ponens**. Any argument in the modus ponens form is valid—if the premises are true, the conclusion absolutely must be true. This means that if "If p, then q" and "p" are both true, the conclusion has to be true also. These facts, then, provide a way to quickly size up an argument. If it's in the form of modus ponens, it's valid, regardless of the content of the statements.

Another common argument form is called **denying the consequent**, or **modus tollens**:

> *If Austin is happy, then Barb is happy.*
> *Barb is not happy.*
> *Therefore, Austin is not happy.*

The form of modus tollens is:

> If *p*, then *q*.
> Not *q*.
> Therefore, not *p*.

Like modus ponens, modus tollens is always valid. If the premises are true, the conclusion must be true. So any argument that's in the modus tollens pattern is valid.

A third common argument form is called **hypothetical syllogism**. "Hypothetical" is just another term for conditional. A **syllogism** is a deductive argument made up of three statements—two premises and a conclusion. (Modus ponens and modus tollens are also syllogisms.) In a hypothetical syllogism, all three statements are conditional, and the argument is always valid:

> *If the ball drops, the lever turns to the right.*
> *If the lever turns to the right, the engine will stop.*
> *Therefore, if the ball drops, the engine will stop.*

Here's the symbolized version:

> If *p*, then *q*.
> If *q*, then *r*.
> Therefore, if *p*, then *r*.

People often use hypothetical syllogisms to reason about causal chains of events. They try to show that one event will lead inexorably to a sequence of events, finally concluding in a single event that seems far removed from the first. This linkage has prompted some to label hypothetical syllogisms "chain arguments."

A fourth common argument form is known as **disjunctive syllogism**. It's valid and extremely simple:

> *Either Ralph walked the dog, or he stayed home.*
>
> *He didn't walk the dog.*
>
> *Therefore, he stayed home.*

The symbolized form:

> Either *p* or *q*.
>
> Not *p*.
>
> Therefore, *q*.

Keep in mind that in a disjunctive syllogism, either disjunct can be denied, not just the first one.

There are two common argument forms that are *not* valid, though they strongly resemble valid forms. One is called **denying the antecedent**. For example:

> *If Einstein invented the steam engine, then he's a great scientist.*
>
> *Einstein did not invent the steam engine.*
>
> *Therefore, he is not a great scientist.*

Denying the antecedent is represented like this:

> If *p*, then *q*.
>
> Not *p*.
>
> Therefore, not *q*.

The premises can be true, and the conclusion false. That's what differentiates from denying the consequent.

You can see the problem with this form in the preceding argument. Even if the antecedent is false (if Einstein did not invent the steam engine), that doesn't show that he's not a great scientist because he could be a great scientist on account of some other great achievement. Thus, denying the antecedent is clearly an invalid pattern: It's possible for the premises to be true and the conclusion false.

Here's another example of this form:

> *If science can prove that God is dead, then God is dead.*
>
> *Science cannot prove that God is dead.*
>
> *Therefore, God is not dead.*

Even if science cannot prove that God is dead, that in itself does not show that God is not dead. Perhaps God is dead even though science cannot prove it. In other words, it's possible for both premises to be true while the conclusion is false.

The other common invalid form is called **affirming the consequent**. Here's an instance of this form:

If Buffalo is the capital of New York, then Buffalo is in New York.

Buffalo is in New York.

Therefore, Buffalo is the capital of New York.

We represent this form like this:

If *p*, then *q*.

q.

Therefore, *p*.

Obviously, in this form it's possible for the premises to be true while the conclusion is false, as this example shows. This pattern, therefore, is invalid.

These six deductive argument forms (four valid ones and two invalid ones) can help you streamline the process of argument evaluation. If you want to find out quickly if a deductive argument is valid, you can use these patterns to do that. (Remember, a good deductive argument has both a valid form and true premises.) You need only to see if the argument fits one of the forms. If it fits a valid form, it's valid. If it fits an invalid form, it's invalid. If it doesn't fit any of the forms, then you need to find another way to evaluate the argument. The easiest way to regularly apply this form-comparison technique is to memorize all six forms so you can identify them whenever they arise.

Sometimes you can see right away that an argument has a valid or invalid form. At other times, you may need a little help figuring this out, or you may want to use a more explicit test of validity. In either case, the *counterexample method* can help. With this technique you check for validity by simply devising a parallel argument that has the same form as the argument you're evaluating (the test argument) but has obviously *true premises and a false conclusion.* Recall that any argument having true premises and a false conclusion cannot be valid. So if you can invent such an argument that also has the same pattern as the test argument, you've proved that the test argument is invalid.

Let's say that you are confronted with this argument:

If crime is increasing, then our nation has abandoned God.

Our nation has abandoned God.

Therefore, crime is increasing.

And to check this test argument, you come up with this parallel argument:

If George is a dog, then he is warm-blooded.

George is warm-blooded.

Therefore, he is a dog.

This argument has the same pattern as the previous one—but the premises are true, and the conclusion is false. So the test argument is invalid. You may have already guessed that it is an instance of affirming the consequent. The counterexample method, though, works not just for the deductive forms we've discussed but for all deductive forms.

Consider another counterexample test. The argument in question is:

If Jackson drinks a lot of orange juice, he will get better.

He didn't drink a lot of orange juice.

Therefore, he will not get better.

And the parallel argument is:

If horses could fly, they would be valuable.

But horses cannot fly.

Therefore, horses are not valuable.

The argument to be tested is, of course, an example of denying the antecedent, and the counterexample method shows it to be invalid.

VALID AND INVALID ARGUMENT FORMS

Valid Argument Forms

Affirming the Antecedent (Modus Ponens)

Example:
If Spot barks, a burglar is in the house.
Spot is barking.
Therefore, a burglar is in the house.

If p, then q.

p.

Therefore, q.

continues

VALID AND INVALID ARGUMENT FORMS

continued

Denying the Consequent (Modus Tollens)

Example:
If it's raining, the park is closed.
The park is not closed.
Therefore, it's not raining.

If p, then q.

Not q.

Therefore, not p.

Hypothetical Syllogism

Example:
If Ajax steals the money, he will go to jail.
If Ajax goes to jail, his family will suffer.
Therefore, if Ajax goes to jail, his family will suffer.

If p, then q.

If q, then r.

Therefore, if p, then r.

Disjunctive Syllogism

Example:
Either we light the fire or we will freeze.
We will not light the fire.
Therefore, we will freeze.

Either p or q.

Not p.

Therefore, q.

Invalid Argument Forms

Affirming the Consequent

Example:
If the cat is on the mat, she is asleep.
She is asleep.
Therefore, she is on the mat.

continues

VALID AND INVALID ARGUMENT FORMS

continued

If p, then q.

q.

Therefore, p.

Denying the Antecedent

Example:
If the cat is on the mat, she is asleep.
She is not on the mat.
Therefore, she is not asleep.

If p, then q.

Not p.

Therefore, not q.

Reductio Ad Absurdum

One kind of powerful argument that you frequently encounter is known as reductio ad absurdum (reduction to absurdity). The idea behind it is that if the contradictory (negation) of a statement leads to an absurdity or falsehood, then the negation of the statement is false and the statement itself must be true. You must accept the statement because denying it gets you into logical trouble. So if you want to demonstrate that a statement is true (or false), you assume the statement's negation and show that it leads to an absurd or false statement. Here's the form of this type of argument:

p.

If p, then q.

Not q.

Therefore, not p.

In plain English, this says: Let's suppose that p is true. If p is true, then q must be true. But there's no way that q can be true. (Or q being true is absurd.) So it must not be the case that p is true. For example:

Suppose that water cannot freeze.

If water cannot freeze, then ice cannot exist.

But obviously ice does exist.

Therefore, water can freeze.

KEY WORDS

affirming the antecedent	affirming the consequent	antecedent
conditional	consequent	denying the antecedent
denying the consequent	disjunctive syllogism	hypothetical syllogism
modus ponens	modus tollens	syllogism

EXERCISES

Exercises marked with * have answers in "Answers to Exercises" (Appendix A).

Exercise 4.1

For each of the following arguments, determine whether it is valid or invalid and indicate the argument pattern.

*1. If the Pilgrims built that wall, there would be archeological evidence of that.
   But there is no such evidence.
   So the Pilgrims did not build that wall.

2. If the butler didn't kill the master, then the maid did.
   The butler didn't kill him.
   So the maid killed him.

3. Either John drove home or he stayed late.
   He didn't drive home.
   Therefore, he stayed late.

4. If the South Africans have nuclear weapons, the South African jungle will be radioactive.
   The South African jungle is radioactive.
   Therefore, the South Africans have nuclear weapons.

5. If the South Africans have nuclear weapons, the South African jungle will be radioactive.
   The South Africans do not have nuclear weapons.
   Therefore, the South African jungle is not radioactive.

*6. If CNN News omits important news stories, then it is irresponsible.
   It is not irresponsible.
   So CNN News does not omit important news stories.

7. If ESP (extrasensory perception) were real, psychic predictions would be completely reliable.

Psychic predictions are completely reliable.
Therefore, ESP is real.

8. If ESP (extrasensory perception) were real, psychic predictions would be completely reliable.
ESP is not real.
Therefore, psychic predictions are not completely reliable.

*9. If ESP (extrasensory perception) were real, psychic predictions would be completely reliable.
ESP is real.
Therefore, psychic predictions are completely reliable.

10. If laws could stop crime, there would be no crime.
But there is crime.
Therefore, laws cannot stop crime.

11. If I perceive what appears to be a red door, then there really is a red door there.
There really is a red door there.
Therefore, I perceive what appears to be a red door.

12. If it rains, Alex will get wet.
If Alex gets wet, he will be upset.
Therefore, if it rains, Alex will be upset.

Exercise 4.2

For each of the following premises, fill out the rest of the argument to make it valid in two different ways—modus ponens and modus tollens.

1. If God is in his heaven, then all is right with the world.
*2. If Lino is telling the truth, he will admit to all charges.
3. If some wars are just, then pacifism is false.
4. If the new vaccine prevents the spread of the virus, the researchers who developed the vaccine should get the Nobel Prize.
*5. If religious conflict in Nigeria continues, thousands more will die.
6. If p, then q.
7. If the glaciers are melting, global warming has increased.
8. If there is such a thing as moral progress—that is, social changes in which we judge states of affairs to be "better" now than before—then the Enlightenment ideal of moral perfection is possible.
*9. If solar power can supply six megawatts of power in San Francisco (which is certainly not the sunniest place in the world), then solar power can transform the energy systems in places like Texas and Arizona.
10. If my honorable colleague would stop listening to only his own voice for less than sixty seconds, he would doubtless be astonished that there are other minds in the world with other ideas.

Exercise 4.3

For each of the following passages, list the conclusion and premises.

*1. "There are those who maintain . . . that even if God is not required as the author of the moral law, he is nevertheless required as the enforcer of it, for without the threat of divine punishment, people will not act morally. But this position is [not plausible]. In the first place, as an empirical hypothesis about the psychology of human beings, it is questionable. There is no un-ambiguous evidence that theists are more moral than nontheists. Not only have psychological studies failed to find a significant correlation between frequency of religious worship and moral conduct, but convicted crimi-nals are much more likely to be theists than atheists. Second, the threat of divine punishment cannot impose a moral obligation, for might does not make right. Threats extort; they do not create a moral duty." [*Free Inquiry*, Summer 1997]

2. "I love *Reason* [magazine], but [regarding a previous article by Nick Gillespie] I'm wondering if all the illegal drugs that Nick Gillespie used to take are finally getting to him. He has a right to speak out against President Bush, but when he refers to him as 'the millionaire president who waited out the Vietnam War in the Texas Air National Guard,' it reminds me of the garbage rhetoric that I might see if I were reading Ted Rall, or Susan Sontag, or one of the other hate-mongering, America-bashing, leftist whiners. That kind of ad hominem attack is not only disrespectful to a man who is doing a damned good job as commander-in-chief (with approval ratings of more than 80 percent); it detracts from the whole point of the article." [Letter to the editor, *Reason*, July 2002]

3. "The first thing that must occur to anyone studying moral subjectivism [the view that the rightness or wrongness of an action depends on the beliefs of an individual or group] seriously is that the view allows the possibility that an action can be both right and not right, or wrong and not wrong, etc. This possibility exists because, as we have seen, the subjectivist claims that the moral character of an action is determined by individual subjective states; and these states can vary from person to person, even when directed toward the same action on the same occasion. Hence one and the same action can evidently be determined to have—simultaneously—radically different moral characters. . . .[If] subjectivism . . . does generate such contradictory conclusions, the position is certainly untenable." [Phillip Montague, *Reason and Responsibility*]

Self-Assessment Quiz

Answers appear in "Answers to Self-Assessment Quizzes" in Appendix B.
Identify the following argument patterns.

1. If *p*, then *q*.
   p.
   Therefore, *q*.
2. If *p*, then *q*.
   Not *q*.
   Therefore, not *p*.
3. If *p*, then *q*.
   If *q*, then *r*.
   Therefore, if *p*, then *r*.
4. Either *p* or *q*.
   Not *p*.
   Therefore, q.
5. If *p*, then *q*.
   q.
   Therefore, *p*.
6. If *p*, then *q*.
   Not *p*.
   Therefore, not *q*.
7. *p*.
   If *p*, then *q*.
   Not *q*.
   Therefore, not *p*.
8. Either *p* or *q*.
   Not *p*.
   Therefore, *q*.
9. If *p*, then *q*.
   Not *q*.
   Therefore, not *p*.

Define the following.

10. antecedent
11. weak argument
12. valid argument
13. cogent argument
14. conditional statement
15. consequent

16. deductive argument

17. inductive argument

18. strong argument

19. invalid argument

 Writing Assignments

Select one of the following topics and extract an issue from it that you can write about. Investigate arguments on both sides of the issue, and write a three-page paper defending your chosen thesis.

sexual harassment on college campuses

immigration

the morning-after pill

free speech on college campuses

textbook censorship

cloning humans

American drone strikes of reputed terrorists in foreign countries

North Korea and nuclear weapons

endangered species

animal rights

date rape

Inductive Arguments and Statistics

W̲E NOW PASS FROM AN EXPLORATION OF DEDUCTIVE ARGUMENTS TO A CLOSE examination of inductive ones—a very small step since both these argument types are common features of our everyday lives. Recall that a deductive argument is intended to provide logically conclusive support for its conclusion, being valid or invalid, sound or unsound. An inductive argument, on the other hand, is intended to supply only probable support for its conclusion, earning the label of "strong" if it renders its conclusion very likely to be true and "weak" if it fails to provide such support. The conclusion of an inductively strong argument is much more likely to be true than not—that is, very probable. If the argument's premises are true, it is said to be cogent. Unlike valid deductive arguments, an inductively strong argument cannot guarantee that the conclusion is true—but it can render the conclusion very probably true, even very, very likely to be true. Inductive arguments, then, cannot give us certainty, but they can give us high levels of probability—high enough at least to help us acquire knowledge in everything from physics to bird watching.

Deductive logic is the invisible framework on which much of our reasoning hangs and the solid bond that holds together the logical lattices of mathematics, computer science, and other theoretical or abstract disciplines. Inductive reasoning, though, gives us most of what we know about the empirical workings of the world, allowing us in science and in ordinary experience to soar reliably from what we know to what we don't. It allows us to reason "beyond the evidence"— from bits of what is already known to conclusions about what those bits suggest is probably true. And when we talk of probability, we enter the realm of statistics.

Inductive arguments come in several forms. In this chapter we will examine two of them (enumerative and analogical) and focus on how to evaluate their merits in real-life contexts.

Enumerative Induction

As you may have noticed, sometimes an inductive argument reasons from premises about a group, or class, of things to a conclusion about a single member of the group—that is, from the general to the particular, or the whole to the part. For example:

> *Almost all of the students attending this college are pacifists.*
>
> *Wei-en attends this college.*
>
> *Therefore, Wei-en is probably a pacifist.*

> *Eighty-two percent of residents in this neighborhood have been victims of crimes.*
>
> *Samuel is a resident of this neighborhood.*
>
> *Therefore, Samuel will probably be a victim of a crime.*

Such an inductive argument has been known traditionally as a *statistical syllogism*. The word *syllogism*—which is usually reserved for deductive arguments— refers to the fact that this argument consists of three statements: two premises and a conclusion. *Syllogism* is used to indicate that the generalization expressed in one of the premises is less than universal. But the defining feature of this argument is that its line of reasoning goes from a statement about a group of things to a conclusion about a single member of that group.

Our main concern here, however, is a more common inductive argument that reasons from premises about individual members of a group to conclusions about the group as a whole (from particular to general, or the part to the whole). In such cases we begin with observations about some members of the group and end with a generalization about all of them. This argument pattern is called **enumerative induction**, and it's a way of reasoning that we all find both natural and useful:

> *All the peace activists I know are kind-hearted. So probably all peace activists are kind-hearted.*
>
> *Every Gizmo computer I've bought in the last two years has had a faulty monitor. Therefore, all Gizmo computers probably have faulty monitors.*
>
> *Forty percent of the pickles that you've pulled out of the barrel are exceptionally good. So 40 percent of all the pickles in the barrel are probably exceptionally good.*

More formally, enumerative induction has this form:

> *X percent of the observed members of group A have property P.*
>
> *Therefore, X percent of all members of group A probably have property P.*

In this formal guise, our pickle argument looks like this:

Forty percent of the observed pickles from the barrel are exceptionally good.

Therefore, 40 percent of all the pickles in the barrel are probably exceptionally good.

Enumerative induction comes with some useful terminology. The group as a whole—the whole collection of individuals in question—is called the **target population** or **target group.** The observed members of the target group are called the **sample members** or **sample.** And the property we're interested in is called the **relevant property** or **property in question.** In the foregoing example, the target group is the pickles in the barrel. The sample is the observed pickles. And the property is the quality of being exceptionally good.

Now, using this terminology we can study arguments by enumeration a little more closely. Remember that an inductive argument can not only be strong or weak, but it can also vary in its strength—in the degree of support that the premises give to the conclusion. So argument strength depends on the premises as well as on how much is claimed in the conclusion. Let's look at some examples.

Argument 1

All the corporate executives Jacques has worked for have been crooks.

Therefore, all corporate executives are probably crooks.

The target group is corporate executives, the sample is the corporate executives Jacques has worked for, and the relevant property is being a crook. We don't know how many corporate executives Jacques has worked for, but we must assume from what we know about career paths in corporate America that the number is small, probably no more than a dozen. Neither do we know exactly how many corporate executives there are, but we can safely guess that there are thousands or hundreds of thousands. It should be obvious then that this enumerative inductive falls short on at least one score: The sample is too small. We simply cannot draw reliable conclusions about all corporate executives based on a mere handful of them. The argument is weak.

With such a small sample of the target group, we can't even conclude that *most* corporate executives are crooks. But we can make argument 1 strong by revising the conclusion like this: "*Some* corporate executives are probably crooks." This is a much more limited generalization that requires a more limited supporting premise.

We can fault this argument on another count: The sample is not representative of the target group. With thousands of corporate executives working for thousands of corporations, we must assume that corporate executives—in temperament, morality, demographics, and many other factors—are a diverse lot. It is therefore highly unlikely that Jacques's former bosses are representative of all corporate executives in their crookedness (the relevant property). And if the sample is not representative of the whole, we cannot use it to draw accurate conclusions about the whole. Argument 1 is weak for this additional reason.

Consider this one:

Argument 2

All of the blue herons that we've examined at many different sites in the nature preserve (about two hundred birds) have had birth defects.

Therefore, most of the blue herons in the nature preserve probably have birth defects.

In this argument the target group is the blue herons in the nature preserve, the sample is the two hundred blue herons examined, and the relevant property is having birth defects. We would normally consider this a very strong enumerative induction. Assuming that the premise is true, we would probably be surprised to discover that only a tiny minority of the target group had birth defects. Since the sample was drawn from many parts of the preserve, we would deem it representative of the target group. And due to the general uniformity of characteristics among birds in the wild, we would assume that a sample of two hundred birds would be large enough to strongly support the conclusion. As it stands, argument 2 is strong.

On the other hand, a conclusion asserting that *all* of the target group had birth defects would normally go beyond what the evidence in the premise would support. There could easily be at least some blue herons in the preserve (assuming it to be sufficiently large) that don't have birth defects, even if most do.

So you can see that an enumerative inductive argument can fail to be strong in two major ways: Its sample can be (1) too small or (2) not representative. Of course, it's possible for an enumerative induction to be perfectly strong—but have false premises, in which case the argument isn't cogent. That is, the data (or evidence) stated in the premises could have been misinterpreted, fabricated, or misstated.

Sample Size

Let's say that you decide to conduct a survey of college students to determine their attitude toward federal deficits. So you stand around in the student center and query the first five students that pass by. Four out of the five say that deficits don't matter. You conclude: Eighty percent of the student body believe that deficits don't matter. Should you send your findings to the school newspaper—or to CNN?

No way. This survey is a joke—the sample is much too small to yield any reliable information about the attitudes of the students as a whole. This verdict may seem obvious, but just about everyone at one time or another probably makes this kind of mistake, an error known as **hasty generalization**. We're guilty of hasty generalization whenever we draw a conclusion about a target group based on an inadequate sample size. People regularly make this mistake when dealing with all sorts of enumerative inductive evidence—political polls, consumer opinion surveys, scientific studies (especially medical research), quality-control checks, anecdotal reports, and many others.

In our everyday experience, we may casually make, hear, or read hasty generalizations like this:

> *You should buy a Dell computer. They're great. I bought one last year, and it has given me nothing but flawless performance.*
>
> *The only male professor I've had this year was a chauvinist pig. All the male professors at this school must be chauvinist pigs.*
>
> *Psychology majors are incredibly ignorant about human psychology. Believe me, I know what I'm talking about: My best friend is a psych major. What an ignoramus!*
>
> *The French are snobby and rude. Remember those two high-and-mighty guys with really bad manners? They're French. I rest my case.*
>
> *The food at Pappie's Restaurant is awful. I had a sandwich there once, and the bread was stale.*

In general, the larger the sample, the more likely it is to reliably reflect the nature of the larger group. In many cases our common sense tells us when a sample is or is not large enough to draw reliable conclusions about a particular target group. A good rule of thumb is this: *The more homogeneous a target group is in traits relevant to the property in question, the smaller the sample can be; the less homogeneous, the larger the sample should be.*

For example, if we want to determine whether cottontail rabbits have teeth, we need to survey only a tiny handful of cottontail rabbits (maybe even just one) because cottontail rabbits are fairly uniform in their physical characteristics. In this sense, if you've seen one cottontail rabbit, you've seen them all. On the other hand, if we want to know the sexual preferences of Hispanics who live in North American suburbs, surveying just a few won't do. Questioning a sample of two or twenty or even two hundred North American suburban Hispanics will not give us a reliable read on the sexual preferences of the target group. In social, psychological, and cultural properties, people are too diverse to judge a large target group by just a few of its members. In biological properties, however, *Homo sapiens* is relatively uniform. We need to survey only one normal member of the species to find out if humans have ears.

Representativeness

In addition to being the proper size, a sample must be a **representative sample**—it must resemble the target group in all the ways that matter. If it does not properly represent the target group, it's a **biased sample.** An enumerative inductive argument is strong only if the sample is representative of the whole.

Many arguments using unrepresentative samples are ludicrous; others are more subtle.

> *College students are glad that Congress is controlled by Republicans. Surveys of the members of Young Republican clubs on dozens of college campuses prove this.*
>
> *Most nurses in this hospital are burned out, stressed out, and overworked. Just ask the ones who work in the emergency department. They'll tell you they're absolutely miserable.*
>
> *No one is happy. Almost everyone is complaining about something. Just look at the letters to the editor in any big-city newspaper. Complaints, complaints, complaints.*

To be truly representative, the sample must be like the target group by (1) having all the same relevant characteristics and (2) having them in the same proportions that the target group does. The "relevant characteristics" are features that could influence the property in question. For example, let's say that you want to survey adult residents of Big City to determine whether they favor distributing condoms in high schools. Features of the residents that could influence whether they favor condom distribution include political party affiliation, ethnic background, and being Catholic. So the sample of residents should have all of these features and have them in the same proportions as the target group (residents of Big City). If half the adult residents of Big City are Catholic, for example, then half the sample should consist of residents who are Catholic.

Say that we want to determine how the ten thousand eligible voters in a small town intend to vote in an upcoming presidential election. We survey one thousand of them, which should be more than enough for our purposes. But the voters we poll are almost all over seventy years old and live in nursing homes. Our sample is biased because it does not reflect the makeup of the target group, most of whom are people under forty-five who live in their own homes, work in factories or offices, and have school-age children. Any enumerative argument based on this survey would be weak.

We are often guilty of biased sampling in everyday situations. One way this happens is through a phenomenon called *selective attention*, the tendency to focus intensely on particular things—to observe or remember them—while ignoring or suppressing others. We may tell our friends that *Stranger Things* is a lousy TV series because we remember that three episodes were boring—but we conveniently forget the four other episodes that we thought were superb. Or we may be convinced that Dr. Jones is one of the legendary "absent-minded professors." But this generalization seems plausible to us only because we're on the lookout for instances in which the professor's behavior seems to fit the stereotype, and we don't notice instances that contradict the stereotype.

MEAN, MEDIAN, AND MODE

If you read enough opinion polls, you will surely encounter one of these terms: mean, median, or mode. These concepts are invaluable in expressing statistical facts, but they can be confusing. Mean is simply an average. The mean of these four numbers—6, 7, 4, and 3—is 5 (6 + 7 + 4 + 3 = 20 divided by 4). The median is the middle point of a series of values, meaning that half the values are above the point and half the values are below the point. The median of these eleven values—3, 5, 7, 13, 14, 17, 21, 23, 24, 27, 30—is 17 (the number in the middle). The mode is the most common value. The mode in this series of values—7, 13, 13, 13, 14, 17, 21, 21, 27, 30, 30—is 13 (the most frequently appearing value).

The notions of mean, median, and mode are often manipulated to mislead people. For example, let's say that the dictator of Little Island Nation (population one thousand) proposes a big tax cut for everyone, declaring that the mean tax savings will be $5,000 (the total tax cut divided by one thousand taxpayers). The Islanders begin to gleefully envision how they will spend their $5,000. But then they learn that the mean figure has been skewed higher because of a few millionaires whose tax savings will be $100,000 or more. The tax savings for the vast majority of taxpayers is actually less than $500. The $5,000 figure that the dictator tossed out is the true mean—but painfully misleading. To the Islanders, the median tax savings is much more revealing: The median is $400. The mode, the most common figure, is $300. When they get all the facts, the Islanders stage a revolt—the first one in history caused by a better understanding of statistics.

Opinion Polls

Enumerative inductions reach a high level of sophistication in the form of opinion polls conducted by professional polling organizations. Opinion polls are used to arrive at generalizations about everything from the outcome of presidential elections to public sentiments about cloning babies to the consumer's appetite for tacos. But as complex as they are, opinion polls are still essentially inductive arguments (or the basis of inductive arguments) and must be judged accordingly.

So as inductive arguments, opinion polls should (1) be strong and (2) have true premises. More precisely, any opinion poll worth believing must (1) use a large enough sample that accurately represents the target population in all the relevant population features and (2) generate accurate data (the results must correctly reflect what they purport to be about). A poll can fail to meet this latter requirement through data-processing errors, botched polling interviews, poorly phrased questions, and the like.

In national polling, samples need not be enormous to be accurate reflections of the larger target population. Modern sampling procedures used in national polls can produce representative samples that are surprisingly small. Polling organizations such as Gallup and Harris regularly conduct polls in which the target group is American adults (more than 242 million in 2013), and the representative sample consists of only one thousand to fifteen hundred individuals.

How can a sample of one thousand be representative of almost two hundred million people? This can be achieved by using **random sampling**. To ensure that a sample is truly representative of the target group, the sample must be selected *randomly* from the target group. In a simple random selection, every member of the target group has an equal chance of being selected for the sample. Imagine that you want to select a representative sample from, say, one thousand people at a football game, and you know very little about the characteristics of this target population. Your best bet for getting a representative sample of this group is to choose the sample members at random. Any nonrandom selection based on preconceived notions about what characteristics are representative will likely result in a biased sample.

Selecting a sample in truly random fashion is easier said than done (humans have a difficult time selecting anything in a genuinely random way). Even a simple process such as your trying to arbitrarily pick names off a list of registered voters is not likely to be truly random. Your choices may be skewed, for example, by unconscious preferences for certain names or by boredom and fatigue. Researchers and pollsters use various techniques to help them get close to true randomization. They may, for instance, assign a number to each member of a population and then use a random-number generator to make the selections.

One approach that definitely does *not* yield a random sample is allowing survey subjects to choose themselves. The result of this process is called a **self-selecting sample**—a type of sample that usually tells you very little about the target population. We would get a self-selecting sample if we publish a questionnaire in a magazine and ask readers to fill it out and mail it in, or if during a TV or radio news broadcast we ask people to cast their vote on a particular issue by clicking options on a website or emailing their responses. In such cases, the sample is likely to be biased in favor of subjects who, for example, just happen to be especially opinionated or passionate; who may have strong views about the topic of the survey and are eager to spout off; or who may simply like to fill out questionnaires. Magazines, newspapers, talk shows, and news programs sometimes acknowledge the use of self-selecting samples by labeling the survey in question as "unscientific." But whether or not that term is used, the media frequently tout the results of such distorted surveys as though the numbers actually proved something.

HOW SURVEY QUESTIONS GO WRONG

Many opinion polls are untrust-worthy because of flaws in the way the questions are asked. The sample may be large enough and representative in all the right ways, but the poll is still dubious. Here are a few of the more common problems.

Question Phrasing

Poll results can be dramatically skewed simply by the way the questions are worded. A poll might ask, for example, "Are you in favor of a woman's right to kill her unborn child?" The question is ostensibly about a woman's right to terminate a pregnancy through abor-

Poll results can be dramatically skewed simply by the way the questions are worded. A poll might ask, for example, "Are you in favor of a woman's right to kill her unborn child?" The question is ostensibly about a woman's right to terminate a pregnancy through abortion and is supposed to be a fair measure of attitudes on the question. But the wording of the question practically guarantees that a very large percentage of respondents will answer "no."

tion and is supposed to be a fair measure of attitudes on the question. But the wording of the question practically guarantees that a very large percentage of respondents will answer "no." The controversial and emotionally charged characterization of abortion as the killing of an unborn child would likely persuade many respondents to avoid answering "yes." More neutral wording of the question would probably elicit a very different set of responses.

Another example: A 1995 poll of African Americans discovered that 95 percent of the sample group approved of a local school voucher program. To get this huge approval rating, the survey question was worded like this: "Do you think that parents in your area should or should not have the right to choose which local schools their children will attend?" Who would want to give up such a right? No wonder the question elicited an overwhelming number of "shoulds."

Such biased wording is often the result of pollster sloppiness. Many other times it's a deliberate attempt to manipulate the poll results. The crucial test of polling questions is whether they're likely to bias responses in one direction or another. Fair questions aren't skewed this way—or are skewed as little as possible.

Question Ordering

The order in which questions are asked in a poll can also affect the poll results. Pollsters know that if the economy is in bad shape and they ask people about the economic mess first and then ask them how they like the

continues

HOW SURVEY QUESTIONS GO WRONG

continued

president, the respondents are likely to give the president lower marks than if the order of the questions was reversed. Likewise, if you're asked specific questions about crimes that have been committed in your home-town and then you're asked if you feel safe from crime, you're more likely to say no than if you're asked the questions in reverse order.

Restricted Choices

Opinion polls frequently condense broad spectrums of opinions on issues into a few convenient choices. Some of this condensation is necessary to make the polling process manageable. But some of it is both unnecessary and manipulative, seriously distorting the opinions of those polled. Daniel Goleman of the *New York Times* offers this example: "In one survey . . . people were asked if they felt 'the courts deal too harshly or not harshly enough with criminals.' When offered just the two options, 6 percent said 'too harshly' and 78 percent answered 'not harshly enough.' But when a third alternative was added—'don't have enough information about the courts to say'—29 percent took that option, and 60 percent answered 'not harshly enough.'"

So a well-conducted poll using a random sample of one thousand to fifteen hundred people can reliably reflect the opinions of the whole adult population. Even so, if a second well-conducted poll is done in exactly the same way, the results will not be identical to that of the first poll. The reason is that every instance of sampling is only an approximation of the results that you would get if you polled every single individual in a target group. And, by chance, each attempt at sampling will yield slightly different results. If you dipped a bucket into a pond to get a one gallon sample of water, each bucketful would be slightly different in its biological and chemical content—even if the pond's content was very uniform.

Such differences are referred to as the **margin of error** for a particular sampling or poll. Competently executed opinion polls will state their results along with a margin of error. A presidential poll, for example, might say that Candidate X will receive 62 percent of the popular vote, plus or minus 3 points (a common margin of error for presidential polls). The usual way of expressing this number is 62 percent ±3. This means that the percentage of people in the target population who will likely vote for Candidate X is between 59 and 65 percent.

Connected to the concept of margin of error is the notion of **confidence level.** In statistical theory, the confidence level is the probability that the sample will accurately represent the target group within the margin of error. A confidence level of 95 percent (the usual value) means that there is a 95 percent chance that the results from polling the sample (taking into account the margin of error) will accurately reflect the results that we would get if we polled the entire target population. So if our aforementioned presidential poll has a 95 percent confidence level, we know that there's a 95 percent chance that the sampling results of 62 percent ±3 points will accurately reflect the situation in the whole target group. Of course, this confidence level also means that there's a 5 percent chance that the poll's results will *not* be accurate.

Note that "confidence level" refers only to sampling error, the probability of the sample not accurately reflecting the true values in the target population. It doesn't tell you anything about any other kinds of polling errors such as bias that can occur because of poorly worded questions or researchers who may consciously or unconsciously influence the kinds of answers received.

Sample size, margin of error, and confidence level are all related in interesting ways.

- Up to a point, the larger the sample, the smaller the margin of error because the larger the sample, the more representative it is likely to be. Generally, for national polls, a sample size of six hundred yields a margin of error of ±5 points; a sample of one thousand, ±4 points; and a sample of fifteen hundred, ±3 points. But increasing the sample size substantially to well beyond one thousand does not substantially decrease the margin of error. Boosting the sample from fifteen hundred to ten thousand, for example, pushes the margin of error down to only 1 percent.
- The lower the confidence level, the smaller the sample size can be. If you're willing to have less confidence in your polling results, then a smaller sample will do. If you can accept a confidence level of only 90 percent (a 10 percent chance of getting inaccurate results), then you don't need a sample size of fifteen hundred to poll the adult population.
- The larger the margin of error, the higher the confidence level can be. With a large margin of error (±8, for example), you will naturally have more confidence that your survey results will fall within this wide range. This idea is the statistical equivalent of a point made earlier: You can have more confidence in your enumerative inductive argument if you qualify, or decrease the precision of, the conclusion.

To sum up: An enumerative induction, like any other inductive argument, must be strong and have true premises for us to be justified in accepting the conclusion. A strong enumerative induction must be based on a sample that is both large enough and representative. An opinion poll, as a sophisticated enumerative

Thank you for taking part in this poll, sir. Here's the first question: What the heck makes you so arrogant to think your opinion could have any kind of importance, sir?

induction, must use a sufficiently large and representative sample and ensure that the gathered data accurately reflect what's being measured.

Analogical Induction

An **analogy** is a comparison of two or more things alike in specific respects. In literature, science, and everyday life, analogies are used to explain or describe something. Analogies (often in the form of similes) can be powerful literary devices, both unforgettable and moving:

> . . . *the evening is spread out against the sky*
> *Like a patient etherized upon a table* . . .
>
> *[T. S. Eliot]*

> *As cold waters to a thirsty soul,*
> *so is good news from a far country.*
>
> *[Proverbs 25:25]*

> . . . *Out, out brief candle!*
> *Life's but a walking shadow, a poor player*
> *That struts and frets his hour upon the stage*

And then is heard no more. It is a tale
Told by an idiot, full of sound and fury,
Signifying nothing.

[**Macbeth,** *Act V*]

But an analogy can also be used to *argue inductively for a conclusion*. Such an argument is known as an **analogical induction**, or simply an **argument by analogy**. An analogical induction reasons this way: Because two or more things are similar in several respects, they are likely to be similar in some further respect.

For example:

Humans can move about, solve mathematical equations, win chess games, and feel pain.

Robots are like humans in that they can move about, solve mathematical equations, and win chess games.

Therefore, it's probable that robots can also feel pain.

This argument says that because robots are like humans in several ways (ways that are already known or agreed on), they must be like humans in yet another way (a way that the argument is meant to establish).

So analogical induction has this pattern:

Thing A has properties P1, P2, P3 plus the property P4.

Thing B has properties P1, P2, and P3.

Therefore, thing B probably has property P4.

Argument by analogy, like all inductive reasoning, can establish conclusions only with a degree of probability. The greater the degree of similarity between the two things being compared, the more probable the conclusion is.

Arguments by analogy are probably used (and misused) in every area of human endeavor—but especially in law, science, medicine, ethics, archeology, and forensics. Here are a few examples.

Argument 1: Medical Science

Mice are mammals, have a mammalian circulatory system, have typical mammalian biochemical reactions, respond readily to high blood pressure drugs, and experience a reduction in blood cholesterol when given the new Drug Z. Humans are mammals, have a mammalian circulatory system, have typical mammalian biochemical reactions, and respond readily to high blood pressure drugs. Therefore, humans will also experience a reduction in blood cholesterol when given the new Drug Z.

Argument 2: Religion

A watch is a mechanism of exquisite complexity with numerous parts precisely arranged and accurately adjusted to achieve a purpose—a purpose imposed by the watch's designer. Likewise the universe has exquisite complexity with count-less parts—from atoms to asteroids—that fit together precisely and accurately to produce certain effects as though arranged by plan. Therefore, the universe must also have a designer.

Argument 3: Law

The case before the court involves a school-sponsored charity drive at which school officials led a public prayer. At issue is whether the school officials were in violation of the Constitutional ban on government support of religion. A simi-lar case—a relevant precedent—involved school-sponsored prayer at a school soccer game, and again at issue was whether the school was in violation of the Constitutional ban on government support of religion. In that case, the high court ruled that the school-sponsored prayer was unconstitutional. Therefore, the high court should also rule in the charity-drive case that the officially led prayer is unconstitutional.

Argument 4: Forensics

Whenever we have observed this pattern in the spatter of blood, we have subse-quently learned that the gunshot victim was about four feet from the gun when it was fired and that the victim was facing away from the assailant. In this crime scene, we have exactly the same pattern of blood spatter. Therefore, the victim was about four feet from the gun when it was fired and was facing away from the assailant.

Arguments by analogy are easy to formulate—perhaps too easy. To use an analogy to support a particular conclusion, all you have to do is find two things with some similarities and then reason that the two things are similar in yet an-other way. You could easily reach some very loopy conclusions. You could argue this, for instance: Birds have two legs, two eyes, breathe air, and fly; and humans have two legs, two eyes, and breathe air; therefore, humans can also fly. So the question is, how do we sort out the worthy analogical inductions from the un-worthy (or really wacky)? How do we judge which ones have conclusions worth accepting and which ones don't?

Fortunately, there are some criteria we can use to judge the strength of argu-ments by analogy:

1. Relevant similarities
2. Relevant dissimilarities
3. The number of instances compared
4. Diversity among cases

If you find yourself thinking that they make perfect sense, that's probably because you already use these criteria in your own arguments by analogy.

Relevant Similarities

The more relevant similarities there are between the things being compared, the more probable the conclusion. Consider this argument:

> *In the Vietnam War, the United States had not articulated a clear rationale for fighting there, and the United States lost. Likewise, in the present war the United States has not articulated a clear rationale for fighting. Therefore, the United States will lose this war, too.*

There is just one relevant similarity noted here (the lack of rationale). As it stands, this argument is weak; the two wars are only dimly analogous. A single similarity between two wars in different eras is not enough to strongly support the conclusion. But watch what happens if we add more similarities:

> *In the Vietnam War, the United States had not articulated a clear rationale for fighting, there was no plan for ending the involvement of US forces (no exit strategy), US military tactics were inconsistent, and the military's view of enemy strength was unrealistic. The United States lost the Vietnam War. Likewise, in the present war, the United States has not articulated a clear rationale for fighting, there is no exit strategy, US tactics are inconsistent, and the military's view of enemy strength is naive. Therefore, the United States will also lose this war.*

With these additional similarities between the Vietnam War and the current conflict, the argument is considerably stronger. (The premises, of course, may be false, rendering the argument not cogent, even if the inference were strong.) Arguments 1–4 (medical science, religion, law, and forensics) can also be strengthened by citing additional relevant similarities between the things compared.

Notice that this first criterion involves *relevant* similarities. The similarities cited in an analogical induction can't strengthen the argument at all if they have nothing to do with the conclusion. A similarity (or dissimilarity) is relevant to an argument by analogy if it has an effect on whether the conclusion is probably true. The argument on war that was just given mentions five different similarities between the Vietnam War and the present war, and each similarity is relevant because it has some bearing on the probability of the conclusion. But what if we added these similarities?

1. In both wars, some combatants have green eyes.
2. In both wars, some soldiers are taller than others.
3. In both wars, ticket sales to movies in the United States increase.

These factors would make no difference to the probability of the conclusion. They're irrelevant and can neither strengthen nor weaken the argument.

Relevant Dissimilarities

Generally, the more relevant dissimilarities, or disanalogies, there are between the things being compared, the less probable the conclusion. Dissimilarities weaken arguments by analogy. Consider argument 1 (regarding Drug Z). What if we discover that cholesterol-lowering drugs that work in mice almost never work in humans? This one dissimilarity would severely weaken the argument and make the conclusion much less probable.

Pointing out dissimilarities in an analogical induction is a common way to undermine the argument. Sometimes finding one relevant dissimilarity is enough to show that the argument should be rejected. A familiar response to argument 2 (the watch argument) is to point out a crucial dissimilarity between a watch and the universe: The universe may resemble a watch (or mechanism) in some ways, but it also resembles a living thing, which a watch does not.

The Number of Instances Compared

The greater the number of instances, or cases, that show the relevant similarities, the stronger the argument. In the war argument, for example, there is only one instance that has all the relevant similarities: the Vietnam War. But what if there were five additional instances—five different wars that have the relevant similarities to the present war? The argument would be strengthened. The Vietnam War, though it is relevantly similar to the present war, may be an anomaly, a war with a unique set of properties. But citing other cases that are relevantly similar to the present war shows that the relevant set of similarities is no fluke.

Argument 4 (the forensics induction) is an especially strong argument in part because it cites numerous cases. It implies the existence of such instances when it says, "Whenever we have observed this pattern . . ."

Diversity Among Cases

As we've seen, dissimilarities between the things being compared weaken an argument by analogy. Such dissimilarities suggest that the things being compared are not strongly analogous. And we've noted that several cases (instead of just one) that exhibit the similarities can strengthen the argument. In this criterion, however, we focus on a very different point: The greater the diversity among the cases that exhibit the relevant similarities, the stronger the argument. Take a look at this argument:

> (1) In the 1990s a US senator, a Republican from Virginia, was chairman of the commerce committee, had very close ties to Corporation X, had previously worked for Corporation X before coming to office, and was found to have been taking bribes from Corporation X.

(2) In the 1980s another US senator, a Democrat from Texas, was chairman of the commerce committee, had very close ties to Corporation X, had previously worked for Corporation X before coming to office, and was found to have been taking bribes from Corporation X.

(3) In the 1970s another US senator, an Independent from Arkansas with strong religious values, was chairman of the commerce committee, had very close ties to Corporation X, had previously worked for Corporation X before coming to office, and was found to have been taking bribes from Corporation X.

(4) Now the newly elected Senator Jones, a Democrat from New York with strong support from labor unions, is chairman of the commerce committee, has very close ties to Corporation X, and has previously worked for Corporation X before coming to office.

(5) Therefore, Senator Jones will take bribes from Corporation X.

Here we have several similarities in question, and they exist between the Senator Jones situation (described in premise 4) and three other cases (detailed in premises 1–3). But what makes this argument especially strong is that the cases are diverse despite the handful of similarities—one case involves a Republican senator from Virginia; another, a Democratic senator from Texas; and finally a religious Independent senator from Arkansas. This state of affairs suggests that the similarities are not accidental or contrived but are strongly linked even in a variety of situations.

As you know, an inductive argument cannot guarantee the truth of the conclusion, and analogical inductions are no exception. But by carefully applying the foregoing criteria, we can increase our chances of arriving at well-supported conclusions (or of identifying those conclusions that are not). This is happily the case—even though there is no magic formula for using the criteria in real-life situations.

 KEY WORDS

analogical induction	analogy	argument by analogy
biased sample	confidence level	enumerative induction
hasty generalization	margin of error	property in question
random samplimg	relevant property	representative sample
sample	sample members	self-selecting sample
target group	target population	

EXERCISES

Exercises marked with * have answers in "Answers to Exercises" (Appendix A).

Exercise 5.1

For each of the following enumerative inductions, (1) identify the target group, sample, and relevant property; (2) indicate whether the argument is strong or weak; and (3) if it's weak, say whether the problem is a sample that's too small, not representative, or both. Assume that the information provided in the premises of each argument is true.

*1. Two-thirds of the adults in New York City identify themselves as "pro-choice" in the abortion debate. And almost 70 percent of adults in San Francisco do. This makes the situation perfectly clear: A large majority of the people in this country are pro-choice.

2. Most people are fed up with celebrities who get on their soapbox and air their political opinions. When people on the street have been asked by TV reporters how they feel about this issue, they almost always say that they wish celebrities would keep their opinions to themselves.

3. Doctors used to think that antiarrhythmic drugs were the cure for irregular heartbeats. They overprescribed these drugs and fifty thousand patients died. Doctors used to believe that the cure for ulcers was a bland diet, but that turned out to be wrong, too. Every new treatment we see these days sounds great. But history tells us that they will all turn out to be worthless.

*4. I've asked at least a dozen first-year students at this university whether the United States should go to war with "terrorist" countries, and they all have said no. So most of the students at this university are against such a militant policy.

5. A random, nationwide poll of several thousand gun owners shows that 80 percent of them are opposed to gun-control laws. Thus, most adults oppose gun-control laws.

6. In every winter for the past twenty years, Buffalo has received several feet of snow. Therefore, Buffalo is likely to get several feet of snow in the next fifty winters.

7. Most newspaper reports of crimes in Chicago involve alleged perpetrators who belong to racial minorities. Therefore, most crimes in Chicago are committed by racial minorities.

*8. Eighty-five percent of dentists who suggest that their patients chew gum recommend Brand X gum. Therefore, 85 percent of dentists recommend Brand X gum.

9. Two hundred samples of water taken from many sites all along the Charles River show unsafe concentrations of toxic chemicals. Obviously the water in the Charles River is unsafe.

10. Clearly there is an epidemic of child abductions in this country. In the past year, major network news organizations have reported five cases of children who were abducted by strangers.

11. University fraternities are magnets for all sorts of illegal activity. Last year several frat brothers were arrested at a frat-house party. And this year a fraternity was actually kicked off campus for violating underage drinking laws.

*12. Most Americans are happy with their jobs and derive a great deal of satisfaction from them. A survey of fifteen hundred adults with an annual income of $48,000 to $60,000, employed in various occupations, supports this assertion. When these subjects were asked if they were happy and satisfied with their jobs, 82 percent said yes.

Exercise 5.2

For each of the enumerative inductions in Exercise 5.1, indicate whether the argument is strong or weak. If it's strong, explain how the sample could be modified to make the argument weak. If it's weak, explain how the sample could be modified to make the argument strong. Keep the modifications as realistic as possible. Answers are provided for 1, 4, 8, and 12.

Exercise 5.3

For each of the following opinion polls, (1) determine whether the poll results offer strong support for the pollster's conclusion, and, if they don't, (2) specify the source of the problem (sample too small, unrepresentative sample, or nonrandom sampling). Assume that the conducting of each survey is free of technical errors such as mistakes in data processing or improper polling interviews.

*1. An Internet site featuring national and world news asks visitors to participate in the site's "instant daily poll" of hot topics. The current polling question is: "Should the words 'under God' be stricken from the Pledge of Allegiance if its recitation is required of public school children?" Twelve thousand people visit the site on the day that the poll is taken. Of those, seven thousand answer no to the question. The site concludes that 58 percent of Americans oppose modifying the Pledge.

2. Anita conducts a survey to determine if Americans are willing to support the arts by contributing money directly to local theater groups. One night she and her assistants interview five hundred people who are attending a performance of a musical at the city's biggest theater. To help

ensure random selection, they purposely select every other patron they encounter for interviewing. There is only one interview question: "Are you willing to support the arts by giving money to local theater groups?" Ninety-four percent of the interviewees answer yes. Anita later reports that a large majority of Americans are willing to support the arts by giving money to local theater groups.

3. A prominent sociologist wants to determine the sexual attitudes of women aged twenty-five to forty-five. The main question to be explored is whether heterosexual women in this age group feel satisfied with their partners' sexual performance. The sociologist interviews two hundred of her friends who belong to the target group. She also asks two hundred of her female colleagues at her college to complete and return a survey asking the key question. She gets seventy-eight completed surveys back from women in the target group. She finds that 75 percent of all the interviewees say that they are not satisfied with their partners' performance. She concludes that most heterosexual women aged twenty-five to forty-five aren't happy with the sexual performance of their partners.

4. A national polling organization surveys fifteen hundred obstetrician-gynecologists chosen randomly from a national registry of this medical specialty. The survey question is whether obstetrician-gynecologists provide quality care for pregnant women. Ninety-eight percent of those surveyed say yes. The pollsters conclude that almost all physicians think that obstetrician-gynecologists provide quality care for pregnant women.

5. A national women's magazine publishes a questionnaire on sexual harassment in the workplace. Respondents are asked to complete the questionnaire and mail it in to the magazine. The magazine receives over twenty thousand completed questionnaires in the mail. Sixty-two percent of the respondents say that they've been sexually harassed at work. The magazine reports that most women have been sexually harassed at work.

Exercise 5.4

For each of the following arguments, indicate which conclusions from the accompanying list would be strongly supported by the premise given. Assume that all statements are true.

*1. Seventy-two percent of the three hundred university students who responded to a questionnaire published in the campus newspaper are opposed to the US president's economic policies.

   a. Some readers of the campus newspaper are opposed to the US president's economic policies.
   b. Seventy-two percent of the students attending this school are opposed to the US president's economic policies.

    c. Some students attending this school are opposed to the US president's economic policies.

    d. Most readers of the campus newspaper are opposed to the US president's economic policies.

    e. Seventy-two percent of the readers of the campus newspaper are opposed to the US president's economic policies.

2. By listening to music, 43 percent of arthritis patients at the Drexell Clinic experience a decrease in pain in their knee and finger joints.

    a. By listening to music, 43 percent of arthritis patients can experience a decrease in pain in their knee and finger joints.

    b. By listening to music, some arthritis patients can experience a decrease in pain in their knee and finger joints.

    c. By listening to music, some arthritis patients at the Drexell Clinic can experience a decrease in pain in their knee and finger joints.

    d. By listening to music, many arthritis patients can experience a decrease in pain in their knee and finger joints.

3. Four out of five of the college's English majors hate anything written by William Faulkner.

    a. Eighty percent of the college's English majors hate anything written by William Faulkner.

    b. Most students at this college hate anything written by William Faulkner.

    c. Most college students hate anything written by William Faulkner.

    d. English majors at this college hate anything written by William Faulkner.

4. Alonzo has been driving his Dodge Spirit for seven years without any problems. His friend has the same kind of car and has been driving it for five years trouble-free.

    a. Dodge Spirits are trouble-free cars.

    b. Most Dodge Spirits are trouble-free cars.

    c. Some Dodge Spirits are trouble-free cars.

    d. Many Dodge Spirits are trouble-free cars.

5. Seventy-seven percent of adults interviewed in three Philadelphia shopping malls (650 people) say they will vote Democratic in the next presidential election.

    a. Most people will vote Democratic in the next presidential election.

    b. Seventy-seven percent of adult residents of Philadelphia will vote Democratic in the next presidential election.

    c. Many people in Philadelphia will vote Democratic in the next presidential election.

    d. A substantial percentage of people who shop at malls in Philadelphia will vote Democratic in the next presidential election.

Exercise 5.5

Evaluate each of the following passages and indicate whether it contains (a) an argument by analogy, (b) a literary analogy, or (c) an enumerative induction. If the passage contains an argument by analogy, indicate the total number of things (instances) being compared, the relevant similarities mentioned or implied, the conclusion, and whether the argument is strong or weak.

1. "The moon was a ghostly galleon tossed upon cloudy seas." [Alfred Noyes].

*2. "Duct tape is like the force. It has a light side, a dark side, and it holds the universe together." [Carl Zwanzig]

3. Girls are smarter than boys. Girls in the debate club always argue better than boys. And the mean grade-point average of the girls in the glee club is higher than that of the boys in the club.

4. "Howard Hughes was able to afford the luxury of madness, like a man who not only thinks he is Napoleon but hires an army to prove it." [Ted Morgan]

5. "Look around the world: contemplate the whole and every part of it: you will find it to be nothing but one great machine, subdivided into an infinite number of lesser machines, which again admit of subdivisions, to a degree beyond what human senses and faculties can trace and explain. All these various machines, and even their most minute parts, are adjusted to each other with an accuracy, which ravishes into admiration all men who have ever contemplated them. The curious adapting of means to ends, through-out all nature, resembles exactly, though it much exceeds, the production of human contrivance; of human design, thought, wisdom, and intelligence. Since therefore the effects resemble each other, we are led to infer, by all the rules of analogy, that the causes also resemble; and that the Author of Nature is somewhat similar to the mind of men; though possessed of much larger faculties, proportioned to the grandeur of the work, which he has executed. By this argument *a posteriori*, and by this argument alone, do we prove at once the existence of a Deity, and his similarity to human mind and intelligence." [David Hume]

*6. My brother was always good at arithmetic, so he'll be a whiz at algebra.

7. Tolerating a vicious dictator is like tolerating a bully on the block. If you let the bully push you around, sooner or later he will beat you up and take everything you have. If you let a dictator have his way, he will abuse his people and rob them of life and liberty. If you stand up to the bully just once or—better yet—knock him senseless with a stick, he will never bother you again. Likewise, if you refuse to be coerced by a dictator or if you attack him, his reign will be over. Therefore, the best course of action for people oppressed by a dictator is to resist and attack.

*8. I like sausage, and I like ham, and I like pork chops. So I will like chitlins.

9. "The brain secretes thought as the stomach secretes gastric juice, the liver bile, and the kidneys urine." [Karl Vogt]

10. George has loved every Chevrolet he has owned in the past five years. So he will probably love the Chevrolet he bought yesterday.

11. How does one know that there exist in the world other minds—that is, others having feelings and other subjective experiences? One can observe that one's own experiences are connected to publicly observable phenomena, that other people exhibit publicly observable phenomena, and therefore other people also must have subjective experiences. For example, one may observe that when one stubs a toe, one feels pain and cries "ouch." Then if other people—who are physically similar to oneself—also stub their toes and cry "ouch," one can conclude that they also experience pain.

*12. "Character is the foundation stone upon which one must build to win respect. Just as no worthy building can be erected on a weak foundation, so no lasting reputation worthy of respect can be built on a weak character." [R. C. Samsel]

Exercise 5.6

Evaluate each of the following arguments by analogy, indicating (1) the things (instances) being compared, (2) the relevant similarities mentioned or implied, (3) whether diversity among multiple cases is a significant factor, (4) the conclusion, and (5) whether the argument is strong or weak.

*1. Like former president Ronald Reagan, president X is a staunch conservative, has strong Christian values, and adheres almost dogmatically to certain conservative principles. President Reagan allowed his fierce fidelity to his principles and values to lead him into a foreign policy disaster, the Iran-Contra debacle. President X will likely be involved in a similar foreign policy mess for similar reasons.

2. The United Nations failed to intervene in Cambodia to prevent massive human rights violations and ethnic cleansing. It also failed to act to stop the murders of close to a million innocent people in Rwanda. The UN will not intervene to stop any widespread slaughter of innocents in Nigeria.

3. "If a single cell, under appropriate conditions, becomes a person in the space of a few years, there can surely be no difficulty in understanding how, under appropriate conditions, a cell may, in the course of untold millions of years, give origin to the human race." [Herbert Spencer]

4. The casinos in Atlantic City have brought a tremendous amount of revenue into both area businesses and local government, without inviting the evils of organized crime and causing the degradation of law and order or quality of life. The same can be said for the Turning Stone casino in upstate New York, as well as for Casino Niagara in Niagara Falls, Canada. A casino

built in Buffalo, New York, will provide all the same benefits without the disadvantages.

*5. A well-established moral principle is that one is morally justified in using deadly force in self-defense when one is threatened with death or great pain from an assailant. A disease such as terminal cancer can also threaten one with death or great pain. So suicide—a use of deadly force—must sometimes be morally justified when it is an act of self-defense against an assailant (terminal disease) that threatens death or great pain.

6. "If we survey the universe, so far as it falls under our knowledge, it bears a great resemblance to an animal or organized body, and seems actuated with a like principle of life and motion. A continual circulation of matter in it produces no disorder: a continual waste in every part is incessantly repaired: The closest sympathy is perceived throughout the whole system. And each part or member, in performing its proper offices, operates both to its own preservation and to that of the whole. The world, therefore, I infer, is an animal, and the Deity is the soul of the world, activating it and activated by it." [Philo, in Hume's *Dialogues Concerning Natural Religion*]

7. "The mass of men serve the State thus, not as men mainly, but as machines, with their bodies. They are the standing army, and the militia, jailers, constables, *posse comitatus*, &c. In most cases there is no free exercise whatever of the judgment or of the moral sense; but they put themselves on a level with wood and earth and stones, and wooden men can perhaps be manufactured that will serve the purpose as well. Such command no more respect than men of straw, or a lump of dirt." [Henry David Thoreau]

 Self-Assessment Quiz

Answers appear in "Answers to Self-Assessment Quizzes" in Appendix B.

1. What is enumerative induction? How is it indicated schematically?
2. In enumerative induction, what are the target group, the sample, and the relevant property?
3. What are the two major ways in which an enumerative induction can fail to be strong?
4. What is analogical induction? How is it indicated schematically?

For each of the following enumerative inductions, indicate whether the argument is strong or weak. If it's weak, say whether the problem is a sample that's too small, not representative, or both.

5. All the women in my yoga class are against the war. Ninety percent of the members of a national women's group (twelve thousand members) are against the war. And all my women friends are against the war. The fact is, almost all American women oppose this war.

6. Recently there was a racially motivated murder in Texas. Two white men killed a black man. Then another murder of a black man by some racist whites occurred in Louisiana. And in Mississippi an admitted racist finally was convicted of the murder of a black man that occurred years ago. The South has more racist killers than any other part of the country.

7. Most professors at this college are not grading as strictly as they used to. They now give B's for work to which they used to assign C's. The grading standards in American colleges are dropping.

8. The first time Ariana encountered trigonometry, she couldn't understand it. And the first time she read Shakespeare, she didn't get it. She will never understand anything.

9. Americans are quite satisfied with the administration's recent foreign policy decisions. An "instant poll" conducted yesterday on the CNN website got fifteen thousand responses from site visitors—and 95 percent of them said that American foreign policy was on the right track.

10. Judging from what I've seen, antiwar demonstrators are just a bunch of peaceniks left over from the Vietnam War era.

Evaluate each of the following arguments by analogy, indicating (1) the two things being compared, (2) the conclusion, and (3) whether the argument is strong or weak.

11. "Suppose that someone tells me that he has had a tooth extracted without an anesthetic, and I express my sympathy, and suppose that I am then asked, 'How do you know that it hurt him?' I might reasonably reply, 'Well, I know that it would hurt me. I have been to the dentist and know how painful it is to have a tooth stopped without an anesthetic, let alone taken out. And he has the same sort of nervous system as I have. I infer, therefore, that in these conditions he felt considerable pain, just as I should myself.'" [Alfred J. Ayer]

12. "As for one who is choosy about what he learns . . . we shall not call him a lover of learning or a philosopher, just as we shall not say that a man who is difficult about his food is hungry or has an appetite for food. We shall not call him a lover of food but a poor eater. . . . But we shall call a philosopher the man who is easily willing to learn every kind of knowledge, gladly turns to learning things, and is insatiable in this respect." [Socrates]

13. "Let us begin with a parable [showing that statements about God have no meaning]. . . . Once upon a time two explorers came upon a clearing in the jungle. In the clearing were growing many flowers and many weeds. One explorer says, 'Some gardener must tend this plot.' The other disagrees, 'There is no gardener.' So they pitch their tents and set a watch. No gardener is ever seen. 'But perhaps he is an invisible gardener.' So they set up a barbed-wire fence. They electrify it. . . . But no shrieks ever suggest that some intruder has received a shock. No movements of the wire ever

betray an invisible climber. . . . Yet still the Believer is not convinced. 'But there is a gardener, invisible, intangible, insensible.' . . . At last the Sceptic despairs, 'But what remains of your original assertion? Just how does what you call an invisible, intangible, eternally elusive gardener differ from an imaginary gardener or even from no gardener at all?'" [Antony Flew]

Evaluate each of the following passages and indicate whether it contains (a) an argument by analogy, (b) a literary analogy, or (c) an enumerative induction. If the passage contains an argument by analogy, indicate the total number of things (instances) being compared, the relevant similarities mentioned or implied, the conclusion, and whether the argument is strong or weak.

14. "The moon was a ghostly galleon tossed upon cloudy seas." [Alfred Noyes]
15. "Duct tape is like the force. It has a light side, a dark side, and it holds the universe together." [Carl Zwanzig]
16. Howard Hughes was able to afford the luxury of madness, like a man who not only thinks he is Napoleon but hires an army to prove it." [Ted Morgan]
17. My brother was always good at arithmetic, so he'll be a whiz at algebra.
18. I like sausage, and I like ham, and I like pork chops. So I will like chitlins.
19. "Vigorous writing is concise. A sentence should contain no unnecessary words, a paragraph no unnecessary sentences, for the same reason that a drawing should have no unnecessary lines and a machine no unnecessary parts." [E. B. White]
20. "Character is the foundation stone upon which one must build to win respect. Just as no worthy building can be erected on a weak foundation, so no lasting reputation worthy of respect can be built on a weak character." [R.C. Samsel]

 ## Writing Assignments

Extract a manageable thesis from the following general claims and write a three-page essay defending it. Look to chapter 12 for guidance.

- Men are better at science than women are.
- Everyone does what is in his or her own best interests.
- It's wrong for the government to tax citizens to support people who are poor and needy.
- Deadbeat dads (fathers who don't or won't pay child support that they are legally obligated to pay) should be put in jail.
- Sexual harassment is not a problem on this campus.
- Competition is always a good thing.
- Pornography should never be banned on a college campus.

Evidence and Experts

IF WE CARE WHETHER OUR BELIEFS ARE TRUE OR RELIABLE, WHETHER WE CAN SAFELY use them to guide our steps and inform our choices, then we must care about the reasons for accepting those beliefs. The better the reasons for acceptance, the more likely are the beliefs, or statements, to be true. Inadequate reasons, no reasons, or fake reasons should lead us not to accept a statement, but to doubt it.

As we saw in earlier chapters, the reasons for accepting a statement are often spelled out in the form of an argument, with the statement being the conclusion. The reasons and conclusion together might compose a deductive argument or an inductive argument. In such cases, the reasons are normally there in plain sight. But in our daily lives, statements or claims usually confront us alone without any accompanying stated reasons. An unsupported claim may be the premise of an argument (and its truth value may then determine whether the argument is sound or cogent). Or it may simply be a stand-alone assertion of fact. Either way, if we care whether the claim is acceptable, we must try to evaluate the claim as it stands.

Of course, it helps to be knowledgeable about the subject matter of a claim. But understanding and applying some critical thinking principles for assessing unsupported claims can be even more useful.

When Claims Conflict

Suppose you come across this claim in a reputable local newspaper:

[Claim 1] The historic Sullivan Building at the corner of Fifth and Main Streets was demolished yesterday to make way for a parking lot.

But say you have very good reasons to believe this claim:

[Claim 2] The historic Sullivan Building at the corner of Fifth and Main Streets was NOT demolished yesterday to make way for a parking lot.

What do you make of such a conflict between claims? Well, as a good critical thinker, you can know at least this: You have good reason to doubt claim 1 and therefore have no good grounds for accepting it. You have good reason to doubt it because it conflicts with another claim you have good reason to believe (claim 2). When two claims conflict, they simply cannot *both* be true; at least one of them has to be false. So this principle comes into play:

If a claim conflicts with other claims we have good reason to accept, we have good grounds for doubting it.

With conflicting claims, you are not justified in believing either one of them until you resolve the conflict. Sometimes this job is easy. If, for example, the competing claims are reports of personal observations, you can often decide between them by making further observations. If your friend says that your dog is sleeping atop your car, and you say that your dog is not sleeping atop your car (because you checked a short time ago), you can see who's right by simply looking at the roof of your car. (Remember, though, that even personal observations can sometimes mislead us, as we'll soon see.)

 FACT AND OPINION

When we evaluate claims, we often are concerned with making a distinction between facts and opinions. But just what is the difference? We normally use the term *fact* in two senses. First, we may use it to refer to a state of affairs—as in, "Examine the evidence and find out the facts." Second, and more commonly, we use *fact* to refer to *true statements*—as in, "John smashed the dinnerware—that's a fact." Thus, we say that some claims, or statements, are facts (or factual) and some are not. We use the word *opinion*, however, to refer to a *belief*—as in, "It's John's opinion that he did not smash the dinnerware." Some opinions are true, so they are facts. Some opinions are not true, so they are not facts.

Sometimes we may hear somebody say, "That's a matter of opinion." What does this mean? Often it's equivalent to something like "Opinions differ on this issue" or "There are many different opinions on this." But it also frequently means that the issue is not a matter of objective fact but is entirely subjective, a matter of individual taste. Statements expressing matters of opinion in this latter sense are not the kinds of things that people can disagree on, just as two people cannot sensibly disagree about whether they like chocolate ice cream.

Many times, however, sorting out conflicting claims requires a deeper inquiry. You may need to do some research to see what evidence exists for each of the claims. In the best-case scenario, you may quickly discover that one of the claims is not credible because it comes from an unreliable source (a subject taken up in the next few pages).

Now suppose that you're confronted with another type of conflict—this time a conflict between a claim and your **background information**. Background information is that huge collection of very well-supported beliefs that we all rely on to inform our actions and choices. A great deal of this lore consists of basic facts about everyday things, beliefs based on very good evidence (including our own personal observations and the statements of excellent authorities), and strongly justified claims that we would regard as "common sense" or "common knowledge." Background beliefs include obvious claims such as "The sun is hot," "The Easter bunny is not real," "Humans are mortal," "Fire burns," and "George Washington lived in the eighteenth century." Suppose then that you're asked to accept this unsupported claim:

Some babies can bench-press a 500-pound weight.

You are not likely to give much credence to this claim for the simple reason that it conflicts with an enormous number of your background beliefs concerning human physiology, gravity, weight lifting, and who knows what else.

Or how about this claim:

The president of the United States is entirely under the control of the chief justice of the Supreme Court.

This claim is not as outlandish as the previous one, but it too conflicts with our background beliefs, specifically those having to do with the structure and workings of the US government. So we would have good reason to doubt this one also.

The principle exemplified here is:

If a claim conflicts with our background information, we have good reason to doubt it.

Other things being equal, the more background information the claim conflicts with, the more reason we have to doubt it. We would normally—and rightfully—assign a low probability to any claim that conflicts with a great deal of our background information.

You would be entitled, for example, to have some doubt about the claim that Joan is late for work if it conflicts with your background information that Joan has never been late for work in the ten years you've known her. But you are entitled to have very strong doubts about, and to assign very low credibility to, the claim that Luis can turn a stone into gold just by touching it. You could even reasonably dismiss the claim out of hand. Such a claim conflicts with too much of what we know about the physical world.

It's always possible, of course, that a conflicting claim is true and some of our background information is unfounded. So many times it's reasonable for us to examine a conflicting claim more closely. If we find that it has no good reasons in its favor, that it is not credible, we may reject it. If, on the other hand, we discover that there are strong reasons for accepting the new claim, we may need to revise our background information. For example, we may be forced to accept the claim about Luis's golden touch (and to rethink some of our background information) if it is backed by strong supporting evidence. Our background information would be in need of some serious revision if Luis could produce this stone-to-gold transformation repeatedly under scientifically controlled conditions that rule out error, fraud, and trickery.

We need to keep in mind that although our background information is generally trustworthy, it is not infallible. What we assume is a strongly justified belief may be nothing more than prejudice or dogma. We should therefore be willing to reexamine background beliefs that we have doubts about—and to be open to reasonable doubts when they arise.

So it is not reasonable to accept a claim if there is good reason to doubt it. And sometimes, if the claim is dubious enough, we may be justified in dismissing a claim out of hand. But what should we believe about a claim that is not quite dubious enough to summarily discard yet not worthy of complete acceptance? We should measure out our belief according to the strength of reasons. That is,

We should proportion our belief to the evidence.

The more evidence a claim has in its favor, the stronger our belief in it should be. Weak evidence for a claim warrants weak belief; strong evidence warrants strong belief. And the strength of our beliefs should vary across this spectrum as the evidence dictates.

Implicit in all of the foregoing is a principle that deserves to be explicit because it's so often ignored:

It's not reasonable to believe a claim when there is no good reason for doing so.

The twentieth-century philosopher Bertrand Russell tried hard to drive this idea home. As he put it, "It is undesirable to believe a proposition when there is no ground whatever for supposing it true." Russell claimed that if the use of this principle became widespread, social life and political systems would be transformed.

Experts and Authorities

When an unsupported claim doesn't conflict with what we already know, we are often justified in believing it *because it comes from experts.* An **expert** is someone who is more knowledgeable in a particular subject area or field than most others are. Experts in professions and fields of knowledge provide us with reasons for believing a claim because, in their specialty areas, they are more likely to be right than we are. They are more likely to be right because (1) they have access to more information on the subject than we do and (2) they are better at judging that information than we are. Experts are familiar with the established facts and existing data in their field *and* know how to properly evaluate that information. Essentially, this means that they have a handle on the information and know how to assess the evidence and arguments for particular claims involving that information. They are true authorities on a specified subject. Someone who knows the lore of a field but can't evaluate the reliability of a claim is no expert.

In a complex world where we can never be knowledgeable in every field, we must rely on experts—a perfectly legitimate state of affairs. But good critical thinkers are careful about expert opinion, guiding their use of experts by some commonsense principles. One such principle is this:

> *If a claim conflicts with expert opinion, we have good reason to doubt it.*

This tenet follows from our definition of experts. If they really are more likely to be right than nonexperts about claims in their field, then any claim that conflicts with expert opinion is at least initially dubious.

Here's the companion principle to the first:

> *When the experts disagree about a claim, we have good reason to doubt it.*

If a claim is in dispute among experts, then nonexperts can have no good reason for accepting (or rejecting) it. Throwing up your hands and arbitrarily deciding to believe or disbelieve the claim is not a reasonable response. The claim must remain in doubt until the experts resolve the conflict or you resolve the conflict yourself by becoming informed enough to competently decide on the issues and evidence involved—a course that's possible but usually not feasible for nonexperts.

Sometimes we may have good reason to be suspicious of unsupported claims even when they are purportedly derived from expert opinion. Our doubt is justified when a claim comes from someone deemed to be an expert who in fact is *not* an expert. When we rely on such bogus expert opinion, we make the mistake known as the **fallacious appeal to authority**.

The fallacious appeal to authority usually happens in one of two ways. First, we may find ourselves disregarding this important rule of thumb: *Just because someone is an expert in one field, he or she is not necessarily an expert in another.* The opinion of experts generally carries more weight than our own—but only in their areas of expertise. Any opinions that they proffer outside their fields are no more authoritative than those of nonexperts. Outside their fields, they are not experts.

We needn't look far for real-life examples of such skewed appeals to authority. Any day of the week we may be urged to accept claims in one field based on the opinion of an expert from an unrelated field. An electrical engineer or Nobel Prize–winning chemist may assert that herbs can cure cancer. A radio talk-show host with a degree in physiology may give advice in psychology. A former astronaut may declare that archeological evidence shows that Noah's ark now rests on a mountain in Turkey. A botanist may say that the evidence for the existence of ESP is conclusive. The point is not that these experts can't be right, but that their expertise in a particular field doesn't give us reason to believe their pronouncements in another. There is no such thing as a general expert, only experts in specific subject areas.

Second, we may fall into a fallacious appeal to authority by regarding a nonexpert as an expert. We forget that a nonexpert—even one with prestige, status, or sex appeal—is still a nonexpert. Movie stars, TV actors, renowned athletes, and famous politicians endorse products of all kinds in TV and print advertising. But when they speak outside their areas of expertise (which is almost always the case), they give us no good reason for believing that the products are as advertised. Advertisers, of course, know this, but they hope that we will buy the products anyway because of the appeal or attractiveness of the celebrity endorsers.

Historically the regarding of a nonexpert as an expert has probably been the most prevalent form of the appeal to authority—with disastrous results. Political, religious, tribal, and cultural leaders often have been designated as authorities not because they knew the facts and could correctly judge the evidence but because culture, tradition, or whim dictated that they be regarded as authorities. When these "authorities" spoke, people listened and believed—then went to war, persecuted unbelievers, or undertook countless other ill-conceived projects. If we are to avoid this trap, we must look beyond mere labels and titles and ask, *"Does this person provide us with any good reasons or evidence?"*

This question, of course, is just another way of asking if someone is a true expert. How can we tell? To be considered an expert, someone must have shown that he or she can assess relevant evidence and arguments and arrive at well-supported conclusions in a particular field. What are the indicators that someone has this essential kind of expertise? There are several that provide clues to someone's ability but do not guarantee the possession of true expertise.

In most professional fields, the following two indicators are considered minimal prerequisites for being considered an expert:

1. Education and training from reputable institutions or programs in the relevant field (usually evidenced by degrees or certificates)
2. Experience in making reliable judgments in the field (generally the more years of experience the better)

But, unfortunately, people can have the requisite education and experience and still not know what they're talking about in the field in question. Woe be to us, for in the real world there are well-trained, experienced auto mechanics who do terrible work—and tenured PhDs whose professional judgment is iffy. Two additional indicators, though, are more revealing:

1. Reputation among peers (as reflected in the opinions of others in the same field, relevant prestigious awards, and positions of authority)
2. Professional accomplishments

These two indicators are more helpful because they are very likely to be correlated with the intellectual qualities expected in true experts. People with excellent reputations among their professional peers and with significant accomplishments to their credit usually are true experts.

Biased Opinions

As we've seen, we are often justified in believing an unsupported claim because it's based on expert opinion. But if we have reason to doubt the opinion of the experts, then we are not justified in believing the claim based on that opinion. And chief among possible reasons for doubt (aside from conflicting expert opinion) is bias. When experts are biased, they are motivated by something other than the search for the truth—perhaps financial gain, loyalty to a cause, professional ambition, emotional needs, political outlook, sectarian dogma, personal ideology, or some other judgment-distorting factor. Therefore, if we have reason to believe that an expert is biased, we are not justified in accepting the expert's opinion.

But how can we tell when experts are biased? There are no hard-and-fast rules here. In the more obvious cases, we often suspect bias when an expert is being paid by special-interest groups or companies to render an opinion, or when the expert expresses very strong belief in a claim even though there is no evidence to support it, or when the expert stands to gain financially from the actions or policies that he or she supports.

It's true that many experts can render unbiased opinions and do high-quality research even when they have a conflict of interest. Nevertheless, in such situations we have reasonable grounds to suspect bias—unless we have good reason to believe that the suspicion is unwarranted. These good reasons might include the fact that the expert's previous opinions in similar circumstances have been reliable or that he or she has a solid reputation for always offering unbiased assessments.

There are, of course, many other possible reasons to doubt the opinion of experts. Any blatant violation of the critical thinking principles discussed in this text, for example, would give us good reason to question an authority's reliability. Among the more common tip-offs of dubious authority are these:

- The expert is guilty of simple factual or formal errors.
- The expert's claims conflict with what you have good reason to believe.
- The expert does not adequately support his or her assertions.

- The expert's writing contains logical contradictions or inconsistent statements.
- The expert does not treat opposing views fairly.
- The expert is strongly biased, emotional, or dismissive.
- The expert relies on information you know is out of date.
- Most other experts in the same field disagree.

The amount of weight you give to any one of these factors—and the subsequent degree of doubt you attach to an expert's opinion—will vary in each case. In general, a single minor error of fact or style does not justify dismissing an expert's entire article that is otherwise excellent. But doubt is cumulative, and as reasons for doubt are added, you may rightfully decide that you are not justified in believing any part of an expert's testimony, regardless of his or her credentials. Depending on your aims, you may decide to check the expert's assertions against other sources or to consult an authority with much less evidential or rhetorical baggage.

Finally, keep in mind that there are certain kinds of issues that we probably don't want experts to settle for us. Indeed, in most cases the experts *cannot* settle them for us. These issues usually involve moral, social, or political questions. If we're intellectually conscientious, we want to provide our own final answers to such questions, though we may draw heavily on the analyses and arguments provided by experts. We may study what the experts have to say and the conclusions they draw. But we want ultimately to come to our own conclusions. We prefer this approach in large part because the questions are so important and because the answers we give help define who we are. What's more, the experts typically disagree on these issues. So even if we wanted the experts to settle one of these questions for us, they probably couldn't.

The Evidence of Personal Experience

We accept a great many claims because they are based on personal experience—our own or someone else's. Personal experience, broadly defined, arises from our senses, our memory, and our judgment involved in those faculties. In countless cases, personal experience is our evidence (or part of the evidence) that something is or is not the case. You believe that Jack caused the traffic accident because you, or someone else, witnessed it. You think that the herbal tea cured your headache because the pain went away after you drank it. You believe that your friend can bend spoons with her mind because you saw her do it at a party. You're sure that the other guy threw the first punch, not you, because that's how you remember the incident. Or you vote to convict the defendant because eyewitness testimony puts him at the scene of the crime with a gun in his hand. But can you trust personal experience to reveal the truth?

The answer is a *qualified* yes. And here's the qualification in the form of an important principle:

> It's reasonable to accept the evidence provided by personal experience only if there's no good reason to doubt it.

If we have no good reason to doubt what our personal experience reveals to us, then we're justified in believing it. This means that if our faculties are working properly and our use of them is unimpeded by anything in our environment, we're entitled to accept what our personal experience tells us. If we seem to see a cat on the mat under good viewing conditions—that is, we have no reason to believe that our observations are impaired by, say, poor lighting, cracked glasses, or too many beers—then we're justified in believing that there's a cat on the mat.

The problem is that personal experience, though generally reliable, is not infallible. Under certain circumstances, our senses, memory, and judgment can't be trusted. It's easy enough to identify these circumstances in an abstract way. The harder job is (1) determining when they actually occur in real-life situations and (2) avoiding them or taking them into account. The rest of this section is a rundown of some of the more common factors that can give us good reason to doubt the reliability of personal experience.

Impairment

This should be obvious: If our perceptual powers are somehow impaired or impeded, we have reason to doubt them. The unambiguous cases are those in which our senses are debilitated because we are ill, injured, tired, stressed out, excited, drugged, drunk, distracted, or disoriented. And just as clear are the situations that interfere with sensory input—when our environment is, say, too dark, too bright, too noisy, or too hazy. If any of these factors are in play, the risk of misperception is high, which gives us reason to doubt the trustworthiness of what we experience.

 I JUST *KNOW!*

Suppose you make a claim that you have neither evidence nor argument to back up, and someone asks, "How do you know?" And you say, "I just know," or "My gut (or intuition) tells me it's true." In such situations, do you really know—do you really possess knowledge? Many epistemologists (philosophers who study knowledge) would argue that you do not, unless your ordinary means of acquiring knowledge (reason and observation) have validated the reliability of your intuition or gut. Nevertheless, many people believe that their gut is a reliable way of knowing. Here's a famous

continues

I JUST *KNOW!*

continued

case of "gut knowing" that has been criticized by several authors, including the philosopher Stephen Law:

Did the United States go to war in Iraq mainly because of President George W. Bush's "gut"? If so, was trusting his gut an irresponsible act? Why or why not?

> Notoriously, during George W. Bush's presidency, Bush's gut became the oracle of the state. Bush was distrustful of book learning and those with established expertise in a given area. When he made the decision to invade Iraq, and was subsequently confronted by a skeptical audience, Bush said that ultimately, he just *knew in his gut* that invading was the right thing to do. . . .
>
> The invasion went ahead. A few months later, Senator Joe Biden told Bush of his growing worries about the aftermath. In response, Bush again appealed to the reliability of his "instincts." . . .
>
> How did Bush suppose his gut was able to steer the ship of state? He supposed it was functioning as a *sort of God-sensing faculty.* Bush believed that by means of his gut he could sense what God wanted of him. . . . Those who, like George W. Bush, place a simple trusting faith in their gut, or wherever else they think their *sensus divinitatis* is located, are being irresponsible and foolish.[1]

Assuming this account of George Bush's thinking is accurate, do you think he really *knew* that invading Iraq was the right thing to do? If so, how does this kind of intuitive knowing work? Exactly how is knowledge gained this way? If not, where do you think Bush's error lies? What is wrong with "knowing in your gut"?

Memories can be affected by many of the same factors that interfere with accurate perception. They are especially susceptible to distortion if they are formed during times of stress—which helps explain why the memories of people who witness crimes or alleged ghosts are so often unreliable. These situations are understandably stressful.

The impairment of our faculties is complicated by the peculiar way they operate. Contrary to what many believe, they are not like recording devices that make exact mental copies of objects and events in the world. Research suggests that they are more like artists who use bits of sensory data or memory fragments to concoct creative representations of things, not exact replicas. Our perception and memory are *constructive*, which means that what we perceive and remember is to some degree fabricated by our minds. Some of the more blatant examples: You see a man standing in the shadows by the road—then discover when you get closer that the man is a tree stump. You anxiously await a phone call from Aunt Mary, and when the call comes and you hear the person's voice, you're sure it's her—then realize that it's some guy asking for a charitable donation. While in the shower you hear the phone ring—but no one is calling, and the ringing is something your mind is making up.

The constructive workings of our minds help us solve problems and deal effectively with our environment. But they can also hinder us by manufacturing too much of our experiences using too little data. Unfortunately, the constructive tendency is most likely to lead us astray precisely when our powers of perception and memory are impaired or impeded. Competent investigators of alleged paranormal phenomena understand this and are rightfully skeptical of paranormal claims based on observations made under dubious conditions like those mentioned here. Under the right conditions, the mind is very good at showing us UFOs and midnight ghosts that aren't there. Likewise, juries are expected to be suspicious of the testimony of eyewitnesses who swear they plainly saw the dirty deed committed but were frightened, enraged, or a little tipsy at the time.

Expectation

A tricky thing about perception is that we often perceive exactly what we expect to perceive—regardless of whether there's anything there to detect. Ever watch the second hand on an electric clock move—then suddenly realize that the clock is not running at all? Ever been walking through a crowd looking for a friend and hear her call your name—then find out later that she was ten blocks away at the time? Such experiences—the result again of the constructive tendencies of the mind—are common examples of how expectation can distort your perceptions.

Scientific research shows that expectation can have a more powerful effect on our experiences than most people think. In numerous studies, subjects who expected to see a flash of light, smell a certain odor, or feel an electric shock did indeed experience these things—even though the appropriate stimuli were never present. The mere suggestion that the stimuli would occur was enough to cause the subjects to perceive, or apparently perceive, things that did not exist.

Our tendency to sometimes perceive things that are not really there is especially pronounced when the stimuli are vague or ambiguous. For example, we may perceive completely formless stimuli—clouds, smoke, "white noise," garbled voices, random-patterned wallpaper, blurry photos, lights in the night sky, stains on the ceiling—yet think we observe very distinct images or sounds.

In the formlessness we may see ghosts, faces, and words and hear songs, screams, or verbal warnings. We may see or hear exactly what we expect to see or hear. Or the mere suggestion of what we should perceive helps us perceive it. This phenomenon is a kind of illusion known as *pareidolia*. It's the reason some people claim to hear Satanic messages when rock music is played backward, or to observe a giant stone face in fuzzy pictures of the surface of Mars, or to see the perfect likeness of Jesus in the skillet burns on a tortilla.

Scientists are keenly aware of the possible distorting influence of expectancy, so they try to design experiments that minimize it. We too need to minimize it as much as possible. Our strong expectations are a signal that we should double-check our sensory information and be careful about the conclusions we draw from it.

Innumeracy and Probability

When we make an off-the-cuff judgment about the chances of something happening (whether an event in the past or one in the future), we should be extra careful. Why? Because, generally, we humans are terrible at figuring probabilities.

Here's a classic example. Imagine that your classroom has twenty-three students present, including yourself. What are the chances that at least two of the students have exactly the same birthday? (Not the same *date of birth*, but the same birthday out of the 365 possible ones.) The answer is neither 1 chance in 365 (1/365) nor 1 in 52 (1/52). It's *1 chance in 2* (1/2, or fifty-fifty)—a completely counterintuitive result.

A common error is the misjudging of coincidences. Many of us often believe that an event is simply too improbable to be a mere coincidence, that something else surely must be going on—such as paranormal or supernatural activity. But we mustn't forget that amazing coincidences occur all the time and, in fact, *must* occur according to elementary laws of statistics. The probability that a particular strange event will occur—say, that an ice cube tossed out of an airplane will hit the roof of a barn—may be extremely low, maybe one in a billion. But that same event given enough opportunities to occur may be highly probable over the long haul. It may be unlikely in any given instance for you to flip a coin and get tails seven times in a row. But this "streak" is virtually certain to happen if you flip the coin enough times.

What are the odds that someone will be thinking of a person she knew, or knew of, from the past twenty-five years and then suddenly learn that the person is seriously ill or dead? Believe it or not, such a strange event is likely to occur several times a day. If we make the reasonable assumption that someone would recognize the names of a few thousand people (both famous and not so famous) from the past twenty-five years and that a person would learn of the illness or death of each of those few thousand people in the twenty-five years, then the chances of our eerie coincidence happening to someone somewhere are pretty good. We could reasonably expect that each day several people would have this experience.

Another error is to think that previous events can affect the probabilities in the random event at hand. This mistake is known as the **gambler's fallacy.** Let's say you toss an unbiased coin six times in a row. On the first toss, the odds are, of course, 1 in 2, or fifty-fifty, that it will land tails. It lands tails. Astoundingly, on the other five tosses the coin also lands tails. That's six tails in a row. So what are the odds that the coin will land tails on the seventh toss? Answer: fifty-fifty. Each toss has exactly the same probability of landing tails (or heads): fifty-fifty. The coin does not remember previous tosses. To think otherwise is to commit the gambler's fallacy. You see it a lot in casinos, sporting events, and—alas—everyday decision making.

The lesson here is not that we should mistrust all judgment about probabilities, but that we shouldn't rely solely on our intuitive sense in evaluating them. Relying entirely on intuition, or "gut feeling," in assessing probabilities is usually not a reason to trust the assessment, but to doubt it.

Advertising and Persuasion

Advertising is like air: It is everywhere, so pervasive and so natural that we forget it's there, yet penetrating and changing us every day. Advertising messages hit us rapid-fire and nonstop from blogs, podcasts, cell phones, television, radio, email, websites, movie theaters, magazines, newsletters, newspapers, book covers, junk mail, telephones, fax machines, product labels, billboards, vehicle signs, T-shirts, wall posters, flyers, and who knows what else. Ads permeate all media—print, film, video, television, radio, and the Internet. Caught in this whirl of words and sounds and images, we can easily overlook the obvious and disconcerting facts behind them: (1) All advertising is designed to influence, persuade, or manipulate us; (2) to an impressive degree and in many ways, it *does* successfully influence, persuade, or manipulate us; and (3) we are often oblivious to—or in outright denial about—how effectively advertising influences, persuades, or manipulates us.

The purpose of advertising is to sell products and services, promote causes or candidates, or alter attitudes and opinions. How well advertising does these jobs can be measured in money. Advertising in most media can cost a great deal. A single full-page magazine ad can cost tens of thousands of dollars; a thirty-second TV ad can run into the millions (especially on Super Bowl Sunday). But companies are willing to pay the price because advertising works. The revenues garnered from advertising can outweigh its costs by wide margins; in the case of a magazine ad or a TV spot, the gain could easily be hundreds of thousands or millions of dollars. In addition, advertisers and advertising agencies invest heavily each year in scientific consumer research to determine how to configure ads precisely to elicit the desired response from people. Again, they make these investments because there is a sure payoff: Consumers usually respond just as the research says they will. How do your eyes track across a newspaper ad when you are looking at it? Would you respond better to a TV commercial if the voice-over came from Anderson Cooper or from Lady Gaga? Would the magazine ad be more likely to sell you the cottage cheese if the headline used the word *creamy* instead of *smooth*? Would the ad copy on the junk-mail envelope increase sales if it were red instead of blue? You may not care about any of this, but advertisers do because such seemingly trivial bits of information can help them influence you in ways you barely suspect.

However averse we are (or think we are) to advertising or to its aims, we cannot deny its appeal. We like advertising, at least some of it. We easily can point to ads that annoy us or insult our intelligence, but most of us can also recall ones that are entertaining, funny, inspiring, even informative.

How, then, should good critical thinkers think about advertising? Our guiding principle should be:

> We generally have good reason to doubt advertising claims and to be wary of *advertising's persuasive powers.*

This means that usually the most reasonable response to advertising is a degree of suspicion. If we prefer truth over falsehood, if we would rather not be mistaken or bamboozled, if we want to make informed choices involving our time and money, then a general wariness toward advertising ploys is justified. This principle does not assume that all ad claims are false or that advertising cannot be genuinely informative or useful. It simply says that we should not accept uncritically an ad's message or impact on us.

There are several reasons for this cautious approach. First, recall the purpose of advertising—to *sell or promote something*, whether a product, service, person, or idea. To put the point bluntly, though advertising can be both truthful and helpful, its primary function is *not* to provide objective and accurate information to consumers. Advertisers will tell you many good things about their products but are unlikely to mention all the bad. Their main job is *not* to help consumers make fully informed, rational choices about available options. Advertising is advertising—it is not intended to be an impartial search for facts or a program of consumer protection. We are therefore justified in maintaining the same attitude toward advertising that we would toward a complete stranger who wants to sell us a widget: His motives are obviously pecuniary while his commitment to honesty is unknown.

Second, advertising has a reputation for—and a history of—misleading messages. The world is filled with ads that make dubious or false claims, use fallacious arguments (stated or implied), and employ psychological tricks to manipulate consumer responses.

Some of these methods fit neatly in our rundown of fallacies and persuaders in chapter 10. Ads frequently employ fallacious appeals to authority ("As an Olympic gold medal winner, I can tell you that PowerVitamin 2000 really works!"), appeals to emotion ("Enjoy the goodness and warmth of Big-Brand Soup, just like mother used to make"), appeals to popularity ("CNN, America's number-one source for news"), hasty generalizations ("Mothers everywhere will love Softie Diapers—our test mothers sure did!"), and faulty analogies ("As a businessman, I saved General Motors. As president, I can save this country.").

But advertisers also use an array of other persuasive techniques, most of which do not involve making explicit claims or providing good reasons for acting or choosing. The following are some of the more common ones.

Identification

Many ads persuade by simply inviting the consumer to identify with attractive people (real or imagined) or groups. Most ads featuring celebrity endorsements use this ploy. The idea is to get you to identify so strongly with a celebrity that you feel his or her product choices are *your* preferred choices. Without providing a single good reason or argument, endorsement ads say, in effect, that if Christina Aguilera prefers Pepsi, if Halle Berry likes Revlon, if Michael Jordan loves Nike, maybe you should, too.

Slogans

Catchy, memorable phrases are the stock-in-trade of advertising. How can we forget "Nike. Just do it" (Nike); "Reach out and touch someone" (AT&T); "Like a rock" (Chevrolet); "Don't leave home without it" (American Express); "Built Ford tough!" (Ford); "Obey your thirst" (Sprite); or "An army of one" (US Army)? Such catchphrases may not say much, but they do get our attention, engender appealing emotions or concepts, and associate them with products or companies—again and again and again. Through repetition that seems to embed themselves in our brains, slogans surreptitiously get us to feel that one product or brand is better than another.

Misleading Comparisons

In advertising, comparisons can mislead in many ways. Consider these examples:

1. BeSure Tampons are 30 percent more absorbent.
2. Big sale! The SuperX CD Player for less than the suggested retail price!
3. Simply better-tasting tacos. No question.
4. X Phone lets you call anywhere cheaper. Just 5 cents per minute compared with Y Phone, which charges 10 cents a minute.

The problem with Example 1 is its vagueness, which is, of course, deliberate. What does "30 percent more absorbent" mean? Thirty percent more absorbent than they used to be? Thirty percent more absorbent than similar products are? If the latter, what similar products are we talking about? Are BeSure Tampons being compared to the *least* absorbent tampons on the market? The *30 percent* may seem impressive—until we know to what it actually refers. (Another relevant question is how absorbency was determined. As you might imagine, there are many ways to perform such tests, some of them likely to yield more impressive numbers than others.)

The claim in Example 2 may or may not be touting a true bargain. We would probably view the "Big sale" in a different light if we knew whether the store's *regular* prices are below the suggested retail prices or if *all* stores sell the CD player below the suggested retail.

Example 3 contains the same sort of vagueness we find in Example 1 plus an additional sort of emptiness. The phrase "better-tasting tacos" is a claim about a subjective state of affairs—a claim that *anyone* could make about his or her own gustatory experience. You and a thousand other people might try the tacos and think they taste terrible. So the claim tells you nothing about whether you will like the tacos. The claim would be empty even if it were stretched to "The best-tasting tacos on earth!" In the ad world, such exaggerations are known as *puffery*, which is regarded in advertising law as hype that few people take seriously.

Example 4 is misleading because it tries to compare apples and oranges. The service offered by X Phone is not like that offered by Y Phone. The former gives you bare-bones service for 5 cents a minute; the latter gives you the same plus caller ID, call waiting, and free long distance on weekends. So comparing the two according to the per-minute charge alone is deceptive.

Weasel Words

When advertisers want to *appear* to make a strong claim but avoid blatant lying or deception, they use what are known as *weasel words*. Weasel words water down a claim in subtle ways—just enough to ensure that it is technically true but superficially misleading. Consider:

1. You may have already won a new 2007 Ford pickup truck!
2. Some doctors recommend ginseng for sexual dysfunction.
3. Relieves up to 60 percent of headaches in chronic headache sufferers.

Example 1 is typical junk-mail hype that seems to promise a valuable prize. But the weasel word *may* weakens the claim. Technically, you *may* have actually won since your winning is at least (remotely) possible. But in the typical sweepstakes, the odds of your winning anything are millions to one. Yes, you may have already won—and you are just as likely to get hit by an asteroid tomorrow.

Example 2 plays on the weasel word *some*. It is probably true that *some* (meaning at least one) doctors recommend ginseng for sexual dysfunction, but a huge majority of them do not. Using *some*, we could craft an infinite number of technically true but misleading (and ridiculous) claims about what doctors do and don't do. In Example 3 the weasel words are *up to*. Notice that many states of affairs would be consistent with this (vague) statement. It would be true even if just 1 percent of headaches were relieved in almost all headache sufferers.

Other weasels include *as many as, reportedly, possibly, virtually, many, seems*, and *perhaps*. Such words, of course, can have perfectly respectable uses as necessary qualifiers in many contexts. The problems arise when they are used not to qualify but to misguide.

Evaluating Sources: The Internet and Beyond

So here are the hard, elementary facts about the news media, social media, the Internet, and the print world:

- Alas, not everything you read is true.
- Countless sources on the Internet and in conventional media are unreliable.
- It's often difficult to tell the difference between fake or false news and real news.
- Advertising cannot be trusted to give you unbiased information.
- A great deal of what you read online is false, misleading, vicious, self-serving, clueless, or crazy.

What's a critical thinker to do? For starters, you can try bravely and conscientiously to do the following:

- **Read critically.** Cultivate a skeptical, vigilant, but inquiring attitude toward what you read. Critically examine claims and evidence and be open to changing your mind as the facts warrant. Do not give in to two of the most damaging ideas in contemporary culture—that there's no such thing as truth or that telling fact from fiction is impossible.
- **Size up authors, bloggers, and publishers.** Do not thoughtlessly assume that what a writer says must be true or that every source disseminates trustworthy information. Evaluate the author's credentials, bias, affiliations, assumptions, motives, and sources. Be suspicious if the author demonstrates poor critical thinking. Gauge sources mainly by the claims they convey—do the claims conflict with expert opinion, with what you have good reason to believe, with the assertions of other (reputable) publishers, with logic and common sense?
- **Sort out claims.** Ultimately the credibility of a source comes down to the credibility of its claims, including those used as premises and conclusions of arguments. So correctly judging the plausibility of statements is

the essential skill in evaluating sources. Remember: It is reasonable (1) to accept claims that fit very well with your background information or that you know are supported independently by authorities or evidence, (2) to accept claims that are adequately supported by the source itself through citations to other credible sources (experts, research, reports, etc.) or through references to supporting facts, (3) to reject claims when there is good reason for believing them false, and (4) to suspend judgment on claims that you are unsure of, for it is unreasonable to accept a claim without good reasons. The only cure for uncertainty about a source's claims is further research and reflection.

- **Compare sources.** Relying exclusively on one source for information is usually a mistake. Consulting a variety of sources helps you put the information in proper perspective, uncover errors and bias, pinpoint consensus and disagreement among experts, and find out where the preponderance of evidence points. Certainly your hunt for sources should be carefully planned and limited, but examining too few of them can lead to views that are one-sided, incomplete, and wrong.

- **Try to discern the source's purpose.** Is the purpose advertising, fundraising, opinion, news, advocacy, entertainment, venting, trolling, commerce?

- **Check alternative news sources.** How can you tell if the news you're getting is incomplete—if there's important news you're not seeing? You can't, unless you check alternative news sources for any missing stories. Reading a variety of newspapers, newsmagazines, blogs, websites, and journals of opinion is the best way to ensure that you're getting the big picture. To avoid confirmation bias, and to ensure that you're fully informed, you should read not only those sources that agree with you but also those that don't. Don't get trapped in an echo chamber. The air inside is decidedly unhealthy.

 FAKE NEWS AND CRITICAL THINKING

Fake news—bogus news stories that masquerade as truthful reporting—has been around for a long time. But thanks to social media, fake news now spreads faster and more cleverly than ever. It was a force to be reckoned with in the 2016 presidential campaign and will continue to deceive, provoke, and harm society indefinitely. Typically it shows up on sites that look legitimate but aren't. The "news" presented can be completely made up, or it can be so partisan that it says only good things about one political perspective and only bad things about another, or it can be a strange but plausible blend of fact and fiction, or it can be satirical—good fun perhaps, except for those who don't get the joke.

continues

FAKE NEWS AND CRITICAL THINKING

continued

It's easy to fall for the misinformation, partly because of the nature of the material and partly because of the way we humans are. We are prone to confirmation bias and to group thinking. You come across a compelling news story that confirms exactly what you want to believe. It reinforces the perspective and prejudices of your group. It seems to be evidence that you have been right all along. So you skip critical thinking and share the story with your like-minded friends, and thousands of people become believers. But for all you know the story

"Fake news" can easily entrap us because of our human tendency toward confirmation bias and group thinking.

may be fake—and you have no good reason for believing it true or false.

Fortunately there are ways to avoid the traps of fake news, and the general strategies for doing so are the same ones highlighted in this chapter. But there are also tips for spotting fake news. Here are some from FactCheck.org:

> **Consider the source.** . . . Clearly, some [fake news] sites do provide a "fantasy news" or satire warning, like WTOE 5, which published the bogus headline, "Pope Francis Shocks World, Endorses Donald Trump for President, Releases Statement." Others aren't so upfront, like the Boston Tribune, which doesn't provide any information on its mission, staff members, or physical location—further signs that maybe this site isn't a legitimate news organization. The site, in fact, changed its name from Associated Media Coverage, after its work had been debunked by fact-checking organizations.
>
> Snopes.com, which has been writing about viral claims and online rumors since the mid-1990s, maintains a list of known fake news websites, several of which have emerged in the past two years.
>
> **Read beyond the headline.** If a provocative headline drew your attention, read a little further before you decide to pass along the shocking information. Even in legitimate news stories, the headline doesn't always tell the whole story. But fake news, particularly

continues

FAKE NEWS AND CRITICAL THINKING

continued

efforts to be satirical, can include several revealing signs in the text. That abcnews.com.co story that we checked, headlined "Obama Signs Executive Order Banning the Pledge of Allegiance in Schools Nationwide," went on to quote "Fappy the Anti-Masturbation Dolphin." We have to assume that the many readers who asked us whether this viral rumor was true hadn't read the full story.

What's the support? Many times these bogus stories will cite official—or official-sounding—sources, but once you look into it, the source doesn't back up the claim. For instance, the Boston Tribune site wrongly claimed that President Obama's mother-in-law was going to get a lifetime government pension for having babysat her granddaughters in the White House, citing "the Civil Service Retirement Act" and providing a link. But the link to a government benefits website doesn't support the claim at all.

The banning-the-pledge [of allegiance] story cites the number of an actual executive order—you can look it up. It doesn't have anything to do with the Pledge of Allegiance.

Check your biases. We know this is difficult. Confirmation bias leads people to put more stock in information that confirms their beliefs and discount information that doesn't. But the next time you're automatically appalled at some Facebook post concerning, say, a politician you oppose, take a moment to check it out.

Try this simple test: What other stories have been posted to the "news" website that is the source of the story that just popped up in your Facebook feed? You may be predisposed to believe that Obama bought a house in Dubai, but how about a story on the same site that carries this headline: "Antarctica 'Guardians' Retaliate Against America With Massive New Zealand Earthquake." That, too, was written by the prolific "Sorcha Faal, and as reported to her Western Subscribers."[2]

KEY WORDS

background information   expert
fallacious appeal to authority   gambler's fallacy

EXERCISES

Exercises marked with * have answers in "Answers to Exercises" (Appendix A).

Exercise 6.1

1. What is a person's background information?
2. What is the most reasonable attitude toward a claim that conflicts with other claims you have good reason to believe?
3. What degree of probability should we assign to a claim that conflicts with our background information?
*4. What is the most reasonable attitude toward a claim that is neither worthy of acceptance nor deserving of outright rejection?
5. What is an expert?
6. What should be our attitude toward a claim that conflicts with expert opinion?
7. What should be our attitude toward a claim when experts disagree about it?
8. What is the fallacious appeal to authority?
9. According to the text, in most fields, what are the two minimal prerequisites for being considered an expert?
*10. According to the text, beyond the minimal prerequisites, what are two more telling indicators that someone is an expert?
11. Under what three circumstances should we suspect that an expert may be biased?
12 When is it reasonable to accept the evidence provided by personal experience?
13. What are two factors that can give us good reason to doubt the reliability of personal experience?
14. What is the gambler's fallacy?
15. What are some ways that people resist contrary evidence?
16. What is confirmation bias?
*17. How can critical thinkers counteract confirmation bias?
18. What is the availability error?
19. What is the connection between availability error and hasty generalization?
20. What principle should guide our judgments about advertising?

Exercise 6.2

Based on claims you already have good reason to believe, your background information, and your assessment of the credibility of any cited experts, indicate for each of the following claims whether you would accept it, reject it, or proportion your belief to the evidence. Give reasons for your answers. If you decide to proportion your belief to the evidence, indicate generally what degree of plausibility you would assign to the claim.

1. Israeli psychic Uri Geller can bend spoons with his mind.
2. In Russia, some people live to be 150 years old.
3. Every year in the United States over three hundred people die of leprosy.
*4. According to Dr. Feelgood, the spokesperson for Acme Mattresses, the EasyRest 2000 from Acme is the best mattress in the world for back-pain sufferers.
5. Some bars in the suburbs of Chicago have been entertaining their nightly patrons with pygmy hippo tossing.
*6. Every person has innate psychic ability that, when properly cultivated, can enable him or her to read another person's mind.
7. The prime minister of Canada works with the government of the United States to suppress the economic power of French Canadians.
8. Molly, a thirty-four-year-old bank manager, says that stock prices will plummet dramatically in two months and will trigger another deep year-long recession.
9. Humans use only about 10 percent of the brain's capacity for thinking and creating.
*10. Fifteen women have died after smelling a free perfume sample that they received in the mail.
11. A chain letter describing the struggles of a nine-year-old girl with incurable cancer is circulating on the Internet. The more people who receive the letter, the better the little girl's chances of survival.
12. A report from the National Institutes of Health says that there is no evidence that high doses of the herb ephedra can cure cancer.
13. Giant albino alligators crawl through the underground sewers of New York City.
*14. Crop circles—large-scale geometric patterns pressed into crop fields—are the work of space aliens.
15. Crop circles are the work of human hoaxers.
16. North Korea is a communist paradise where everyone prospers and human rights are respected.
*17. Dr. Xavier, a world-famous astrologer, says that the position of the sun, planets, and stars at your birth influences your choice of careers and your marital status.
18. Eleanor Morgan, a Nobel Prize–winning economist, says that modern democratic systems (including developed nations) are not viable.
19. Eating meat rots your colon.
20. The highway speed limit in New York is 65 mph.

Exercise 6.3

For each of the following claims, decide whether you agree or disagree with it. If you agree with it, indicate what evidence would persuade you to reject the statement. If you disagree with it, indicate what evidence would persuade you to accept the statement. In each case, ask yourself if you would really change your mind if presented with the evidence you suggested.

1. Affirmative action should be abolished at all state colleges.
2. Gay marriages should be banned in the United States.
*3. An alien spacecraft crashed in Roswell, New Mexico, in 1947.
4. Earth is only ten thousand years old.
5. There is life on Mars.
6. Some people can twist their heads around on their necks a complete 360 degrees.
7. On Tuesday, a new computer virus will shut down every network and every PC in the world.
*8. Meditation and controlled breathing can shrink cancerous tumors.
9. All swans are white.
10. "Corporate welfare"—tax breaks and other special considerations for businesses—should be discontinued.

Exercise 6.4

Examine the following news story and answer the questions that follow.

Work Farce

June 26, 2003—Brazen Department of Education construction employees ripped off the city by clocking in but doing little or no work—instead spending their days at the gym, shopping or moonlighting, a sting operation by Schools Investigator Richard Condon's office found.

Checks of 13 workers—some chosen randomly, others on the basis of complaints—who were monitored beginning last August found eight of them doing little or no work.

The slackers will soon find themselves in handcuffs and unemployment lines, authorities said. . . . Condon charged that time cheating by phantom workers is "common practice."

"Time abuse is a financial drain on the city's public school system. No doubt it plays a role in the overtime that is paid to skilled trade workers," Condon said. . . . Condon did not release the names of the slackers because they're about to be arrested, he said. Chancellor Joel Klein said they will be fired "immediately."[3]

1. Is the story slanted toward or against a particular group mentioned in the story? How?
2. Are there instances of biased language or emotional appeals in the story or headline? If so, give examples.
3. What is the main source for this story?

 ## Self-Assessment Quiz

Answers appear in "Answers to Self-Assessment Quizzes" in Appendix B.

1. How should a critical thinker regard an unsupported claim that conflicts with a great deal of her background information?
2. State in your own words Bertrand Russell's principle regarding unsupported claims.
3. Name four factors to consider in deciding whether someone should be considered an expert.
4. According to the text, what are some telltale signs that an expert may be biased?
5. Name three types of perceptual impairment that can give us good reason to doubt the reliability of our personal experience.

For each of the following situations and the claim associated with it, indicate whether there may be good reasons to doubt the claim and, if so, specify the reasons.

6. Standing on a street corner in heavy fog, Eve thinks that she sees an old friend walking away from her on the other side of the street. She says to herself, "That's Julio Sanchez."
7. While playing an old rock tune backwards, Elton thinks that he hears a sentence on the tape. It's almost inaudible, but he thinks it says, "Hello, Elton, long time no see."
8. Detective Jones views the videotape of the robbery at the Seven-Eleven, which occurred last night. He sees the robber look into the camera. "I know that guy," he says. "I put him away last year on a similar charge."

For each of the following claims, indicate whether it is: (a) probably true, (b) probably false, (c) almost certainly true, (d) almost certainly false, or (e) none of the above.

9. "Most people are not aware that the cartoonish 'Bigfoot' figure is a distorted product of ancient and modern stories describing a real but unacknowledged species that is still occasionally observed today in North American forests." [The Bigfoot Field Researchers Organization]

10. "The actual risk of falling ill from a bioterrorist attack is extremely small." [American Council on Science and Health]
11. Nobody in the world is truly altruistic. Everyone is out for himself alone.
12. School violence is caused mainly by hypocrisy on the part of teachers and school administrators.
13. "The world shadow government behind the U.S. government is at it again, destroying U.S. buildings and killing people with staged acts of terrorism [on 9/11/01], the intent of which being—among other things—to start WW III." [Website devoted to 9/11 theories]
14. "What is Pre-Birth Communication? It's something that many people experience, yet very few talk about—the sense that somehow we are in contact with a being who is not yet born! It may be a vivid dream, the touch of an invisible presence, a telepathic message announcing pregnancy, or many other types of encounter. It is a mystery, one that challenges our ideas about ourselves and our children." [Website on "pre-birth communication"]
15. Physicians, drug companies, the food industry, the National Cancer Institute, and the American Cancer Society are all fighting to prevent "natural" cancer cures such as vitamin supplements and herbs from being used by cancer patients.
16. Medieval history is a lie—or, rather, it doesn't exist. Monks made it up based on a corrupt copy of ancient history.

Read the following news story and then answer questions 17–20.

Soldiers Sweep Up Saddam's Hit Goons

July 1, 2003—WASHINGTON—U.S. troops captured 319 suspected Ba'ath Party murderers as part of a tough new crackdown on regime diehards yesterday, as Defense Secretary Donald Rumsfeld forcefully denied that the United States is getting into a "quagmire" in Iraq.

Military officials said U.S. forces carried out 27 raids and also seized more than $9 million in cash as well as hundreds of machine guns and grenade launchers over the past two days as part of Operation Sidewinder.

The military offensive is a get-tough display of American power aimed at defeating Saddam Hussein's loyalists and outside terrorists responsible for hit-and-run attacks on U.S. troops and sabotage of Iraq's power and water services. But the Iraqi goon squads continued their guerrilla-style campaign yesterday, ambushing a U.S. Avenger air-defense vehicle in the ultra-tense town of Fallujah, wounding Jeremy Little, an Australian-born sound man for NBC news.

The Pentagon says 65 soldiers have been killed and scores more wounded in a series of ambushes and attacks by Saddam loyalists since the war was declared over May 1.

But at a Pentagon briefing, Rumsfeld tried to counter growing criticism in Congress and in the media over the U.S. policy toward Iraq and angrily denied that the U.S. is getting into another Vietnam War quagmire. . . .

Rumsfeld admitted that fighting in Iraq "will go on for some time," but said "more and more Iraqis" are starting to cooperate with coalition forces in their hunt for Saddam's goon squads.[4]

17. Is the story slanted toward or against a particular group mentioned in the story? How?
18. Are there instances of loaded or biased language or emotional appeals in the story or headline? If so, give examples.
19. What is the main source for this story?
20. Is this story lacking another perspective on the events? Is there more to the story that isn't mentioned? If so, explain.

 Writing Assignments

Select one of the following topics and extract an issue from it that you can write about. Investigate arguments on both sides of the issue, and write a three-page paper defending your chosen thesis.

the right to carry handguns on college campuses
"fake news"
a ban on Muslims entering the country
the federal deficit
religious liberty
sexual harassment in the workplace
animal rights
hate speech

Causal Arguments

OUR WORLD IS A SHIFTING, MULTIFARIOUS, COMPLICATED WEB OF CAUSES AND effects—and that's an oversimplification. Incredibly, the normal human response to the apparent causal chaos is to jump in and ask what causes what. What causes breast cancer? What made Malcolm steal the car? What produced that rash on Norah's arm? What brought the universe into existence? When we answer such questions (or try to), we make a **causal claim**—a statement about the causes of things. And when we try to prove or support a causal claim, we make a **causal argument**—an inductive argument whose conclusion contains a causal claim.

Causal arguments, being inductive, can give us only probable conclusions. If the premises of a strong causal argument are true, then the conclusion is only probably true, with the probability varying from merely likely to highly probable. The probabilistic nature of causal arguments, however, is not a failing or weakness. Causal reasoning is simply different from deductive reasoning, and it is our primary method of acquiring knowledge about the workings of the world. The great human enterprise known as science is concerned mainly with causal processes and causal arguments, and few people would consider this work inferior or unreliable because it was not deductively unshakeable.

Causal arguments can come in several inductive forms, some of which you already know about. For example, we sometimes reason about cause and effect using enumerative induction:

One time, when I made the aluminum rod come in contact with the rotating circular-saw blade, sparks flew.

Another time, when I made the aluminum rod come in contact with the rotating circular-saw blade, sparks flew.

Many other times, when I made the aluminum rod come in contact with the rotat-ing circular-saw blade, sparks flew.

Therefore, making the aluminum rod come in contact with the rotating circular-saw blade always causes sparks to fly.

Occasionally, we may argue to a causal conclusion using analogical induction:

Ten years ago a massive surge in worldwide oil prices caused a recession.

Five years ago a massive surge in worldwide oil prices caused a recession.

Therefore, the current massive surge in worldwide oil prices will cause a recession.

Most often, though, we use another type of induction in which we reason to a causal conclusion by pinpointing the best explanation for a particular effect. Let's say that after a hailstorm you discover that the roof of your car, which you had left parked outside in the driveway, has a hundred tiny dents in it. You might reason like this: The dents could have been caused by the mischievous kids next door, or by a flock of lunatic woodpeckers, or by the hailstorm. After considering these options (and a few others), you decide that the best explanation (or hypoth-esis) for the dents is the hailstorm. So you conclude that the hailstorm caused the dents in your car's roof.

This is a very powerful and versatile form of inductive reasoning called **inference to the best explanation.** (We'll discuss it in more detail in the next chapter.) It's the essence of scientific thinking and a mainstay of our everyday problem-solving and knowledge acquisition (whether causal or noncausal).

Testing for Causes

English philosopher John Stuart Mill (1806–1873) noted several ways of evaluat-ing causal arguments and formulated them into what are now known as "Mill's methods" of inductive inference. Despite their fancy name, however, the meth-ods are basically common sense and are used by just about everyone. They also happen to be the basis of a great deal of scientific testing. Let's look at a few of the more important ones.

Agreement or Difference

A modified version of Mill's *Method of Agreement* says that if two or more occur-rences of a phenomenon have only one relevant factor in common, that factor must be the cause.

Imagine that dozens of people stop into Elmo's corner bar after work as they usually do and that ten of them come down with an intestinal illness one hour after leaving the premises. What caused them to become ill? There are a lot of possibilities. Maybe a waiter who had a flu-like illness sneezed into their drinks, or the free tacos had gone bad, or another patron had a viral infection and passed it along via a handshake. But let's say that there is only one relevant factor that's common to all ten people who got sick: They all had a drink from the same bottle of wine. We could then plausibly conclude that something in the wine probably caused the illness.

Public health officials often use the Method of Agreement, especially when they're trying to determine the cause of an unusual illness in a population of several thousand people. They might be puzzled, say, by an unusually large number of cases of rare liver disease in a city. If they discover that all the affected people have the same poison in their bloodstreams—and this is the only common relevant factor—they have reason to believe that the poison is the cause of the liver disease. In such situations, the poison may turn out to have an industrial or agricultural source.

Mill's (modified) *Method of Difference* says that the relevant factor present when a phenomenon occurs, and absent when the phenomenon does not occur, must be the cause. Here we look not for factors that the instances of the phenomenon have in common, but for factors that are points of difference among the instances.

Suppose that the performance of football players on a major league team has been consistently excellent except for six players who've recently been playing the worst games of their careers. The only relevant difference between the high- and low-performing players is that the latter have been taking daily doses of Brand X herbal supplements. If the supplement dosing is really the only relevant difference, we could plausibly conclude that the supplements are causing the lousy performance. (Finding out if the supplements are indeed the only relevant difference, of course, is easier said than done.)

Both Agreement and Difference

If we combine these two reasoning patterns, we get a modified version of what Mill called the *Joint Method of Agreement and Difference*. Using this joint method is, obviously, just a matter of applying both methods simultaneously—a procedure that generally increases the probability that the conclusion is true. This combined method, then, says that the likely cause is the one isolated when you (1) identify the relevant factors common to occurrences of the phenomenon (the Method of Agreement) and (2) discard any of these that are present even when there are no occurrences (the Method of Difference).

Let's apply this combined method to the mystery illness at Elmo's bar. Say that among the ten patrons who become ill, the common factors are that they all drank from the same bottle of wine, and they all had the free tacos. So we reason that the likely cause is either the wine or the tacos. After further investigation, though, we find that other patrons who ate the tacos did not become ill. We con-clude that the wine is the culprit.

You can see the Joint Method of Agreement and Difference at work in modern controlled trials used to test the effectiveness of medical treatments. In these exper-iments, there are two groups of subjects—one known as the experimental group; the other, the control group. The experimental group receives the treatment being tested, usually a new drug. The control group receives a bogus, or inactive, treat-ment (referred to as a placebo). This setup helps ensure that the two groups are as similar as possible and that they differ in only one respect—the use of the genuine treatment. A controlled trial, then, reveals the relevant factor *common* to the oc-currence of the effect, which is the subjects' response to the treatment (Method of Agreement). And it shows the only important difference between the occurrence and nonoccurrence of the effect: the use of the treatment being tested.

Correlation

In many cases, relevant factors aren't merely present or absent during occur-rences of the phenomenon—they are closely *correlated* with the occurrences. The cause of an occurrence varies as the occurrence (effect) does. For such situations Mill formulated the *Method of Concomitant Variation*. This method says that when two events are correlated—when one varies in close connection with the other—they are probably causally related.

If you observe that the longer you boil eggs, the harder they get (and no other relevant factors complicate this relationship), you can safely conclude that this correlation between boiling and hardening is a causal connection. You have good evidence that the boiling causes the hardening.

In medical science, such correlations are highly prized because direct evi-dence of cause and effect is so hard to come by. Correlations are often indirect evidence of one thing causing another. In exploring the link between cigarette smoking and lung cancer, for example, researchers discovered first that people who smoke cigarettes are more likely to get lung cancer than those who don't smoke. But later research also showed that the more cigarettes people smoke, the higher their risk of lung cancer. Medical scientists call such a correlation a *dose–response relationship.* The higher the dose of the element in question (smok-ing), the higher the response (the more cases of lung cancer). This dose–response relationship between cigarette smoking and lung cancer is, when combined with other data, strong evidence that smoking causes lung cancer.

A very important cautionary note must accompany this discussion of correla-tion: Correlation, of course, does not always mean that a causal relationship is present. A correlation could just be a coincidence. An increase in home PC sales is correlated with a rise in the incidence of AIDS in Africa, but this doesn't mean that one is in any way causally linked with the other.

Causal Confusions

Mill's methods and other forms of causal reasoning may be common sense, but they're not foolproof. No inductive procedure can guarantee the truth of the conclusion. More to the point, it's easy to commit errors in cause-and-effect reasoning—regardless of the method used—by failing to take into account pertinent aspects of the situation. This section describes some of the more common causal blunders to which we're all prey.

Misidentifying Relevant Factors

A key issue in any type of causal reasoning is whether the factors preceding an effect are truly relevant to that effect. In the Method of Agreement, for example, it's easy to find a preceding factor common to all occurrences of a phenomenon. But that factor may be irrelevant. In the case of Elmo's bar, what if all those who became ill had black hair? So what? We know that hair color is very unlikely to be related to intestinal illness. *Relevant* factors include only those things that could possibly be causally connected to the occurrence of the phenomenon being studied. We could reasonably judge that factors relevant to the intestinal illness would include all the conditions that might help transmit bacteria or viruses.

Your ability to identify relevant factors depends mostly on your background knowledge—what you know about the kinds of conditions that could produce the occurrences in which you're interested. Lack of background knowledge might lead you to dismiss or ignore relevant factors or to assume that irrelevant factors must play a role. The only cure for this inadequacy is deeper study of the causal possibilities in question.

Mishandling Multiple Factors

Most of the time, the biggest difficulty in evaluating causal connections is not that there are so few relevant factors to consider—but that there are so many. Too often the Method of Agreement and the Method of Difference are rendered useless because they cannot, by themselves, narrow the possibilities to just one. At the same time, ordinary causal reasoning is frequently flawed because of the failure to consider *all* the relevant antecedent factors. (The next chapter will refer to this problem as the failure to consider alternative explanations.)

Sometimes this kind of oversight happens because we simply don't look hard enough for possible causes. At other times, we miss relevant factors because we don't know enough about the causal processes involved. This again is a function of skimpy background knowledge. Either way, there is no countermeasure better than your own determination to dig out the whole truth.

COINCIDENCE, BIRTH DATES, AND US PRESIDENTS

When we're tempted to say that the conjunction of two events "couldn't be just coincidence," we should think twice. People are often lousy at determining the true likelihood of events. Recall the birth-date problem mentioned earlier. It's the classic example of misjudged probabilities: In a random selection of twenty-three people, what is the probability that at least two of them will have the same birth date? The answer: 50 percent, or 50-50. People are usually shocked when they hear the answer. Part of the reason is that they typically underestimate how often oddball coincidences occur and fail to see that such strange conjunctions *must* occur from time to time. Here's a succinct explanation of the problem from social psychologist David G. Myers:

> We've all marveled at such coincidences in our own lives. Checking out a photocopy counter from the Hope College library desk, I confused the clerk when giving my six-digit department charge number—which just happened at that moment to be identical to the counter's six-digit number on which the last user had finished. Shortly after my daughter, Laura Myers, bought two pairs of shoes, we were astounded to discover that the two brand names on the boxes were "Laura" and "Myers."

Certain facts about John F. Kennedy and Abraham Lincoln point to some strange coincidences. But what do the coincidences prove?

continues

COINCIDENCE, BIRTH DATES, AND US PRESIDENTS

continued

And then there are those remarkable coincidences that, with added digging, have been embellished into really fun stories, such as the familiar Lincoln–Kennedy coincidences (both with seven letters in their last names, elected 100 years apart, assassinated on a Friday while beside their wives, one in Ford's theater, the other in a Ford Motor Co. car, and so forth). We also have enjoyed newspaper accounts of astonishing happenings, such as when twins Lorraine and Levinia Christmas, driving to deliver Christmas presents to each other near Flitcham, England, collided.

My favorite is this little known fact: In Psalm 46 of the King James Bible, published in the year that Shakespeare turned 46, the 46th word is "shake" and the 46th word from the end is "spear." (More remarkable than this coincidence is that someone should have noted this!) . . .

"In reality," says mathematician John Allen Paulos, "the most astonishingly incredible coincidence imaginable would be the complete absence of all coincidences." When Evelyn Marie Adams won the New Jersey lottery twice, newspapers reported the odds of her feat as 1 in 17 trillion—the odds that a given person buying a single ticket for two New Jersey lotteries would win both. But statisticians Stephen Samuels and George McCabe report that, given the millions of people who buy U.S. state lottery tickets, it was "practically a sure thing" that someday, somewhere, someone would hit a state jackpot twice. Consider: An event that happens to but one in a billion people in a day happens 2000 times a year. A day when nothing weird happened would actually be the weirdest day of all.[1]

Being Misled by Coincidence

Sometimes ordinary events are paired in unusual or interesting ways: You think of Hawaii, then suddenly a TV ad announces low-cost fares to Maui; you receive some email just as your doorbell sounds and the phone rings; or you stand in the lobby of a hotel thinking of an old friend—then see her walk by. Plenty of interesting pairings can also show up in scientific research. Scientists might find, for example, that men with the highest rates of heart disease may also have a higher daily intake of water. Or women with the lowest risk of breast cancer may own Toyotas. Such pairings are very probably just coincidence, merely interesting correlations of events. A problem arises, though, when we think that there nevertheless must be a causal connection involved.

For several reasons, we may very much want a coincidence to be a cause-and-effect relationship, so we come to believe that the pairing is causal. Just as often we may mistake causes for coincidences because we're impressed or excited about the conjunction of events. The pairing of events may seem "too much of a coincidence" to be coincidence, so we conclude that one event must have caused the other. You may be thinking about how nice it would be for your sister to call you from her home in Alaska—then the phone rings, and it's her! You're tempted to conclude that your wishing caused her to call. But such an event, though intriguing and seemingly improbable, is not really so extraordinary. Given the ordinary laws of statistics, incredible coincidences are common and must occur. Any event, even one that seems shockingly improbable, is actually very probable over the long haul. Given enough opportunities to occur, events like this surprising phone call are virtually certain to happen to *someone*.

People are especially prone to "it can't be just coincidence" thinking because, for several psychological reasons, they misjudge the probabilities involved. They may think, for example, that a phone call from someone at the moment they're thinking of that person is incredible—but only because they've forgotten about all the times they've thought of that person and the phone *didn't* ring.

Unfortunately, there is no foolproof way to distinguish coincidence from cause and effect. But this rule of thumb can help:

> *Don't assume that a causal connection exists unless you have good reason for doing so.*

Generally, a good reason consists of the passing of one or more standard causal tests (such as the ones we've been discussing)—and being able to rule out any relevant factors that might undermine the verdict of those tests. Usually, when a cause–effect connection is uncertain, only further evaluation or research can clear things up.

Confusing Cause with Temporal Order

A particularly prevalent type of misjudgment about coincidences is the logical fallacy known as **post hoc, ergo propter hoc** ("after that, therefore because of that"). We believe that a cause must precede its effect. But just because one event precedes another that doesn't mean that the earlier one *caused* the later. To think so is to be taken in by this fallacy. Outrageous examples of post hoc arguments include: "The rooster crowed, then the sun came up, so the rooster's crowing caused sunrise!" and "Jasmine left her umbrella at home Monday, and this caused it to rain." You can clearly see the error in such cases, but consider these arguments:

Argument 1

After the training for police officers was enhanced, violent crime in the city decreased by 10 percent. So enhanced training caused the decline in violent crime.

Argument 2

An hour after Julio drank the cola, his headache went away. The cola cured his headache.

Argument 3

As soon as Smith took office and implemented policies that reflected his conservative theory of economics, the economy went into a downward slide characterized by slow growth and high unemployment. Therefore, the Smith policies caused the current economic doldrums.

Argument 4

I wore my black shirt on Tuesday and got an F on a math quiz. I wore the same shirt the next day and flunked my psych exam. That shirt's bad luck.

The conclusion of argument 1 is based on nothing more than the fact that the enhanced training preceded the reduction in violent crime. But crime rates can decrease for many reasons, and the enhanced training may have had nothing to do with the decline in crime. For the argument to be strong, other considerations besides temporal order would have to apply—for example, that other possible causes or antecedent factors had been ruled out; that there was a close correlation between amount of training and decline in crime rates; or that in previous years (or in comparable cities) enhanced training was always followed by decreased violent crime (or no change in training was always followed by steady crime rates).

Argument 2 is also purely post hoc. Such reasoning is extremely common and underlies almost all folk remedies and a great deal of quackery and bogus self-cures. You take a vitamin E capsule, and eight hours later your headache is gone. But was it really the vitamin E that did the trick? Or was it some other overlooked factor such as something you ate, the medication you took (or didn't take), the nap you had, the change in environment (from, say, indoors to outdoors), or the stress reduction you felt when you had pleasant thoughts? Would your headache have gone away on its own anyway? Was it the *placebo effect*—the tendency for people to feel better when treated even when the treatment is fake or inactive? A chief function of controlled medical testing is to evaluate cause-and-effect relationships by systematically ruling out post hoc thinking and irrelevant factors.

Argument 3 is typical post hoc reasoning from the political sphere. Unless there are other good reasons for thinking that the economic policy is causally connected to specific economic events, the argument is weak and the conclusion unreliable.

Argument 4 is 100 percent post hoc and undiluted superstition. There is no difference in kind between this argument and much of the notorious post hoc reasoning of centuries ago: "That girl gave me the evil eye. The next day I broke my leg. That proves she's a witch, and the Elders of Salem should have her put to death!"

THE DEADLY POST HOC FALLACY

Despite a growing body of scientific research showing no connection between a measles vaccine and autism in young children, many people have insisted that the vaccine causes the disorder. Some parents of autistic children reasoned that since autism symptoms arose after the children were vaccinated, the vaccine was to blame. As evidence builds against a causal link, the reasoning looks more and more post hoc—and dangerous. A recent study confirms previous findings:

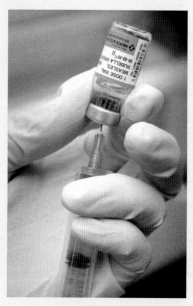

> Scientists who tried to replicate a study that once tied a measles vaccine with autism said on Wednesday they could not find any link and hope their study will encourage parents to vaccinate their children to combat a rash of measles outbreaks.

Does a measles vaccine cause autism in children? Science says no, but the *post hoc* fallacy can trick you into thinking yes.

Parents' refusals to have their children vaccinated against measles have contributed to the highest numbers of cases seen in the United States and parts of Europe in many years.

Measles kills about 250,000 people a year globally, mostly children in poor nations.

Public health officials have been stressing the safety of the combined measles-mumps-rubella, or MMR, shot and other childhood vaccines in the face of vocal groups who claim the immunizations may cause autism and other problems.

The U.S. Institute of Medicine has issued several definitive reports showing no connection between autism and any vaccinations.[2]

Confusing Cause and Effect

Sometimes we may realize that there's a causal relationship between two factors—but we may not know which factor is the cause and which is the effect. We may be confused, in other words, about the answers to questions like these:

Does your coffee drinking cause you to feel stressed out—or do your feelings of being stressed out cause you to drink coffee?

Does participation in high-school sports produce desirable virtues such as courage and self-reliance—or do the virtues of courage and self-reliance lead students to participate in high school sports?

Does regular exercise make people healthy—or are healthy people naturally prone to regular exercise?

As you can see, it's not always a simple matter to discern what the nature of a causal link is. Again, we must rely on our rule of thumb: *Don't assume that a causal connection exists unless you have good reason for doing so.* This tenet applies not only to our ordinary experience but to all states of affairs involving cause and effect, including scientific investigations.

In everyday life, sorting cause from effect is often easy because the situations we confront are frequently simple and familiar—as when we're trying to discover what caused the kettle to boil over. Here, we naturally rely on Mill's methods or other types of causal reasoning. But as we've seen, in many other common circumstances, things aren't so simple. We often cannot be sure that we've identified all the relevant factors, or ruled out the influence of coincidence, or correctly distinguished cause and effect. Our rule of thumb, then, should be our guide in all the doubtful cases.

Science faces all the same kinds of challenges in its pursuit of causal explanations. And despite its sophisticated methodology and investigative tools, it must expend a great deal of effort to pin down causal connections. Identifying the cause of a disease, for example, usually requires not one study or experiment, but many. The main reason is that uncovering relevant factors and excluding irrelevant or misleading factors is always tough. This is why we should apply our rule of thumb even to scientific research that purports to identify a causal link.

Necessary and Sufficient Conditions

Another useful kind of causal argument is built on the concepts of **necessary condition** and **sufficient condition**. We sometimes speak of the conditions (or features) that a thing *must* have in order to be that thing. These are called necessary conditions. For example, being a bird is a necessary condition for being an eagle; the presence of oxygen is a necessary condition for combustion to occur; and being male is a necessary condition for being an uncle. An eagle is an eagle only if it is a bird; combustion can occur only if oxygen is present; and someone can be an uncle only if he is male. A thing often has more than one necessary condition. The necessary conditions for combustion to occur are oxygen, heat, and fuel. If even one of these conditions is absent, combustion will not occur.

Often we are also interested in the conditions that *guarantee* that something exists or is a certain kind of thing. These are known as sufficient conditions. Being a human male with a niece or nephew is a sufficient condition for being an uncle. The sufficient condition for combustion is the combination of all the necessary conditions.

Conditions can also be *both* necessary and sufficient. Fuel being heated to a certain temperature in the presence of oxygen is both a necessary and sufficient condition for combustion.

Now suppose someone argues for the conclusion that a person becomes a criminal if and only if he or she is raised in a single-parent home. That is, she asserts that the necessary and sufficient condition for becoming a criminal is to have been raised in a household headed by just one parent. To refute this claim, all you have to do is show that this condition is *not* necessary and sufficient for becoming a criminal. You just have to produce one example of someone who is a criminal but did not come from a household headed by just one parent. And, of course, such examples abound and can be incorporated into your counterargument.

 KEY WORDS

causal argument	causal claim	inference to the best explanation
necessary condition	post hoc, ergo propter hoc	sufficient condition

 EXERCISES

Exercises marked with * have answers in "Answers to Exercises" (Appendix A).

Exercise 7.1

Analyze each of the following causal arguments. Identify the conclusion and whether the argument appeals to the method of agreement, the method of difference, the joint method of agreement and difference, or correlation. In some cases the conclusion may be implied but not stated. Indicate whether the argument is strong or weak.

1. Forty-five patients were admitted to Mercy Hospital for pneumonia in December. They were all given standard treatment for pneumonia. After five days, thirty of them were well enough to go home. The other fifteen, however, somehow acquired other infections and were not well enough to be released for fourteen days. The only relevant factor common to these fifteen is this: They all stayed in the same ward (different from the ward that the other group stayed in). Something about staying in that ward is the cause of the prolonged illness.

*2. Research suggests that eating lots of fruits and vegetables may provide some protection against several types of cancer. Studies have revealed that the risk of getting cancer associated with the lowest intakes of fruits and vegetables is twice as high as that associated with the highest intakes. This association holds for several types of cancer, including cancers of the breast, colon, pancreas, and bladder.

3. "An experimental vaccine prevented women from becoming persistently infected with a [type of human papilloma virus called HPV-16] that is associated with half of all cervical cancers, researchers reported. . . . The study involved 2,392 women from 16 to 23 years in age. Participants were randomly assigned to receive three shots of either an HPV-16 vaccine or a placebo (a dummy substance). The study was double-blinded—that is, neither the investigators nor the study participants knew who got the vaccine and who got the placebo. Participants were followed for an average of 17 months after getting the third shot. . . . [Forty-one] women developed HPV-16 infection—all of these women were in the placebo group. . . . By comparison, no one who got all three vaccine shots developed an HPV-16 infection." [National Cancer Institute]

4. Getting the endorsement of the teachers' union in this town is absolutely essential to being elected to the school board in this city. No one has ever won a seat on the school board without an endorsement from the teachers' union.

5. For most of the school year the number of disciplinary actions taken weekly because of student misconduct at North High School has remained about the same—roughly ten a week. But for the last month the number of actions per week has gone down considerably—to about six per week. There can be only one reason: Last month the Ten Commandments were posted in the hallway outside the principal's office. This posting was the only significant recent change in the school.

6. In Instance 1, when factors X, Y, and Z were present, E happened. In Instance 2, when factors X, Y, and P were present, E happened. In Instance 3, when factors X and Z were present, E did not happen. In Instance 4, when Z and P were present, E did not happen. And in Instance 5, when X, Z, and P were present, E did not happen. Therefore, Y caused E.

*7. Educators have frequently noted the connection between education level and salary. The higher a person's education level is, the higher his or her annual salary is likely to be. Education increases people's earning power.

8. On Tuesday fifty-two people ate ham sandwiches at Johnny's Deli, and half of these came down with hepatitis. The board of health discovered that the people who became ill had their ham sandwiches made by Johnny's brother, who had hepatitis at the time. This was the only relevant common element among those who got sick. Seems Johnny's brother was the cause of this outbreak.

9. Scientists wanted to see whether giving prepuberty children dietary supplements of calcium could significantly increase the density of the children's bones. (Bone density is a key part of bone strength.) So they selected seventy-one pairs of identical twins and gave one twin of each pair a daily supplement of extra calcium and the other twin a sugar pill (placebo). All the twins had diets that contained adequate amounts of all nutrients. The investigators monitored the twins and their diets for three years. The only relevant difference between the twins was the extra calcium that half of them received. At the end of the three years, the scientists found that the twins who had received the extra calcium had significantly greater bone density. They concluded that the extra calcium caused the increased density.

Exercise 7.2

For each argument in Exercise 7.1, identify errors in causal reasoning that are most likely to occur in the circumstances indicated. The possibilities include (a) misidentifying or overlooking relevant factors, (b) being misled by coincidence, (c) falling for the post hoc fallacy, and (d) confusing cause and effect. Answers are provided for 2 and 7.

Exercise 7.3

For each of the following causal statements, indicate whether the specified cause is (a) a necessary condition, (b) a sufficient condition, (c) a necessary and sufficient condition, or (d) neither a necessary nor a sufficient condition.

*1. Sylvia's being exposed to the influenza virus caused her to get the flu.

2. Sergio's eagerness to get to the airport caused him to get a speeding ticket.

3. Giving the roses water and nourishing soil caused them to flourish.

*4. Chopping off the head of the king put an end to him.

5. The mighty Casey hit the ball out of the park, winning the game by one run.

6. The straw broke the camel's back.

7. The proper combining of sodium and chlorine produced salt, sodium chloride.

8. Johann got a good grade on the exam because he studied the night before.

*9. A single spark started the internal combustion engine.

10. Simone lost weight by exercising regularly.

 ## Self-Assessment Quiz

Answers appear in "Answers to Self-Assessment Quizzes" in Appendix B. Analyze each of the following causal arguments. Identify the conclusion and whether the argument is weak or strong. If it's weak, explain why with reference to the material in this chapter.

1. School violence is caused mainly by teens playing violent video games. Incidents of violence in schools have increased as more and more teens are playing violent video games, as the video games themselves have become more graphically and realistically violent, and as the number and variety of video games have expanded dramatically.

2. Smoking and exposure to secondhand smoke among pregnant women pose a significant risk to both infants and the unborn. According to numerous studies, each year the use of tobacco causes thousands of spontaneous births, infant deaths, and deaths from SIDS. Death rates for fetuses are 35 percent higher among pregnant women who smoke than among pregnant women who don't smoke.

3. Why are crime rates so high, the economy so bad, and our children so prone to violence, promiscuity, and vulgarity? These social ills have arisen—as they always have—from the "moral vacuum" created when Americans turn away from religion. Our current slide into chaos started when prayer was banned from public schools and secular humanism swooped in to replace it. And as God has slowly faded from public life, we have got deeper in the hole.

4. The twelve of us went on a hike through the mountains. We all drank bottled water except Lisa, who drank from a stream. Later she got really sick. Some intestinal thing. But the rest of us were fine. We've repeated this adventure many times on other hikes, with all but one of us drinking bottled water and one drinking from a stream. Everything else was the same. Each time, the person who drank from the stream got really ill. Drinking from streams on these hikes causes intestinal illness. Don't do it.

5. Ever since I started drinking herbal tea in the morning, my energy level has improved and I'm a lot calmer during the day. That stuff works.

6. Yesterday my astrological chart—prepared by a top astrologer—said that I would meet an attractive person today, and I did. Last week, it said I'd come into some money, and I did. (Jack paid me that hundred dollars he owed me.) Now I'm a believer. The stars really do rule.

7. Most of the terminal cancer patients in this ward who had positive attitudes about their disease lived longer than expected. Most of the negative-attitude patients didn't live as long as expected. A positive attitude can increase the life expectancy of people with terminal cancer.

Analyze each of the following causal arguments. Identify the conclusion and whether the argument appeals to the method of agreement, the method of difference, the joint method of agreement and difference, or correlation. In some cases the conclusion may be implied but not stated. Indicate whether the argument is strong or weak.

8. "On the 20th May, 1747, I took twelve patients [with] scurvy on board the *Salisbury* at sea. Their cases were as similar as I could have them. They all in general had putrid gums, the spots and lassitude, with weakness of their knees. They lay together in one place, being a proper apartment for the sick in the fore-hold; and had one diet in common to all. . . . Two of these were ordered each a quart of cider a day. Two others took [twenty-five drops of] vitriol three times a day. . . . Two others took two spoonfuls of vinegar three times a day. . . . Two of the worst patients [were given a half pint of sea water daily]. . . . Two others had each two oranges and one lemon given them everyday. . . . The two remaining patients took [small doses of nutmeg, garlic, mustard seed, and a few other ingredients]. The consequence was that the most sudden and visible good effects were perceived from the use of the oranges and lemons; one of those who had taken them being at the end of six days fit for duty. . . . The other was the best recovered of any in his condition, and being now deemed pretty well was appointed nurse to the rest of the sick. As I shall have occasion elsewhere to take notice of the effects of other medicines in this disease, I shall here only observe that the result of all my experiments was that oranges and lemons were the most effectual remedies for this distemper at sea." [James Lind, *Of the Prevention of the Scurvy*, 1753]

9. On Tuesday fifty-two people ate ham sandwiches at Johnny's Deli, and half of these came down with hepatitis. The board of health discovered that the people who became ill had their ham sandwiches made by Johnny's brother, who had hepatitis at the time. This was the only relevant common element among those who got sick. Seems Johnny's brother was the cause of this outbreak.

10. Scientists wanted to see whether giving prepuberty children dietary supplements of calcium could significantly increase the density of the

children's bones. (Bone density is a key part of bone strength.) So they selected seventy-one pairs of identical twins and gave one twin of each pair a daily supplement of extra calcium and the other twin a sugar pill (placebo). All the twins had diets that contained adequate amounts of all nutrients. The investigators monitored the twins and their diets for three years. The only relevant difference between the twins was the extra calcium that half of them received. At the end of the three years, the scientists found that the twins who had received the extra calcium had significantly greater bone density. They concluded that the extra calcium caused the increased density.

11. For years vehicular accidents at the intersection of Fifth and Main Streets have consistently averaged two to four per month. Since a traffic light was installed there, the rate has been one or two accidents every three months. That new traffic light has made quite a difference.

12. The risk of atherosclerosis (a.k.a. hardening of the arteries) is linked to the amount of cholesterol in the bloodstream (called serum cholesterol). The higher the serum cholesterol levels, the greater the risk of atherosclerosis. There's a causal connection between serum cholesterol levels and risk of atherosclerosis.

13. Investigators tested the performance of four gasoline-powered lawnmowers before and after a tune-up. The machines differed in age, manufacturer, engine type, and controls. The performance of every mower was better after the tune-up, leading the testers to conclude that tune-ups can improve the performance of lawnmowers.

14. The reason there have been so many terrorist attacks in Western countries in the past ten years is that the rights of Palestinians have been violated by Westerners. Every time large numbers of innocent Palestinians have been jailed, persecuted, or killed in Western countries, there has been a terrorist attack in the West.

15. Charlie was pretty happy all week, but then he started moping around like he'd lost his dog or something. I think he's upset because he got word that his grades weren't good enough to get into med school.

16. The price of a barrel of oil on the world market has hit $40 only twelve times in the last thirty years. Sometimes major world economies were in recession, and sometimes they weren't. Sometimes oil production was down; sometimes up. US oil reserves were sometimes sold off; sometimes not. But one thing that was always present when oil hit $40 was that there was a major war going on somewhere in the world.

17. Sometimes my television reception is excellent, and sometimes it's terrible. There's only one important factor that seems to make a difference. When the reception is excellent, no other major appliances are running in the house. When it's terrible, at least one major appliance—like the dishwasher—is

running. For some reason, running a major appliance interferes with my TV reception.

18. In our test, after people washed their hands with Lather-Up Germicidal Soap, no germs whatsoever could be detected on their hands. But under exactly the same conditions, after they washed their hands with Brand X germicidal soap, plenty of germs were found on their hands. Lather-Up is better.

19. Just five people got A's on the midterm exam. The only common factor in their success is that they all studied the night before and reviewed their notes just before walking into class to take the test.

20. The cause of Jackie M's criminal behavior—his involvement in petty theft and assaults—is no mystery. Jackie commits most of his criminal acts when the outdoor temperatures are highest. When outdoor temperatures are lowest, he behaves himself. In fact, the incidence of his criminal behavior rises as the temperature rises. Jackie's problem is that he has a heat-sensitive personality.

 ## Writing Assignments

1. Argue for a claim that you think you can defend in a three-page essay. Use the following statements as starting points to extract a manageable thesis.
   • People (including college students) have a right not to be offended.
   • People have a right to voice their opinions, even very offensive opinions.
   • Everyone does what is in his or her own best interests.
   • It's wrong for the government to tax citizens to support people who are poor and needy.
   • Deadbeat dads (fathers who don't or won't pay child support that they are legally obligated to pay) should be put in jail.
   • Sexual harassment is not a problem on this campus.
   • Animals have rights.
   • Muslims are not terrorists.
   • Guns should not be allowed on college campuses (except by security personnel).

2. Select a causal argument on a political issue from recent op-ed pages (in newspapers or on websites). Then critique it, explaining why it's strong or weak, specifically noting whether it misidentifies or overlooks relevant factors, confuses cause with coincidence, commits the post hoc fallacy, confuses cause and effect, or mishandles or misunderstands necessary and sufficient conditions.

Inference to the Best Explanation

L ET'S TAKE STOCK OF THE INDUCTIVE TERRAIN TRAVELED THUS FAR. IN THE PRECEDING chapters, we closely examined the nature and uses of inductive reasoning. We were reminded that a deductive argument, unlike an inductive one, is intended to provide logically conclusive support for its conclusion. If it succeeds in providing such support, it's said to be valid; if not, invalid. If a valid argument has true premises, it's said to be sound. But an inductive argument is intended to supply only probable support for its conclusion. If it manages to render the conclusion very likely to be true, it's said to be strong; if not, weak. The conclusion of an inductively strong argument is much more likely to be true than not. If a strong argument has true premises, it's said to be cogent.

We also saw that inductive arguments come in several forms. One of them is enumerative induction, in which we reason from premises about *some* members of a group to a conclusion, or generalization, about the group *as a whole.* All the swans you have ever seen are white, so *all* swans are probably white. Forty percent of the students at your college have a driver's license, so 40 percent of all students everywhere must have a driver's license. (Whether these enumerative inductive arguments are strong or cogent is another matter.)

Another kind of inductive argument is argument by analogy (or analogical induction), in which we reason that since two or more things are similar in several respects, they must be similar in some additional respect. In an analogical induction, you might argue that (1) since humans can move about, solve mathematical equations, win chess games, and feel pain, *and* (2) since computers (or robots) are like humans in that they can move about, solve mathematical equations, and win chess games, it's therefore probable that computers can also feel pain. Analogical induction, like all inductive reasoning, can establish conclusions only with a degree of probability.

Finally, we saw that causal arguments—inductive arguments whose conclusions contain causal claims—can be enumerative inductions, analogical inductions, or arguments that rely on Mill's methods and similar kinds of inferences. Reasoning well about causal connections means avoiding numerous common errors, including misidentifying or overlooking relevant factors, confusing coincidence with cause, and committing the post hoc fallacy.

We noted only in passing that there is another kind of inductive reasoning called **inference to the best explanation.** Now it's time to delve deep into this kind of inductive reasoning, perhaps the most commonly used form of inference and arguably the most empowering in daily life.

Explanations and Inference

Recall from chapter 1 that an explanation is a statement (or statements) asserting why or how something is the case. For example: The bucket leaks because there's a hole in it. He was sad because his dog died. She broke the pipe by hitting it with a wrench. These explanations and all others are intended to clarify and elucidate, to increase our understanding. Remember too our discussion of the important distinction between an explanation and an argument. While an explanation tells us *why or how something is the case*, an argument gives us reasons for believing *that something is the case.*

As you've probably already guessed, there are also different kinds of explanations. For instance, some explanations are what we might call procedural—they try to explain how something is done or how an action is carried out. ("She opened up the engine, then examined the valves, then checked the cylinders.") Some are interpretive—they try to explain the meaning of terms or states of affairs. ("This word means 'dashing' or 'jaunty.'") And some are functional—they try to explain how something functions. ("The heart circulates and oxygenates the blood.")

But the kind of explanation we're concerned with here—and the kind we bump into most often—is what we'll call, for lack of something snappier, a *theoretical explanation.* Such explanations are theories, or hypotheses, that try to explain why something is the way it is, why something is the case, why something happened. In this category, we must include all explanations intended to explain the cause of events—the causal explanations that are so important to both science and daily life. Theoretical explanations, of course, are claims. They assert that something is or is not the case.

Now, even though an explanation is not an argument, an explanation can be *part* of an argument. It can be the heart of the kind of inductive argument known as inference to the best explanation. And in this kind of inference, the explanations we use are theoretical explanations.

In inference to the best explanation, *we reason from premises about a state of affairs to an explanation for that state of affairs.* The premises are statements about observations or other evidence to be explained. The explanation is a claim about why the state of affairs is the way it is. The key question that this type of inference tries to answer is, What is the best explanation for the existence or nature of this state of affairs? The best explanation is the one most likely to be true, even though there is no guarantee of its truth as there is in deductive inference.

So inference to the best explanation has this pattern:

Phenomenon Q.

E provides the best explanation for Q.

Therefore, it is probable that E is true.

For example:

The new quarterback dropped the ball again. The best explanation for that screw-up is that he's nervous. So he's definitely nervous.

The best explanation for Maria's absence today is that she's angry at the boss. Yep, she's mad at the boss.

The defendant's fingerprints were all over the crime scene, the police found the victim's blood on his shirt, and he was in possession of the murder weapon. The only explanation for all this that makes any sense is that the defendant actually committed the crime. He's guilty.

If the explanations in these arguments really are the best, then the arguments are inductively strong. And if the premises are also true, then the arguments are cogent. If cogent, we are justified in believing that the explanations for the phenomena are in fact correct.

Notice that an inference to the best explanation always goes "beyond the evidence"—it tries to explain facts but does so by positing a theory that is not derived entirely from those facts. It tries to understand the known by putting forth—through inference and imagination—a theoretical pattern that encompasses both the known and unknown. It proposes a plausible pattern that expands our understanding.

The fact that there are *best* explanations, of course, implies that not all explanations for a state of affairs are created equal; some are better than others. Just because you've devised an explanation for something doesn't mean that you're justified in believing that the explanation is the right one. If other explanations are just as good, your explanation is in doubt. If other explanations are better than yours, you are not justified in believing it. But much of the time, after further study or thought, you can reasonably conclude that a particular explanation really is the best explanation. (More on how to evaluate the relative worth of explanations later.) In this way, you can come to understand the state of affairs more than you did before.

Inference to the best explanation probably seems very familiar to you. That's because you use it all the time—and need it all the time. Often when we try to understand something in the world, we construct explanations for why this something is the way it is, and we try to determine which of these is the best.

Devising explanations helps increase our understanding by fitting our experiences and background knowledge into a coherent pattern. At every turn, we are confronted with phenomena that we can only fully understand by explaining them.

Sometimes we're barely aware that we're using inference to the best explanation. If we awaken and see that the streets outside are wet, we may immediately posit this explanation: It's been raining. Without thinking much about it, we may also quickly consider whether a better explanation is that a street-sweeper machine has wet the street. Just as quickly we may dismiss this explanation because we see that the houses and cars are also wet. After reasoning in this fashion, we may decide to carry an umbrella that day.

Let's consider a more elaborate example. Say that you discover that your car won't start in the morning (the phenomenon to be explained). You would like to know why it won't start (the explanation for the failure) because you can't repair the car unless you know what the problem is. You know that there are several possible explanations or theories.

1. The battery is dead.
2. The fuel tank is empty.
3. The starter has malfunctioned.
4. A vandal has sabotaged the car.
5. All or several of the above.

So you try to figure out which theory is the most plausible, that is, most likely to be true. You see right away that there is snow around the car from yesterday's snowstorm—but there are no tracks (not even yours) and no signs of tampering anywhere. So you dismiss theory 4. You remember that you filled up the gas tank yesterday, the fuel gauge says that the tank is full, and you don't see any signs of leakage. So you can safely ignore theory 2. You notice that the lights, heater, and radio work fine, and the battery gauge indicates a fully charged battery. So you discard theory 1. When you try to start the car, you hear a clicking sound like the one you heard when the starter had failed previously. Among the theories you started with, then, theory 3 now seems the most plausible. This means that theory 5 cannot be correct since it entails two or more of the theories.

If you wanted to, you could state your argument like this:

(1) Your car won't start in the morning.

(2) The theory that the starter has malfunctioned is the best explanation for the car's not starting in the morning.

(3) Therefore, it's probable that the malfunctioning starter caused the car not to start in the morning.

In science, where inference to the best explanation is an essential tool, usually the theories of interest are causal theories, in which events are the things to be explained and the proposed causes of the events are the explanations. Just as we do in everyday life, scientists often consider several competing theories for the same event or phenomenon. Then—through scientific testing and careful thinking—they systematically eliminate inadequate theories and eventually arrive at the one that's rightly regarded as the best of the bunch. Using this form of inference, scientists discover planets, viruses, cures, subatomic particles, black holes—and many things that can't even be directly observed.

And then there are all those other professionals who rely on inference to the best explanation. Physicians use it to pinpoint the cause of multiple symptoms in patients. Police detectives use it to track down law breakers. Judges and juries use it to determine the guilt or innocence of accused persons. And philosophers use it to assess the worth of conceptual theories.

With so many people in so many areas of inquiry using inference to the best explanation, you'd expect the world to be filled with countless theories proposed by innumerable people looking to explain all sorts of things. And so there are.

Of course, it's often easy to make up theories to explain things we don't understand. The harder job is sorting out good theories from bad, and that's the topic of the next few pages.

 DARWIN AND THE BEST EXPLANATION

Charles Darwin (1809–1882) offered the theory of evolution by natural selection as the best explanation for a wide variety of natural phenomena. He catalogued an extensive list of facts about nature and showed that his theory explains them well. He argued, however, that the alternative theory of the day—the view that God independently created species—does not explain them. Darwin declared:

> It can hardly be supposed that a false theory would explain, in so satisfactory a manner as does the theory of natural selection, the several large classes of facts above specified. It has recently been objected that this is an unsafe method of arguing; but it is a method used in judging of the common events of life, and has often been used by the greatest natural philosophers.[1]

Theories and Consistency

Very often we may propose a theory as an explanation for a phenomenon, or we may have a theory thrust upon us for consideration. In either case, we will likely be dealing with an argument in the form of inference to the best explanation. The conclusion of the argument will always say, in effect, *this* theory is the best explanation of the facts. And we will be on the hot seat trying to decide if it really is. How do we do that?

The work is not always easy, but there are special criteria we can use to get the job done. Before we apply these criteria, though, we have to make sure that the theory in question meets the minimum requirement of *consistency.* A theory that does not meet this minimum requirement is worthless, so there is no need to use the special criteria to evaluate the theory. A theory that meets the requirement is eligible for further consideration. Here we are concerned with both *internal* and *external* consistency. A theory that is internally consistent is consistent with itself—it's free of contradictions. A theory that is externally consistent is consistent with the data it's supposed to explain—it fully accounts for the phenomenon to be explained.

If we show that a theory contains a contradiction, we have refuted it. A theory that implies that something both is and is not the case cannot possibly be true. By exposing an internal contradiction, Galileo once refuted Aristotle's famous theory of motion, a venerable hypothesis that had stood tall for centuries. He showed that the theory implied that one falling object falls both faster and slower than another one.

If a theory is externally inconsistent, we have reason to believe that it's false. Suppose you leave your car parked on the street overnight and the next morning discover that (1) the windshield is broken, (2) there's blood on the steering wheel, and (3) there's a brick on the front seat. And let's say that your friend Charlie offers this theory to explain these facts: Someone threw a brick through your windshield. What would you think about this theory?

You would probably think that Charlie had not been paying attention. His theory accounts for the broken windshield and the brick—but not the blood on the steering wheel. You would likely toss his theory out and look for one that was complete. Like this one: A thief broke your windshield with a brick then crawled through the broken window, cutting himself in the process.

Theories and Criteria

For a moment let's return to our example of the car that won't start. Recall that we examined five possible explanations for the nonstart phenomenon:

1. The battery is dead.
2. The fuel tank is empty.
3. The starter has malfunctioned.
4. A vandal has sabotaged the car.
5. All or several of the above.

But what if someone suggested that our analysis of this problem was incomplete because we failed to consider several other possible theories that are at least as plausible as these five? Consider these, for example:

6. Each night, you are sabotaging your own car while you sleepwalk.
7. Your ninety-year-old uncle, who lives a thousand miles away from you, has secretly been going for joyrides in your car, damaging the engine.
8. A poltergeist (a noisy, mischievous ghost) has damaged the car's carburetor.
9. Yesterday, you accidentally drove the car through an alternative space-time dimension, scrambling the electrical system.

What do you think of these theories? More specifically, are the last four theories *really* at least as plausible as the first five? If you think so, *why?* If you think not, *why not?* Remember that a theory's strangeness is no good reason to discount it. It will not do to say that theories 6–9 are too weird to be true. In the history of science, plenty of bizarre theories have turned out to be correct. (Quantum theory in physics, for example, is about as weird as you can get.) Earlier we concluded that theory 3 was better (more likely to be true) than 1, 2, 4, and 5. But what criteria did we use to arrive at this judgment? And on the basis of what criteria can we say that theory 3 is any better than theories 6–9? There must be *some* criteria because it is implausible that every theory is equally correct. Surely there is a difference in quality between a theory that explains rainfall by positing some natural meteorological forces and one that alleges that Donald Duck causes weather phenomena.

A simplified answer to the problem of theory choice is this: Just weigh the evidence for each theory, and the theory with the most evidence wins. As we will soon see, the amount or degree of evidence that a theory has is indeed a crucial factor—but it cannot be the sole criterion by which we assess explanations. Throughout the history of science, major theories—from the heliocentric theory of the solar system to Einstein's general theory of relativity—have never been established by empirical evidence alone.

The task of determining the best explanation has another complication. If we accept such extraordinary theories as 6–9 as legitimate possibilities, there must be no end to the number of theories that we could devise to explain the data at hand. In fact, we could come up with an infinite number of possible theories for any phenomenon simply by repeatedly adding one more element. For example, we could propose the one-poltergeist theory (a single entity causing the trouble), a two-poltergeist theory, a three-poltergeist theory, and so on.

Fortunately, despite these complications, there are reasonable criteria and reliable procedures for judging the merits of eligible theories and for arriving at a defensible judgment of which theory is best. Enter: the **criteria of adequacy**. The criteria of adequacy are the essential tools of science and have been used by scientists throughout history to uncover the best explanations for all sorts of events and states of affairs. Science, though, doesn't own these criteria. They are as useful—and as used—among nonscientists as they are among men and women of science.

Applying the criteria of adequacy to a set of theories constitutes the ultimate test of a theory's value, for *the best theory is the eligible theory that meets the criteria of adequacy better than any of its competitors.* Here, "eligible" means that the theory has already met the minimum requirement for consistency.

All of this implies that the evaluation of a particular theory is not complete until alternative, or competing, theories are considered. As we've seen, there is an indefinite number of theories that could be offered to explain a given set of data. The main challenge is to give a fair assessment of the relevant theories in relation to each other. To fail to somehow address the alternatives is to overlook or deny relevant evidence, to risk biased conclusions, and to court error. Such failure is probably the most common error in the appraisal of theories.

A theory judged by these criteria to be the best explanation for certain facts is worthy of our belief, and we may legitimately claim to know that such a theory is true. But the theory is not then necessarily or certainly true in the way that a sound deductive argument's conclusion is necessarily or certainly true. Inference to the best explanation, like other forms of induction, cannot guarantee the truth of the best explanation. That is, it is not truth preserving. The best theory we have may actually be false. Nevertheless, we would have excellent reasons for supposing our best theory to be a true theory.

The criteria of adequacy are *testability, fruitfulness, scope, simplicity,* and *conservatism.* Let's examine each one in detail.

Testability

Most of the theories that we encounter every day and all the theories that scientists take seriously are **testable**—*there is some way to determine whether the theories are true or false.* If a theory is untestable—if there is no possible procedure for checking its truth—then it is worthless as an explanatory theory. Suppose someone says that an invisible, undetectable spirit is causing your headaches. What possible test could we perform to tell if the spirit actually exists? None. So the spirit theory is entirely empty. We can assign no weight to such a claim.

Here's another way to look at it. Theories are explanations, and explanations are designed to increase our understanding of the world. But an untestable theory does not—and cannot—explain anything. It is equivalent to saying that an unknown thing with unknown properties acts in an unknown way to cause a phenomenon—which is the same thing as offering no explanation at all.

We often run into untestable theories in daily life, just as scientists sometimes encounter them in their work. Many practitioners of alternative medicine claim that health problems are caused by an imbalance in people's *chi,* an unmeasurable form of mystical energy that is said to flow through everyone. Some people say that their misfortunes are caused by God or the Devil. Others believe that certain events in their lives happen (and are inevitable) because of fate. And parents may hear their young daughter say that she did not break the lamp, but her invisible friend did.

Many theories throughout history have been untestable. Some of the more influential untestable theories include the theory of witches (some people called witches are controlled by the Devil), the moral fault theory of disease (immoral behavior causes illness), and the divine placement theory of fossils (God created geological fossils to give the false impression of an ancient Earth).

But what does it mean for a theory to be testable or untestable? A theory is testable *if it predicts something other than what it was introduced to explain.* Suppose your electric clock stops each time you touch it. One theory to explain this event is that there is an electrical short in the clock's wiring. Another theory is that an invisible, undetectable demon causes the clock to stop. The wiring theory predicts that if the wiring is repaired, the clock will no longer shut off when touched. So it is testable—there is something that the theory predicts other than the obvious fact that the clock will stop when you touch it. But the demon theory makes no predictions about anything, *except* the obvious, the very fact that the theory was introduced to explain. It predicts that the clock will stop if you touch it, but we already know this. So our understanding is not increased, and the demon theory is untestable.

Now, if the demon theory says that the demon can be detected with x-rays, then there is something the theory predicts other than the clock's stopping when touched. You can x-ray the clock and examine the film for demon silhouettes. If the theory says that the demon can't be seen but can be heard with sensitive sound equipment, then you have a prediction, something to look for other than clock stoppage.

So other things being equal, testable theories are superior to untestable ones; they may be able to increase our understanding of a phenomenon. But an untestable theory tells us nothing. An untestable theory is just an oddity.

Fruitfulness

Imagine that we have two testable theories, theory 1 and theory 2, that attempt to explain the same phenomenon. Theory 1 and theory 2 seem comparable in most respects when measured against the criteria of adequacy. Theory 1, however, successfully predicts the existence of a previously unknown entity, say, a star in an uncharted part of the sky. What would you conclude about the relative worth of these two theories?

If you thought carefully about the issue, you would probably conclude that theory 1 is the better theory—and you would be right. Other things being equal, theories that perform this way—that successfully predict previously unknown phenomena—are more credible than those that don't. They are said to be **fruitful**, to yield new insights that can open up whole new areas of research and discovery. This fruitfulness suggests that the theories are more likely to be true.

If a friend of yours is walking through a forest where she has never been before, yet she seems to be able to predict exactly what's up ahead, you would probably conclude that she possessed some kind of accurate information about the forest, such as a map. Likewise, if a theory successfully predicts some surprising state of affairs, you are likely to think that the predictions are not just lucky guesses. All empirical theories are testable (they predict something beyond the thing to be explained). But fruitful theories are testable and then some. They not only predict something, they predict something that no one expected. The element of surprise is hard to ignore.

Decades ago Einstein's theory of relativity gained a great deal of credibility by successfully predicting a phenomenon that was extraordinary and entirely novel. The theory predicts that light traveling close to massive objects (such as stars) will appear to be bent because the space around such objects is curved. The curve in space causes a curve in nearby light rays. At the time, however, the prevailing opinion was that light always travels in straight lines—no bends, no curves, no breaks. In 1919 the physicist Sir Arthur Eddington devised a way to test this prediction. He managed to take two sets of photographs of exactly the same portion of the sky—when the sun was overhead (in daylight) and when it was not (at night). He was able to get a good photo of the sky during daylight because there was a total eclipse of the sun at the time. If light rays really were bent when they passed near massive objects, then stars whose light passes near the sun should appear to be shifted slightly from their true position (as seen at night). Eddington discovered that stars near the sun did appear to have moved and that the amount of their apparent movement was just what the theory predicted. This novel prediction then demonstrated the fruitfulness of Einstein's theory, provided a degree of confirmation for the theory, and opened up new areas of research.

So the moral is that other things being equal, fruitful theories are superior to those that aren't fruitful. Certainly many good theories make no novel predictions but are accepted nonetheless. The reason is usually that they excel in other criteria of adequacy.

Scope

Suppose theory 1 and theory 2 are two equally plausible theories to explain phenomenon X. Theory 1 can explain X well, and so can theory 2. But theory 1 can explain or predict *only* X, whereas theory 2 can explain or predict X—as well as phenomena Y and Z. Which is the better theory?

We must conclude that theory 2 is better because it explains more diverse phenomena. That is, it has more **scope** than the other theory. The more a theory explains or predicts, the more it extends our understanding. And the more a theory explains or predicts, the less likely it is to be false because it has more evidence in its favor.

A major strength of Newton's theory of gravity and motion, for example, was that it explained more than any previous theory. Then came Einstein's theory of relativity. It could explain everything that Newton's theory could explain plus many phenomena that Newton's theory could not explain. This increased scope of Einstein's theory helped convince scientists that it was the better theory.

Here's a more down-to-earth example. For decades psychologists have known about a phenomenon called *constructive perception*. In constructive perception what we perceive (see, hear, feel, etc.) is determined in part by what we expect, know, or believe. Studies have shown that when people expect to perceive a certain stimulus (say, a flashing light, a certain color or shape, a shadow), they often *do* perceive it, even if there is no stimulus present. The phenomenon of constructive perception then can be used to explain many instances in which people seem to perceive something when it is not really there or when it is actually very different from the way people think it is.

One kind of case that investigators sometimes explain as an instance of constructive perception is the UFO sighting. Many times people report seeing lights in the night sky that look to them like alien spacecraft, and they explain their perception by saying that the lights were caused by alien spacecraft. So we have two theories to explain the experience: constructive perception and UFOs from space. If these two theories differ only in the degree of scope provided by each one, however, we must conclude that the constructive-perception theory is better. (In reality, theories about incredible events usually differ on several criteria.) The constructive-perception theory can explain not only UFO sightings but all kinds of ordinary and extraordinary experiences—hallucinations, feelings of an unknown "presence," misidentification of crime suspects, contradictory reports in car accidents, and more. The UFO theory, however, is (usually) designed to explain just one thing: an experience of seeing strange lights in the sky.

Scope is often a crucial factor in a jury's evaluation of theories put forth by both the prosecution and the defense. The prosecution will have a very powerful case against the defendant if the prosecutor's theory (that the defendant did it) explains all the evidence and many other things while the defense theory (innocence) does not. The defendant would be in big trouble if the prosecutor's theory explains the blood on the defendant's shirt, the eyewitness accounts, the defendant's fingerprints on the wall, and the sudden change in his usual routine—*and* the innocence theory renders these facts downright mysterious.

Other things being equal, then, the best theory is the one with the greatest scope. And if other things aren't equal, a theory with superior scope doesn't necessarily win the day because it may do poorly on the other criteria—or another theory might do better.

Simplicity

Let's return one last time to the scenario about the nonstarting car. Recall that the last four theories are:

6. Each night, you are sabotaging your own car while you sleepwalk.
7. Your ninety-year-old uncle, who lives a thousand miles away from you, has secretly been going for joyrides in your car, damaging the engine.

8. A poltergeist (a noisy, mischievous ghost) has damaged the car's carburetor.

9. Yesterday, you accidentally drove the car through an alternative space-time dimension, scrambling the electrical system.

By now you probably suspect that these explanations are somehow unacceptable, and so they are. One important characteristic that they each lack is **simplicity**. Other things being equal, the best theory is the one that is the simplest—that is, the one that makes the fewest assumptions. The theory making the fewest assumptions is less likely to be false because there are fewer ways for it to go wrong. Another way to look at it is that since a simpler theory is based on fewer assumptions, less evidence is required to support it.

Explanations 8 and 9 lack simplicity because they each must assume the existence of an unknown entity (poltergeists and another dimension that scrambles electrical circuits). Such assumptions about the existence of unknown objects, forces, and dimensions are common in occult or paranormal theories. Explanations 6 and 7 assume no new entities, but they do assume complex chains of events. This alone makes them less plausible than the simple explanation of 3, starter malfunction.

The criterion of simplicity has often been a major factor in the acceptance or rejection of important theories. For example, simplicity is an important advantage that the theory of evolution has over creationism, the theory that the world was created at once by a divine being (see chapter 9). Creationism must assume the existence of a creator and the existence of unknown forces (supernatural forces used by the creator). But evolution does not make either of these assumptions.

Scientists eventually accepted Copernicus's theory of planetary motion (heliocentric orbits) over Ptolemy's (Earth-centered orbits) because the former was simpler. In order to account for apparent irregularities in the movement of certain planets, Ptolemy's theory had to assume that planets have extremely complex orbits (orbits within orbits). Copernicus's theory, however, had no need for so much extra baggage. His theory could account for the observational data without so many orbits-within-orbits.

Sometimes a theory's lack of simplicity is the result of constructing ad hoc hypotheses. An **ad hoc hypothesis** is one that cannot be verified independently of the phenomenon it's supposed to explain. If a theory is in trouble because it is not matching up with the observational data of the phenomenon, you might be able to rescue it by altering it—by positing additional entities or properties that can account for the data. Such tinkering is legitimate (scientists do it all the time) if there is an independent way of confirming the existence of these proposed entities and properties. But if there is no way to verify their existence, the modifications are ad hoc hypotheses. Ad hoc hypotheses always make a theory less simple—and therefore less credible.

THERE'S NO THEORY LIKE A CONSPIRACY THEORY

Conspiracy theories try to explain events by positing the secret participation of numerous conspirators. The assassination of JFK, the terrorist attacks of 9/11, the death of Elvis Presley, the UFO crash at Roswell, the Great Recession of 2008, the NASA moon landings, the bloodline of Jesus Christ—all these and more have been the subject of countless conspiracy theories, both elaborate and provocative. Some conspiracy theories, of course, have been found to be true after all. But most of them are implausible or absurd. The main problem with them is that they fail the criterion of *simplicity*. They would have us make numerous assumptions that raise more questions than they answer: How do the conspirators manage to keep their activities secret? How do they control all the players? Where is the evidence that all the parts of the conspiracy have come together just so?

The terrorist attacks of September 11, 2001, are a favorite topic of conspiracy theorists. Many of them allege, on flimsy evidence, that the attacks were an inside job: the Bush administration either allowed the attacks to happen or actively orchestrated them.

As we have seen, for any set of facts, it is shockingly easy to devise a theory that fits them, but this fit alone cannot establish the truth of the theory. That's why we must apply the criteria of adequacy to sort out the plausible theories from the implausible. Very often the set of alleged facts that are supposed to back up the theory are not facts at all. They are unsupported assertions coughed up by a fevered social media and red-hot political conflicts.

For those who eagerly believe them, conspiracy theories are what scientists call *nonfalsifiable hypotheses*: there is no possible evidence that believers would accept as counting against their beloved theory. Every piece of counterevidence is dismissed, ignored, chalked up to a government cover-up, or interpreted as actually confirming the theory.

There is no escape from this prison of the mind except through critical thinking—through a fair weighing of the evidence, a careful consideration of alternative theories, and an unwillingness to believe without good reason.

Conservatism

What if a trusted friend told you that—believe it or not—some dogs lay eggs just as chickens do? Let's assume that your friend is being perfectly serious and believes what she is saying. Would you accept this claim about egg-laying dogs? Not likely. But why not?

Probably your main reason for rejecting such an extraordinary claim would be that it fails the criterion of **conservatism**, though you probably wouldn't state it that way. (Note: This sense of "conservatism" *has nothing to do with political parties*.) This criterion says that other things being equal, *the best theory is the one that fits best with our well-established beliefs*—that is, with beliefs backed by excellent evidence or very good arguments. We would reject the canine-egg theory because, among other things, it conflicts with our well-founded beliefs about mammals, evolution, canine anatomy, and much more. Humans have an enormous amount of experience with dogs (scientific and otherwise), and none of it suggests that dogs can lay eggs. In fact, a great deal of what we know about dogs suggests that they *cannot* lay eggs. To accept the canine-egg theory despite its conflicting with a mountain of solid evidence would be irrational—and destructive of whatever understanding we had of the subject.

Perhaps one day we may be shocked to learn that—contrary to all expectations and overwhelming evidence—dogs do lay eggs. But given that this belief is contrary to a massive amount of credible experience, we must assign a very low probability to it.

What kind of beliefs fall into the category of "well-established" knowledge? For starters, we can count beliefs based on our own everyday observations that we have no good reasons to doubt (such as "It's raining outside," "The parking lot is empty," and "The train is running late today"). We can include basic facts about the world drawn from excellent authority ("The Earth is round," "Men have walked on the moon," and "Cairo is the capital of Egypt"). And we can include a vast array of beliefs solidly supported by scientific evidence, facts recognized as such by most scientists ("Cigarettes cause lung cancer," "Vaccines prevent disease," "Dinosaurs existed," and "Germs cause infection").

Many of our beliefs, however, cannot be regarded as well established. Among these, of course, are all those we have good reasons to doubt. But there is also a large assortment of beliefs that occupy the middle ground between those we doubt and those we have excellent reasons to believe. We may have some reasons in favor of these beliefs, but those reasons are not so strong that we can regard the beliefs as solid facts. We can only proportion our belief to the evidence and be open to the possibility that we may be wrong. Very often such claims reside in areas that are marked by controversy—politics, religion, ethics, economics, and more. Among these notions, we must walk cautiously, avoid dogmatism, and follow the evidence as best we can. We should not assume that the claims we have absorbed from our upbringing and culture are beyond question.

That being said, there are good reasons for respecting the criterion of conservatism, properly understood. We are naturally reluctant to accept explanations that conflict with what we already know, and we should be. Accepting beliefs that fly in the face of our knowledge has several risks:

1. The chances of the new belief being true are not good (because it has no evidence in its favor, while our well-established beliefs have plenty of evidence on their side).
2. The conflict of beliefs undermines our knowledge (because we cannot know something that is in doubt, and the conflict would be cause for doubt).
3. The conflict of beliefs lessens our understanding (because the new beliefs cannot be plausibly integrated into our other beliefs).

So everything considered, the more conservative a theory is, the more plausible it is.[2]

Here's another example. Let's say that someone claims to have built a perpetual motion machine. A perpetual motion machine is supposed to function without ever stopping and without requiring any energy input from outside the machine; it is designed to continuously supply its own energy.

Now, this is an intriguing idea—that we shouldn't take too seriously. The problem is that the notion of a perpetual motion machine is not conservative at all. It conflicts with a very well-established belief—namely, one of the scientific laws of thermodynamics. The law of conservation of mass-energy says that mass-energy cannot be created or destroyed. A perpetual motion machine, though, would have to create energy out of nothing. Like any law of nature, however, the law of conservation of mass-energy is supported by a vast amount of empirical evidence. We must conclude, then, that it is extremely unlikely that anyone could escape the law of conservation of mass-energy through the use of any machine. (This fact, however, has not stopped countless optimistic inventers from claiming that they've invented such devices. When the devices are put to the test, they invariably fail to perform as advertised.)

It's possible, of course, that a new theory that conflicts with what we know could turn out to be right and a more conservative theory wrong. But we would need good reasons to show that the new theory was correct before we would be justified in tossing out the old theory and bringing in the new.

Science looks for conservative theories, but it still sometimes embraces theories that are departures (sometimes *radical* departures) from the well-worn, accepted explanations. When this dramatic change happens, it's frequently because other criteria of adequacy outweigh conservatism. We'll explore the creation and evaluation of scientific theories in the next chapter.

Occult or paranormal theories often run afoul of the criterion of conservatism. Take *dowsing*, for instance. Dowsing is the practice of detecting underground water by using a Y-shaped stick (known as a divining rod or dowsing rod), a pendulum, or another device. It's a folk tradition that's hundreds of years old. Dowsers claim to be able to detect the presence of underground water by walk-ing over a given terrain and holding the two branches of the dowsing rod (one in each hand) with its point facing skyward away from the body. (This claim, as it turns out, is unsupported.) When the point of the rod dips toward the ground, that's supposed to indicate that water is beneath the dowser. It seems to the dowser (and sometimes to observers) that the rod moves on its own, as though under the influence of some hidden force.

One theory to account for the rod's movements is this: an unknown form of radiation emanating from the underground water pulls on the divining rod, causing it to move. (A well-supported alternative theory is that the movement of the divining rod in the dowser's hands is caused by suggestion and unconscious muscular activity in the dowser.) As it stands, the radiation theory is not testable, fruitful, or simple. But its major failing is its lack of conservatism. The claim about the strange, occult radiation conflicts with what scientists know about energy, radiation, and human sensory systems. It is possible that the dowser's radiation exists, but there is no reason to believe that it does and good reason to doubt it.

We will look at many more examples shortly, but before we go any further, you need to fully understand two crucial points about the nature of theory appraisal.

First, there is no strict formula or protocol for applying the criteria of adequacy. In deductive arguments, there are rules of inference that are precise and invariable. But inference to the best explanation is a different animal. There are no precise rules for applying the criteria, no way to quantify how a theory measures up according to each criterion, and no way to rank each criterion according to its importance. Sometimes we may assign more weight to the criterion of scope if the theory in question seems comparable to other theories in terms of all the re-maining criteria. Other times we may weight simplicity more when considering theories that seem equally conservative or fruitful. The process of theory evalu-ation is not like solving a math problem—but more like diagnosing an illness or making a judicial decision. It is rational but not formulaic, and it depends on the dynamics of human judgment. The best we can do is follow some guide-lines for evaluating theories generally and for applying the criteria of adequacy. Fortunately, this kind of help is usually all we need. (You'll get this kind of guid-ance in the following pages.)

Second, despite the lack of formula in theory assessment, the process is far from sub-jective or arbitrary. There are many distinctions that we successfully make every day that are not quantifiable or formulaic—but they are still objective. We cannot say exactly when day turns into night or when a person with a full head of hair becomes bald or when a puddle in the rain becomes a pond, but our distinctions between night and day or baldness and hirsuteness or puddles and ponds are clearly objective. Of course, there are cases that are not so clear-cut that give rise to reasonable disagreement among reasonable people. But there are also many instances that are manifestly unambiguous. Pretending that these states of affairs are unclear would be irrational. It would simply be incorrect to believe that broad daylight is nighttime or that a puddle is a pond.

Telling Good Theories from Bad

Many (perhaps most) explanatory theories that you run into every day are easy to assess. They are clearly the best (or not the best) explanations for the facts at hand. The dog barked because someone approached the house. Your friend blushed because he was embarrassed. The senator resigned because of a scandal. In such cases, you may make inferences to the best explanation (using some or all of the criteria of adequacy) without any deep reflection. But at other times, you may need and want to be more deliberate, to think more carefully about which explanation is really best. In either case, it helps to have a set of guidelines that tells you how your inquiry *should* proceed if you're to make cogent inferences. Here, then, is the **TEST formula**, four steps to finding the best explanation:

Step 1. State the **T**heory and check for consistency.
Step 2. Assess the **E**vidence for the theory.
Step 3. **S**crutinize alternative theories.
Step 4. **T**est the theories with the criteria of adequacy.

(In the next chapter, you will see that this formula is also one way of describing the general approach used in science to evaluate sets of theories.)

Step 1. State the theory and check for consistency. Before you can evaluate an explanatory theory, you must express it in a statement that's as clear and specific as possible. Once you do this, you can check to see if the theory meets the minimum requirement for consistency. If it fails the consistency test, you can have no good grounds for believing that it's correct. And, obviously, if the theory fails step 1, there's no reason to go to step 2.

Step 2. Assess the evidence for the theory. To critically evaluate any theory, you must understand any reasons in its favor—the empirical evidence or logical arguments that may support or undermine it. Essentially, this step involves an honest assessment of the empirical evidence relevant to the truth (or falsity) of the theory. To make this assessment, you must put to use what you already know about the credibility of sources, causal reasoning, and evidence from personal and scientific observations.

In this step, you may discover that the evidence in favor of a theory is strong, weak, or nonexistent. You may find that there is good evidence that seems to count against the theory. Or you may learn that the phenomenon under investigation did not occur at all. Whatever the case, you must have the courage to face up to reality. You must be ready to admit that your favorite theory has little to recommend it.

Step 3. Scrutinize alternative theories. Inference to the best explanation will not help us very much if we aren't willing to consider alternative explanations. Simply examining the evidence relevant to an eligible theory is not enough.

Theories can often appear stronger than they really are if we don't bother to compare them with others. To take an outrageous example, consider this theory designed to explain the popularity and seeming omnipresence of an American icon: Mickey Mouse is not an animated character but a living, breathing creature that lives in Hollywood. The evidence for this explanation is the following: (1) Millions of people (mostly children) worldwide believe that Mickey is real; (2) Walt Disney (Mickey's alleged creator) always talked about Mickey as if the mouse was real; (3) millions of ads, books, movies, and TV shows portray Mickey as real; (4) it's possible that through millions of years of Earth history a biological creature with Mickey's physical characteristics could have evolved; and (5) some say that if enough people believe that Mickey is real, then—through psychic wish fulfillment or some other paranormal process—he will become real.

Now, you don't believe that Mickey is real (do you?), even in the face of reasons 1–5. But you might admit that the Mickey theory is starting to sound more plausible. And if you never hear any alternative explanations, you might eventually become a true believer. (Anthropologists can plausibly argue that various cultures have come to believe in many very unlikely phenomena and exotic deities in large part because of *a lack of alternative explanations.*)

When you do consider an alternative explanation—for example, that Mickey is an imaginary character of brilliant animation marketed relentlessly to the world—the Mickey-is-real theory looks a little silly. And once you consider the evidence for this alternative theory (for example, documentation that Walt Disney created Mickey with pen and ink and that countless marketing campaigns have been launched to promote his creation), the other explanation looks even sillier.

Step 3 requires us to have an open mind, to think outside the box, to ask if there are other ways to explain the phenomenon in question and to consider the evidence for those theories. Specifically, in this step we must conscientiously look for competing theories, *then apply both step 1 and step 2 to each one of them.* This process may leave us with many or few eligible theories to examine. In any case, it's sure to tell us something important about the strength or weakness of competing theories.

Many times the criteria of adequacy can help us do a preliminary assessment of a theory's plausibility without our surveying alternative theories. For example, a theory may do so poorly regarding a particular criterion that we can conclude that, whatever the merits of alternative explanations, the theory at hand is not very credible. Such a clear lack of credibility is often apparent when a theory is obviously neither simple nor conservative.

Skipping step 3 is an extremely common error in the evaluation of explanations of all kinds. It is a supreme example of many types of errors discussed in earlier chapters—overlooking evidence, preferring available evidence, looking only for confirming evidence, and denying the evidence.

Step 3 goes against our grain. The human tendency is to grab hold of a favorite theory—and to halt any further critical thinking right there. Our built-in bias is to seize on a theory immediately—because we find it comforting or because we just "know" it's the right one—then ignore or resist all other possibilities. The result is a greatly increased likelihood of error and delusion and a significantly decreased opportunity to achieve true understanding.

Failure to consider alternative theories is the archetypal mistake in inquiries into the paranormal or supernatural. The usual pattern is this: (1) You come across an extraordinary or impressive phenomenon, (2) you can't think of a natural explanation of the facts, and (3) you conclude that the phenomenon must not be natural but paranormal or supernatural. This conclusion, however, would be unwarranted. Just because you can't think of a natural explanation doesn't mean that there isn't one. You may simply be unaware of the correct natural explanation. In the past, scientists have often been confronted with extraordinary phenomena that they couldn't explain—phenomena that were later found to have a natural explanation.

Step 4. Test the theories with the criteria of adequacy. As we've seen, simply toting up the evidence for each of the competing theories and checking to see which one gets the highest score will not do. We need to measure the plausibility of the theories using the criteria of adequacy. The criteria can help us put any applicable evidence in perspective and allow us to make a judgment about theory plausibility even when there's little or no evidence to consider.

By applying the criteria to all the competing theories, we can often accomplish several important feats. We may be able to eliminate some theories immediately, assign more weight to some than others, and distinguish between theories that at first glance seem equally strong.

The best way to learn how to do step 4, as well as steps 1–3, is by example. Watch what happens when we assess the plausibility of theories for the following two phenomena.

A Doomed Flight

In 1996, a Boeing 747 jetliner known famously as TWA flight 800 crashed in the Atlantic Ocean off Long Island, New York, killing all 230 people onboard. The incident, like most airline disasters, prompted a search for explanations for the crash and the proliferation of numerous explanatory theories, some of them alleging conspiracy, cover-up, and dark deeds. The FBI, the National Transportation Safety Board (NTSB), and others launched investigations, relying heavily on the criteria of adequacy to sort through competing theories. After many months of inquiry and debate, experts concluded that the probable cause of the crash was mechanical failure.

A Boeing 747 in trouble; from the movie *Eraser*.

Using this incident as inspiration and guide, let's devise another story of a mysterious jetliner crash and examine the main theories to explain it. We will assume that all the facts in the case are known, that all relevant reports are honest (no intent to deceive), and that no other information is forthcoming. In other words, this is a very contrived case. But it suits our purposes here just fine. Here goes.

The (made-up) facts of the case are these: At 7:30 p.m. flight 200, a Boeing 747, departed JFK airport in New York on its way to London and then crashed into the Atlantic about thirty miles off the coast. While in flight, the plane exploded, sending debris over a wide area. The crash happened during a time of heightened awareness of possible terrorist attacks on aircraft.

Now let's try steps 1–4 on a supposedly popular theory and some of its leading alternatives. Here's the pop theory in question. Theory 1: *A missile fired by a terrorist brought down the plane.* This one meets the requirement for consistency, so our first concern is to assess the evidence for the theory. Those who favor this theory point to several pieces of evidence. Eyewitnesses said that they had seen a bright streak of light or flame speeding toward the plane. A few people said that they thought they were watching a missile intercept the plane. And a journalist reported on the Internet that the plane had been shot down by a missile fired from a boat.

There are, however, some problems with this evidence. Eyewitness reports of the movements of bright lights in a dark sky are notoriously unreliable, even when the eyewitnesses are experts. Under such viewing conditions, the actual size of a bright object, its distance from the observer, its speed, and even whether it's moving are extremely difficult to accurately determine by sight.

Also another phenomenon could have easily been mistaken for a speeding missile: It's known that an explosion rupturing a fuel tank on a 747's wing can ignite long streams of fuel, which from the ground may look like a missile heading toward the plane. In addition, US Coast Guard and Navy ships were in sight of every ship and boat in the area and report no firing of missiles or any other pyrotechnics. Because of the distances involved and other factors, firing a missile from the ground at flight 200 and hitting it was virtually impossible. Finally, an unsupported allegation—whether from a journalist or anyone else—is not good evidence for anything.

Then we have this explanation. Theory 2: *An alien spacecraft shot down the plane.* For the sake of illustration, we will assume that this explanation meets the consistency requirement. The evidence is this: Several people say that they saw a UFO fly near the plane just before the plane exploded. And tapes of radar images show an unknown object flying close to the 747.

These eyewitness accounts suffer from the same weakness as those mentioned in theory 1. Observations under the conditions described are not reliable. Thus, many alleged alien craft have turned out to be airplanes, helicopters, blimps, meteors, and even the planet Venus, an extremely bright object in the sky. Radar tapes may show many objects that are "unknown" to untrained observers but are identified precisely by experts. The radar evidence would be more impressive if flight controllers could not account for an object flying close to flight 200.

Theory 3: *A bomb on board the plane exploded, bringing the aircraft down.* This explanation is internally and externally consistent. The main evidence for it is the existence of trace amounts of explosive residue on a few of the recovered aircraft parts. Also, the story of the crash of flight 200 resembles the media account of the crash of another jetliner that's known to have been brought down by an onboard bomb.

This resemblance, though, is only that—it's not evidence that counts in favor of the bomb theory. And the explosive residue is not so telltale after all. Investigators determined that the residues are most likely left over from a security training exercise conducted on the plane a week earlier. Moreover, examination of the wreckage and patterns of damage to it suggests that a bomb was not detonated inside the aircraft.

Theory 4: *A mechanical failure involving the fuel tanks caused the explosion that brought the plane down.* This is an eligible theory. It's backed by evidence showing that an explosion occurred in one of the plane's fuel tanks. Experts know that a short circuit in wiring outside a fuel tank can cause excess voltage in wiring that's inside the tank, igniting the fuel. Investigators found that there was indeed a short circuit in some of the fuel tank wiring. In addition, explosions in several other 747s, some smaller planes, and various machine engines have been linked to faulty wiring in fuel tanks.

Theory 5: *A solar flare disrupted electrical circuits in the plane, releasing a spark that made the fuel tanks explode.* This too is an eligible theory. Solar flares are massive electromagnetic explosions on the surface of the sun. They can sometimes disrupt radio communications, even cause radio blackouts. Theory 5 says that a solar flare so dramatically affected electrical circuits in the plane that a spark was emitted that ignited the fuel. The rationale behind this theory is that flying planes, being closer to the sun, are more susceptible to the powerful effects of solar flares.

The evidence for this theory, however, is nil. There is no good reason to believe that a solar flare could ever cause a spark in an electrical circuit.

Now let's apply the criteria of adequacy to these explanations. We can see right away that all the theories do equally well in terms of testability and fruitfulness. They're all testable, and none has yielded any surprising predictions.

Except for theory 4, they also have equal scope because they explain only the phenomenon they were introduced to explain, the crash of flight 200 (and perhaps similar airline crashes). Theory 4, however, has a slight edge because it can explain certain airline crashes as well as explosions in other systems that have wired fuel tanks. So if we are to distinguish between the theories, we must rely on the other criteria.

This is bad news for theories 2 and 5 because they fail the criteria of simplicity and conservatism. The evidence in favor of the alien spacecraft theory is extremely weak. Even worse, it conflicts with a great deal of human experience regarding visitors from outer space. We simply have no good evidence that anyone has ever detected any beings or technology from outer space. Moreover, the probability of Earth being visited by beings from outer space must be considered low (but not zero) in light of what we know about the size of the universe and the physical requirements of space travel. Likewise, the solar flare theory has no evidence to support it, and it too conflicts with what we know. There are no documented cases of solar flares causing sparks in electrical wiring. And neither theory is simple. Theory 2 assumes an unknown entity (aliens), and theory 5 assumes unknown processes (solar flares causing sparks in wiring). These are excellent grounds for eliminating theories 2 and 5 from the running.

That leaves theories 1, 3, and 4, which we must also sort out using the criteria of simplicity and conservatism. They fare equally well in terms of simplicity because none assumes any unknown or mysterious entities or processes. Conservatism, though, is a different story. Neither theory 1 nor 3 accords with the evidence. In each case, existing evidence counts *against* the theory. Theory 4, though, accords well with the evidence. It not only doesn't conflict with what we know, but the evidence also supports the theory in important ways. Theory 4, then, is the best explanation for the crash of flight 200 and the theory most likely to be true. And the explanation we started with, theory 1, is implausible.

An Amazing Cure

Homeopathy is an old theory that currently occupies an honored place among advocates of what is often called "alternative medicine"—health practices and hypotheses that are, for the most part, outside the realm of conventional medicine and medical science. Homeopathy is based on the idea that extremely tiny doses of substances that cause disease symptoms in a healthy person can alleviate similar symptoms in a sick person. Samuel Hahnemann (1755–1843), a German physician, was the first to apply this notion systematically. He also added what he called the "law of infinitesimals," the proposition that—contrary to the findings of science—the smaller the dose, the more powerful the medicine. So he treated people with drastically diluted substances—so diluted that, in many homeopathic medicines, not even one molecule of the substance remained. Hahnemann acknowledged this fact but believed that the substances somehow left behind an imperceptible "spirit-like" essence, or memory, that effected cures. This essence was supposed to revitalize the "vital force" in the body.

To be more precise, we can state the homeopathic theory like this: *Extremely dilute solutions of substances that produce symptoms in a healthy person can cure those same symptoms in a sick person.* This hypothesis is offered as an explanation of why people taking homeopathic remedies seem to get better. They get better because homeopathy works.

The leading alternative theory is this: *People taking homeopathic remedies feel better because of the placebo effect.* That is, homeopathy does not work as advertised, but people think that it does because of the power of placebos (inactive or fake treatments). The placebo effect is a very well-documented phenomenon in which people given a placebo respond with improvements in the way they feel. Scientists disagree over how much placebos can affect clinical conditions, but there is little doubt that placebos can have at least a modest impact on how people feel, especially their experience of pain.[3] Because placebos can have an effect, they are used in all well-designed clinical trials—that is, studies testing the effectiveness of treatments. There are other plausible alternative theories (such as the idea that people feel better because of the natural course of the disease), but we will restrict our analysis to the homeopathy and placebo theories.

Both are eligible theories. They are also both testable, so we must turn to the other criteria to help us judge their worth. The homeopathy theory has yielded no observable, surprising predictions, so it has no advantage in fruitfulness. The placebo theory has yielded several predictions (that a certain percentage of people who suffer from a particular illness and who get a placebo will feel better), but none of these are particularly surprising. The homeopathy theory has no scope because it tries to explain events by positing unknown forces and processes—which doesn't explain anything. The placebo theory, though, does have scope, explaining why people may feel better after trying a homeopathic remedy as well as why people with a variety of illnesses feel better after taking a placebo.

But in terms of simplicity, the homeopathy theory is in trouble. Homeopathy postulates both an undetectable essence and an unknown mysterious force. These assumptions alone are serious problems for the theory. The placebo theory, on the other hand, assumes no unknown forces, entities, or processes.

Finally, homeopathy runs afoul of the criterion of conservatism. It conflicts with a massive amount of scientific evidence in biochemistry and pharmacology. There is no verified instance of any substance having a stronger effect the more diluted it becomes. There isn't a single documented case of an extremely diluted solution (one in which not one molecule of the original substance remains) affecting any biological system. In addition, all available scientific evidence on the question gives little or no support to homeopathy. (Many studies have been conducted on homeopathic remedies, but several scientific reviews have concluded that the studies are seriously flawed or weak, offering no significant support to the theory.)[4]

We can lay out these assessments as in the following table:

Criteria	Homeopathy	Placebo
Testable	Yes	Yes
Fruitful	No	No
Scope	No	Yes
Simple	No	Yes
Conservative	No	Yes

In the absence of a formula for weighting or ranking criteria, what plausible judgments can we make about the relative strengths of these two theories? It seems that we can ignore the criteria of testability and fruitfulness because both theories seem roughly even on these criteria—or at least no theory has a clear advantage over the other. We have decided, however, that homeopathy has no scope, while the placebo theory does.

Things become clearer when we consider the remaining criteria. There are stark differences between the two theories in simplicity and conservatism. Homeopathy is not simple, and any theory that posits an unknown entity is less plausible than one that does not—unless the other criteria of adequacy can somehow offset this disadvantage. But the other criteria are not much help for homeopathy. This judgment—the lack of simplicity and the resulting lower plausibility—seems clear-cut and is based on an unambiguous state of affairs. The homeopathy theory's lack of conservatism is also evident. The plausibility of any theory that flies in the face of such a mountain of established fact is near zero. So homeopathy's score must also be near zero. It is, therefore, a very poor explanation and strikingly inferior to the alternative explanation.

Without a detailed formula, without a weighting system, and without quantifying any criteria, we have arrived at a verdict regarding two competing theories. Deciding among theories is not always so straightforward, of course. But this lack of clear-cut answers is what gives rise to more research and more critical thinking.

KEY WORDS

ad hoc hypothesis	conservatism	criteria of adequacy
fruitful	inference to the best explanation	scope
simplicity	testable	TEST formula

EXERCISES

Exercises marked with * have answers in "Answers to Exercises" (Appendix A).

Exercise 8.1

1. What is an explanation?
2. What is inference to the best explanation?
3. Is inference to the best explanation inductive or deductive?
* 4. According to the text, what is a theoretical explanation?
5. What is the basic logical pattern of inference to the best explanation? for enumerative induction? for analogical induction?
6. According to the text, under what circumstances can an inference to the best explanation be deemed strong? cogent?
7. Did the fictional Sherlock Holmes use deduction or induction in his crime-solving?
* 8. What is a causal explanation? Are causal explanations used in inference to the best explanation?
9. What is an untestable theory?
10. Have you used inference to the best explanation today? If so, how did you use it? (Supply an example from the events of your day.)

Exercise 8.2

1. When you are trying to decide between two theories, can you always rely on evidence alone to determine which theory is better?
*2. In theory evaluation, what is the minimum requirement of consistency?

3. According to the text, what is a "best theory"?
4. According to the text, what are the criteria of adequacy?
5. What does it mean for a theory to be testable? fruitful? conservative?
*6. What does it mean to say that a theory does not have much scope?
7. According to the text, are theories that posit paranormal entities simple? If not, why not?
8. What are the risks involved in accepting a nonconservative theory?

Exercise 8.3

For each of the following explanations, indicate what state of affairs is being explained and what the explanation is.

1. Most students drop Professor Graham's class because he is so boring.
*2. We all know that the spotted owl is endangered, and the only explanation for that is the political clout of the logging industry.
3. Why did James say that he saw a ghost in his bedroom? Because he drinks too much and has a vivid imagination.
4. Crimes committed by high school students are increasing because school districts refuse to mandate harsh punishments for criminal acts.
*5. I'll tell you why the incidence of robbery is up: There aren't enough gun owners in the population.
6. Binge drinking is on the rise at women's colleges. This can best be explained by the permissive attitudes of the deans.
7. Americans are fond of the death penalty, but Europeans are not. Americans just never got over the old Wild West eye-for-an-eye mentality. Europeans never had a Wild West.
*8. I believe that psychics really can predict the future because many things that psychics have told me have come true.
9. Rock stars make more money than teachers because they are smarter than teachers.
10. Global terrorism is caused by worldwide injustice and deprivation.

Exercise 8.4

In each of the following examples, a state of affairs is described. Devise two theories to explain each one. Include one theory that you consider plausible and one theory that you think is not plausible.

1. Mutilated cows have been found in several pastures in the western United States. In each case organs are missing from the carcasses. There are never any signs of vehicle tracks or footprints. The cause of death is unknown. The method used to remove the organs is also unknown, although the wounds show indications of precision surgical tools.

*2. When Jack came home, he noticed the window in the kitchen was broken, there were muddy footprints on the kitchen floor, and some valuable silverware was missing.

3. Maria awoke yesterday and found that the furniture in her room had been completely rearranged while she slept.

4. José discovered this morning that the roof and hood of his car bore dozens of tiny dents.

5. In the 1980s the number of homeless people in the United States increased dramatically.

*6. Alice has been taking vitamin C every day for a year, and during that time she has not had a cold or a sore throat.

7. Teenagers are now having sex at earlier ages.

8. Scientists have discovered that there is a direct correlation between fat in people's diets and heart disease. The more fat, the greater the risk of heart disease.

9. The incidence of violent crimes in the United States has decreased in recent years.

Exercise 8.5

Read each of the following passages and answer these questions:

1. What is the phenomenon being explained?
2. What theory is suggested as a possible explanation for the phenomenon?
3. Is the theory plausible? If not, why not?
4. Is there a plausible theory that the writer has overlooked? If so, what is it?

PASSAGE 1

Many people believe that drinking a warm glass of milk at bedtime helps them fall asleep. The reason must be the tryptophan in the milk. Tryptophan is an essential amino acid that is converted into serotonin. Serotonin affects sleep patterns and the perception of pain.

PASSAGE 2

"Shark attacks around the world declined in 2003 for a third straight year, partly because swimmers and surfers grew more accustomed to thinking of the ocean as a wild and dangerous place. . . .

"The University of Florida, which houses the International Shark Attack File, said there were 55 unprovoked attacks worldwide, down from 63 reported in 2002 and lower than the previous year's 68 attacks.

"Four people were killed, compared to three in 2002, four in 2001 and 11 in the year 2000.

"Normally, scientists do not put much stock in year-to-year fluctuations in the number of attacks because they can be affected by such things as the weather and oceanographic conditions that drive bait fish closer to shore.

"But the third consecutive year of decline could indicate a longer term trend, the university said.

"'I think people are beginning to get a little more intelligent about when and where they enter the water,' George Burgess, director of the International Shark Attack File, said in a statement.

"'There seems to be more of an understanding that when we enter the sea, it's a wilderness experience and we're intruders in that environment.'"[5]

PASSAGE 3

"Women who have been coloring their hair for 24 years or more have a higher risk of developing a cancer called non-Hodgkin lymphoma, researchers reported.

"They said their study of 1,300 women could help explain a mysterious rise in the number of cases of the cancer that affects the lymphatic system.

"Writing in the *American Journal of Epidemiology*, they said women who dyed their hair starting before 1980 were one-third more likely to develop non-Hodgkin lymphoma, or NHL, and those who used the darkest dyes for more than 25 years were twice as likely to develop the cancer.

"'Women who used darker permanent hair coloring products for more than 25 years showed the highest increased risk,' Tongzhang Zheng, associate professor of epidemiology and environmental health at Yale School of Medicine, said in a statement.

"Cancer experts note that a person's absolute risk of developing lymphoma is very low, so doubling that risk still means a woman who dyes her hair is very unlikely to develop lymphoma."[6]

PASSAGE 4

Spontaneous human combustion (SHC) is the theory that under certain rare circumstances, a human body mysteriously ignites, burns, and is almost entirely consumed. Investigators have encountered a few cases in which the burnt remains of a human body (usually only a limb or two) are found in an enclosed room, with nearby flammable objects completely unaffected by fire. The other parts of the body, including the torso, are entirely incinerated. There is usually, or always, a source of flame in the room—a lit pipe or candle, for example. And the victim is often elderly, alcoholic, or in some way incapacitated. SHC is the only reasonable explanation for these strange facts.

Exercise 8.6

Following are several pairs of theories used to explain various phenomena. For each pair, determine (1) which theory is simpler and (2) which one is more conservative.

1. Phenomenon: A sudden remission of cancer in a patient.
   Theories: Part of the natural cycle of the disease; the result of taking an elixir with "healing properties" unknown to science.

*2. Phenomenon: The survival of a group of sailors whose ship sank at sea.
   Theories: Quick action by a group of magic dolphins; quick action by the Coast Guard rescue team.

3. Phenomenon: The winning of an election by a relatively unknown candidate.
   Theories: A last-minute blitz of TV ads; the candidate's endorsement by a famous convicted murderer.

*4. Phenomenon: A "precognitive" dream (having one's dream come true).
   Theories: Coincidence; psychic energy emanating from the dreamer.

5. Phenomenon: The sudden friendliness of the North Korean government toward the United States.
   Theories: A big change in the leadership of the government; North Korea's realization that democratic capitalism is the way to go.

6. Phenomenon: The bizarre and dangerous behavior of your best friend.
   Theories: An allergy attack; the result of taking LSD.

*7. Phenomenon: A hurricane hitting south Florida.
   Theories: El Niño; radiation from outer space.

8. Phenomenon: A huge drop in the incidence of childhood disease over the last fifty years.
   Theories: Mandatory immunization; lower levels of air pollution.

Exercise 8.7

Evaluate the following theories using the TEST formula. As part of your evaluation:

a. State the claim to be evaluated.
b. Indicate what phenomenon is being explained.
c. Specify at least one alternative theory.
d. Use the criteria of adequacy to assess the two theories and determine which one is more plausible.
e. Write a paragraph detailing your reasons for your choice. Use your background knowledge to fill in any information about the theories and how well they do regarding each criterion.

1. A religious sect based in Boston predicts that the end of the world will occur on January 1, 2001. The world, of course, did not end then. The leader of the sect explains that the prophecy failed to come true because members of the sect did not have enough faith in it.

2. A small, secret society of corporate CEOs and international bankers runs the economies of the United States and Europe. For its own benefit and for its own reasons, the society decides when these nations go into and come out of recession, what levels of production will be achieved by the oil industry, and what each country's gross national product will be. Members of the society are so rich and powerful that they are able to hide the society's activities from public view and operate without the knowledge of governments and ordinary citizens.

3. What is the greatest influence on the course of human history, its social and cultural development? Some say it's powerful ideas like socialism, democracy, human dignity, and scientific method. Some say it's the social movements that embody and promote these ideas. But the greatest influences are wrought by great leaders, who are not necessarily great thinkers. Throughout history, every time a great leader appeared—Moses, Alexander, Caesar, Napoleon, and the like—the world was irrevocably changed regardless of what ideas or social movements were in existence.

4. The primary cause of all wars is fear. When people are afraid of others— because of ignorance or perceived threats—they naturally respond with belligerence and acts of violence. If they have no fear of others, they tend to react rationally and calmly and to seek some sort of fair accommodation.

5. Scientists studied twenty terminal cancer patients, taking note of the overall mental attitudes of the patients. Some of them were characterized as having negative attitudes; they were often angry at their situation and experienced feelings of hopelessness and regret. But other patients were thought to have positive attitudes; they were generally upbeat, optimistic about their treatment, and hopeful. Most of those with positive attitudes lived longer than most of those with negative attitudes. A positive attitude can lengthen cancer patients' lives.

6. Anaïs said farewell to her favorite uncle as he boarded a plane for Paris. That night she dreamed that he was flying in a jetliner that suddenly ran into a powerful thunderstorm and extreme turbulence. The plane rocked from side to side, then descended rapidly into the night. The jetliner crashed into a mountain, killing all onboard. When she awoke the next day, she learned that her uncle's plane had encountered violent turbulence on the way to Paris and that several passengers, including her uncle, had been injured during the flight. She had just had one of those rare experiences known as a prophetic dream.

Self-Assessment Quiz

Answers appear in "Answers to Self-Assessment Quizzes" in Appendix B.

1. What is the basic pattern of inference to the best explanation? How does this pattern differ from that of enumerative induction? analogical induction?
2. What is the minimum requirement for consistency?
3. What are the criteria of adequacy?
4. According to the text, what does it mean for a theory to be testable or untestable?
5. What is the TEST formula?
6. According to the text, in theory evaluation, when is a theory properly considered the best?

Each of the following theories is offered to explain John's apparently prophetic dream that a distant cousin would die in a plane crash. Indicate which theory (a) lacks simplicity, (b) is not conservative, (c) is untestable, and (d) has the most scope. (Some theories may merit more than one of these designations.)

7. The fact that John's dream happened to be about a plane crash involving his cousin was coincidence. We have many dreams, and some are likely to match real events from time to time.
8. In his dream, John was able to see into the future and "view" the plane crash.
9. The incident was an example of "synchronicity," in which events are paired in unusual but predetermined ways by cosmic forces.
10. John had calculated the odds of the crash even before he dreamed about it, so the dream was not a prophecy, but a memory of his calculation.

Indicate which theory in each of the following groups is most plausible.

11. Phenomenon: The rise in popularity of a newly elected president. Theories: (1) The so-called honeymoon effect in which a new president enjoys popularity until he or she is involved in serious or controversial decisions, (2) the systematic manipulation of all polling organizations by the president's staff, (3) the influence of a powerful secret society controlling the media.
12. Phenomenon: Your friend has been skipping class, and you haven't seen her in days. Theories: (1) She's in bed with the flu, (2) she has been kidnapped, (3) she has inherited millions of dollars and has decided to hang out with a better class of friends.
13. Phenomenon: Ships, boats, and planes have been disappearing off the coast of Florida for years. Theories: (1) Considering the meteorological and atmospheric conditions of the area, it's normal for some craft to be lost from time to time; (2) the craft have been hijacked; (3) the ships, boats, and planes are simply off course.

14. Phenomenon: The rapid spread of an unknown, dangerous, viral disease throughout North America. Theories: (1) The lack of awareness and defenses against a new mutated virus, (2) bureaucratic bungling at the Centers for Disease Control and Prevention, (3) a massive conspiracy of doctors who want higher fees for treating seriously ill patients.

Evaluate the following theories using the TEST formula. As part of your evaluation, (1) state the claim to be evaluated, (2) indicate what phenomenon is being explained, (3) specify at least one alternative theory, and (4) use the criteria of adequacy to assess the two theories and determine which one is more plausible.

15. People buy high-ticket merchandise because of subliminal advertising—their minds are being influenced by imperceptible stimuli designed by ad execs.
16. Skeptical scientists have never been able to find evidence for cold fusion, try as they may. That's because their skepticism skews their observations.
17. Eleanor won the state lottery twice in nine months. She must have a system that enables her to pick winning numbers.
18. He embezzled that money because his parents were divorced when he was very young.
19. Schoolchildren who do poorly in school are not dumb or handicapped. They perform poorly for one reason only: low or negative expectations of their teachers.
20. The woman has been displaying bizarre behavior for years, but recently she seems worse than ever. She sometimes suddenly begins screaming, saying that there are snakes crawling on the walls. She shakes uncontrollably at the slightest noise. And she has started to bleed from her palms. The priest says that she's possessed by demons, and he's right.

 ## Writing Assignments

1. In a one-page essay, evaluate the theory that all major decisions made by the current US president are politically motivated and have very little to do with the merits of ideas or programs. Use the TEST formula.
2. Think of the last time you caught a cold or the flu. Write a one-page paper evaluating at least two theories that explain how you first came in contact with the virus. Use the TEST formula.
3. Write a three-page paper in which you use the TEST formula to assess two theories meant to explain the existence of the pictures, videos, and rocks that NASA says were acquired on the moon.
4. Using the TEST formula, evaluate the theory that people are more likely to behave strangely or violently during a full moon than at other times. Do some research to uncover any evidence pertaining to this theory. Write a 200-word report summarizing your findings.

Judging Scientific Theories

SO THE WORLD IS CHOCKABLOCK WITH CLAIMS IN THE FORM OF EXPLANATIONS— *theoretical explanations*, to be more precise, about why something is the case or why something happens. An overwhelming number of such theories are offered to explain the cause of events: why the window broke, why the moon looks so pale, why Ralph stole the bike, why the stock market tanked. As critical thinkers, we do the best we can in evaluating these theories that come our way, testing them if possible, looking for alternative theories, and applying the criteria of adequacy. As it turns out, science is in the same line of work.

Science seeks to acquire knowledge and understanding of reality, and it does so through the formulation, testing, and evaluation of theories. When this kind of search for answers is both systematic and careful, science is being done. And when we ourselves search for answers by scrutinizing possible theories—and we do so systematically and carefully—we are searching scientifically.

Let's examine the scientific process more closely.

Science and Not Science

First, let's explore what science is *not.*[1]

Science is not technology. Science is a *way* of searching for truth—a way that uses what's often referred to as *the scientific method.* Technology is not a search for truth; it's the production of products—DVDs, cell phones, wireless computers, robots that sweep the carpet, self-driving cars, better mousetraps. Technology applies knowledge acquired through science to practical problems that science generally doesn't care about, such as the creation of electronic gadgets. Technology seeks facts to use in producing stuff. Science tries to understand how the world works not by merely cataloging specific facts but by identifying general principles that both explain and predict phenomena.

This nice distinction gets blurry sometimes when technologists do scientific research in order to build a better product or scientists create gadgets in order to do better scientific research. But, in general, science pursues knowledge; technology makes things.

Science is not ideology. Some people say that science is not a way of finding out how the world works, but a worldview affirming how the world is, just as Catholicism or socialism affirms a view of things. To some, science is not only an ideology, but a most objectionable one—one that posits a universe that is entirely material, mechanistic, and deterministic. On this "scientific view," the world—including us—is nothing more than bits of matter forming a big machine that turns and whirs in predetermined ways. This mechanistic notion is thought to demean humans and human endeavors by reducing us to the role of cogs and sprockets.

But we can't identify science with a specific worldview. At any given time, a particular worldview may predominate in the scientific community, but this fact doesn't mean that the worldview is what science is all about. Predominant worldviews among scientists have changed over the centuries, but the general nature of science as a way of searching for truth has not. For example, the mechanistic view of the universe, so common among scientists in the seventeenth century, has now given way to other views. Discoveries in quantum mechanics (the study of subatomic particles) have shown that the old mechanistic perspective is incorrect.

Science is not scientism. One definition of *scientism* is the view that science is the only reliable way to acquire knowledge. Put another way, science is the only reliable road to truth. But in light of the reliability of our sense experience under standard, unhindered conditions, this claim is dubious. We obviously do know many things without the aid of scientific methodology.

But there is a related point that is not so dubious. Science may not be the only road to truth, but it is an extremely reliable way of acquiring knowledge about the empirical world. (Many philosophers of science would go a step further and say that science is our *most reliable* source of knowledge about the world.) Why is science so reliable? Science embodies to a high degree what is essential to reliable knowing of empirical facts: systematic consideration of alternative solutions or theories, rigorous testing of them, and careful checking and rechecking of the conclusions.

Some would say that science is reliable because it is self-correcting. Science does not grab hold of an explanation and never let go. Instead, it looks at alternative ways to explain a phenomenon, tests these alternatives, and opens up the conclusions to criticism from scientists everywhere. Eventually, the conclusions may turn out to be false, and scientists will have to abandon the answers they thought were solid. But usually, after much testing and thinking, scientists hit upon a theory that does hold up under scrutiny. They are then justified in believing that the theory is true, even though there is some chance that it is flawed.

The Scientific Method

The scientific method cannot be identified with any particular set of experimental or observational procedures because there are many different methods to evaluate the worth of a hypothesis. In some sciences such as physics and biology, hypotheses can be assessed through controlled experimental tests. In other sciences such as astronomy and geology, hypotheses usually must be tested through observations. For example, an astronomical hypothesis may predict the existence of certain gases in a part of the Milky Way, and astronomers can use their telescopes to check whether those gases exist as predicted.

The scientific method, however, does involve several steps, regardless of the specific procedures involved:

1. Identify the problem or pose a question.
2. Devise a hypothesis to explain the event or phenomenon.
3. Derive a test implication or prediction.
4. Perform the test.
5. Accept or reject the hypothesis.

Scientific inquiry begins with a problem to solve or a question to answer. So in step 1 scientists may ask: What causes X? Why did Y happen? Does hormone therapy cause breast cancer? Does aspirin lower the risk of stroke? How is it possible for whales to navigate over long distances? How did early hominids communicate with one another? Was the Big Bang an uncaused event?

In step 2 scientists formulate a hypothesis that will constitute an answer to their question. In every case there are facts to explain, and the hypothesis is an explanation for them. The hypothesis guides the research, suggesting what kinds of observations or data would be relevant to the problem at hand. Without a hypothesis, scientists couldn't tell which data are important and which are worthless.

Where do hypotheses come from? One notion is that hypotheses are generated through induction—by collecting the data and drawing a generalization from them to get a hypothesis. But this can't be the way that most hypotheses are formulated because they often contain concepts that aren't in the data. (Remember, theories generally reach beyond the known data to posit the existence of things unknown.) The construction of hypotheses is not usually based on any such mechanical procedure. In many ways, they are created just as works of art are created. Scientists dream them up. They, however, are guided in hypothesis creation by certain criteria—namely, the criteria of adequacy we examined in the last chapter. With testability, fruitfulness, scope, simplicity, and conservatism as their guide, they devise hypotheses from the raw material of the imagination.

Remember, though, that scientists must consider not just their favorite hypothesis, but alternative hypotheses as well. The scientific method calls for consideration of competing explanations and for their examination or testing at some point in the process. Sometimes applying the criteria of adequacy can immediately eliminate some theories from the running, and sometimes theories must be tested along with the original hypothesis.

In step 3 scientists derive implications, or consequences, of the hypothesis to test. As we've seen, sometimes we can test a theory directly, as when we simply check the lawnmower's gas tank to confirm the theory that it won't run because it's out of gas. But often theories cannot be tested directly. How would we directly test, for example, the hypothesis that chemical X is causing leukemia in meno-pausal women? We can't.

So scientists test indirectly by first deriving a test implication from a hypoth-esis and then putting that implication to the test. Deriving such an observational consequence involves figuring out what a hypothesis implies or predicts. Scien-tists ask, "If this hypothesis were true, what consequences would follow? What phenomena or events would have to obtain?"

Recall that we derived test implications in the problem of the car that wouldn't start in chapter 8. One hypothesis was that the car wouldn't start because a vandal had sabotaged it. We reasoned that if a vandal had indeed sabotaged the car, there would be tracks in the snow around it. But there were no tracks, discon-firming the sabotage hypothesis.

The logic of hypothesis testing, then, works like this. When we derive a test implication, we know that if the hypothesis to be tested (H) is true, then there is a specific predicted consequence (C). If the consequence turns out to be false (it does not obtain as predicted), then the hypothesis is probably false, and we can reject it. The hypothesis, in other words, is disconfirmed. We can represent this outcome in a conditional, or hypothetical, argument:

> If H, then C.
>
> Not-C.
>
> Therefore, not-H.

This is, remember, an instance of modus tollens, a valid argument form. In this case, H would be false even if only one of several of its consequences (test implications) turned out to be false.

On the other hand, we would get a very different situation if C turned out to be true:

> If H, then C.
>
> C.
>
> Therefore, H.

Notice that this is an instance of affirming the consequent, an invalid argu-ment form. So just because C is true, that doesn't necessarily mean that H is true. If a consequence turns out to be true, that doesn't *prove* that the hypothesis is correct. In such a result, the hypothesis is confirmed, and the test provides at least some evidence that the hypothesis is true. But the hypothesis isn't then established. If other consequences for the hypothesis are tested, and all the results are again positive, then there is more evidence that the hypothesis is correct. As more and more consequences are tested, and they are shown to be true, we can have increasing confidence that the hypothesis is in fact true. As this evidence accumulates, the likelihood that the hypothesis is actually false decreases—and the probability that it's true increases.

In step 4 scientists carry out the testing. Usually this experimentation is not as simple as testing one implication and calling it quits. Scientists may test many consequences of several competing hypotheses. As the testing proceeds, some hypotheses are found wanting, and they're dropped. If all goes well, eventually one hypothesis remains, with considerable evidence in its favor. Then step 5 can happen, as the hypothesis or hypotheses are accepted or rejected.

Because scientists want to quickly eliminate unworthy hypotheses and zero in on the best one, they try to devise the most telling tests. This means that they are on the lookout for situations in which competing hypotheses have different test consequences. If hypothesis 1 says that C is true, and hypothesis 2 says that C is false, a test of C can then help eliminate one of the hypotheses from further consideration.

As we've seen, implicit in all this is the fact that no hypothesis can ever be *conclusively* confirmed. It's always possible that we will someday find evidence that undermines or conflicts with the evidence we have now.

Likewise, no hypothesis can ever be *conclusively* confuted. When scientists test hypotheses, they never really test a single hypothesis—they test a hypothesis together with a variety of background assumptions and theories. So a hypothesis can always be saved from refutation by making changes in the background claims. (As we detailed in the previous chapter, sometimes these changes are made by constructing ad hoc hypotheses—by postulating unverifiable entities or properties.) In such situations, no amount of evidence logically compels us to conclusively reject a hypothesis.

But our inability to conclusively confirm or confute a hypothesis does not mean that all hypotheses are equally acceptable. Maintaining a hypothesis in the face of mounting negative evidence is unreasonable, and so is refusing to accept a hypothesis despite accumulating confirming evidence. Through the use of carefully controlled experiments, scientists can often affirm or deny a hypothesis with a high degree of confidence.

Testing Scientific Theories

Let's see how we might use the five-step procedure to test a fairly simple hypothesis. Suppose you hear reports that some terminal cancer patients have lived longer than expected because they received high doses of vitamin C. And say that the favored hypothesis among many observers is that the best explanation for the patients' surviving longer is that vitamin C is an effective treatment against cancer. So you decide to test this hypothesis: High doses of vitamin C can increase the survival time of people with terminal cancer. (Years ago, this hypothesis was actually proposed and tested in three well-controlled clinical trials.[2]) An obvious alternative hypothesis is that vitamin C actually has no effect on the survival of terminal cancer patients and that any apparent benefits are due mainly to the placebo effect (the tendency for people to temporarily feel better after they're treated, even if the treatment is a fake). The placebo effect could be leading observers to believe that people taking vitamin C are being cured of cancer and are thus living longer. Or the placebo effect could be making patients feel better, enabling them to take better care of themselves (by eating right or complying with standard medical treatment, for example), increasing survival time.

Now, if your hypothesis is true, what would you expect to happen? That is, what test implication could you derive? If your hypothesis is true, you would expect that terminal cancer patients given high doses of vitamin C would live longer than terminal cancer patients who didn't receive the vitamin (or anything else).

How would you conduct such a test? To begin with, you could prescribe vitamin C to a group of terminal cancer patients (called the experimental group) but not to another group of similar cancer patients (called the control group) and keep track of their survival times. Then you could compare the survival rates of the two groups. But many people who knowingly receive a treatment will report feeling better—even if the treatment is an inactive placebo. So any positive results you see in the treated group might be due not to vitamin C but to the placebo effect.

To get around this problem, you would need to treat both groups, one with vitamin C and the other with a placebo. That way, if most of the people getting the vitamin C live longer than expected and fewer of those in the placebo group do, you can have a slightly better reason for believing that vitamin C works as advertised.

But even this study design is not good enough. It's possible for the people conducting the experiment, the experimenters, to unknowingly bias the results. Through subtle behavioral cues, they can unconsciously inform the test subjects which treatments are real and which ones are placebos—and this, of course, would allow the placebo effect to have full rein. Also, if the experimenters know which treatment is the real one, they can unintentionally misinterpret or skew the study results in line with their own expectations.

This problem can be solved by making the study *double-blind*. In double-blind experiments, neither the subjects nor the experimenters know who receives the real treatment and who the inactive one. A double-blind protocol for your vitamin study would ensure that none of the subjects would know who's getting vitamin C, and neither would the experimenters.

What if you have a double-blind setup but most of the subjects in the vitamin C group were sicker to begin with than those in the placebo control group? Obviously, this would bias the results, making the vitamin C treatment look less effective—even if it *is* effective. To avoid this skewing, you would need to ensure that each group is as much alike as possible to start—with all subjects being around the same age, same physical condition, same stage of cancer, and so on.

Finally, you would need to run some statistical tests to ensure that your results are not a fluke. Even in the most tightly controlled studies, it's possible that the outcome is the result of random factors that cannot be controlled. Statisticians have standard methods for determining when experiment results are likely, or not likely, to be due to chance.

Suppose you design your study well and you conduct it. The results: The patients receiving the high doses of vitamin C did not live longer than the placebo group. In fact, all the subjects lived about the same length of time. Therefore, your hypothesis is disconfirmed. On the other hand, the alternative hypothesis—that vitamin C has no measurable effect on the survival of terminal cancer patients—is confirmed.

Should you now reject the vitamin C theory? Not yet. Even apparently well-conducted studies can have hidden mistakes in them, or there can be factors that the experimenters fail to take into account. This is why scientists insist on study *replication*—the repeating of an experiment by different groups of scientists. If the study is replicated by other scientists, and the study results hold up, then you can be more confident that the results are solid. In such a case, you could safely reject the vitamin C hypothesis. (This is, in fact, what scientists did in the real-life studies of vitamin C and cancer survival.)

At this point, when evidence has been gathered that can bear on the truth of the hypothesis in question, good scientific judgment is crucial. It's here that consideration of other competing hypotheses and the criteria of adequacy again come into play. At this stage, scientists need to decide whether to reject or accept a hypothesis—or modify it to improve it.

 NONINTERVENTION (POPULATION) STUDIES

Not all medical hypotheses are tested by treating (or not treating) groups of patients and analyzing the results (as in the vitamin C example). Many are tested without such direct intervention in people's lives. The former type of study is known as an intervention, or controlled, trial, while the latter is called, not surprisingly, a *nonintervention* study (also an *observational* or *population* study). The basic idea in a nonintervention study is to track the interplay of disease and related factors in a specified population, uncovering associations among these that might lead to better understanding or control of the disease process.

continues

NONINTERVENTION (POPULATION) STUDIES

continued

A typical nonintervention study might go like this: For seven years scientists monitor the vitamin E intake (from food and supplements) and the incidence of heart disease of 90,000 women. Evaluation of this data shows that the women with the highest amounts of vitamin E in their diets have a 40 percent lower incidence of heart disease. That is, for reasons unknown, a lower risk of heart disease is associated with a higher intake of vitamin E in women. This study does not show that higher intakes of vitamin E *cause* less heart disease, only that there is a link between them. Perhaps some other factor merely associated with vitamin E is the true protector of hearts, or maybe women who take vitamin E are more likely to do other things (such as exercise) that lower their risk of heart disease.

Generally, nonintervention studies cannot establish cause-and-effect relationships, though they may hint that a causal relationship is present. And sometimes multiple nonintervention studies yielding the same results can make a strong case for a causal connection. Intervention trials, however, *can* establish cause and effect.

Nonintervention studies have led scientists to some of the most important findings in preventive health. It was a series of such studies done over decades, coupled with other kinds of scientific data, that revealed that cigarette smoking caused cancer. And it was such investigations that showed that high blood pressure, high cholesterol, overweight, and smoking are risk factors for heart disease.

Note to critical thinkers: Very often the media misreport the results of nonintervention studies, reading cause and effect into a mere association. For example, if a single nonintervention study finds a link between chewing gum and better eyesight, a headline in a blog or the morning paper (or a TV newscaster) may proclaim that "Gum-chewing improves your eyesight!" Maybe, maybe not—but the study would not justify that conclusion.

Judging Scientific Theories

As you can see, theory testing is part of the broader effort to assess the merits of one theory against a field of alternatives. And as you know by now, this broader effort will always involve, explicitly or implicitly, the application of the criteria of adequacy to the theories in question:

- Testability: Whether there's some way to determine if a theory is true
- Fruitfulness: The number of novel predictions made
- Scope: The amount of diverse phenomena explained
- Simplicity: The number of assumptions made
- Conservatism: How well a theory fits with existing knowledge

Let's study two important examples to see how scientists manage this task: The first is a classic case from the history of science; the second, a contemporary tale of what many perceive as a battle between science and religion. Notice that the steps itemized by the TEST formula are implicit in the evaluation process.

Copernicus Versus Ptolemy

Consider the historic clash between the geocentric (Earth-centered) and the heliocentric (sun-centered) theories of planetary motion. It's difficult to imagine two rival theories that have more profoundly influenced how humanity views itself and its place in the universe.

In the beginning was the geocentric view. Aristotle got things going by putting forth the theory that a spherical Earth was at the center of a spherical universe consisting of a series of concentric, transparent spheres. On one celestial sphere we see the sun, the moon, and the known planets. On the outermost sphere we behold the stars. All the heavenly bodies rotate in perfect circles around the stationary Earth. The heavenly bodies are pure, incorruptible, and unchanging; the Earth, impure, corruptible, and transient.

Then came the great astronomer and mathematician Ptolemy, who flourished in Alexandria between 127 and 148 C.E. He discovered inconsistencies in the traditional geocentric system between the predicted and observed motions of the planets. He found, in other words, that Aristotle's theory was not conservative, a crucial failing. So he fine-tuned the old view, adding little circular motions (called epicycles) along the planet orbits and many other minor adjustments. He also allowed for an odd asymmetry in which the center of planet orbits was not exactly the center of Earth—all this so the theory would match up to astronomical observations. By the time Ptolemy finished tinkering he had posited eighty circles and epicycles—eighty different planetary motions—to explain the movements of the sun, moon, and five known planets.

The result was a system far more complex than Aristotle's was. But the revised theory worked well enough for the times, and it agreed better than the earlier theory did with observational data. Despite the complications, learned people could use Ptolemy's system to calculate the positions of the planets with enough accuracy to effectively manage calendars and astrological charts. So for fifteen centuries astronomers used Ptolemy's unwieldy, complex theory to predict celestial events and locations. In the West, at least, Earth stood still in the center of everything as the rest of the universe circled around it.

The chief virtue of the Ptolemaic system, then, was conservatism. It fit, mostly, with what astronomers knew about celestial goings-on. It was also testable, as any scientific theory should be. Its biggest failing was simplicity—or the lack thereof. The theory was propped up by numerous assumptions for the purpose of making the theory fit the data.

Enter Nicolaus Copernicus (1473–1543). He was disturbed by the complexity of Ptolemy's system. It was a far cry from the simple theory that Aristotle bequeathed to the West. Copernicus proposed a heliocentric theory in which Earth and the other planets orbit the sun, the true center of the universe. In doing so, he greatly simplified both the picture of the heavens and the calculations required to predict the positions of planets.

Copernicus's theory was simpler than Ptolemy's on many counts, but one of the most impressive was retrograde motion, a phenomenon that had stumped astronomers for centuries. From time to time, certain planets seem to reverse their customary direction of travel across the skies—to move backward! Ptolemy explained this retrograde motion by positing yet more epicycles, asserting that planets orbiting Earth will often orbit around a point on the larger orbital path. Seeing these orbits within orbits from Earth, an observer would naturally see the planets sometimes backing up.

But the Copernican theory could easily explain retrograde motion without all those complicated epicycles. As the outer planets (Mars, Jupiter, Saturn) orbit the sun, so does Earth, one of the inner planets. The outer planets, though, move much slower than Earth does. On its own orbital track, Earth sometimes passes the outer planets as they lumber along on their orbital track, just as a train passes a slower train on a parallel track. When this happens, the planets appear to move backward, just as the slower train seems to reverse course when the faster train overtakes it.

Copernicus's theory, however, was not superior on every count. It explained a great many astronomical observations, but Ptolemy's theory did too, so they were about even in scope. It had no big advantage in fruitfulness over the Ptolemaic system. It made no impressive predictions of unknown phenomena. Much more troubling, it seemed to conflict with some observational data.

One test implication of the Copernican theory is the phenomenon known as *parallax*. Critics of the heliocentric view claimed that if the theory were true, then as Earth moved through its orbit, stars closest to it should seem to shift their position relative to stars farther away. There should, in other words, be parallax. But no one had observed parallax.

Copernicus and his followers responded to this criticism by saying that stars were too far away for parallax to occur. As it turned out, they were right about this, but confirmation didn't come until 1832 when parallax was observed with more powerful telescopes.

Another test implication seemed to conflict with the heliocentric model. Copernicus reasoned that if the planets rotate around the sun, then they should show phases just as the moon shows phases due to the light of the sun falling on it at different times. But in Copernicus's day, no one could see any such planetary phases. Fifty years later, though, Galileo used his new telescope to confirm that Venus had phases.

Ultimately, scientists accepted the Copernican model over Ptolemy's because of its simplicity—despite what seemed at the time like evidence against the theory. As Copernicus said, "I think it is easier to believe this [sun-centered view] than to confuse the issue by assuming a vast number of Spheres, which those who keep the Earth at the center must do."[3]

 ARE YOU SCIENTIFICALLY LITERATE?

Surveys conducted by the National Science Foundation (NSF) have consistently shown that Americans' understanding of science and the scientific process is limited and that belief in such things as psychic powers and UFOs is more widespread than we might expect in a scientifically advanced culture. For years the NSF has been gauging public understanding of science using a nine-question knowledge survey. In 2012 Americans scored a 5.8 out of the 9 questions (65 percent). Here's the survey so you can test your own scientific literacy. Answers are at the end. (*Note:* More than 25 percent of respondents got question 3 wrong!)

Many people are ignorant of basic scientific facts while strongly believing in scientifically debunked phenomena.

1. The center of the Earth is very hot. True or false?
2. The continents have been moving their location for millions of years and will continue to move. True or false?
3. Does the Earth go around the sun, or does the sun go around the Earth?
4. All radioactivity is man-made. True or false?
5. Electrons are smaller than atoms. True or false?
6. Lasers work by focusing sound waves. True or false?
7. It is the father's gene that decides whether the baby is a boy or a girl. True or false?
8. Antibiotics kill viruses as well as bacteria. True or false?
9. Human beings, as we know them today, developed from earlier species of animals. True or false?

Answers: 1. True; 2. True; 3. The Earth goes around the sun; 4. False; 5. True; 6. False; 7. True; 8. False; 9. True.

Evolution Versus Creationism

Few scientific theories have been more hotly debated among nonscientists than evolution and its rival, creationism (or creation science). Both theories purport to explain the origin and existence of biological life on Earth, and each claims to be a better explanation than the other. Can science decide this contest? Yes. Despite the complexity of the issues involved and the mixing of religious themes with the nonreligious, good science can figure out which theory is best. Remember that the best theory is the one that explains the phenomenon and measures up to the criteria of adequacy better than any of its competitors. There is no reason that the scientific approach cannot provide an answer here—even in this thorniest of thorny issues.

Neither the term "evolution" nor the concept began with Charles Darwin (1809–1882), the father of evolutionary theory. The word showed up in English as early as 1647. The ancient Greek philosopher Anaximander (c. 611–547 B.C.E.) was actually the first evolutionary theorist, inferring from some simple observations that humans must have evolved from an animal and that this evolution must have begun in the sea. But in his famous book *On the Origin of Species* (1859), Darwin distilled the theory of evolution into its most influential statement.

 CAN YOU SEE EVOLUTION?

Critics of the theory of evolution often ask, "If evolution occurs, why can't we see it?" Here's how the National Academy of Sciences responds to this objection (https://www.nap.edu/read/11876/chapter/4#39ml):

> Thus, for many areas of science, scientists have not directly observed the objects (such as genes and atoms) or the phenomena (such as the Earth going around the Sun) that are now well-established facts. Instead, they have confirmed them indirectly by observational and experimental evidence. Evolution is no different. Indeed . . . evolutionary science provides one of the best examples of a deep understanding based on scientific reasoning.
>
> This contention that nobody has seen evolution occurring further ignores the overwhelming evidence that evolution has taken place and is continuing to occur. The annual changes in influenza viruses and the emergence of bacteria resistant to antibiotics are both products of evolutionary forces. Another example of ongoing evolution is the appearance of mosquitoes resistant to various insecticides, which has contributed to a resurgence of malaria in Africa and elsewhere.

continues

CAN YOU SEE EVOLUTION?

continued

> The transitional fossils that have been found in abundance since Darwin's time reveal how species continually give rise to successor species that, over time, produce radically changed body forms and functions. It also is possible to directly observe many of the specific processes by which evolution occurs. Scientists regularly do experiments using microbes and other model systems that directly test evolutionary hypotheses.

Scientists have been fine-tuning the theory ever since, as new evidence and new insights pour in from many different fields, such as biochemistry and genetics. But the basic idea has not changed: Living organisms adapt to their environments through inherited characteristics, which results in changes in succeeding generations. Specifically, the offspring of organisms differ physically from their parents in various ways, and these differences can be passed on genetically to their offspring. If an offspring has an inherited trait (such as sharper vision or a larger brain) that increases its chances of surviving long enough to reproduce, the individual is more likely to survive and pass the trait on to the next generation. After several generations, this useful trait, or adaptation, spreads throughout a whole population of individuals, differentiating the population from its ancestors. *Natural selection* is the name that Darwin gave to this process.

Creation science, on the other hand, maintains that (1) the universe and all life was created suddenly, out of nothing, only a few thousand years ago (six thousand to ten thousand is the usual range); (2) natural selection could not have produced living things from a single organism; (3) species change very little over time; (4) man and apes have a separate ancestry; and (5) the Earth's geology can be explained by catastrophism, including a worldwide flood.[4]

The first thing we should ask about these two theories is whether they're testable. The answer is yes. Recall that a theory is testable if it predicts or explains something other than what it was introduced to explain. On this criterion, evolution is surely testable. It explains, among other things, why bacteria develop resistance to antibiotics, why there are so many similarities between humans and other primates, why new infectious diseases emerge, why the chromosomes of closely related species are so similar, why the fossil record shows the peculiar progression of fossils that it does, and why the embryos of related species have such similar structure and appearance.

Creationism is also testable. It too explains something other than what it was introduced to explain. It claims that Earth's geology was changed in a worldwide flood, that the universe is only a few thousand years old, that all species were created at the same time, and that species change very little over time.

Innumerable test implications have been derived from evolutionary theory, and innumerable experiments have been conducted, confirming the theory. For example, if evolution is true, then we would expect to see systematic change in the fossil record from simple creatures at the earlier levels to more complex individuals at the more recent levels. We would expect not to see a reversal of this configuration. And this sequence is exactly what scientists see time and time again.

Creationism, however, has not fared as well. Its claims have not been borne out by evidence. In fact, they have consistently conflicted with well-established scientific findings.

This latter point means that creationism fails the criterion of conservatism—it conflicts with what we already know. For example, the scientific evidence shows that Earth is not six thousand to ten thousand years old—but billions of years old. According to the National Academy of Sciences:

> There are no valid scientific data or calculations to substantiate the belief that Earth was created just a few thousand years ago. [There is a] vast amount of evidence for the great age of the universe, our galaxy, the Solar system, and Earth from astronomy, astrophysics, nuclear physics, geology, geochemistry, and geophysics. Independent scientific methods consistently give an age for Earth and the Solar system of about 5 billion years, and an age for our galaxy and the universe that is two to three times greater.[5]

Creationism also fails the criterion of conservatism on the issue of a geology-transforming universal flood. Again, the National Academy of Sciences:

> Nor is there any evidence that the entire geological record, with its orderly succession of fossils, is the product of a single universal flood that occurred a few thousand years ago, lasted a little longer than a year, and covered the highest mountains to a depth of several meters. On the contrary, intertidal and terrestrial deposits demonstrate that at no recorded time in the past has the entire planet been under water. . . . The belief that Earth's sediments, with their fossils, were deposited in an orderly sequence in a year's time defies all geological observations and physical principles concerning sedimentation rates and possible quantities of suspended solid matter.[6]

Has either theory yielded any novel predictions? Evolution has. It has predicted, for example, that new species should still be evolving today; that the fossil record should show a movement from older, simpler organisms to younger, more complex ones; that proteins and chromosomes of related species should be similar; and that organisms should adapt to changing environments. These and many other novel predictions have been confirmed. Creationism has made some novel claims, as we saw earlier, but none of these have been supported by good evidence. Creationism is not a fruitful theory.

"IT'S BLACK, AND IT LOOKS LIKE A HOLE.
I'D SAY IT'S A BLACK HOLE."

The criterion of simplicity also draws a sharp contrast between the two theories. Simplicity is a measure of the number of assumptions that a theory makes. Both theories make assumptions, but creationism assumes much more. Creationism assumes the existence of a creator and unknown forces. Proponents of creationism readily admit that we do not know how the creator created nor what creative processes were used.

In this contest of theories, the criterion of scope—the amount of diverse phenomena explained—is probably more telling than any of the others. Biological evolution explains a vast array of phenomena in many fields of science. In fact, a great deal of the content of numerous scientific fields—genetics, physiology, biochemistry, neurobiology, and more—would be deeply perplexing without the theory of evolution. As the eminent geneticist Theodosius Dobzhansky put it, "Nothing in biology makes sense except in the light of evolution."[7]

Virtually all scientists would agree—and go much further:

It helps to explain the emergence of new infectious diseases, the development of antibiotic resistance in bacteria, the agricultural relationships among wild and domestic plants and animals, the composition of Earth's atmosphere, the molecular machinery of the cell, the similarities between human beings and other primates, and countless other features of the biological and physical world.[8]

Creationism, however, can explain none of this. And it provokes, not solves, innumerable mysteries: What caused the worldwide flood? Where did all that water come from? Where did it all go? Why does Earth seem so ancient (when it's said to be so young)? How did the creator create the entire universe suddenly—out of nothing? Why does the fossil record seem to suggest evolution and not creation? So many questions are an indication of diminished scope and decreased understanding.

Good scientists must be prepared to admit this much: If creationism meets the criteria of adequacy as well as evolution does, then creationism must be as good a theory as evolution. But creationism fails to measure up to the criteria of adequacy. On every count it shows itself to be inferior. Scientists then are justified in rejecting creationism in favor of evolution. And this is exactly what they do.

Science and Weird Theories

What good is science and inference to the best explanation in the realm that seems to lie *beyond* common sense and scientific inquiry—the zone of the extraordinary, the paranormal, and the supernatural? In this land of the wonderfully weird—the interesting and mysterious domain of UFOs, ESP, ghosts, psychic predictions, tarot card readings, and the like—exactly what work can science do?

From the preceding chapter, you probably have already guessed that science and critical reasoning can be as useful in assessing weird claims as they are in sizing up mundane ones. Inference to the best explanation—whether wielded in science or everyday life—can be successfully applied to extraordinary theories of all kinds. Fortunately for critical thinkers, the TEST formula outlined in chapter 8 for finding the best theoretical explanation is not afraid of ghosts, monsters, or space aliens. In the next few pages, we will get a good demonstration of these points by examining some extraordinary theories in much greater detail than we have previously.

Science has always been interested in the mysterious, and from time to time it has also ventured into the weird. In the past 150 years, scientists have tested spiritualism, clairvoyance, telepathy, telekinesis (moving physical objects with the mind alone), astrology, dowsing, the Loch Ness monster, faith healing, fire walking, and more. Among these we should also count some bizarre phenomena that scientists never tire of studying—black holes, alternative dimensions of space, and the microworld of subatomic particles (the weirdest of the weird) where the laws of physics are crazy enough to make Alice in Wonderland scream.

But why should anyone bother to learn how to evaluate weird claims in the first place? Well, for one thing, they are widely believed and often difficult to ignore. They are, after all, heavily promoted in countless websites, television programs, movies, books, magazines, and tabloids. And—like claims in politics, medicine, and many other fields—they can dramatically affect people's lives, for better or worse. It's important then for anyone confronted with such popular and influential claims to be able to assess them carefully.

In addition, if you really care whether an extraordinary claim is true or false, there is no substitute for the kind of critical evaluation discussed here. Accepting (or rejecting) a weird claim solely because it's weird will not do. A horselaugh is not an argument, and neither is a sneer. Weird claims often turn out to be false, and, as the history of science shows, they sometimes surprise everyone by being true.

Making Weird Mistakes

So in science and in our own lives, the critical assessment of weird theories is possible—but that doesn't mean the process is without risks. It's easy for a scientist or anyone else to err when thinking about extraordinary claims. Weird claims and experiences have a way of provoking strong emotions, preconceived attitudes, and long-held biases. In the world of the weird, people (including scientists and other experts) are often prone to the kinds of errors in reasoning we discussed in chapter 2, including resisting contrary evidence, looking for confirming evidence, and preferring available evidence. Those who contemplate extraordinary things also seem to be especially susceptible to the following errors.

Leaping to the Weirdest Theory

When people have an extraordinary experience, they usually try to make sense of it. They may have a seemingly prophetic dream, see a ghostly shape in the dark, watch their astrologer's prediction come true, think that they've witnessed a miracle, or feel that they have somehow lived another life centuries ago. Then they cast about for an explanation for such experiences. And when they cannot think of a natural explanation, they often conclude that the explanation must be paranormal or supernatural. This line of reasoning is common but fallacious. *Just because you can't think of a natural explanation doesn't mean that there isn't one.* You may just be ignorant of the correct explanation. Throughout history, scientists have often been confronted with astonishing phenomena that they could not explain in natural terms at the time. But they didn't assume that the phenomena must be paranormal or supernatural. They simply kept investigating—and they eventually found natural explanations. Comets, solar eclipses, meteors, mental illness, infectious diseases, and epilepsy were all once thought to be supernatural or paranormal but were later found through scientific investigation to have natural explanations.

When confronted then with a phenomenon that you don't understand, the most reasonable response is to search for a natural explanation.

The leap to a nonnatural explanation is an example of the fallacy known as the appeal to ignorance. People think that since a paranormal or supernatural explanation has not been shown to be false, it must be true. This line, though logically fallacious, can be very persuasive.

The failure to consider alternative explanations is probably the most common error in assessing paranormal claims. As we've seen, this failure can be willful: People can refuse to consider seriously a viable alternative. But honest and intelligent people can also simply be unaware of possible natural explanations. Looking for alternative explanations requires imagination and a deliberate attempt to "think outside the box."

Mixing What Seems with What Is

Sometimes people leap prematurely to an extraordinary theory by ignoring this elementary principle: *Just because something seems real doesn't mean that it is.* Because of the nature of our perceptual equipment and processes, we humans are bound to have many experiences in which something appears to be real but is not. The corrective for mistaking the unreal for the real is applying another important principle that we discussed earlier: It's reasonable to accept the evidence provided by personal experience only if there's no good reason to doubt it. We have reason to doubt if our perceptual abilities are impaired (we are under stress, drugged, afraid, excited, etc.), we have strong expectations about a particular experience (we strongly expect to see a UFO or hear spooky noises, for example), and observations are made under poor conditions (the stimuli are vague and ambiguous or the environment is too dark, too noisy, too hazy, etc.). Scientists can falter here just as anyone else can, which is why they try to use research methods that minimize reasons for doubt.

Misunderstanding the Possibilities

Debates about weird theories often turn on the ideas of possibility and impossibility. Skeptics may dismiss a weird theory by saying, "That's impossible!" Believers may insist that a state of affairs is indeed possible, or they may proclaim, "*Anything* is possible!" Such protestations, however, are often based on misunderstandings.

The experts on the subject of possibility (namely, philosophers) often talk about *logical possibility* and *logical impossibility.* Something is logically impossible if it violates a principle of logic (that is, it involves a logical contradiction). Something is logically possible if it does not violate a principle of logic (does not involve a logical contradiction). Anything that is logically impossible can't exist. We know, for example, that there are no married bachelors because these things involve logical contradictions (male humans who are both married and not married). Likewise we know that there are no square circles because they involve logical contradictions (things that are both circles and not circles). We must conclude from all this that, despite what some people sincerely believe, it is not the case that anything is possible. If a weird phenomenon is logically impossible, we needn't investigate it further because it can't exist. Most alleged paranormal phenomena, however, are not logically impossible. ESP, UFOs, reincarnation, dowsing, spontaneous human combustion, out-of-body experiences, and many more generally do not involve any logical contradiction.

Philosophers also refer to *physical possibility* and *physical impossibility*. Something is said to be physically impossible if it violates a law of science. We know that traveling faster than the speed of light is physically impossible because such an occurrence violates a law of science. Perpetual motion machines are physically impossible because they violate the law of science known as the conservation of mass-energy. Thus, scientists are skeptical of any extraordinary phenomenon that is said to be physically impossible.

Yet whether an event violates a law of nature is very difficult—perhaps impossible—to prove. The philosopher of science Theodore Schick, Jr., explains why:

> No event . . . can provide sufficient grounds for believing that a miracle [a violation of scientific law] has occurred, because its seeming impossibility may simply be due to our ignorance of the operative laws. . . . We would be justified in believing that an apparent violation of a natural law was a miracle only if we were justified in believing that no natural law would ever be discovered to explain the occurrence. But we can never be justified in believing that, because no one can be sure what the future will bring. We can't rule out the possibility that a natural explanation will be found for an event, no matter how incredible.[9]

Some things that are logically possible are physically impossible. It's logically possible for Vaughn's dog to fly to another galaxy in sixty seconds. This astounding performance does not violate a principle of logic. But it does violate laws of science pertaining to speed-of-light travel and gravitation. It is therefore physically impossible. The upshot of all this is that, contrary to what some people would have us believe, if something is logically possible, that doesn't mean it's physically possible. That is, if something is logically possible, that doesn't mean it's actual. Many logically possible things may not be real.

Judging Weird Theories

Now let's do a detailed evaluation of two extraordinary theories using the TEST formula from chapter 8. Recall the procedure's four steps:

Step 1. State the theory and check for consistency.
Step 2. Assess the evidence for the theory.
Step 3. Scrutinize alternative theories.
Step 4. Test the theories with the criteria of adequacy.

Science uses such a procedure to assess all manner of extraordinary explanations, and—by proceeding carefully and systematically—so can you.

Crop Circles

Crop circles are large-scale geometric designs pressed or stamped into fields of grain. They are often circular but can be almost any shape, ranging from simple patterns to complex pictograms or symbols. They can measure a few feet in diameter or span the length of several football fields. The wave of popular interest in crop circles began in the 1970s when they started mysteriously appearing overnight in the grain fields of southern England. The crops would be neatly flattened with the stalks pressed together and sometimes impressively interlaced. In the 1980s and 1990s, interest in the phenomenon grew as crop circles proliferated throughout the world, showing up in Europe, Africa, Australia, the United States, and elsewhere. In 2002 Hollywood got into the act by releasing the movie *Signs* starring Mel Gibson. He plays a Pennsylvania farmer who discovers massive crop circles in his fields and is soon drawn into encounters with extraterrestrial beings.

From the beginning, crop circles have been both intriguing and controversial. The controversy has centered mostly on one question: What theory best explains the existence of crop circles? Many explanations for the cause of the phenomenon have been offered and debated, with plenty of people making the case for their

Crop circles in wheat fields near Alton Barnes, Wiltshire, UK.

favorite theory through books, magazine articles, and, of course, the Internet. Let's examine some of these theories and see if we can separate the good from the bad.

Step 1. We begin with a theory that has gotten a great deal of attention from skeptics and believers alike.

Theory 1: Crop circles are created by small whirlwinds of electrified air (a.k.a. wind vortices). The idea here is that crop circles are made by columns of whirling, charged air similar to dust devils or miniature tornadoes. These vortices form above grain fields and then plunge to the ground, discharging the electricity and flattening the grain in swirled patterns. But unlike tornadoes, wind vortices leave the stalks of grain undamaged.

Step 2. What is the evidence for this theory? The evidence is indirect. Natural crop-circle vortices are unknown to science, but similar vortices are reported to have been produced artificially in laboratories. A few people claim to have seen the vortices in open fields. An electrified vortex might produce light during discharge, and sure enough eyewitnesses have reported seeing "balls of light" and other light phenomena in or near crop circles. Many crop-circle enthusiasts (known as "cereologists" or "croppies") have photographed what they claim are mysterious lights near crop circles, and the photographs show impressive balls of light and strange glowing arcs. Some croppies also report hearing strange sounds near crop circles (humming noises, for example). Finally, some cereologists have reported that the plants in crop circles differ anatomically from those outside the circles. The joints in stalks, for example, may be bigger in crop-circle plants than in plants growing elsewhere.

This evidence, however, is weak. Producing a vortex in a laboratory does not prove that it exists "in the wild." In fact, there is no good evidence that crop-circle vortices exist in nature. As with most unfamiliar and provocative phenomena, eyewitness accounts of vortices are generally unreliable, especially since people generally don't know what a true crop-circle vortex looks like. Sightings of various light phenomena are not direct evidence for the existence of vortices because they can be explained in alternative ways. The lights could come from many other sources, including ball lightning (a documented phenomenon), commercial aircraft, military aircraft, the parachute flares of pranksters, and the flashlights of people making crop circles (there are plenty of people who make crop circles as hoaxes or works of art). The photographs of light phenomena also have alternative explanations. The arcs and balls of light in these photos can be easily produced when the flash reflects off of the camera strap, insects, droplets of water, and the like. Photos of weird lights are also easily faked. Reports of strange sounds, like the reports of weird lights, are not good evidence of vortices at work because the sounds could have several alternative causes (farm machinery, wind, etc.). And even if there are anatomical differences between crop-circle plants and noncircle plants, this would not show that crop circles are made by vortices. At most, it would suggest only that crop-circle plants are different, however the circles are made. (This same point applies to claims about other kinds of differences between crop-circle areas and noncircle locations, including alleged magnetic or soil anomalies. The anomalies, if they exist, do not confirm that crop circles are made in any particular way.)

The biggest problem for the crop-circle vortex theory is that it doesn't explain the evidence. The theory seems adequate to explain circular crop-circle designs (a whirlwind would seem to be just the thing to make a circle on the ground), but not all crop circles are circular. Many are incredibly complex amalgams of squares, triangles, straight lines, and shapes that have no names.

Step 3. Now let's examine a popular alternative theory.

Theory 2: Crop circles are made by extraterrestrial beings (space aliens). This explanation asserts only that crop circles are the work of aliens; it does not specify how the aliens do it. The circles could be created by alien spacecraft, energy beams from space, or "thought energy" from places unknown. This theory has seemed plausible to some people in light of the intricacy and beauty of crop-circle pictograms, with a few croppies insisting that aliens must be communicating in geometrical language. To some, the circles have seemed much too complicated and elegant to be the result of human ingenuity.

The evidence for this alien explanation? The elegant complexity of crop circles has been thought to be pretty good support for the theory. Who else but aliens would create such brilliant masterpieces on such a large scale—masterpieces that are best viewed from the air or space itself? A few people have announced that they found very intricate mathematics in the more elaborate crop-circle designs. Also, some have reported seeing odd lights in the vicinity of crop circles, and others have claimed that they saw actual alien craft in the night sky not far from the crop-circle fields. A few cereologists have even claimed that they caught sight of UFOs in the process of making crop circles.

This evidence, however, is problematic and has some of the same weaknesses as the wind vortex evidence. The complexity and beauty of crop circles do not lend support to the alien theory because the artistry of the crop formations has an obvious alternative explanation: Humans made them. There are numerous documented cases of humans—either hoaxers or artists—creating stunningly exquisite and elaborate crop circles, some with plenty of mathematics built in. Because the human artist explanation is at least as plausible as the alien artist one, the artistic or intellectual impressiveness of crop circles can give no weight to the alien theory. As mentioned earlier, light phenomena near crop circles also have alternative explanations. Nighttime UFO sightings might seem to be good evidence that aliens are up to something. But they are susceptible to many of the doubt-producing factors that we discussed in chapter 6: darkness, ambiguous stimuli, lack of cues to the true position and size of moving objects, perceptual construction, stress, strong emotions, expectancy, and more. Eyewitness reports of aliens actually constructing crop circles constitute very weak evidence for theory 2. Such extraordinary reports require reliable corroborating evidence, but no alien activity of any kind has ever been scientifically documented, despite allegations to the contrary.

Many people favor a more down-to-earth theory.

Theory 3: Crop circles are made by humans using ordinary means. This explanation encompasses the creation of crop circles by hoaxers, artists, or any other humans. The relevant evidence suggests that many crop circles have indeed been produced by humans. In 1991 two English artists with a sense of humor, Doug Bower and Dave Chorley, declared that they had been making crop circles for years to fool gullible people who believed in UFOs. They demonstrated their circle-making skills for reporters and television audiences, easily producing very elaborate crop circles in a short time. To create their designs, they used only ropes and planks. They showed that crop circles thought to be way beyond human ability were in fact made by humans using incredibly simple techniques. Their formations fooled many people including at least one prominent cereologist. Many circle-watchers conceded that human hoaxers were making crop circles and that distinguishing "true" circles from fake ones is no cinch. A leading cereologist admitted that 80 percent of crop circles in Britain were made by humans.

It is clear, however, that Bower and Chorley could not have created all the known crop circles. From southern England, crop-circle creation spread all over the globe, appearing in increasing numbers. This spread of the phenomenon, though, seemed to correlate with increased international media coverage of crop circles, suggesting that other humans may have been inspired to copy English circle-making. In addition, many artists have been fascinated by the aesthetics of crop circles and have generated their own masterpieces in grain.

Croppies have argued that humans can't be responsible for some crop circles because there are often no signs of human activity at formation sites (no footprints, paths through the grain, etc.). But as the circle-building of hoaxers suggests, crop circles can be produced by humans without leaving evidence of human activity behind. Hoaxers, for example, can often avoid leaving footprints in a grain field by walking along tramlines, the narrow footpaths created by farm machinery.

Also, as suggested earlier, physical anomalies in crop-circle plants or soil do not prove that crop circles are made in any particular way. It's possible that anomalies are produced by the techniques used in human circle-making. Some have suggested, for example, that enlarged joints in grain stalks are the result of the bent stalks baking in the hot sun.

Step 4. Now let's see what happens when we apply the criteria of adequacy to these three theories. Theories 1 and 3 seem equal in terms of testability. Both predict something other than what they were introduced to explain. Theory 1, for example, predicts that in the creation of a crop circle, an electrified vortex forms above the formation area—something that should be detectable by the right kind of scientific instruments. Theory 3 is certainly testable because human activity is detectable and measurable. Theory 2 (aliens) may or may not be testable, depending on how alien activity is construed. We will give the theory the benefit of the doubt and say that it too is testable.

Theories 1 and 2 are not fruitful, for they have yielded no surprising predictions. We could argue, though, that theory 3 is fruitful because the creation of specific crop circles at designated times and places has been successfully predicted by hoaxers (the ones who created the circles).

In terms of scope, neither theory 1 nor 2 gets any points. The vortex theory does not explain anything other than the creation of crop circles. Theory 2 could be construed as explaining many things in which aliens are involved (UFO sightings, abductions, UFO crashes, etc.). But positing the existence of mysterious beings that act in mysterious ways for mysterious reasons does not seem to explain much of anything. Theory 3, on the other hand, can be used to explain many strange phenomena because humans, after all, are responsible for many hoaxes and bizarre happenings.

As far as simplicity is concerned, theories 1 and 2 are in deep trouble. Like most paranormal explanations, they both posit the existence of unknown entities (charged, naturally occurring vortices and space aliens). Theory 3 sticks with known entities and processes.

On the criterion of conservatism, theories 1 and 2 are again in trouble. There is no good evidence that the hypothesized vortex has ever occurred anywhere. And we have no good reason to believe that either space aliens or alien technology has ever visited Earth, let alone created some nice designs in a wheat field.

We can summarize these judgments as in the following table:

Criteria	Vortices	Aliens	Humans
Testable	Yes	Yes	Yes
Fruitful	No	No	Yes
Scope	No	No	Yes
Simple	No	No	Yes
Conservative	No	No	Yes

We can see immediately that the three theories are equal in testability, but theory 3 wins on all other counts. It is clearly the superior theory. Both the vortex theory and the alien theory fail the test of fruitfulness, scope, simplicity, and conservatism. Of these four criteria, simplicity and conservatism carry the most weight here. In general, the plausibility of a theory is weakened considerably when it posits unknown entities and processes. Likewise, a theory that doesn't fit with what we already know takes a hit in credibility. An unconservative theory, of course, can acquire some credibility if it excels in the other criteria of adequacy. But theories 1 and 2 fall short in all the criteria except testability. We can see then that theories 1 and 2 are not good explanations for crop circles. They are most likely false. Theory 3—human creation of crop circles—is a much better theory.

There are other crop-circle theories that we haven't examined. None of them seem to measure up to the criteria of adequacy as well as theory 3 does. If this is the case, then we can give an even stronger endorsement of theory 3: Crop circles are probably human-made.

EYEWITNESS TESTIMONY AND EXTRAORDINARY THINGS

A great deal of the evidence for paranormal phenomena is eyewitness testimony. Unfortunately, research suggests that eyewitness testimony generally can't be trusted—especially when the testimony concerns the paranormal. For example, in some studies people who had participated in séances later gave wildly inaccurate descriptions of what had transpired. Researchers have found that people's beliefs and expectations seem to play a big role in the unreliability of testimony about the paranormal.

Spoon-bending—bending metal spoons allegedly using only mental powers—used to be a popular feat performed by self-proclaimed psychics. But then magicians got into the act and showed that they too could bend spoons—not through psychic powers but with simple magic tricks.

Different people clearly have different beliefs and expectations prior to observing a supposed psychic—skeptics might expect to see some kind of trickery; believers may expect a display of genuine psi [parapsychological phenomena]. Some seventy years ago Eric Dingwall in Britain speculated that such

continues

EYEWITNESS TESTIMONY AND EXTRAORDINARY THINGS

continued

expectations may distort eyewitness testimony: The frame of mind in which a person goes to see magic and to a medium cannot be compared. In one case he goes either purely for amusement or possibly with the idea of discovering "how it was done," whilst in the other he usually goes with the thought that it is possible that he will come into direct contact with the other world.

Recent experimental evidence suggests that Dingwall's speculations are correct. Richard Wiseman and Robert Morris in Britain carried out two studies investigating the effect that belief in the paranormal has on the observation of conjuring tricks. Individuals taking part in the experiment were first asked several questions concerning their belief in the paranormal. On the basis of their answers they were classified as either believers (labeled "sheep") or skeptics (labeled "goats").

In both experiments individuals were first shown a film containing fake psychic demonstrations. In the first demonstration the "psychic" apparently bent a key by concentrating on it; in the second demonstration he supposedly bent a spoon simply by rubbing it.

After they watched the film, witnesses were asked to rate the "paranormal" content of the demonstrations and complete a set of recall questions. Wiseman and Morris wanted to discover if, as Richard Hodgson and Dingwall had suggested, sheep really did tend to misremember those parts of the demonstrations that were central to solving the tricks. For this reason, half of the questions concerned the methods used to fake the phenomena. For example, the psychic faked the key-bending demonstration by secretly switching the straight key for a pre-bent duplicate by passing the straight key from one hand to the other. During the switch the straight key could not be seen. This was clearly central to the trick's method; and one of the "important" questions asked was whether the straight key had always remained in sight. A second set of "unimportant" questions asked about parts of the demonstration that were not related to the tricks' methods. Overall, the results suggested that sheep rated the demonstrations as more "paranormal" than goats did, and that goats did indeed recall significantly more "important" information than sheep. There was no such difference for the recall of the "unimportant" information.[10]

Talking with the Dead

Some people claim that they can communicate with the dead, providing impressive and seemingly accurate information about a person's dead loved ones. They are called psychics (a century ago they were called mediums), and they have gained the respect of many who have come to them in search of messages from the deceased. They have appeared on television programs, published books, and offered seminars to thousands. The most famous among these modern-day mediums were psychics James Van Praagh, Sylvia Browne, and John Edward. Their performances assured many people that their loved ones who "have passed over" are fine and that any unsettled issues of guilt and forgiveness can be resolved.

What is the best explanation for these otherworldly performances in which the psychics appear to be in contact with the dead? Several theories have been proposed. One is that the psychics are getting information about the dead and their loved ones ahead of time (before the performances begin). Another is that the psychics are using telepathy to read the minds of the living to discover facts about the dead. But for simplicity's sake let's narrow the list of theories down to the two leading ones.

Step 1. Here's the psychics' theory.
Theory 1: The psychics are communicating information or messages to and from the disembodied spirits of people who have died. In other words, the psychics are doing exactly what they claim to be doing. They are somehow identifying the appropriate deceased spirit, receiving and decoding transmissions from that spirit, conveying the information to the living, and sending messages back to the dead.

Step 2. The main evidence in support of this theory is the psychics' performance. They typically perform before an audience and talk to audience members who have lost loved ones. The psychics appear to know facts about the dead that they could only know if they were actually communicating with the dead. They also seem to inexplicably know things about members of the audience. Often they also provide incorrect information (such as saying that a member of the audience has lost her mother when in fact the mother is very much alive). But their "hits" (times when they produce correct information) occur often enough and seem to be specific enough to impress.

Psychics have rarely been tested scientifically. The few experiments conducted to date have been severely criticized for sloppy methodology. So there is no good scientific evidence to support theory 1. Investigators who have seen the psychics' live performances (not just the edited versions of the TV programs) report that the hit rates (the percentage of hits out of the total number of statements or questions) are actually much lower than most people realize. They have found hit rates as low as 5 percent with the highest being well under 50 percent.

The low hit rate, though, may not be apparent on TV shows because misses are often edited out. Psychics tend to explain their misses with ad hoc hypotheses (explanations that cannot be verified).

Step 3. Here's the main alternative to the psychics' theory.

Theory 2: The psychics are doing "cold reading." Cold reading is a very old skill practiced by fortune-tellers, tarot-card readers, and mentalists (performers who pretend to read minds). When done well, cold reading can astonish and appear to be paranormal. In cold reading, the psychic reader surreptitiously acquires information from people (the subjects) by asking them questions, making statements, observing how people behave, and listening to what they say. Good cold readers always give the impression that the information actually comes from some mysterious source such as the spirits of the departed. Anyone can learn to do cold reading. It doesn't require any exotic skills or special powers. All that's needed is the practiced ability to deftly manipulate a conversation to elicit information from the subject.

Note that theory 2 does not say that the cold reading is necessarily done to deliberately deceive an audience. Cold reading can be done either consciously or unconsciously. It's possible for people to do cold reading while believing that they are getting information via their psychic powers.

To get the relevant information (or appear to have it), a psychic reader can use several cold-reading techniques. These include the following.

1. The reader encourages the subject to fill in the blanks.

    READER: I'm sensing something about the face or head or brow.

    SUBJECT: You're right, my father used to have terrible headaches.

    READER: I'm feeling something about money or finances.

    SUBJECT: Yes, my mother always struggled to pay the bills.

2. The reader makes statements with multiple variables so that a hit is very likely.

    READER: I'm feeling that your father was dealing with a lot of frustration, anguish, or anger.

    SUBJECT: Yes, he was always arguing with my brother.

3. The reader makes accurate and obvious inferences from information given by the subject.

    READER: Why was your father in the hospital?

    SUBJECT: He had had a heart attack.

    READER: Yes, he struggled with heart disease for years and had to take heart medication for a long time. You were really worried that he would have another heart attack.

4. The reader asks many questions and treats answers as though they confirmed the reader's insight.

READER: Who was the person who got a divorce?

SUBJECT: That was my daughter. She divorced her husband in 1992.

READER: Because I feel that the divorce was very painful for her, that she was sad and depressed for a while.

5. The reader makes statements that could apply to almost anyone.

READER: I'm sensing something about a cat or a small animal.

SUBJECT: Yes, my mother owned a poodle.

With such cold-reading techniques a reader can appear to read minds. Theory 2 is bolstered by the fact that the psychics' amazing performances can be duplicated by anyone skilled in the use of cold reading. In fact, magicians, mentalists, and other nonpsychic entertainers have used cold-reading techniques to give performances that rival those of the top psychics. Regardless of their authenticity, the performances of Van Praagh, Edward, and other psychics seemed to be indistinguishable from those based on cold reading. The psychics may indeed be communicating with the dead, but they look like they're using cold-reading techniques.

Step 4. Now we can apply the criteria of adequacy to these two competing explanations. Both theories are testable, and neither has yielded any novel predictions. So we must judge the theories in terms of scope, simplicity, and conservatism. And on each of these criteria, theory 2 is clearly superior. Theory 1 explains only the psychics' performances as described earlier, but theory 2 explains these performances plus other kinds of seemingly psychic readings, including tarot-card reading, fortune-telling, mentalist acts, and old-fashioned spiritualist séances. Theory 1, of course, fails the criterion of simplicity because it assumes unknown entities (disembodied spirits with certain abilities) and unknown processes (communication to and from the dead). Theory 2 makes no such assumptions. Finally, theory 1 is not conservative. It conflicts with everything we know about death, the mind, and communication. Theory 2, though, fits with existing knowledge just fine.

Here are these judgments in table form:

Criteria	Theory 1	Theory 2
Testable	Yes	Yes
Fruitful	No	No
Scope	No	Yes
Simple	No	Yes
Conservative	No	Yes

We must conclude that theory 1 is a seriously defective theory. It is unlikely to be true. Theory 2, however, is strong. It is not only superior to theory 1, but it is also a better explanation than other competing theories we haven't discussed in that it can explain most or all of the psychics' hits. If the cold-reading theory really is better than all these others, then we have good reasons to believe that Van Praagh, Edward, and other psychics performed their amazing feats through simple cold reading.

 EXERCISES

Exercises marked with * have answers in "Answers to Exercises" (Appendix A).

Exercise 9.1

1. How does science differ from technology?
2. What is the scientific method?
3. Can science be identified with a particular worldview?
4. According to the text, what is scientism?
5. According to the text, why is science such a reliable way of knowing?
*6. What are the five steps of the scientific method?
7. Can hypotheses be generated through induction? Why or why not?
8. What does it mean to derive a test implication from a theory?
*9. What is the conditional argument reflecting the fact that a theory is disconfirmed?
10. What is the conditional argument reflecting the fact that a theory is confirmed?
11. Can theories be conclusively confirmed? Why or why not?
*12. Can theories be conclusively disconfirmed? Why or why not?
13. According to the text, is creationism as good a scientific theory as evolution? Why or why not?

Exercise 9.2

For each of the following phenomena, devise a hypothesis to explain it and derive a test implication to test the hypothesis.

1. In a recent study of scientific literacy, women performed better than men in understanding the scientific process and in answering questions about basic scientific facts and concepts.
*2. Jamal found giant footprints in his backyard and mysterious tufts of brown fur clinging to bushes in the area. Rumors persist that Bigfoot, the giant primate unknown to science, is frequenting the area. Two guys living nearby also claim to be perpetrating a hoax about the existence of the creature.

3. A man with a gun entered a mall in Chicago and began shooting randomly at shoppers, shouting something about demons using his body to commit horrible acts.

4. For years after the tragedy of September 11, 2001, there were no major terrorist attacks in the United States.

5. The CIA reviewed the president's State of the Union speech before he made it and verified that the intelligence information in the speech was correct. Later it was found that some of the information was erroneous and based on dubious sources.

*6. Weight trainers swear that the supplement creatine dramatically increases their performance.

7. Many people who take B vitamins for their headaches report a lower incidence of headaches.

8. Recent research confirms a link between diets high in saturated fat and a higher risk of coronary artery disease.

9. When John got home, he found that the lock on his door had been broken and his color TV was missing.

10. The economic gap between the very rich and the very poor widened considerably in 2014.

Exercise 9.3

Using your background knowledge and any other information you may have about the subject, devise a competing theory for each of the following and then apply the criteria of adequacy to both of them—that is, ascertain how well each theory does in relation to its competitor on the criteria of testability, fruitfulness, scope, simplicity, and conservatism.

1. Phenomenon: People report feeling less pain after trying acupuncture.
   Theory: Treatment with acupuncture needles can alleviate pain.

2. Phenomenon: In the United States in 2014, a few people contracted the Ebola virus even though none of them had traveled recently to places in Africa known to be the source of the virus.
   Theory: The virus was carried from Africa to the United States by trade winds in the Atlantic Ocean.

*3. Phenomenon: The unexpected melting of massive chunks of the world's glaciers.
   Theory: Local climate changes.

4. Phenomenon: A rare species of fungus grows in only one place in the world—the wing tips of a beetle that inhabits caves in France.
   Theory: Evolution.

5. Phenomenon: As the job market worsens, blacks lose jobs faster than whites.
   Theory: Racial prejudice.

6. Phenomenon: The psychic was able to recount a number of personal details about a recently deceased person he never met.
   Theory: Psychic ability.

*7. Phenomenon: Almost all of the terrorist attacks in the world in the past five years have been perpetrated by religious fanatics.
   Theory: Religion fosters terrorism.

8. Phenomenon: Twenty patients with severe arthritis pain were prayed for by fifty people, and fourteen out of those twenty reported a significant lessening of pain.
   Theory: Prayer heals.

9. Phenomenon: Over the past year, two terminally ill cancer patients in Broderick Hospital were found to be cancer-free.
   Theory: Treatment with a new type of chemotherapy works.

10. Phenomenon: Air pollution levels in San Francisco are at their highest levels in years.
   Theory: Increased numbers of SUVs being driven in the San Francisco area.

Exercise 9.4

For each of the following theories, derive a test implication and indicate whether you believe that such a test would likely confirm or disconfirm the theory.

1. Elise has the power to move physical objects with her mind alone.
*2. Ever since the city installed brighter street lights, the crime rate has been declining steadily.
3. The Ultra-Sonic 2000 pest-control device can rid a house of roaches by emitting a particular sound frequency that humans can't hear.
4. The Dodge Intrepid is a more fuel-efficient car than any other on the road.
5. Practitioners of transcendental meditation (TM) can levitate—actually ascend unaided off the ground without physical means of propulsion.
*6. Eating foods high in fat contributes more to overweight than eating foods high in carbohydrates.
7. Lemmings often commit mass suicide.
8. The English sparrow will build nests only in trees.

Exercise 9.5

Read the following passages and answer the following questions for each one:

1. What is the phenomenon being explained?
2. What theories are advanced to explain the phenomenon? (Some theories may be unstated.)
3. Which theory seems the most plausible and why? (Use the criteria of adequacy.)

4. Regarding the most credible theory, is there a test implication mentioned? If so, what is it? If not, what would be a good test implication for the theory?
5. What test results would convince you to change your mind about your preferred theory?

PASSAGE 1

"In the past several years, a researcher named David Oates has been advocating his discovery of a most interesting phenomenon. Oates claims that backward messages are hidden unintentionally in all human speech. The messages can be understood by recording normal speech and playing it in reverse. . . . [According to Oates] 'Any thought, any emotion, any motive that any person has can appear backwards in human speech. The implications are mind boggling because reverse speech opens up the Truth.'. . . To our knowledge there is not one empirical investigation of reverse speech in any peer-reviewed journal. If reverse speech did exist it would be, at the very least, a noteworthy scientific discovery. However, there are no data to support the existence of reverse speech or Oates's theories about its implications."[11]

PASSAGE 2

"Michael Behe, a Lehigh University biochemist, claims that a light-sensitive cell, for example, couldn't have arisen through evolution because it is 'irreducibly complex.' Unlike the scientific creationists, however, he doesn't deny that the universe is billions of years old. Nor does he deny that evolution has occurred. He only denies that every biological system arose through natural selection.

"Behe's favorite example of an irreducibly complex mechanism is a mouse trap. A mouse trap consists of five parts: (1) a wooden platform, (2) a metal hammer, (3) a spring, (4) a catch, and (5) a metal bar that holds the hammer down when the trap is set. What makes this mechanism irreducibly complex is that if any one of the parts were removed, it would no longer work. Behe claims that many biological systems, such as cilia, vision, and blood clotting, are also irreducibly complex because each of these systems would cease to function if any of their parts were removed.

"Irreducibly complex biochemical systems pose a problem for evolutionary theory because it seems that they could not have arisen through natural selection. A trait such as vision can improve an organism's ability to survive only if it works. And it works only if all the parts of the visual system are present. So, Behe concludes, vision couldn't have arisen through slight modifications of a previous system. It must have been created all at once by some intelligent designer. . . .

"Most biologists do not believe that Behe's argument is sound, however, because they reject the notion that the parts of an irreducibly complex system could not have evolved independently of that system. As Nobel

Prize–winning biologist H. J. Muller noted in 1939, a genetic sequence that is, at first, inessential to a system may later become essential to it. Biologist H. Allen Orr describes the processes as follows: 'Some part (A) initially does some job (and not very well, perhaps). Another part (B) later gets added because it helps A. This new part isn't essential, it merely improves things. But later on A (or something else) may change in such a way that B now becomes indispensable.' For example, air bladders—primitive lungs—made it possible for certain fish to acquire new sources of food. But the air bladders were not necessary to the survival of the fish. As the fish acquired additional features, however, such as legs and arms, lungs became essential. So, contrary to what Behe would have us believe, the parts of an irreducibly complex system need not have come into existence all at once."[12]

PASSAGE 3

"A Ouija board is used in divination and spiritualism. The board usually has the letters of the alphabet inscribed on it, along with words such as 'yes,' 'no,' 'goodbye' and 'maybe.' A planchette (a slidable 3-legged device) or pointer of some sort is manipulated by those using the board. The users ask the board a question and together or one of them singly moves the pointer or the board until a letter is 'selected' by the pointer. The selections 'spell' out an answer to the question asked.

"Some users believe that paranormal or supernatural forces are at work in spelling out Ouija board answers. Skeptics believe that those using the board either consciously or unconsciously select what is read. To prove this, simply try it blindfolded for some time, having an innocent bystander take notes on what letters are selected. Usually, the result will be unintelligible nonsense.

"The movement of the planchette is not due to paranormal forces but to unnoticeable movements by those controlling the pointer, known as the *ideo-motor* effect. The same kind of unnoticeable movement is at work in dowsing.

"The Ouija board was first introduced to the American public in 1890 as a parlor game sold in novelty shops."[13]

 Self-Assessment Quiz

Answers appear in "Answers to Self-Assessment Quizzes" in Appendix B.

1. What is a test implication?
2. Are hypotheses generated purely through induction? Why or why not?
3. When a test implication is disconfirmed, what conditional argument is exemplified?
4. When a test implication is confirmed, what conditional argument is exemplified?

5. Why can't scientific hypotheses be conclusively confirmed?
6. Why can't scientific hypotheses be conclusively disconfirmed?

For each of the following phenomena, devise a hypothesis to explain it and derive a test implication to test the hypothesis.

7. Automobile accidents on Blind Man's Curve have increased lately, especially since the street light was broken and not replaced.
8. Juan was found two hours after the fatal stabbing, sitting in Central Park with blood on his shirt.
9. Mysterious lights appeared in the night sky. They looked like alien spacecraft.

For each of the following phenomena, indicate (1) a possible hypothesis to explain it, (2) a possible competing hypothesis, (3) a test implication for each hypothesis, and (4) what testing results would confirm and disconfirm the hypothesis.

10. While camping in the state park, Maria came down with a gastrointestinal illness.
11. The students who were put in a class with two teachers instead of one showed an improvement in their grades.
12. Public health officials report a significant increase in levels of stress in people who live or work in New York City.
13. Since the Vaughn family started using Super Cold-Stopper With Beta-Carotene they have suffered 50 percent fewer colds.

For each of the following hypotheses, specify a test implication and indicate what evidence would convince you to accept the hypothesis.

14. Esther stole the book from the library.
15. Most people—both white and black—are economically better off now than their parents were thirty years ago.
16. The health care system in this country is worse now than it was when Barack Obama was president.

Each of the theories that follow is offered to explain why an astrological reading by a famous astrologer turned out to be wildly inaccurate. Based on a person's horoscope, he had predicted that the person was a nice man who could work with other people very well. The person turned out to be Josef Mengele, the Nazi mass murderer. Indicate which theory (a) lacks simplicity, (b) is not conservative, (c) is untestable, and (d) has the most scope. (Some theories may merit more than one of these designations.)

17. Theory: Astrology—the notion that the position of the stars and planets at your birth controls your destiny—has no basis in fact.
18. Theory: Astrology works, but the astrologer read the horoscope wrong.
19. Theory: An unknown planetary force interfered with the astrological factors that normally determine a person's destiny.

Evaluate the following theory using the TEST formula. Indicate what phenomenon is being explained. Use your background knowledge to assess the evidence. Specify one alternative theory, use the criteria of adequacy to assess the two theories, and determine which one is more plausible.

20. Joseph has acted strangely for years—always wearing black clothes and sometimes having seizures in public. He's possessed.

 ## Writing Assignments

1. In a two-page essay evaluate the following theories using the TEST formula:
   a. **Phenomenon:** People report feeling less arthritis pain after taking fish oil capsules.
      Theory 1: Fish oil relieves joint pain.
      Theory 2: The placebo effect.
   b. **Phenomenon:** A temporary drop in the crime rate in Des Moines, Iowa, just after a transcendental meditation (TM) group meditated for three days on a lower crime rate.
      Theory 1: TM meditation lowers crime rates.
      Theory 2: Normal fluctuations in Des Moines crime rate.
   c. **Phenomenon:** Fifty patients with severe arthritis pain were prayed for by one hundred people, and twenty-five out of those fifty patients reported a significant lessening of pain.
      Theory 1: Prayer heals.
      Theory 2: Normal pain remission that is characteristic of arthritis.

2. Devise two theories to explain the low test scores of most of the students in your calculus course, and then write a two-page paper evaluating the worth of the two theories.

3. Do Internet research on conspiracy theories concerning the September 11, 2001, attack on the United States. They posit explanations of why or how the attack happened—explanations that are usually shockingly different from the explanations accepted by most Americans. Select one of these alternative theories and compare it to the prevailing standard explanation. Using the TEST formula, decide which theory is more plausible.

Fallacies and Persuaders

A N ARGUMENT IS MEANT TO PROVE A POINT—TO PROVIDE GOOD REASONS FOR accepting a claim. As you know, sometimes an argument succeeds, and sometimes it doesn't. When it doesn't, the problem will be that the premises are false, the reasoning is faulty, or both. In any case, the argument is defective, bad, or bogus—call it what you will. There are countless ways that an argument can be defective. But there are certain types of defective arguments that recur so frequently that they have names (given to them, in many cases, by ancient philosophers or medieval scholars) and are usually gathered into critical thinking texts so students can become aware of them. Such common, flawed arguments are known as fallacies, and they are therefore said to be fallacious.

Fallacies are often beguiling; they can *seem* plausible. Time and again they are *psychologically* persuasive, though *logically* impotent. The primary motivation for studying fallacies, then, is to be able to detect them so you're not taken in by them.

We can divide fallacies into two broad categories: (1) those that have irrelevant premises and (2) those that have unacceptable premises.[1] Irrelevant premises have no bearing on the truth of the conclusion. An argument may seem to offer reasons for accepting the conclusion, but the "reasons" have nothing to do with the conclusion. Unacceptable premises are relevant to the conclusion but are nonetheless dubious in some way. An argument may have premises that pertain to the conclusion, but they do not adequately support it. Premises can be unacceptable because they are as dubious as the claim they're intended to support, because the evidence they offer is too weak to adequately support the conclusion, or because they're otherwise so defective that they provide no support at all.

Alas, critical thinking is undone by more than just fallacies. It is easily weakened or wrecked by subtler means—by rhetoric, the use of nonargumentative,

219

emotive words and phrases to persuade or influence an audience. Arguments try to persuade through logic and reasons, but rhetoric tries to persuade primarily through the artful use of emotion-laden language. Fallacies at least have the semblance of arguments, but rhetorical devices are nonargument persuaders. There's nothing inherently wrong with using rhetoric. Its use can become worrisome, though, when there's an attempt to persuade or coerce through rhetoric alone.

In this chapter we examine numerous fallacies of both types as well as some of the more popular rhetorical ploys. Once again the key to immunizing yourself against manipulation by fallacies or rhetoric is practice in identifying the species and subspecies when you see them.

Fallacies: Irrelevant Premises

Genetic Fallacy

The term **genetic fallacy** has both a general and specific meaning. In the general sense—that is, when it applies to arguments that a claim is true or false solely because of its origin—it refers to nonhuman and abstract origins (such as a group of people or a piece of writing) as well as to particular individuals (such as John Smith). But to avoid confusion, it's best to restrict *genetic fallacy* to nonhuman and abstract origins, and to use the terms *appeal to the person* or *ad hominem* (discussed later) to refer to individual persons.

So the following are examples of the genetic fallacy (restricted sense):

You can safely dismiss that alternative energy plan. It's the brainchild of a liberal think tank in Washington.

We should reject that proposal for solving the current Social Security mess. It comes straight from the Republican Party.

Russell's idea about tax hikes for the middle class came to him in a dream, so it must be bunk.

These arguments fail because they reject a claim based solely on where it comes from, not on its merits. In most cases, the source of an idea is irrelevant to its truth. Good ideas can come from questionable sources. Bad ideas can come from impeccable sources. Generally, judging a claim only by its source is a recipe for error.

Composition

The fallacy of **composition** is arguing that what is true of the parts must be true of the whole. The error here is thinking that the characteristics of the parts are some-how transferred to the whole, something that is not always the case. Likewise, the error is committed whenever we assume that what's true of a member of a group is true of the group as a whole. For example,

> *The atoms that make up the human body are invisible. Therefore, the human body is invisible.*
>
> *Each member of the club is productive and effective. So the club will be productive and effective.*
>
> *Each note in the song sounds great. Therefore, the whole song will sound great.*
>
> *Every part of this motorcycle is lightweight; therefore, the whole motorcycle is lightweight.*

Sometimes, of course, the parts do share the same characteristics as the whole. We may safely conclude that since all the parts of the house are made of wood, the house itself is made of wood. We commit the fallacy of composition, though, when we assume that a particular case must be like this.

The fallacy of composition often shows up in statistical arguments. Consider:

> *The average small investor puts $2,000 into the stock market every year. The average large investor puts $100,000 into stocks each year. Therefore, the group of large investors as a whole invests more money in the stock market than the small-investor group does.*

Just because the average small investor invests less than the average large investor does not mean that small investors as a group invest less than large investors as a group. After all, there may be many more small investors than large investors.

Division

The flip side of the fallacy of composition is the fallacy of **division**—arguing that what is true of the whole must be true of the parts. The fallacy is also committed when we assume that what is true of a group is true of individuals in the group.

> *This machine is heavy. Therefore, all the parts of this machine are heavy.*
>
> *Since the committee is a powerful force in Washington politics, each member of the committee is a powerful force in Washington politics.*
>
> *University students study every conceivable subject. So that university student over there also studies every conceivable subject.*

These arguments are fallacious because they assume that characteristics of the whole must transfer to the parts or that traits of the group must be the same as traits of individuals in the group.

Like the fallacy of composition, the fallacy of division is frequently used in statistical arguments:

> *The average SAT test score of seniors [as a group] is higher than the average SAT score of sophomores. Therefore, this senior's test score must be higher than the score of that sophomore.*

Just because the average score for seniors is higher than the average score for sophomores doesn't mean that any individual senior must have a higher score than any sophomore. The scores of individuals, which make up the average, may vary greatly.

Appeal to the Person

The fallacy of **appeal to the person** (or **ad hominem**, meaning "to the man") is rejecting a claim by criticizing the person who makes it rather than the claim itself. For example:

> *Jones has argued for a ban on government-sanctioned prayer in schools and at school-sponsored events. But he's a rabid atheist without morals of any kind. Anything he has to say on the issue is bound to be a perversion of the truth.*

> *We should reject Chen's argument for life on other planets. He dabbles in the paranormal.*

> *You can't believe anything Morris says about welfare reform. He's a bleeding-heart liberal.*

Such arguments are fallacious because they attempt to discredit a claim by appealing to something that's almost always irrelevant to it: a person's character, motives, or personal circumstances. Claims must be judged on their own merits; they are not guilty by association. We are never justified in rejecting a claim because of a person's faults unless we can show how a person's faults translate into faults in the claim—and this is almost never the case. Even when a person's character is relevant to the truth of claims (as when we must consider the merits of testimonial evidence), we are not justified in believing a claim false just because the person's character is dubious. If the person's character is dubious, we are left with no reason to think the claim either true *or* false

The fallacy of appeal to the person comes in several varieties. One is the personal attack, often simply consisting of insults. The gist is familiar enough: Reject X's claims, ideas, or theories because X is a radical, reactionary, extremist, right-winger, left-winger, fool, bonehead, moron, nutbar, or scum of the earth. Whatever psychological impact such terms of abuse may have, logically they carry no weight at all.

Another form of this fallacy emphasizes not a person's character but his or her circumstances. Here someone making a claim is accused of inconsistency—specifically, of maintaining a view that is inconsistent with his or her previous views or social or political commitments.

> *Edgar asserts that evolution is true, but he's an ordained minister in a fundamentalist church that has taken a firm stand against evolution. So he can't accept this theory; he must reject it.*

> *Madison says she's opposed to abortion, but you can't take her seriously. Her view goes against everything her party stands for.*

These arguments are fallacious if they're implying that a claim must be true (or false) just because it's inconsistent with some aspect of the claimant's circumstances. The circumstances are irrelevant to the truth of the claim.

When such arguments are put forth as charges of hypocrisy, we get another ad hominem fallacy known as *tu quoque* (or "you're another"). The fallacious reasoning goes like this: Ellen claims that X, but Ellen doesn't practice/live by/ condone X herself—so X is false. Look:

> *Alice, the town liberal, tells us that we shouldn't drive SUVs because the cars use too much gas and are bad for the environment. But she drives an SUV herself. What a hypocrite! I think we can safely reject her stupid pronouncements.*

But whether someone is hypocritical regarding their claims can have no bearing on the truth of those claims. We may, of course, condemn someone for hypocrisy, but we logically cannot use that hypocrisy as a justification for rejecting her views. Her views must stand or fall on their own merits.

In another variation of circumstantial ad hominem reasoning, someone might deduce that a claim is false because the person making it, given his or her circumstances, would be expected to make it. For example:

> *Wilson claims that the political system in Cuba is exemplary. But he has to say that. He's a card-carrying communist. So forget what he says.*

But whether Wilson is a communist, and whether he would be expected or required to have certain views because of his connection to communism, is irrelevant to the truth of his claim.

Finally, we have the ad hominem tactic known as "poisoning the well." In this one, someone argues like this: X has no regard for the truth or has nonrational motives for espousing a claim, so nothing that X says should be believed— including the claim in question. The idea is that just as you can't get safe water out of a poisoned well, you can't get reliable claims out of a discredited claimant. This tack is fallacious because the fact that someone might have dubious reasons for making a claim does not show that the claim is false, nor does it mean that everything that comes out of the "poisoned well" can be automatically dismissed.

Equivocation

The fallacy of **equivocation** is the use of a word in two different senses in an argument. For example:

> *The end of everything is its perfection.*
> *The end of life is death.*
> *Therefore, death is the perfection of life.*

> *Only man is rational.*
> *No woman is a man.*
> *Therefore, no woman is rational.*

> *Laws can only be created by law-givers.*
> *There are many laws of nature.*
> *Therefore, there must be a Law-Giver, namely, God.*

In the first argument, *end* is used in two different senses. In the first premise it means purpose, but in the second it means termination. Because of this flip-flop in meanings, the conclusion doesn't follow from the premises—but it looks as if it should.

In the second argument, *man* is the equivocal term. In the first premise it means humankind, but in the second, male. So the conclusion doesn't follow, making it appear that a sound argument has banished women's rationality.

In the third argument, *laws* is used in two senses—rules of human behavior in the first premise, regularities of nature (as in "law of gravity") in the second. Consequently, the conclusion trying to establish the existence of God doesn't follow.

The fallacy of equivocation occurs whenever a word has one meaning in one premise and another meaning in another premise or the conclusion. This switch of senses always invalidates the argument.

Appeal to Popularity

The fallacy of the **appeal to popularity** (or to the masses) is arguing that a claim must be true merely because a substantial number of people believe it. The basic pattern of this fallacy is "Everyone (or almost everyone, most people, many people) believes X, so X must be true." For example:

> *Most people approve of the government's new security measures, even though innocent people's privacy is sometimes violated. So I guess the measures must be okay.*

> *Of course the war is justified. Everyone believes that it's justified.*

> *The vast majority of Americans believe that there's a supreme being, so how could you doubt it?*

These arguments are fallacious because they assume that a proposition is true merely because a great number of people believe it. But as far as the truth of a claim is concerned, what many people believe is irrelevant. Many people used to believe that certain women were witches and should be burned, that slavery was perfectly acceptable, that Earth was the center of the universe, and that bleeding and purging were cures for just about every ill. Large groups of people are no more infallible than an individual is. Their belief in a proposition, by itself, is no indication of truth.

What many other people believe, however, can be an indication of truth if they are experts or have expert knowledge in the issue at hand. If almost all farmers say that the fall harvest will be abundant, ordinarily we should believe them.

Appeal to Tradition

The **appeal to tradition** is arguing that a claim must be true just because it's part of a tradition. For example:

> *Acupuncture has been used for a thousand years in China. It must work.*

> *Of course publishing pornography is wrong. In this community there's a tradition of condemning it that goes back fifty years.*

Such appeals are fallacious because tradition, like the masses, can be wrong. Remember that an established tradition barred women from voting, stripped African Americans of their civil rights, promoted the vengeful policy of "an eye for an eye," and sanctioned the sacrifice of innocents to the gods.

Be careful, though. Automatically rejecting a claim because it's traditional is not reasonable either. The point is that a tradition should be neither accepted nor rejected without good reason. Kneejerk acceptance of tradition is as bad as kneejerk rejection.

Appeal to Ignorance

The **appeal to ignorance** is arguing that a lack of evidence proves something. In one type of this fallacy, the problem arises by thinking that a claim must be true because it hasn't been shown to be false. For example:

> *No one has shown that ghosts aren't real, so they must be real.*

> *It's clear that God exists because science hasn't proved that he doesn't exist.*

> *You can't disprove my theory that JFK was killed by LBJ. Therefore, my theory is correct.*

The problem here is that a lack of evidence is supposed to prove something—but it can't. A lack of evidence alone can neither prove nor disprove a proposition. A lack of evidence simply reveals our ignorance about something.

In another variation of this fallacy, the breakdown in logic comes when you argue that a claim must be false because it hasn't been proved to be true. Look at these:

> No one has shown that ghosts are real, so they must not exist.

> It's clear that God doesn't exist because science hasn't proved that he does.

> You can't prove your theory that JFK was killed by LBJ. Therefore, your theory is false.

Again, the moral is: Lack of evidence proves nothing. It does not give us a reason for believing a claim.

But what if our moral was wrong? If we could prove something with a lack of evidence, we could prove almost anything. You can't prove that invisible men aren't having a keg party on Mars—does this mean that it's true that invisible men are having a keg party on Mars? You can't prove that Socrates belched at his famous trial—does this prove that he didn't belch?

There are cases, however, that may seem like appeals to ignorance but actually are not. Sometimes when we carefully search for something, and such a thorough search is likely to uncover it if there is anything to uncover, the failure to find what we're looking for can show that it probably isn't there. A botanist, for example, may scan a forest looking for a rare plant but not find it even though she looks in all the likely places. In this case, her lack of evidence—her not finding the plant after a thorough search—may be good evidence that the plant doesn't exist in that environment. This conclusion would not rest on ignorance, but on the knowledge that in these circumstances any thorough search would probably reveal the sought-after object if it was there at all.

This kind of inductive reasoning is widespread in science. Drugs, for example, are tested for toxicity on rodents or other animals before the drugs are given to humans. If after extensive testing no toxic effects are observed in the animals (which are supposed to be relevantly similar to humans), the lack of toxicity is considered evidence that the drug will probably not cause toxic effects in humans. Likewise, in the realm of extraordinary claims, some scientists regard the failure to find the Loch Ness monster or Bigfoot after decades of searching to be evidence that these creatures do not exist.

Appeals to ignorance involve the notion of **burden of proof**. Burden of proof is the weight of evidence or argument required by one side in a debate or disagreement (in the critical thinking sense). Problems arise when the burden of proof is placed on the wrong side. For example, if Louise declares that "no one has shown that gremlins aren't real, so they must be real," she implicitly puts the burden of proof on those who don't agree with her. She's asserting, in effect, "I say that gremlins are real, and it's up to you to prove I'm wrong." Or to put it another way, "I'm entitled to believe that gremlins are real unless you prove that they're not." But as we saw earlier, this line is just an appeal to ignorance, and the burden of proof for showing that gremlins are real rests with *her*—not with those who don't share her belief. If her claim is unsupported, you need not accept it. If you take the bait and try to prove that gremlins don't exist, you are accepting a burden of proof that should fall on Louise's shoulders, not yours.

Usually, the burden of proof rests on the side that makes a positive claim—an assertion that something exists or is the case, rather than that something does not exist or is not the case. So in general, if a person (the claimant) makes an unsupported positive claim, he or she must provide evidence for it if the claim is to be accepted. If you doubt the claim, you are under no obligation to prove it wrong. You need not—and should not—accept it without good reasons (which the claimant should provide). Of course, you also should not reject the claim without good reasons. If the claimant does provide you with reasons for accepting the claim, you can either accept them or reject them. If you reject them, you are obligated to explain the reasons for your rejection.

 CAN YOU PROVE A NEGATIVE?

As you might imagine, appeals to ignorance can result in strange (and frustrating) conversations.

> ALICE: Unicorns exist!
>
> YOU: Oh, yeah, can you prove they exist?
>
> ALICE: Can you prove they don't?

Can you prove that unicorns don't exist? If not, does that prove that they do exist?

Alice's appeal to ignorance, of course, does not prove that unicorns exist. (The proper response to her unsupported claim is to point out that the claim is unsupported and that you therefore have been offered no good reason to believe it.) Moreover, her demand for proof that unicorns don't exist is unfair because she is asking you to do the impossible. She is asking you to *prove a universal negative*—a claim that nothing of a certain kind exists. To prove that unicorns do not exist, you would have to search throughout all space and time. But no one can do that. So her request is unreasonable.

It is possible, however, to prove a more limited negative claim, such as "There are no baseballs on this table." Some limited negative claims are very difficult to prove, but not impossible—such as "There are no Chevrolet trucks in this state."

Appeal to Emotion

The fallacy of the **appeal to emotion** is the use of emotions as premises in an argument. That is, it consists of trying to persuade someone of a conclusion solely by arousing his or her feelings rather than presenting relevant reasons. When you use this fallacy, you appeal to people's guilt, anger, pity, fear, compassion, resentment, pride—but not to good reasons that could give logical support to your case. Take a look:

> *You should hire me for this network analyst position. I'm the best person for the job. If I don't get a job soon my wife will leave me, and I won't have enough money to pay for my mother's heart operation. Come on, give me a break.*
>
> *Political ad: If school music programs are cut as part of the new district budget, we will save money—and lose our children to a world without music, a landscape without song. Let the children sing. Vote no on Proposition 13.*

As arguments, these passages are fallacious not just because they appeal to strong emotions, but because they appeal to almost *nothing but* strong emotions. They urge us to accept a conclusion but offer no good reasons for doing so. We may feel compassion for the job hunter and his mother, but those feelings have no bearing on whether he is truly the best person for the job. We may recoil from the idea of children in a stark, tuneless world, but that overblown image and the emotions it evokes in us provide no logical support for the conclusion.

Good writers often combine arguments with emotional persuasion in the same piece of writing, and no fallacy need enter the picture. A strong argument is presented, and it's reinforced by strong feelings. Consider this piece of persuasive prose:

> I am a mother though my child is dead. He did not die of an incurable disease, of a virus beyond the ken of medical science. He was not taken from me by a foreign enemy while defending his country. No, he was needlessly slaughtered on the highway. A drunk driver ran broadside into his motorcycle. My son was shot fifty feet through the air by the collision and hit the blacktop at forty-five miles per hour.
>
> My son's assassin is not yet out of high school and yet that boy was able to walk into a liquor store and purchase two six packs of beer, most of which he drank that evening. This boy does not have the mental capability to graduate from high school in the prescribed time (he was held back in his senior year), and yet the law has given him the right to purchase alcohol and decide for himself what is appropriate behavior with regard to alcoholic consumption. I do not trust most of my adult friends to make such mature judgments. How can anyone trust the eighteen-year-old?
>
> The law must change. Statistics have shown that states which have a minimum drinking age of twenty-one years also have significantly fewer

automobile accidents caused by drunken teenagers. I lost my son, but why do any of the rest of us have to suffer as I have? Please, support legislation to increase the drinking age to twenty-one.[2]

This passage evokes sympathy and indignation—but also gives an argument using statistics to support a conclusion about the need for new legislation.

As you would expect, appeals to emotion come in different flavors, some of which are identified by name:

APPEAL TO PITY: the attempt to persuade people to accept a conclusion by evoking their pity, compassion, or empathy. Example: *I should get this merit scholarship. I'm homeless and penniless, so the money would be put to good use.*

APPLE POLISHING: the attempt to persuade people to accept a conclusion by flattering them. Example: *I know you'll vote for me in the upcoming election because you have the true American spirit and the genuine wisdom that comes from faith and hard work.*

SCARE TACTICS: the attempt to persuade people to accept a conclusion by engendering in them an unwarranted fear. Example: *Unless we defeat Proposition 13, the homosexual agenda will be taught in our schools, and more kids will want to become gay.*

Red Herring

Perhaps the most blatant fallacy of irrelevance is the **red herring**, the deliberate raising of an irrelevant issue during an argument. This fallacy gets its name from the practice of dragging a smelly fish across a trail to throw a hunting dog off the scent. The basic pattern is to put forth a claim and then couple it with additional claims that may seem to support it but in fact are mere distractions. For instance:

Every woman should have the right to an abortion on demand. There's no question about it. These anti-abortion activists block the entrances to abortion clinics, threaten abortion doctors, and intimidate anyone who wants to terminate a pregnancy.

The legislators should vote for the three-strikes-and-you're-out crime control measure. I'm telling you, crime is a terrible thing when it happens to you. It causes death, pain, and fear. And I wouldn't want to wish these things on anyone.

Notice what's happening here. In the first example, the issue is whether women should have the right to abortion on demand. But the arguer shifts the subject to the behavior of anti-abortion activists, as though their behavior has some bearing on the original issue. Their behavior, of course, has nothing to do

with the main issue. The argument is bogus. In the second example, the issue is whether the legislators should vote for a three-strikes crime bill. But the subject gets changed to the terrible costs of crime, which is only remotely related to the main issue. (There's also an appeal to fear.) We can all agree that crime can have awful consequences, but this fact has little to do with the merits and demerits of enacting a three-strikes law.

Straw Man

Related to red herring is the fallacy of the **straw man**—the distorting, weakening, or oversimplifying of someone's position so it can be more easily attacked or refuted. A straw-man argument works like this: Reinterpret claim X so that it becomes the weak or absurd claim Y. Attack claim Y. Conclude that X is unfounded. For example:

> *David says that he's opposed to the new sodomy laws that make it illegal for consenting adult homosexuals to engage in sex acts in their own homes. Obviously he thinks that gay sex is something special and should be protected so it's allowed to take place just about anywhere. Do you want gays having sex all over town in full view of your children? David does, and he's dead wrong.*

> *Senator Jones is opposed to the military spending bill, saying that it's too costly. Why does he always want to slash everything to the bone? He wants a pint-sized military that couldn't fight off a crazed band of terrorists, let alone a rogue nation.*

> *Lawyers for the ACLU have sued to remove the massive Ten Commandments monument from the lobby of the courthouse. As usual, they are as anti-religious as ever. They want to remove every vestige of religion and faith from American life. Don't let them do it. Don't let them win yet another battle in their war to secularize the whole country.*

In the first passage, David is opposed to laws prohibiting sexual activity between consenting, homosexual adults in their own homes. His opponent, however, distorts his view, claiming that David is actually in favor of allowing gay sex virtually anywhere, including in public. David, of course, is not asserting this (few people would). This distorted version of David's position is easy to ridicule and reject, allowing his actual view to be summarily dismissed.

In the second passage, Senator Jones is against the military spending bill on the grounds that it costs too much. His position, though, is twisted into the claim that the military should be pared down so drastically that it would be ineffective even against small groups of terrorists. The senator's views on military spending are thus made to appear extreme or ludicrous. But it is unlikely that Senator Jones (or any other senator) wants to see the US military reduced to such a level. He simply wants a less expensive military—not necessarily an ineffective one.

The third passage is typical of the kind of fallacious arguments that crop up in debates over church-state separation. Here, the ACLU wants a monument displaying the Ten Commandments removed from the lobby of a government building, a view that is characterized as anti-religious. But a request that a religious symbol be removed from a government context is not, in itself, necessarily antireligious. Many have argued, for example, that such requests should be made to protect freedom of religion by preventing the government from giving preferential treatment to one religion over another. Also, wanting to get rid of a religious display on public property is a far cry from wanting to remove "every vestige of religion and faith from American life." Characterizing the ACLU suit as anti-religious, though, is a way to generate strong opposition to it. Note that in church-state debates, the straw-man tack is also used to bolster the other side of the dispute. Those who favor religious displays on government property are sometimes characterized as fanatics who want to turn the government into a theocracy. But, of course, from the fact that people want to allow such a religious display it does not follow that they want anything like a theocracy.

Two Wrongs Make a Right

Two wrongs make a right is a piece of fallacious reasoning that we are all probably guilty of. It is arguing that doing something morally wrong is justified because someone else has done the same (or similar) thing:

> *I have a clear conscience. I stole his laptop because he took mine a month ago.*
>
> *My wife had an affair, so I'm within my rights to have one, too.*
>
> *Okay, I snatched a few of those little Brach candies at the supermarket. So what? Three other people did, too.*

The idea is that someone else's wrong acts can somehow make yours right. But if your action is morally impermissible, someone else's deed cannot make it otherwise. If your action lacks justification, it cannot acquire justification by what someone else does.

That is not to say that justification for your behavior is impossible to obtain. Most ethicists would say that self-defense against other people's injurious actions can be a legitimate reason for your doing something that normally would be wrong. It surely must be permissible, they would argue, to knock down a mugger who is busy trying to knock you down. Likewise, a nation surely must be justified in going to war against a foreign power that first made war against it. And to many, in the name of justice, punishment by the state for criminal acts can also be justified.

But what about "an eye for an eye" justice? Can't we avenge a wrong done to us by someone else—can't we do unto him as he has done to us? In many cultures, the answer is an emphatic *yes*. If a man kills your goat, you are justified in killing his. If a woman steals your coat, you can legitimately steal hers. But most ethicists would probably say *no*: this "eye for an eye" principle (and similar "two wrongs make a right" views) is not justice but personal vengeance, which is immoral.

Fallacies: Unacceptable Premises

Begging the Question

The fallacy of **begging the question** (or arguing in a circle) is the attempt to establish the conclusion of an argument by using that conclusion as a premise. To beg the question is to argue that a proposition is true because the very same proposition supports it:

> *p*
> Therefore, *p*.

The classic question-begging argument goes like this:

> God exists. We know that God exists because the Bible says so, and we should believe what the Bible says because God wrote it.

Or, more formally:

> The Bible says that God exists.
> The Bible is true because God wrote it.
> Therefore, God exists.

This argument assumes at the outset the very proposition ("God exists") that it is trying to prove. Any argument that does this is fallacious.

Unfortunately, most question-begging arguments are not as obviously fallacious as "*p* is true because *p* is true." They may be hard to recognize because they are intricate or confusing. Consider this argument:

It is in every case immoral to lie to someone, even if the lie could save a life. Even in extreme circumstances a lie is still a lie. All lies are immoral because the very act of prevarication in all circumstances is contrary to ethical principles.

At first glance, this argument may seem reasonable, but it's not. It reduces to this circular reasoning: "Lying is always immoral because lying is always immoral."

Among the more subtle examples of question-begging is this famous one, a favorite of critical thinking texts:

To allow every man unbounded freedom of speech must always be, on the whole, advantageous to the state; for it is highly conducive to the interests of the community that each individual should enjoy a liberty, perfectly unlimited, of expressing his sentiments.[3]

This argument, as well as the one preceding it, demonstrates the easiest way to subtly beg the question: Just repeat the conclusion as a premise, but use different words.

False Dilemma

The fallacy of **false dilemma** is asserting that there are only two alternatives to consider when there are actually more than two. For example:

Look, either you support the war or you are a traitor to your country. You don't support the war. So you're a traitor.

This argument contends that there are only two alternatives to choose from: Either you back the war, or you are a traitor. And since you don't back the war, you must be a traitor. But this argument works only if there really are just two alternatives. Actually there are other plausible possibilities here. Maybe you are loyal to your country but don't want to see it get involved in a costly war. Maybe you are a patriot who simply disagrees with your government's rationale for going to war. Because these possibilities are excluded, the argument is fallacious.

Again:

Either those lights you saw in the night sky were alien spacecraft (UFOs), or you were hallucinating. You obviously weren't hallucinating. So they had to be UFOs.

This argument says that there are only two possibilities: The lights were UFOs, or you hallucinated the whole thing. And they must have been UFOs because you weren't hallucinating. But as is the case with the majority of alleged paranormal events, there are many more possible explanations than most people realize. The lights could have been commercial aircraft, military aircraft, meteors, atmospheric conditions, or the planet Venus (which, believe it or not, is often mistaken for a UFO). Since the argument ignores these reasonable possibilities, it's fallacious.

Finally:

> We must legalize drugs. We either legalize them or pay a heavy toll in lives and the taxpayer's money to continue the war on drugs. And we cannot afford to pay such a high price.

At first glance, these two alternatives may seem to exhaust the possibilities. But there is at least one other option—to launch a massive effort to prevent drug use and thereby reduce the demand for illegal drugs. The argument does not work because it fails to consider this possibility.

Note that these three arguments are expressed in disjunctive (either-or) form. But they can just as easily be expressed in a conditional (if-then) form, which says the same thing:

> Look, if you don't support the war, then you are a traitor to your country. You don't support the war. So you're a traitor.

> If those lights you saw in the night sky were not alien spacecraft (UFOs), then you were hallucinating. You obviously weren't hallucinating. So they had to be UFOs.

> We must legalize drugs. If we don't legalize them, then we will pay a heavy toll in lives and the taxpayer's money to continue the war on drugs. And we cannot afford to pay such a high price.

Sometimes we encounter stand-alone disjunctive phrases, rather than full-blown false dilemma arguments. These are false choices often presented as one-liners or headlines in tabloid newspapers, TV news programs, and magazines. For example:

> Syria: Quagmire or Failure?

> Microsoft: Bad Cop or Evil Giant?

> Is the Administration Incompetent or Just Evil?

By limiting the possibilities, these headlines can imply that almost any outlandish state of affairs is actual—without even directly asserting anything. People are often taken in by false dilemmas because they don't think beyond the alternatives laid before them. Out of fear, the need for simple answers, or a failure of imagination, they don't ask, "Is there another possibility?" To ask this is to think outside the box and reduce the likelihood of falling for simplistic answers.

Decision-Point Fallacy

Finally, here's a variation on the false-dilemma ploy that you will encounter sooner or later, if you haven't already: the **decision-point fallacy** (also called the line-drawing fallacy). For the sake of clarity, let's start with a silly example:

Joe lost the hair on his head. When he had a full head of hair and he lost just a hair or two, he clearly was not bald. If we are to say truthfully that he is bald, there must have been a point in the hair-loss process (a decision point) in which he became bald. (Maybe the loss of one more hair was enough to render him bald.) But obviously there is no such point at which we can legitimately decide that Joe went from not being bald to being bald. Therefore, we must infer that Joe did not become bald at all.

And here are two opposing arguments that are far more serious:

The abortion-rights version: *At conception, an embryo is not a person (not an entity with full moral rights, including a right to life). And in the long process of gestation, there is no precise point at which we can definitively say that the fetus has gone from being a nonperson to being a person. Therefore, the fetus does not become a person at any point in gestation—the fetus is simply not a person.*

The right-to-life version: *In the long process of gestation, there is no point at which we can definitively say that the fetus has become a person. People have suggested different points at which personhood arises (at viability, for example), but none of these is plausible. Conception, however, is plausible as the beginning of personhood, for at that instant the embryo receives what will make it fully human—DNA. Therefore, personhood arises at the moment of conception.*

What's wrong with these decision-point arguments? In many processes, there is no decision point, no dynamic moment that suddenly transforms something into something else—and our concepts are fuzzy to reflect this fact. *Bald* and *hairy* are such terms. But none of this means that those concepts don't sometimes apply. Even though we can't say at what point a man becomes bald, we can normally use the word *bald* just fine to accurately describe a man who has hair loss.

The decision-point fallacy would have us assume that there must be a specific transforming point even though no such point exists or needs to exist. It is often an easy assumption to make—and to avoid.

Slippery Slope

The fallacy of **slippery slope** is arguing, without good reasons, that taking a particular step will inevitably lead to a further, undesirable step (or steps). The idea behind the metaphor, of course, is that if you take the first step on a slippery slope, you will have to take others because, well, the slope is slippery. A familiar slippery-slope pattern is "Doing action A will lead to action B, which will lead to action C, which will result in calamitous action D. Therefore, you should not do action A." It's fallacious when there is no good reason to think that doing action A will actually result in undesirable action D. Take a look at this classic example:

> *We absolutely must not lose the war in Vietnam. If South Vietnam falls to the communists, then Thailand will fall to them. If Thailand falls to them, then South Korea will fall to them. And before you know it, all of Southeast Asia will be under communist control.*

This argument was commonplace during the Cold War. It was known as the domino theory because it asserted that if one country in Southeast Asia succumbed to communism, they all would succumb, just as a whole row of dominoes will fall if the first one is pushed over. It was fallacious because there was no good evidence that the dominoes would inevitably fall as predicted. In fact, after South Vietnam was defeated, they did not fall as predicted.

Here are some more examples:

> *If assault rifles are banned in this country, then handguns will be next. Then sporting rifles will be banned. And ultimately all guns will be banned, and our fundamental freedom to own guns will be canceled out altogether. So if assault rifles are banned, we might as well strike the Second Amendment from the Constitution because it will be worthless.*

> *We must ban pornography in all forms. Otherwise, rape and other sex crimes will be as common as jaywalking.*

> *All Americans should be against laws permitting consensual homosexual sex in one's own home. If that kind of thing is allowed, before you know it anything goes—bestiality, prostitution, illegal drug use, and violence.*

These arguments follow the basic slippery-slope pattern. They are fallacies not because they assert that one event or state of affairs can inevitably lead to others, but because there is no good reason to believe the assertions. Some arguments may look like slippery-slope fallacies but are not because there is good reason to think that the steps are connected as described. Observe:

> *If you have Lyme disease, you definitely should get medical treatment. Without treatment, you could develop life-threatening complications. Man, you could die. You should see your doctor now.*

This is not a fallacious slippery-slope argument. There are good reasons to believe that the series of events mentioned would actually happen.

Hasty Generalization

In chapter 2 we pointed out the connection between the availability error and the fallacy known as **hasty generalization**. Here we need only recall that we are guilty of hasty generalization when we draw a conclusion about a whole group based on an inadequate sample of the group. This mistake is a genuine fallacy of unacceptable premises because the premises stating the sample size are relevant to the conclusion, but they provide inadequate evidence. For example:

> *You should buy an iPhone. They're great. I bought one last year, and it has given me nothing but flawless performance.*

> *The only male professor I've had this year was a chauvinist pig. All the male professors at this school must be chauvinist pigs.*

> *Psychology majors are incredibly ignorant about human psychology. Believe me, I know what I'm talking about: My best friend is a psych major. What an ignoramus!*

> *The French are snobby and rude. Remember those two high-and-mighty guys with really bad manners? They're French. I rest my case.*

> *The food at Pappie's Restaurant is awful. I had a sandwich there once, and the bread was stale.*

Persuaders: Rhetorical Moves

Rhetoric presents us with a large repertoire of techniques for influencing hearts and minds through emotion—while proving nothing through reason. Very often rhetorical devices do nothing more than promote a negative (or positive) attitude toward someone or something, but this ploy can be extraordinarily persuasive. Here are a few of the better known examples.

Innuendo

Innuendo is suggesting something denigrating about a person without explicitly stating it. Through innuendo you can indirectly convey the false claim that someone is bad, though you make only true statements. For example:

> *I'm fairly sure that Senator Johnson's youthful indiscretions involving alcohol, marijuana, and crack cocaine probably have no influence on her current public service.*

> *I think we can assume that Mr. Abernathy absolutely does not embezzle—anymore.*

Innuendo was employed in a notorious smear of Senator John McCain in the South Carolina Republican primary in 2000. In a sham telephone survey, voters were asked, "Would you be more or less likely to vote for John McCain if you knew he had fathered an illegitimate black child?"

Euphemisms and Dysphemisms

Euphemisms are words used to convey positive or neutral attitudes or emotions in place of more negative ones; **dysphemisms** are words used to convey negative attitudes or emotions in place of neutral or positive ones. These rhetorical devices work by using the persuasive force of a word's *connotations*, the feelings and attitudes linked to the word's literal meaning. The devices can mislead, obscure, and confuse. To hide the truth, political, economic, or military leaders might use the euphemism *meaningful downturn in aggregate output* for *recession; revenue enhancement* for *tax increase; downsizing* for *firing; armed reconnaissance* for *bombing; neutralize* for *kill; enhanced interrogation methods* for *torture; collateral damage* for *civilian casualties;* or *soft targets* for *people to kill.*

In debates about gun ownership, those who want to restrict gun ownership may characterize their position as "anti-assault weapon." Those opposed to this position may label it as "anti-self-defense." Both these labels are meant to provoke certain attitudes toward the subject matter—attitudes that may not be supported by any evidence or argument.

Consider the disparate impact on the reader of these pairs of terms, both of which refer to the same thing:

full-figured	fat
guerrillas	freedom fighters
resolute	pigheaded
emphatic	pushy
sweat	perspire

But keep in mind that euphemisms often perform a useful social purpose by allowing us to discuss sensitive subjects in an inoffensive way. We may spare people's feelings by saying that their loved ones "have passed" rather than that they "have died," or that their dog "was put to sleep" rather than "killed." Nevertheless, as critical thinkers, we should be on guard against the deceptive use of connotations. As critical writers, we should rely primarily on argument and evidence to make our case.

Stereotyping

A **stereotype** is an unwarranted conclusion or generalization about an entire group of people. To stereotype someone is to judge her not as an individual, but as part of a group whose members are thought to be all alike. We think because she is a member of the group, and we assume without good reason that all the members are rude and arrogant, that she must also be rude and arrogant. We wrongly assume that because all members of _____ (insert name of any political, ethnic, or class group) are _____ (insert name of any negative attribute), the member of that group standing before us also must have that attribute.

By asserting that someone is part of a hated stereotyped group, a speaker or writer can induce others to form a baseless, negative opinion of that person. This slanted opinion in turn can cause people to react dismissively, disdainfully, or angrily to any member of the disparaged group. This is the well-worn path of bigots of all stripes—and a painful indication that critical thinking is needed.

Stereotypes are especially prevalent in politics, where they are often mixed in with dysphemisms, the straw-man fallacy, innuendo, appeal to the person, and other fallacious thinking. A few examples:

We all know that the Democrats are pro-taxes and anti-rich.

All the Republicans want is a free ride for rich people and no entitlements for the less well off.

Don't elect Southerners. They're all anti-government, states-rights fanatics.

Ridicule

Ridicule is the use of derision, sarcasm, laughter, or mockery to disparage a person or idea. Ridicule succeeds when it gets an emotional reaction from you that leads you to dismiss people or their claims for no good reason. Its aim is to put people or beliefs in a ridiculous or absurd light, to make them a laughing-stock. Look:

Trust the New York Times *to report the news fairly? Right, just like I trust the airlines to be always on time.*

You think Fox News is fair and balanced? Ha!

Remember, when ridicule does its work, it makes no appeal to evidence or argument. It may be interesting or amusing, but it gives you no good reason to believe anything. When the credibility of claims is at stake, ridicule is best seen as an emotional trick.

Rhetorical Definitions

One of the more subtle means of persuasion uses **rhetorical definition**. The point of this tactic is not to accurately define but to influence through an emotion-charged skewed definition. Usually we are most interested in what is called a *lexical definition*, which reports the meaning that a term has among those who use the language. For example, among English-speaking people, the word "rain" is used to refer to (or mean) condensed atmospheric moisture falling in drops, which is the lexical definition. A *stipulative definition* reports a meaning that a term is deliberately assigned, often for the sake of convenience or economy of expression. If you assign a meaning to a familiar term or to a term that you invent, you give a stipulative definition. A *précising* definition reports a meaning designed to decrease ambiguity or vagueness. It qualifies an existing term by giving it a more precise definition. Someone, for example, might offer a précising definition for the word "old" (as it applies to the age of humans) by specifying that "old" refers to anyone over eighty. A rhetorical definition, on the other hand, wants to sway you toward particular attitudes or beliefs.

Someone who opposes abortions for any reason, for example, might rhetorically define "abortion" as "the murder of innocent human beings and the rejection of God." Someone who believes that some abortions are morally permissible might define "abortion" as "the termination of a human embryo or fetus."

Now take a look at these politically motivated rhetorical definitions:

Government entitlements should be discontinued. They're just handouts to people who don't want to work.

For conservatives, tax reform means making the rich richer and the middle class poorer.

Gun control is code for "Let's get rid of every gun in America."

Capital punishment is legalized murder.

KEY WORDS

ad hominem	appeal to emotion	appeal to ignorance
appeal to pity	appeal to popularity (or to the masses)	appeal to the person
appeal to tradition	apple polishing	begging the question
burden of proof	composition	decision-point fallacy
division	dysphemism	equivocation
euphemism	false dilemma	genetic fallacy
hasty generalization	innuendo	red herring
rhetorical definition	ridicule	scare tactics
slippery slope	stereotype	straw man
tu quoque	two wrongs make a right	

EXERCISES

Exercises marked with * have answers in "Answers to Exercises" (Appendix A).

Exercise 10.1

1. What are fallacies of irrelevant premises? What makes them irrelevant?
2. What is the genetic fallacy?
3. Can the origin of a claim ever be relevant to deciding its truth or falsity?
*4. What is the fallacy of composition?

5. What are the two forms of the fallacy of division?
6. Why are appeals to the person fallacious?
7. What type of ad hominem argument is put forth as a charge of hypocrisy?
8. What is the fallacy of poisoning the well?
9. What is the fallacy of equivocation?
*10. Why are appeals to popularity fallacious?
11. Why are appeals to tradition fallacious?
12. What are the two forms of the appeal to ignorance?
13. What is the proper response to an appeal to ignorance?
14. What is rhetoric?
*15. According to the text, is it ever legitimate to use rhetoric and argument together?
16. What is the fallacy of red herring?
17. Why is an argument that relies on the straw-man fallacy a bad argument?
18. What is the fallacy of begging the question?
*19. Why are people often taken in by false dilemmas?
20. What is the burden of proof?
21. What is the fallacy of slippery slope? Can the argument used in the slippery-slope fallacy ever be used legitimately? Why or why not?
22. What is the rhetorical device of innuendo?
23. What is the rhetorical device of stereotyping?

Exercise 10.2

In the following passages, identify any fallacies of irrelevance (genetic fallacy, composition, division, appeal to the person, equivocation, appeal to popularity, appeal to tradition, appeal to ignorance, appeal to emotion, red herring, and straw man). Some passages may contain more than one fallacy, and a few may contain no fallacies at all. Also identify any rhetorical devices highlighted in this chapter.

*1. "Seeing that the eye and hand and foot and every one of our members has some obvious function, must we not believe that in like manner a human being has a function over and above these particular functions?" [Aristotle]
2. The federal budget deficits are destroying this country. Just ask any working stiff; he'll tell you.
3. The hippies of the sixties railed against the materialistic, capitalistic system and everyone who prospered in it. But all their bellyaching was crap because they were a bunch of hypocrites, living off their rich mothers and fathers.
4. Anthony argues that capital punishment should be abolished. But why should we listen to him? He's a prisoner on death row right now.

*5. The *New York Times* reported that one-third of Republican senators have been guilty of Senate ethics violations. But you know that's false—the *Times* is a notorious liberal rag.

6. Geraldo says that students who cheat on exams should not automatically be expelled from school. But it's ridiculous to insist that students should never be punished for cheating.

7. Of course the death penalty is a just punishment. It has been used for centuries.

8. My sweater is blue. Therefore, the atoms that make up the sweater are blue.

9. The prime minister is lying about his intelligence briefings since almost everyone surveyed in national polls thinks he's lying.

*10. Kelly says that many women who live in predominantly Muslim countries are discriminated against. But how the heck would she know? She's not a Muslim.

11. A lot of people think that football jocks are stupid and boorish. That's a crock. Anyone who had seen the fantastic game that our team played on Saturday, with three touchdowns before halftime, would not believe such rubbish.

12. Does acupuncture work? Can it cure disease? Of course. It has been used in China by folk practitioners for at least three thousand years.

13. The arguments of right-to-lifers cannot be believed. They're hypocrites who scream about dead babies but then murder abortion doctors.

*14. "The only proof capable of being given that an object is visible, is that people actually see it. The only proof that a sound is audible, is that people hear it: and so of the other sources of our experience. In like manner, I apprehend, the sole evidence it is possible to produce that anything is desirable, is that people actually desire it." [John Stuart Mill]

15. The new StratoCar is the best automobile on the road. Picture the admiring glances you'll get when you take a cruise in your StratoCar through town. Imagine the power and speed!

16. Gremlins exist, that's for sure. No scientist has ever proved that they don't exist.

17. "The most blatant occurrence of recent years is all these knuckleheads running around protesting nuclear power—all these stupid people who do not research at all and who go out and march, pretending they care about the human race, and then go off in their automobiles and kill one another." [Ray Bradbury]

18. Is the theory of evolution true? Yes. Polls show that most people believe in it.

*19. The former mayor was convicted of drug possession, and he spent time in jail. So you can safely ignore anything he has to say about legalizing drugs.

20. I don't believe in heaven and hell because no one—not even scientists— has ever produced proof that they exist.

21. Professor, I deserve a better grade than a D on my paper. Look, my parents just got a divorce. If they see that I got a D, they will just blame each other, and the fighting will start all over again. Give me a break.

22. Only man has morals. No woman is a man. Therefore, no woman has morals.

23. Every player on the team is the best in the league. So the team itself is the best in the league.

*24. Why are Asians so good at math?

25. I'm sure Senator Braxton would never take a large bribe.

*26. Our administration may need to consider trying some form of revenue enhancement.

Exercise 10.3

In the following passages, identify any fallacies of unacceptable premises (begging the question, false dilemma, slippery slope, and hasty generalization). Some passages may contain more than one fallacy, and a few may contain no fallacies at all.

1. Random drug testing in schools is very effective in reducing drug use because the regular use of the testing makes drug use less likely.

2. If today you can make teaching evolution in public schools a crime, then tomorrow you can make it a crime to teach it in private schools. Then you can ban books and other educational materials that mention evolution. And then you can ban the very word from all discourse. And then the anti-science bigots will have won.

3. Three thieves are dividing up the $7,000 they just stole from the First National Bank. Robber number one gives $2,000 to robber number two, $2,000 to robber number three, and $3,000 to himself. Robber number two says, "How come you get $3,000?" Robber number one says, "Because I am the leader." "How come you're the leader?" "Because I have more money."

*4. Either God exists or he does not exist. If he exists, and you believe, you will gain heaven; if he exists and you don't believe, you will lose nothing. If he does not exist, and you believe, you won't lose much. If he does not exist, and you don't believe, you still won't lose much. The best gamble then is to believe.

5. John is now on trial for murder, but the proceedings are a waste of time and money. Everyone knows he's guilty.

*6. I used to work with this engineering major. And, man, they are really socially inept.

7. I met these two guys on a plane, and they said they were from Albuquerque. They were total druggies. Almost everyone in that city must be on drugs.

8. Some people are fools, and some people are married to fools.
9. Bill is an investment banker, drives a Cadillac, is overweight, and votes Republican. John is also an investment banker, drives a Cadillac, and is overweight. So John probably votes Republican, too.
*10. Either we fire this guy or we send a message to other employees that it's okay to be late for work. Clearly, we need to fire him.

Exercise 10.4

For each of the following claims, devise an argument using the fallacy shown in parentheses. Make the argument as persuasive as possible.

1. The federal budget deficit will destroy the economy. (red herring)
2. *The Hunger Games* is the best movie ever made. (appeal to popularity)
*3. Mrs. Anan does not deserve the Nobel Prize. (appeal to the person)
4. Vampires—the blood-sucking phantoms of folklore—are real. (appeal to ignorance)
5. Internet pornography can destroy this country. (slippery slope)
*6. The Boy Scouts of America should allow gay kids to be members. (begging the question)
7. The United States should attack Iran. (false dilemma)
8. That economics seminar is absolutely the worst course offered at the university. (hasty generalization)
9. Pope John Paul II was a moral giant. (appeal to emotion)
10. The Nigerian court was right to sentence that woman to be stoned to death for adultery. (appeal to popularity)
*11. There are too many guns on the streets because our politicians are controlled by the National Rifle Association and other gun nuts. (red herring)
12. All efforts should be made to ban trade in exotic pets such as tigers. (genetic fallacy)

 ## Self-Assessment Quiz

Answers appear in "Answers to Self-Assessment Quizzes" in Appendix B. Identify the fallacies or rhetorical devices in the following passages.

1. "[Howard] Dean has leapt beyond criticizing Bush and is now embracing terrorists. He has called Hamas terrorists 'soldiers in a war' and said the U.S. should not take sides between Israel and Palestinian suicide bombers." [Ann Coulter]
2. You think that welfare mothers would actually prefer to have jobs? Prove it, and until you do they are all lazy moochers.

3. Civil rights legislation was furiously opposed by Dixiecrat Strom Thurmond—which proves that it was reasonable and moral.

4. "[The president] lies about important things like the economy, his tax cuts, his education, our reasons for going to war and drunk driving. But I think he lies only when he feels he has to. He knows that most of the time Fox News, the *Wall Street Journal*, and Rush Limbaugh are only too glad to do it for him." [Al Franken]

5. "Jews are part of the Soviet people. They are a fine people, intelligent, very valued in the Soviet Union. Therefore, the problem for the Jews in the Soviet Union does not exist." [Mikhail Gorbachev]

6. You can safely ignore Helena's argument for the rights of women because she's a member of the National Organization for Women.

7. You advocate a woman's right to abortion because you do not understand how hideous and monstrous an abortion procedure is, how it tears a living fetus away from the uterine wall, crushes it to bleeding pieces, and sucks it away into oblivion.

8. That is a lousy book. It did not sell well at all.

9. All of us cannot be loved because all of us cannot be the focus of deep affection.

10. "If the parts of the Universe are not accidental, how can the whole Universe be considered as the result of chance? Therefore the existence of the Universe is not due to chance." [Moses Maimonides]

11. This administration is either one of the best or one of the worst. It is certainly not one of the best, so we must count it among those at the bottom of the heap.

12. Atheistic philosophers have been trying for thousands of years to prove that there is no God, and they haven't succeeded yet. This shows that there is indeed a God after all.

13. How can you, with a straight face, argue that animals have rights and expect me to believe you? You eat meat!

14. Judges should not hand down anything but maximum sentences for all convicted criminals. If you start making exceptions, prosecutors will start asking for lighter sentences. Next thing you know, every criminal will be getting off with mere warnings.

15. America—love it or leave it!

16. I cannot wait until the *USA Today* columnist starts acting his age and retires. What a waste of editorial space. His op-ed column on Sunday was absolutely stupid.

17. The biggest threat to the Constitution these days is the destroy-all-guns Left.

18. Children were asked to recite the Pledge of Allegiance every day and to include the phrase "under God." That was dead wrong. No child should have to submit to such brainwashing.

19. Ranjit was caught cheating on his final exam. But why should he be punished when a dozen other people cheated last year in the same course?
20. We all know what "abortion rights activists" really means—it means baby killers.

 Writing Assignments

1. Find a magazine or newspaper letter to the editor that contains at least one fallacy. Identify the fallacy and rewrite the passage to eliminate the fallacy and strengthen the argument. (To effectively rework the argument, you may have to make up some facts.)
2. Select an editorials/letters page from a newspaper (it should contain several opinions on various issues). Scan the entire page, circling and labeling any examples of fallacies. Locate at least three examples.
3. Tune into a TV or radio political talk show—preferably one in which you usually find yourself in strong agreement with the opinions expressed— and identify at least three instances of fallacious reasoning.

Critical Thinking in Morality and the Law

W E HAVE COME FAR. WE HAVE SEEN THAT WE CAN PRODUCTIVELY APPLY CRITICAL thinking to everyday claims, arguments, and problems; to explanations in a wide range of subject areas; to scientific theories of all sorts; and to offbeat theories of the paranormal and supernatural kind. Now we can go even further. We can now venture into a vast and complex sphere that is often thought to be off limits to critical reasoning: *morality*. Morality concerns beliefs about right and wrong, good and bad, and just and unjust. It's an aspect of life that we deal with every day because we have little choice. In countless situations we must decide what we ought to do or not do, what is moral or immoral, and what is good or bad. To do these things, we are forced to accept or reject moral statements, make and criticize moral arguments, and wrestle with moral theories.

In this process of contending with moral issues, we inevitably formulate our own moral theory—our own beliefs about what morality is or is not, what actions are right or wrong, and what things are good or bad. To an astonishing degree, our moral theory charts the course of our lives. If the course matters, then we must try to fashion the best moral theory we can.

If we are to be intellectually mature, we also must try to integrate the results of these moral analyses and deliberations into a comprehensive picture of reality, what is known as a worldview. A **worldview** is a philosophy of life, a set of beliefs and theories that helps us make sense of a wide range of issues in life. It defines for us what exists, what should be, and what we can know. We all have a worldview, and our notions about morality are an important part of it. A good critical thinker tries to ensure that his or her worldview contains no internal contradictions and that it offers reliable guidance in dealing with the world.

So in this chapter, we set out to apply critical thinking to some big ideas and broad questions. We explore procedures for evaluating moral discourse—specifically, moral judgments, principles, arguments, and theories—and look at ways that we can incorporate our understanding into a coherent worldview.

Moral Arguments

A moral argument, like any other kind of argument, has premises and a conclusion. The premises (and sometimes the conclusion) may be implied, not stated, and they may be simple or complex—just as in other arguments. Moral arguments, however, differ from nonmoral ones in that their conclusions are moral statements. In general, a **moral statement** is a statement asserting that an action is right or wrong (moral or immoral) or that something (such as a person or motive) is good or bad. Here are some moral statements:

- Serena should keep her promise to you.
- It is wrong to treat James so harshly.
- Abortion is immoral.
- We ought to protect Liu from the angry mob.
- My father is a good man.

Moral statements are plainly different from nonmoral, or descriptive, statements. Nonmoral statements do not assert that something is right or wrong, good or bad—they simply describe a state of affairs without giving it a value one way or the other. Compare these nonmoral statements with the moral statements just given:

- Serena did not keep her promise to you.
- James was treated harshly.
- Some people think abortion is immoral.
- Liu was protected from the angry mob.
- My father tried to be a good man.

The standard moral argument is a mixture of moral and nonmoral statements. At least one premise is a moral statement that asserts a general moral principle or moral standard. At least one premise makes a nonmoral claim. And the conclusion is a moral statement, or judgment, about a particular case (usually a particular kind of action). For example:

Argument 1

(1) It is wrong to inflict unnecessary pain on a child.

(2) Spanking inflicts unnecessary pain on a child.

(3) Therefore, spanking is wrong.

In this simple argument, premise 1 is a moral statement, affirming a general moral principle. Premise 2 is a nonmoral statement describing the nature of a specific kind of action. And the conclusion is the moral statement that the argument is intended to establish. It is about a specific kind of action.

A standard moral argument has this form for good reason. In a moral argument, we simply cannot establish the conclusion (a moral statement) without a moral premise. A moral argument with only nonmoral premises does not work. To put it another way, we cannot infer what *should be* or *ought to be* (in the conclusion) from statements about *what is*. Suppose the previous argument reads like this (and there are no missing premises):

Spanking inflicts unnecessary pain on a child.

Therefore, spanking is wrong.

The premise doesn't say anything about right or wrong; it just makes a descriptive claim. The conclusion, though, does assert something about right or wrong. So the conclusion is not supported by the premise; it does not follow from the descriptive statement.

Here's another example:

Torturing prisoners of war is a case of intentional mistreatment.

Prisoners of war should not be tortured.

This argument fails because the moral premise is missing. We need a moral premise to connect the nonmoral premise to the conclusion, like this:

Argument 2

No prisoner of war should ever be intentionally mistreated.

Torturing prisoners of war is a case of intentional mistreatment.

Prisoners of war should not be tortured.

In the standard moral argument, we also need a nonmoral premise. Remember that the conclusion is a moral statement (judgment) about a particular kind of action. The moral premise, however, is a statement expressing a general moral principle about a much broader class of actions. In order to infer the narrower conclusion from a much broader premise, we need a nonmoral statement to bridge the gap. For example, from the general moral principle that "no prisoner of war should ever be intentionally mistreated," we cannot conclude that "prisoners of war should not be tortured" unless there is a nonmoral premise stating that torturing prisoners of war is a type of intentional mistreatment. Likewise from the general moral principle that "murder is wrong," we cannot conclude that "abortion is wrong" unless there's a factual premise telling us that abortion is murder.

Now, very often when you encounter moral arguments, they are abbreviated and missing the moral premise (the general moral principle), like the arguments discussed earlier:

Spanking inflicts unnecessary pain on a child.

Therefore, spanking is wrong.

Torturing prisoners of war is a case of intentional mistreatment.

Prisoners of war should not be tortured.

Usually, the moral premise is missing because it's implicit. In such cases, to make sense of the argument, you must supply the implicit premise. Sometimes you may automatically add the implicit premise in your head without bothering to properly fill out the argument. But if you want to carefully evaluate moral arguments, it's best to spell out any missing premises. Implicit moral premises are often dubious and need to be studied closely. General moral principles that are taken for granted may turn out to be unfounded or incomplete. Also, laying everything out on the table like this is essential if you want to improve the argument—an important exercise if you care that your positions on moral issues are well supported.

The simplest approach to identifying implicit premises is to treat moral arguments as deductive. (Notice that arguments 1 and 2 are valid deductive arguments.) Your task, then, is to supply plausible premises that will make the argument valid. (We used this same procedure in chapter 3 for finding implicit premises.) Consider this argument:

Cloning humans is unnatural.

Therefore, cloning humans is morally wrong.

As it stands, this argument is not valid, and we can see right away that the missing premise is a general moral principle. A plausible premise to make this argument valid, then, is "Anything unnatural is morally wrong," a general moral principle. The revised version is:

Argument 3

Anything unnatural is morally wrong.

Cloning humans is unnatural.

Therefore, cloning humans is morally wrong.

Here's another incomplete argument:

Meg lied to her sister for no good reason.

Therefore, Meg should not have lied to her sister.

To make this argument valid and to supply a general moral principle, we can add this premise:

Argument 4

One should not lie without good reason.

Meg lied to her sister for no good reason.

Therefore, Meg should not have lied to her sister.

Another advantage to treating moral arguments as deductive (and to supplying explicit premises that will make the arguments valid) is ease of analysis. Generally, moral arguments are easier to appraise and modify when they are deductive. And if they are deductively valid, you know that any flaws in the arguments will likely be the result of false premises. For example, if you have a deductively valid argument, and the conclusion is false, you know that at least one of the premises is false.

 AGREEMENT IN MORAL DISCOURSE

Despite the prevalence of moral disagreements on countless issues, there is a surprising amount of agreement on basic moral principles. Often, the bone of contention in moral arguments is not the moral premises (which may be widely accepted), but the nonmoral ones. In debates about "pulling the plug" on severely comatose patients, for example, all parties may agree that murder is wrong but disagree about the nature of comatose patients. Some may insist that comatose patients are entities that can be murdered (because they are fully human, true persons, etc.); others, that comatose patients are not the kind of entities that can be murdered (because they are not persons, for example). So there may not be as much moral disagreement in the world as you might think. Here's a list of moral principles that both parties in moral debates often accept:

- **Personal benefit:** Acknowledge the extent to which an action produces beneficial consequences for the individual in question.
- **Principle of benevolence:** Help those in need.
- **Principle of harm:** Do not harm others.
- **Principle of honesty:** Do not deceive others.
- **Principle of lawfulness:** Do not violate the law.
- **Principle of autonomy:** Acknowledge a person's freedom over his/her actions or physical body.
- **Principle of justice:** Acknowledge a person's right to due process, fair compensation for harm done, and fair distribution of benefits.
- **Rights:** Acknowledge a person's rights to life, information, privacy, free expression, and safety.[1]

Moral Premises

In good arguments the inferences are valid or strong and the premises—whether nonmoral or moral—are true. This latter stipulation means that to make good arguments, you must ensure that the premises are backed by good reasons and are not simply assumed without warrant. To evaluate arguments, you must check the premises for these same qualities. As noted in previous chapters, accurately assessing the truth of nonmoral premises depends mostly on your knowledge of the subject matter, including the results of relevant scientific research, the analyses of reliable experts, and the content of your background information. Gauging the truth of moral premises (moral principles) mostly involves examining the support they get from three sources: (1) other moral principles, (2) moral theories, and (3) considered moral judgments.

The appeal to another moral principle (usually a more general or higher level principle) is probably the most common way to support a moral premise. Often the more general principle is extremely credible or accepted by all parties so that further support for it is unnecessary. Sometimes it is controversial so that it too is in need of support. Suppose the moral premise in question is, "A dying patient in intolerable and untreatable pain should be allowed to commit suicide with a physician's help." Some would say that this claim is derived from, or is based on, the higher (and more widely accepted) principle of autonomy—the notion that a person has an inherent right of self-determination, a right to make autonomous choices about his or her own life and death. Others would support the premise by appealing to the principle of beneficence, or mercy: If we are in a position to relieve the severe suffering of another without excessive cost to ourselves, we have a duty to do so. They would interpret this principle as sanctioning the physician's role in helping a competent, hopelessly ill patient to die. To try to show that the premise is false, someone might appeal to a sanctity-of-life principle, asserting that human life is sacred and should be preserved at all costs. When such higher principles are brought in, the truth of the original premise often becomes clear—or not. They cannot be the court of final appeal in ethics, for they too can be tested by reasoned argument showing why they should or should not be believed.

Reasons for accepting or rejecting a moral premise can also come from a moral theory, a general explanation of what makes an action right or what makes a person or motive good (see the next section). For example, traditional utilitarianism is a moral theory asserting that right actions are those that produce the greatest happiness for all concerned. To support the assisted suicide premise, you could appeal to the theory, arguing that the least amount of unhappiness (pain and suffering) for all concerned (patient, physician, and family) would result if the physician helped the patient die. To counter your argument, someone would need to show that your happiness calculations were incorrect (for example, that assisted suicide actually causes more unhappiness in the long run), or that

utilitarianism itself is an inadequate theory, or that other theories or considerations are more important or relevant than utilitarian factors.

A moral premise can also be supported or undermined by our *considered moral
judgments*. These are moral judgments that we consider credible after we carefully
and dispassionately reflect on them. Pertaining to either specific cases or general
statements, they constitute what philosophers have called our moral common
sense. They are not infallible guides to morality, but unless we have good reasons for doubting their soundness, we are entitled to trust them. Some of our
considered judgments may seem undeniable, even self-evident—for example:
"Inflicting unnecessary, undeserved suffering on someone is wrong"; "Torturing
children for the fun of it is immoral"; "Treating people harshly merely because of
the color of their skin is unjust."

Moral principles, theories, and judgments relate to one another in interesting
ways (a topic we explore in the following pages). For now, it's enough to note
that we can evaluate moral premises by seeing if they conflict with principles,
theories, or judgments that we have good reason to trust. Specifically, we can
assess a moral premise the same way we might assess any other kind of universal
generalization—by trying to think of counterexamples to it. Consider this deductively valid argument, a modified version of argument 3:

Argument 5

(1) *The medical cloning of humans is unnatural because it is something that
would not occur without human intervention.*

(2) *All actions that are unnatural and that are not done for religious reasons
should not be done.*

(3) *The medical cloning of humans is never done for religious reasons.*

(4) *Therefore, cloning humans should not be done.*

Premise 2 is the general moral principle here. Is it true? At the very least it is
questionable. We know that it's questionable because we can think of counterexamples to it. That is, we can think of instances in which the principle seems
not to hold. For example, what about the use of antibiotics to treat infections?
The use of antibiotics is unnatural as defined in the argument (they are a good
example of human intervention in the natural course of illness), and few would
claim that antibiotics are employed for religious reasons. (The term "for religious
reasons" is vague, but we will assume for the sake of this example that it means
something like "as an integral part of established religious practice.") But despite
its unnaturalness, the use of antibiotics seems to be morally acceptable to almost
everyone. At any rate, it is difficult to imagine what a plausible argument against
antibiotics would be like. So premise 2 appears to be false. We could probably
refute premise 2 by using many other counterexamples, such as wearing clothes,
drinking bottled water, and riding a bicycle.

Moral Theories

Very often when we assess moral arguments and in other ways think critically about morality, we are trying to come to a moral judgment about a particular issue or kind of action. We deliberate because we want to understand
what's right or wrong, good or bad. Our moral judgments may appear as
premises or conclusions in our arguments or as sturdy pillars of our moral
common sense. They may be justified by appeals to general moral principles,
which in turn may gain credibility from the most reliable of our moral judgments. But what of moral theories? In the previous section we saw how a
moral theory can strengthen or weaken a moral premise. Yet that's only part
of the story.

As we have seen, theories of morality are attempts to explain what makes an
action right or what makes a person or motive good. They try to specify what all
right actions and all good things have in common. As such, they can give support, guidance, or validation to our moral decision making, shaping our moral
principles, judgments, and arguments. Traditional utilitarianism (mentioned
earlier) is a well-known example of a moral theory. Another is the divine command theory, the view that what makes an action right is that God commands it
or wills it. Ethical egoism asserts that right actions are those that promote one's
own best interests.

Interestingly enough, we all have a moral theory. Whether we articulate it or
not, we all have some kind of view of what makes actions right or persons good.
Even the notion that there is no such thing as right or wrong is a moral theory.
Even the idea that all moral theories are worthless or that all moral judgments
are subjective, objective, relative, or meaningless is a moral theory. The critical
question, then, is not whether you have a moral theory but whether the theory
you have is a good one.

Moral theorizing is a fact of the moral life. We do moral theorizing when we
ponder what rightness or goodness means, or try to furnish basic justification for
a moral standard, or resolve a conflict between principles, or gauge the credibility of moral intuitions, or explain why an action is right or wrong. To theorize is
to step back from the specifics of a case and try to see the larger pattern that can
help us make sense of it all.

Despite the importance of moral theories, they are not the ultimate
authority or sole referee in moral reasoning. A theory gives us very general
norms, but morality is about more than just generalities—it's also about
the particulars of individual moral judgments. How do the general and the
particular fit together? Here is one way. Suppose you must decide whether
an action is morally permissible. From a plausible moral theory, you draw
general guidance in the form of moral principles that apply to the case. If
the principles appear to sanction conflicting decisions, you turn again to the

theory for understanding in how to resolve the inconsistency. At the same time you consult your considered moral judgments. If your theory and your considered judgments lead you to the same conclusion, you have good reason to believe that the conclusion is correct. If your theory and considered judgments diverge, you must decide which is more credible. If the implications of your theory seem more plausible, you may decide to revise your considered judgments to cohere better with the theory. If your judgments seem more plausible, you may decide to alter your theory accordingly. If your credible judgments conflict drastically with your theory, you may be justified in giving up the theory altogether.

Evaluating Moral Theories

As you may have gathered, several moral theories vie for our allegiance, each one with a distinctive take on morality and with different implications for moral issues. Moral philosophers remind us that theories also differ in quality: All moral theories are not created equal. Some theories are better than others. This fact immediately prompts two questions: Which moral theory is best, and how can we judge that it is the best? Recall that we asked this type of question in chapters 8 and 9 when we discussed inference to the best explanation and several types of theories (everyday, scientific, and weird). The answer in this chapter is the same as the answer in those chapters: To identify the best theory, we must compare competing theories and use the criteria of adequacy to appraise their worth. The criteria of adequacy that we use in judging moral theories are a little different from those we use to assess other types of theories, though the two sets of criteria have much in common. In significant ways, too, moral theories are much like scientific theories, and the process of theory evaluation is similar in both cases.

How are moral theories like scientific theories? Recall that scientific theories try to explain the causes of events, everything from tumor growth to exploding stars. A plausible scientific theory is one that's consistent with all the relevant data. A theory explaining the cause of a fatal illness, for example, must take into account facts about patient symptoms, medical test results, medical histories, environmental factors, and more. Moral theories, on the other hand, try to explain what makes an action right or what makes a person good. A plausible moral theory must also be consistent with the relevant data. The data that moral theories try to explain are our considered moral judgments, the moral judgments we accept after we reason about them carefully. Any plausible moral theory must be consistent with those considered moral judgments. As we have seen, they are fallible and revisable, but we are entitled to believe them unless we have good reason to doubt them. If a moral theory is seriously inconsistent with them—if, for example, it approves of obviously immoral acts (such as inflicting pain on innocent children for no good reason or treating equals unequally)—it is dubious, perhaps even fatally flawed, and deserving of radical revision or rejection. So the first criterion of adequacy for moral theories is: *consistency with considered moral judgments.*

In science (and many other fields of inquiry) there is an interesting relationship between theory and data. The data have an impact on the theory because the theory explains the data. A good theory, on the other hand, can lead scientists to reject certain data. Scientists want the data and theory to match up as closely as possible. They want the match to be so close that significant changes in either the data or theory aren't necessary. Moral theories work this way, too. As suggested earlier, our moral data (our considered moral judgments) influence our moral theory. And our moral theory can lead us to accept or reject certain data. Ideally, we want the fit between data and theory to be as close as possible. In other words, we want to achieve what moral philosophers refer to as a "reflective equilibrium" between facts and theory. We want the fit to be so close that significant adjustments in either data or theory are not necessary.

In addition to being consistent with the data, a plausible scientific theory must also be conservative. It must be consistent with background information—that is, with well-founded beliefs such as reliable scientific findings and well-established theories. Plausible moral theories must also be consistent with the relevant background information—that is, with our experience of the moral life. Whatever else our moral experience involves, it certainly includes (1) making moral judgments (we do this constantly), (2) having moral disagreements (we occasionally do this), and (3) sometimes acting immorally (we recognize that we are not morally perfect). If a moral theory suggests that we do not have these experiences, we must view the theory with suspicion. Another criterion of adequacy for moral theories, then, is *consistency with our experience of the moral life.*

Now, it's possible that our experience of the moral life is an illusion, only seeming to involve making moral judgments, having moral disagreements, and getting into moral disagreements. But unless we have good reason to believe that our moral experience is an illusion, we are justified in accepting it at face value.

A scientific theory gains in credibility if it helps to solve problems (has fruitfulness and scope). A plausible moral theory must also help to solve problems. That is, it must help us make moral decisions, especially those that involve moral dilemmas, instances where moral principles or moral judgments are in conflict. After all, the reason we want a moral theory is that it helps guide our actions and reconcile clashing moral beliefs. A moral theory that offers no help with such moral problems is said to be *unworkable.* Unworkable moral theories are inferior. So a final criterion of adequacy for moral theories is *workability in real-life situations.*

CRITIQUING MORAL THEORIES

Most moral philosophers don't buy the idea that one moral theory is as good as any other. They spend a good deal of time evaluating moral theories to gauge their worth, and some theories don't fare very well under this scrutiny. Here, for example, are some typical criticisms of three controversial moral theories, two of which we met in chapter 2.

Subjective Relativism

This view states that what makes an action right for someone is that it is approved by that person. Moral judgments are relative to what each person believes. If you say that stealing is wrong, then it's wrong (for you). If someone else says that stealing is right, then it's right (for her). Moral philosophers, though, think that the theory has several problematic implications. For example, the theory implies that each person is morally infallible. If you truly approve of an action, then it's right, and you cannot be wrong. Subjective relativism also makes moral disagreement nearly impossible. You disagree with others when you think they are mistaken. But according to subjective relativism, no one could be mistaken. These and other implications, critics say, render the theory implausible.

Social Relativism

This view claims that what makes an action right is that it's approved by one's society or culture. If your society deems something to be right, it's right. Moral truth is relative to societies or cultures. As you might expect, this view is criticized for many of the same problems that plague subjective relativism. It implies that societies are infallible. This means that if most people living in the so-called Islamic State in the Middle East in 2016 had approved of the extermination of thousands of innocent people in their midst, then the extermination was morally right. It seems, though, that societies are no more infallible than individuals are. What's more, social relativism implies that it would be impossible to disagree with one's society and be right. Social reformers such as Martin Luther King, Jr., or Gandhi could not claim that an action approved by society is wrong, for if society approves of it, the action is right. For these and other reasons, most moral philosophers view social relativism as a questionable moral theory.

Ethical Egoism

In this view, what makes an action right is that it promotes one's own best interests. It doesn't imply that you should do anything you want

continues

CRITIQUING MORAL THEORIES

continued

because, in the long run, that may not be in your own best interest. Ethical egoism could even condone altruism on the grounds that being nice to other people is in your best interest. Critics, however, say that the theory is implausible because it sanctions all sorts of abominable acts. For example, if it's in your best interest to kill your boss, and if you could do it without suffering any negative consequences (such as getting caught), then ethical egoism says that your moral duty is to kill him.

Two Important Theories

Now let's see how we can use these criteria to take the measure of two fundamentally different theories: traditional utilitarianism and Kantian ethics. Traditional utilitarianism was founded by Jeremy Bentham (1748–1832) and later refined by John Stuart Mill (1806–1873). Bentham's idea was that right actions are those that achieve the greatest happiness for the greatest number. He declared that by this simple standard all actions could be judged. Many people embraced the theory, for it seemed so much more rational than moral theories of the time, which often rested on dubious assumptions. In the nineteenth century, traditional utilitarianism inspired reformers who worked to abolish slavery, eliminate child labor, and increase recognition of women's rights.

To be more precise, traditional utilitarianism says that what makes an action right is that it maximizes overall happiness, everyone considered. Acting morally in any given situation, then, involves calculating how much happiness can be produced by several possible actions, identifying the persons who will be affected by those actions, and opting for the one action that produces the greatest amount of happiness in the world. Notice that what matters in utilitarianism is the *consequences* of an action—not whether the action breaks a rule or violates some abstract principle. If happiness is maximized by a particular action, then the action is morally right, regardless of any other considerations. By the lights of utilitarianism, the end justifies the means.

How does traditional utilitarianism fare when judged by the moral criteria of adequacy? For starters, the theory does seem to be consistent with key aspects of our experience of the moral life. The theory assumes that we can and do make moral judgments, have moral disagreements, and act immorally.

Some critics, however, have questioned whether traditional utilitarianism is a workable theory because calculating amounts of happiness seems to be extremely difficult or impossible. For example, each action we perform has consequences indefinitely into the future. If this is the case, then at what point should we make our calculation of the happiness produced? Should we figure into our calculations the happiness that will accrue by next Tuesday? next year? next decade? Some actions may produce very little happiness in the short run but a great deal of happiness over the long haul. Some actions work the other way round—big short-term benefits, no long-term payback. Traditional utilitarianism offers no help in resolving this problem, and so critics have accused the theory of being unworkable.

Many moral philosophers think that the theory faces a much bigger problem than unworkability: It seems to conflict with many of our considered moral judgments. For instance, the theory seems inconsistent with our considered moral judgments involving rights. We tend to think that certain things should not be done to people even if doing them would produce the greatest amount of happiness in the world. We would not think it right to falsely accuse and punish an innocent person just because doing so would make a whole town of people happy. We would not think it right to torture one person just because the action would make a dozen other people extremely happy. Our considered moral judgments say that such actions are wrong, but traditional utilitarianism says they may be right.

Suppose two possible actions will produce exactly the same amount of overall happiness. But one of the actions involves the violation of someone's rights or causes a serious injustice. According to utilitarianism, the two actions are equally right. But to many, this evaluation of the situation seems to conflict with our considered moral judgments.

The same kind of conflict arises in regard to moral duties. Most of us believe that we have certain duties to other people that often seem weightier than considerations of happiness. For example, we believe that in general we have a duty to keep our promises to people. But traditional utilitarianism does not recognize any such duties. It says that our only goal should be to maximize happiness—regardless of whether we have to break a promise to do it.

So for these reasons (and a few others), many critics have accused the theory of being acutely inconsistent with relevant moral data. They believe that any theory that runs afoul of the criterion of consistency in this way cannot be correct.

But take note: Even the fiercest critics of utilitarianism have admitted that the theory does seem to capture something essential to moral theories—the notion that the consequences of actions are indeed relevant to moral judgments. Probably very few people would want to say that in moral decision making the consequences of their actions never matter.

For the record, the sketch of traditional utilitarianism given here has been oversimplified so we can focus on the process of theory assessment. Over the years, utilitarians have modified the theory to make it more plausible. Critics, however, still claim that the theory is flawed . . . but that's another story.

In radical contrast to utilitarianism and other theories basing rightness on the consequences of actions, the moral theory of Immanuel Kant (1724–1804) says that rightness does not depend at all on the production of happiness or on the satisfaction of human desires. For Kant, rightness is not defined by an action's results, but by its form—that is, by the nature of the action itself. Harming the innocent is wrong not because it causes unhappiness, but because of the kind of action it is. Morality is about conforming your actions to universal moral rules derived from reason and doing so for duty's sake alone. Your actions are right only if they are consistent with such rules, and you deserve praise for right actions only if you act solely from a sense of duty.

In Kantian ethics, the moral rules (or duties) are expressed as categorical imperatives—that is, as commands that apply without exception (categorically, or absolutely) and without regard to a person's preferences or goals. Kant says that we can infer all our duties from one moral principle, the ultimate categorical imperative. He formulates it in several ways but supposes that they are all equivalent. His first formulation says, "Act only on that maxim through which you can at the same time will that it should become a universal law."[2] On Kant's view, our actions imply general moral rules, or maxims. To tell a lie for personal gain is essentially to act according to a maxim that says something like "It's morally permissible to lie to someone to promote your own interests." To determine if an action is permissible, we need to ask ourselves if we could consistently will that the maxim of our action become a universal moral law that applies to everyone. We must ask, "Could all humankind, with logical consistency, act on the maxim, and would we be willing to have them do that?" If the answer is yes on both counts, the action is morally permissible; if not, it is prohibited.

Here is Kant's illustration of properly applying this formulation. Suppose that to borrow money from a friend (money that you know you will never pay back), you falsely promise to repay the loan. Is this behavior permissible? To find out, you must ask if you could consistently will that the maxim of your action become a universal law. The maxim of your action is, "Whenever you need money that you know you cannot pay back, make a lying promise to obtain the loan." What would happen if everyone acted according to this maxim? Everyone would make lying promises to get a loan, but everyone would also know that the promises were empty—and the practice of loaning money based on a promise would cease to exist. The result is a contradiction: The universal making of lying promises would end the practice of promising. Thus, you cannot consistently will that the maxim of your action become a universal law, so making a lying promise to borrow money is prohibited.

This bare sketch of only one formulation of the categorical imperative does not do justice to Kant's theory, but it's enough for an illustration of how we might apply the moral criteria of adequacy.

One fact that seems obvious is that the theory easily passes the second criterion: It is generally consistent with our experience of the moral life. According to Kantian ethics, we do form moral judgments, have moral disagreements, and err in our moral beliefs. Any flaws in the theory are more likely to arise from the first criterion; sure enough, critics insist that the theory is not consistent with our considered moral judgments. One argument for this conclusion starts from Kant's claim that the moral rules are absolute—that is, they must be obeyed without exception (or as he says, we have "perfect" duties). He asserts, for example, that we have an absolute duty not to lie or to kill the innocent, regardless of the consequences of observing the rule. Suppose a crazed killer wants to murder an innocent man who takes refuge in your house. The killer knocks at your door and asks you if the man is hiding inside. If you tell the truth, the innocent man will be murdered; if you lie, he will be saved. What would Kant have you do in a case like this? His answer is unequivocal: You must tell the truth though it leads to the murder of an innocent person. How does this absolutism fit with our moral common sense? Not very well, critics say. Our considered moral judgments seem to suggest that, in general, saving an innocent life has far more moral value than blindly adhering to an absolute rule. Moral common sense seems to affirm that doing our duty for duty's sake—though generally a worthy aim—is sometimes less important than avoiding tragic consequences. Kant would have us do our duty though the heavens fall, but that view appears inconsistent with moral judgments that we have good reasons to trust.

Given enough space, we could review the responses that Kant's defenders have offered to this criticism (and to others). And we could dwell on the formulation of the categorical imperative that some consider Kant's greatest insight—the principle of respect for persons. But this brief treatment will have to do.

Between utilitarianism and Kantian ethics, which theory is better and why? An adequate answer to that question would be anything but brief. Comparing the virtues and vices of these two theories, and then deciding which one is preferable, would require a great deal of careful analysis and critical thinking. But however the task proceeds, it is sure to involve applying to both theories some telling criteria of adequacy (either the three criteria discussed here, or variations on them, and perhaps others). Such an investigation would show that neither theory is perfect (no theory is) and would likely yield an edifying conclusion such as (1) one theory is more plausible than the other, or (2) both theories are seriously defective, or (3) the best elements of both can be blended into a new theory, or (4) one of the theories is an especially good candidate for modification to eliminate shortcomings.

Applying the criteria is not like solving a mathematical equation or following a set of instructions to build a gasoline engine. There is no rigid rubric for using or weighting the criteria to sort good theories from bad. But like the scientific criteria of adequacy, these standards do give us guidance in making reasonable judgments about the objective strengths and weaknesses of theories.

Legal Reasoning

Argument and inference play a dynamic role in legal reasoning of all sorts. They are regularly put to use in debates about the making of new laws, in criminal and civil proceedings, and in judicial decision-making. And as in any other field, deductive and inductive patterns form the foundation of the reasoning used. The application of these two forms of argument, however, is not as mechanical or formulaic as some might assume.

Usually when judges decide particular cases, the overarching pattern in their reasoning is deductive (although there is much more to it than that). In a given case, the judge ascertains a relevant rule of law, identifies the facts to which the rule pertains, and applies the rule to the facts. The result is a judicial decision, a ruling, that should reflect both the rule and the facts. When explicitly stated, this line of reasoning might look like this:

> *Those who fail to meet the nation's citizenship requirements cannot be citizens. (the rule)*
>
> *Victor has failed to meet the nation's citizenship requirements. (the facts)*
>
> *Therefore, Victor is not a citizen. (the conclusion, or ruling)*

Or in a conditional mode:

> *If someone fails to meet the nation's citizenship requirements, he or she cannot be a citizen. (the rule)*
>
> *Victoria has failed to meet the nation's citizenship requirements. (the facts)*
>
> *Therefore, Victoria is not a citizen. (the conclusion, or ruling)*

In proceedings at the Supreme Court, critical reasoning—including deductive and inductive argument—is at the heart of judicial decision-making.

Such deductive arguments constitute only the general framework of judicial decision-making. Inside this framework other kinds of inferences and considerations are at work. First, to reach a verdict, a judge cannot simply apply the rule to the facts and get the right answer, as if by formula or computer calculation. Often the rules contain unclear or conflicting statements, or they are inconsistent with other rules, or how the rules are to be applied to the facts may not be apparent, or there may be no rules at all that are relevant to the case at hand. So a judge must interpret the rules or make do when no rule applies. The facts too require some interpretation, for there are usually several different ways to describe them, and it's not always obvious which way is appropriate. Moreover, inductive inference plays an even larger role than deduction does in judicial reasoning.

How so? For one thing, courts must determine what the facts are in cases, and that task must involve inductive reasoning. They have to reason inductively to derive the facts from eyewitness testimony, the testimony of expert witnesses, and physical evidence. Such inferences are often very straightforward: Expert X says that the defendant's DNA was left on the murder weapon; therefore, the defendant's DNA was probably left on the murder weapon.

Also, very often the dominant question before a court is that of causality. Did the driver of the truck cause the accident? Did Johnson burglarize the house? Did the chemical company cause toxic waste to flow into the ground water and did that waste make the residents ill? The main reason that such questions are important is that they are linked to legal responsibility. Those who cause an injury to someone are held legally responsible for it and therefore must face the legal consequences—a judgment of the court that goes against them.

Inductive inferences in the form of arguments from analogy are both common and essential in judicial reasoning. In trial courts, analogical arguments are often used to establish the facts. Expert testimony is assessed by referring to the expert's previous experience in circumstances analogous to those of the present. Evaluating circumstantial evidence requires comparing familiar experiences of the past with analogous experiences relevant to the present case.

More important, reasoning by analogy is central to judicial decision-making. In many systems of justice (notably those of the United States and the United Kingdom), judges must decide cases in light of previous settled cases—in accordance with precedent, especially precedent established by higher courts. That is, courts are required to let their judgments be controlled by decisions handed down in relevantly similar cases. Thus, arguments by analogy arise naturally and take the familiar form discussed in chapter 5. For example:

1. In the cases relevant to the present case, persons with lung cancer sue cigarette manufacturers for causing their cancer, and the courts rule that the persons must be compensated for their illness.
2. In the present case, a person with lung cancer sues a cigarette manufacturer for causing her cancer.

3. Therefore, in the present case, the person with lung cancer should probably be compensated.

As with any other analogical argument, the strength of such inferences depends on relevant similarities and differences. Judges must decide whether prior cases are similar enough (or different enough) in relevant ways to the case at hand. They will follow precedent and treat the cases the same if they think the cases are relevantly similar enough. They will depart from precedent and treat the cases differently if they decide the cases are too dissimilar in relevant aspects.

A Coherent Worldview

Making a coherent and powerful worldview for yourself is the work of a lifetime, requiring reflection, critical thinking, and (often) personal anguish. So there is no way that this chapter—or *any* chapter, book, or person—can provide you with ready-made content for your worldview. But we can trace out some characteristics that any good worldview should possess.

A worldview is a massive intellectual construct with many elements. We can get a handle on it, though, by thinking of it as primarily a composite of theories—theories about morality, God, science, mind, personhood, society, knowledge, and much more. We all have our own beliefs about these things, and our most general beliefs often congeal into theories. Since worldviews are framed out of theories, good worldviews will, as a minimum requirement, consist of good theories. So much of the job of devising a good worldview consists of ensuring that our theories are the best theoretical explanations available. We do that, of course, by putting our theories to the test as we have in previous chapters.

But there's more to crafting a plausible worldview than that. Recall our discussion of theories and inference to the best explanation in chapter 8. We saw that a theory helps increase our understanding by fitting our beliefs into a coherent pattern. When some of our most fundamental beliefs conflict with one another, the relevant theory is in trouble and our understanding is decreased. After all, if two of our beliefs are inconsistent with one another, we know that at least one of them must be false. To achieve true understanding, we must somehow resolve the inconsistency. Likewise, if the theories that make up our worldview are inconsistent with one another, there is obviously something wrong with our worldview. At least one of our theories must be flawed, and some of our beliefs must be wrong. Our understanding of the world is decreased, and our prospects for success (however we define it) are dimmed. A crucial criterion, then, for judging a worldview is *internal consistency*—the requirement that the theories composing our worldview do not conflict.

How can our best theories conflict? Here are some ways:

- *Our moral theory can conflict with our view of human freedom.* Most people believe that persons can be held morally responsible for their actions—as long as they act freely. That is, persons can be praised or blamed only for those actions over which they have control. But many people also think that humans *cannot* act freely, that they do not have free will. They believe in causal determinism, the view that every event in the universe has a cause (is determined). This means that everything that happens (including human actions) has a preceding cause, so that the chain of causes stretches back into the indefinite past—out of our control. Many would see this situation as an unacceptable conflict between their moral theory and their view of the way the world is.

- *Our theory about the existence of God can conflict with our scientific theory about the nature of the universe.* Some people argue that God must exist because everything has a cause, including the universe, and the only thing that could have caused the universe is God. Modern physics, however, shows that some things in the universe (namely, certain subatomic particles) often occur uncaused, so it's not true that everything has a cause. Thus, in this instance science seems to be at odds with a certain brand of theology.

- *Our theory about the mind can be in conflict with theories of personal survival after death.* Some believe that people can live on in some ethereal form (as souls or disembodied minds, for example) after death. This notion accords well with the idea that the mind (our true essence) is the kind of thing that can exist independently of the body. But this kind of survival after death would not be possible if the mind is identical to the body, as some people believe.

The work of building plausible worldviews will always involve eliminating inconsistencies. If you really want to understand the world and your place in it, you must wrestle with these inconsistencies. Reconciling conflicting beliefs (by eliminating them or modifying them) is a necessary condition for creating theories and a worldview that can successfully guide your thinking, your choices, and your deeds.

With this discussion, we now come full circle to a theme that bubbles up in the first few pages of this book and flows through each chapter to this final paragraph: Every statement, every theory, and every worldview is fair game for critical thinking. No claim can be considered immune to critical inquiry, revision, and rejection. We will probably never be able to evaluate the truth of all our beliefs, but we violate the spirit of critical reasoning and do ourselves a disfavor if we cordon them off and post a sign that says "Off Limits!" If truth is what we seek, if knowledge is our goal, we should be willing to turn the light of critical thinking on any dark corner anywhere. This point is especially relevant to the development of worldviews, which too often are thought to be the unalterable givens of clan and culture, ideologies carved in the pillars of the mind forever. Our worldviews are far too important not to subject them to intelligent, reasoned reflection.

KEY WORDS

moral statement   worldview

EXERCISES

Exercises marked with * have answers in "Answers to Exercises" (Appendix A).

Exercise 11.1

1. What is a moral theory?
2. According to the text, what is a worldview?
3. What is a moral statement?
4. What is the basic structure of a standard moral argument?
*5. Why can't we infer a moral statement from nonmoral statements alone?
6. Why is it important to spell out implicit premises in a moral argument?
7. What technique can we use to determine whether a general moral principle is true?
8. What is a moral judgment?
*9. According to the text, what precisely does a moral theory try to explain?
10. According to the text, what are the criteria of adequacy for appraising moral theories?
11. According to the text, how are moral theories like scientific theories?
12. Who founded the moral theory known as traditional utilitarianism?
*13. According to the text, what is a crucial criterion for judging a worldview?
14. How do judges use analogical argument in deciding cases?
15. Why can't judges use deductive reasoning alone in their deliberations?
16. What are considered moral judgments? Are they infallible? How are they used in moral deliberations?
17. What is Kant's theory of ethics?

Exercise 11.2

Specify whether the following statements are moral or nonmoral.

*1. Joan worries whether she's doing the right thing.
2. When the government restricts freedom of the press, it harms every citizen.
3. The government should not restrict freedom of the press.
4. Paul was sure that he saw Gregory steal the book from the library.
5. Because of the terrible results of the bombing, it's clear that the entire war effort was immoral.

*6. The Church should never have allowed pedophile priests to stay in the priesthood.

7. The officer was justified in using deadly force because his life was threatened.

8. The officer used deadly force because his life was threatened.

*9. Lying is wrong unless the lie involves trivial matters.

10. The officials should never have allowed the abuse to continue.

Exercise 11.3

In each of the following passages, add a moral premise to turn it into a valid moral argument.

1. Noah promised to drive Thelma to Los Angeles, so he should stop belly-aching and do it.

2. The refugees were shot at and lied to, and the authorities did nothing to stop any of this. The authorities should have intervened.

3. There was never any imminent threat from the Iraqi government, so the United States should not have invaded Iraq.

*4. The Indian government posed an imminent threat to Pakistan and the world, so the Pakistanis were justified in attacking Indian troops.

5. Burton used a gun in the commission of a crime; therefore, he should get a long prison term.

6. Ellen knew that a murder was going to take place. It was her duty to try to stop it.

7. Ahmed should never have allowed his daughter to receive in vitro fertilization. Such a procedure is unnatural.

8. The doctors performed the experiment on twenty patients without their consent. Obviously, that was wrong.

*9. What you did was immoral. You hacked into a database containing personal information on thousands of people and invaded their privacy.

10. Ling spent all day weeding Mrs. Black's garden for no pay. The least Mrs. Black should do is let Ling borrow some gardening tools.

Exercise 11.4

Use counterexamples to test each of the following general moral principles.

1. Anything that is unnatural is immoral.

2. It is always and everywhere wrong to tell a lie.

*3. In all circumstances the killing of a human being is wrong.

4. In all situations in which our actions can contribute to the welfare, safety, or happiness of others, we should treat all persons equally.

5. Any action that serves one's own best interests is morally permissible.

6. Any action that is approved of by one's society is moral.

*7. Assisted suicide is never morally justified.

8. Whatever action a person approves of is morally right.

9. Making a promise to someone incurs a moral obligation to keep the promise in all circumstances.

10. Any action done for religious reasons is morally acceptable because religious reasons carry more weight than secular ones.

Exercise 11.5

Identify the moral argument in each of the following passages. Specify the premises and the conclusion, adding implicit premises where needed.

1. The movie *Lorenzo's Oil* is about a family's struggle to find a cure for their young son's fatal genetic disease, an illness that usually kills boys before they reach their eleventh birthday. The script is based on the true story of a family's attempt to save Lorenzo, their son, from this fatal genetic disease through the use of a medicinal oil. The movie is a tear-jerker, but it ends on a hopeful note that suggests that the oil will eventually cure Lorenzo and that the oil is an effective treatment for the genetic disease. The problem is, there is no cure for the disease and no good scientific evidence showing that the oil works. But the movie touts the oil anyway—and gives false hope to every family whose son suffers from this terrible illness. Worse, the movie overplays the worth of the oil, seriously misleading people about the medical facts. The movie, therefore, is immoral. It violates the ageless moral dictum to, above all else, "Do no harm." *Lorenzo's Oil* may be just a movie, but it has done harm nonetheless.

2. "I, like many of my fellow Muslims, was appalled by the latest bombings in Saudi Arabia ('Among the Saudis, Attack Has Soured Qaeda Supporters,' front page, Nov. 11). Yet I was disturbed to get the sense that Saudis were angered by this latest act of barbarity because the targets were mainly Arab and Muslim.

"You quote one person as saying of the bombing in Riyadh in May, 'At that time it was seen as justifiable because there was an invasion of a foreign country, there was frustration.' Another says, 'Jihad is not against your own people.'

"Regardless of whether the victims are Muslim or not, the vicious murder of innocent human beings is reprehensible and repugnant, an affront to everything Islam stands for. Any sympathy for Al Qaeda among the minority of Saudis should have evaporated after the May bombings in Riyadh, and it should have surprised no one in Saudi Arabia that Al Qaeda would attack a housing complex full of Arabs and Muslims.

"That is what Al Qaeda is: a band of bloodthirsty murderers." [Letter to the editor, *New York Times*]

3. John and Nancy Jones had a two-year-old son who suffered from a serious but very curable bowel obstruction. For religious reasons, the Joneses decided to treat their son with prayer instead of modern medicine. They refused medical treatment even though they were told by several doctors that the child would die unless medically treated. As it turned out, the boy did die. The Joneses were arrested and charged with involuntary manslaughter. Were the Joneses wrong to refuse treatment for their son? The answer is yes. Regardless of what faith or religious dogma would have the Joneses do, they allowed their child to die. According to just about any moral outlook, the care of a child by the parents is a fundamental obligation. Above all other concerns, parents have a duty to ensure the health and safety of their children and to use whatever means are most likely to secure those benefits. The Joneses ignored this basic moral principle. They were wrong—and deserve whatever punishment the state deems appropriate.

 ## Self-Assessment Quiz

Answers appear in "Answers to Self-Assessment Quizzes" in Appendix B.

1. What is a moral statement?

2. What are the elements of a standard moral argument?

3. According to the text, what are the moral criteria of adequacy?

4. According to the text, how can you test whether a general moral principle is true?

5. Is it possible to derive a moral statement from a nonmoral statement?

In each of the following passages, add a moral premise to turn it into a valid moral argument.

6. Of course we should have offered protection to the Kurds. They were in grave danger, and they asked for our help.

7. The supplement manufacturers knew that the herb ephedra was dangerous, so they should have removed it from the market.

8. The Democrats insulted the president. They should have never been allowed to do that.

9. The Smiths were consenting adults who were having sex in the privacy of their own home. These actions by the Smiths are morally permissible.

10. Randi killed his neighbor, and the killing was not in self-defense. He should not have committed such an act.

Use counterexamples to test each of the following general moral principles.

11. Lying is wrong under all circumstances.

12. People who commit crimes should not be punished—they should be re-trained to act legally.
13. All humans, whatever their circumstances, have full moral rights.
14. All creatures that are alive and sensitive to stimulation are equally valu-able and should be accorded equal respect.
15. The morally right action is the one that produces the most happiness, ev-eryone considered.
16. Right actions are those that are in one's own self-interest.

Defend the following actions from a utilitarian standpoint.

17. Medical experimentation on a patient without her consent.
18. Taking food, shelter, and other resources from rich people and distributing them equally among poor people.

Evaluate each of the following arguments.

19. Any form of expression or speech that offends people of faith should not be tolerated. *Penthouse* magazine definitely offends people of faith. Ban it!
20. Anyone who disagrees with the basic moral dictums of the prevailing cul-ture should be censored. Dr. Tilden's graduation speech clearly was in-consistent with the prevailing moral opinions on campus. She should be reprimanded.

 ## Writing Assignments

1. Write a two-page essay arguing that sometimes it can be morally permis-sible to torture alleged terrorists to elicit information from them about future terrorist attacks. Then write a one-page rebuttal of the essay. For the purposes of this exercise, you can use fabricated—but plausible—facts.
2. Write a two-page assessment of the moral theory known as ethical egoism (discussed in the box "Critiquing Moral Theories"). Use the moral criteria of adequacy.
3. From a newspaper opinion/editorial page (including letters to the editor) select a passage containing a moral argument. Write a brief assessment of the argument, identifying the premises and conclusion, adding implicit premises (to make the argument valid), and stating whether the revised argument is sound or unsound.
4. Go to the opinion/editorial section of http://www.usatoday.com and select a short article on an important moral issue. Analyze the article's ar-gument, identifying premises and the conclusion, and determine whether the argument is a good one.

Writing Argumentative Essays

A S WE NOTE IN CHAPTER 1, AN ARGUMENT IS A GROUP OF STATEMENTS IN WHICH some of them (the premises) are intended to support another of them (the conclusion). This configuration of statements supporting another statement is not only the basic structure of an argument—it's the general design of an argumentative essay. An argumentative essay tries to support a particular conclusion or position on an issue by offering reasons to support that conclusion. Arguments (in the critical thinking sense) are not passionate exchanges of unsupported views, pointless contests of the is-too-is-not variety. And neither are argumentative essays. A mere sequence of statements expressing your views is not an argument, just as several pages of such statements do not constitute an argumentative essay.

So in an argumentative essay, your main task is to provide rational support for a claim. If you are successful, you will have shown that there are good reasons to accept your view of things. Readers who think critically may well be persuaded by your arguments. If you write well, you may be able to make your essay even more persuasive through rhetorical or stylistic devices that add emphasis, depth, and vividness to your prose. No one wants to read a boring essay. What you should not do, however, is rely entirely on nonargumentative elements to persuade your audience. Strong emotional appeals, for example, can indeed persuade some people, but they prove nothing. In truly effective argumentative essays, the primary persuasive device is critical reasoning.

Basic Essay Structure

Good argumentative essays generally contain the following elements, though not necessarily in the order shown here:

- Introduction (or opening)
- Statement of thesis (the claim to be supported)

271

- Argument supporting the thesis
- Assessment of objections
- Conclusion

In the *introduction*, you want to do at least two things: (1) grab the reader's attention and (2) provide background information for the thesis. Effective attention-grabbers include startling statistics, compelling quotations, interesting anecdotes, opinions of experts, shocking or unexpected claims, and vivid imagery. Whatever attention-grabbers you use, *they must relate to the topic of the essay*. No use telling a good story if it has nothing to do with your thesis. Providing background for your thesis often means explaining why your topic is important, telling how you became concerned, or showing that there is a problem to be solved or a question to be answered. Very often the introduction is laid out in the first paragraph of the essay, sometimes consisting of no more than a sentence or two. In general, the briefer the introduction, the better.

The *thesis statement* also usually appears in the first paragraph. It's the statement that you hope to support or prove in your essay, the conclusion of the argument that you intend to present. You want to state the thesis in a single sentence and do so as early as possible in the essay. Your thesis statement is like a compass to your readers, guiding them through your essay from premise to premise, showing them a clear path. It also helps you stay on course, reminding you to keep every part of the essay related to your single unifying idea. Your thesis statement should be restricted to a claim that can be defended in the space allowed (often only 750 to 1,000 words). Not restricted enough: "Tuition is too high." Better: "Tuition increases at Podunk College are unacceptable." Better still: "The recent tuition increase at Podunk College is unnecessary for financial reasons." (More on how to devise a properly restricted thesis statement in a moment.)

The main body of the essay is the fully developed argument supporting the thesis. This means that the basic essay structure consists of the thesis statement followed by each premise or reason that supports the thesis. Each premise in turn is clearly stated, sufficiently explained and illustrated, and supported by examples, statistics, expert opinion, and other evidence. Sometimes you can develop the essay very simply by devoting a single paragraph to each premise. At other times, each premise may demand several paragraphs. In any case, you should develop just one point per paragraph, with every paragraph clearly relating to the thesis statement.

A sketch of the argument for the Podunk College essay, then, might look like this:

Premise: If the college has a budget surplus, then a tuition increase is unnecessary.

Premise: The college has had a budget surplus for the last five years.

Premise: If the college president says that the school is financially in good shape and therefore doesn't need a tuition increase, then it's probably true that the school doesn't need a tuition increase.

Premise: In an unguarded moment, the president admitted that the school is financially in good shape and therefore doesn't need a tuition increase.

Thesis statement: Therefore, the recent tuition increase at Podunk College is probably unnecessary for financial reasons.

Good argumentative essays include an *assessment of objections*—an honest effort to take into account any objections that readers are likely to raise about the thesis statement or its premises. When you deal with such objections in your essay, you lend credibility to it because you're making an attempt to be fair and thorough. In addition, when you carefully examine objections, you can often see ways to make your argument or thesis statement stronger. It isn't necessary to consider every possible objection, just the strongest or the most common ones. Sometimes it's best to deal with objections when you discuss premises that relate to them. At other times it may be better to handle objections near the end of the essay after defending the premises.

Finally, your essay—unless it's very short—must have a *conclusion*. The conclusion usually appears in the last paragraph of the essay. Typically it reiterates the thesis statement (though usually not in exactly the same words). If the argument is complex or the essay is long, the conclusion may contain a summary of the argument. Good conclusions may reassert the importance of the thesis statement, challenge readers to do something about a problem, tell a story that emphasizes the relevance of the main argument, or bring out a disturbing or unexpected implication of a claim defended in the body of the essay.

Guidelines for Writing the Essay

1. *Determine your thesis statement.* Do not write on the first thesis idea that pops into your head. Select a topic you're interested in and narrow its scope until you have a properly restricted thesis statement. Research the topic to find out what issues are being debated. When you think you have an idea for a thesis statement, stop. Dig deeper into the idea by examining the arguments associated with that claim. Choose a thesis statement that you think you can defend. If you come to a dead end, start the process over.

2. *Create an outline.* Establish the basic framework of your outline by writing out your thesis statement and all the premises that support it. Then fill in the framework by jotting down what points you will need to make in defense of each premise. Decide on what objections to your argument you will consider and how you will respond to them.

3. *Write a first draft.* As you write, don't be afraid to revise your outline or even your thesis statement. Writing will force you to think carefully about the strengths and weaknesses of your argument. If need be, write a second draft and a third. Good writers aren't afraid of revisions; they depend on them.

4. *Stay on track.* Make sure that each sentence of your essay relates somehow to your thesis statement and argument.

5. *Zero in on your audience.* Determine for what audience your essay is intended, and write to them. Is it readers of the local paper? fellow students? people who are likely to disagree with you?

6. *Support your premises.* Back up the premises of your argument with examples, expert opinion, statistics, analogies, and other kinds of evidence.

7. *Let your final draft sit.* If possible, when you've finished writing your paper, set it aside and read it the next day. You may be surprised how many mistakes this fresh look can reveal. If you can't set the essay aside, ask a friend to read it and give you some constructive criticism.

From Issue to Thesis

For many students, the biggest challenge in writing an argumentative essay is deciding on an appropriate thesis—the claim, or conclusion, that the essay is designed to support or prove. Very often, when an essay runs off the track and crashes, the derailment can be traced to a thesis that was bad from the beginning.

Picking a thesis out of the air and beginning to write is usually a mistake. Any thesis statement that you craft without knowing anything about the subject is likely to be ill-formed or indefensible. It's better to begin by selecting an issue— a question that's controversial or in dispute—then researching it to determine what arguments or viewpoints are involved. To research it, you can survey the views of people or organizations involved in the controversy. Read articles and books, talk to people, go online. This process should not only inform you about various viewpoints but also tell you what arguments are used to support them. It should also help you narrow the issue to one that you can easily address in the space you have.

Suppose you begin with this issue: whether the United States has serious industrial pollution problems. After investigating this issue, you would probably see that it is much too broad to be addressed in a short paper. You should then restrict the issue to something more manageable—for example: whether recent legislation to allow coal-burning power plants to emit more sulfur dioxide will harm people's health. With the scope of the issue narrowed, you can explore arguments on both sides. You cannot examine every single argument, but you should assess the strongest ones, including those that you devise yourself. You can then use what you've already learned about arguments to select one that you think provides good support for its conclusion. The premises and conclusion of this argument can then serve as the bare-bones outline of your essay. Your argument might look like this:

> [Premise 1] Excessive amounts of sulfur dioxide in the air have been linked to increases in the incidence of asthma and other respiratory illnesses.
>
> [Premise 2] Many areas of the country already have excessive amounts of sulfur dioxide in the air.
>
> [Premise 3] Most sulfur dioxide in the air comes from coal-burning power plants.
>
> [Conclusion] Therefore, allowing coal-burning power plants to emit more sulfur dioxide will most likely increase the incidence of respiratory illnesses.

For the sake of example, the premises of this argument are made up. But your essay's argument must be for real, with each premise that could be called into question supported by an additional argument. After all, your readers are not likely to accept your argument's conclusion if they doubt your premises.

In some cases, your paper may contain more than one argument supporting a single conclusion, or it may offer a critique of someone else's argument. In either case, investigating an issue and the arguments involved will follow the pattern just suggested. In a critique of an argument (or arguments), you offer reasons why the argument fails and thus support the thesis that the conclusion is false.

This process of devising a thesis statement and crafting an argument to back it up is not linear. You will probably have to experiment with several arguments before you find one that's suitable. Even after you decide on an argument, you may later discover that its premises are dubious or that they cannot be adequately supported. Then you will have to backtrack to investigate a better argument. Backtracking in this preliminary stage is relatively easy. If you postpone this rethinking process until you are almost finished with your first draft, it will be harder—and more painful.

From Thesis to Outline

We have just seen that the second step in writing an argumentative essay (after determining your thesis statement, or conclusion) is creating an outline. Outlines are useful because, among other things, they help avert disaster in the essay-writing phase. Imagine writing two-thirds of your essay, then discovering that the second premise of your argument cannot be supported and is in fact false. You might have to throw out the whole argument and start over.

At the head of your outline, insert your thesis statement, articulating it as clearly and as precisely as possible. At every stage of outlining, you can then refer to the statement for guidance. The premises and conclusion of your argument (or arguments) will constitute the major points of your outline. The following, for example, is the preliminary outline for the essay discussed earlier:

> **THESIS:** Allowing coal-burning power plants to emit more sulfur dioxide will most likely increase the incidence of respiratory illnesses.
>
> I. Excessive amounts of sulfur dioxide in the air have been linked to increases in the incidence of asthma and other respiratory illnesses.
> II. Many areas of the country already have excessive amounts of sulfur dioxide in the air.
> III. Most sulfur dioxide in the air comes from coal-burning power plants.
> IV. Therefore, allowing coal-burning power plants to emit more sulfur dioxide will most likely increase the incidence of respiratory illnesses.

After you clearly state the premises, you need to ask yourself whether any of them need to be defended. As discussed earlier, any premise likely to be questioned by your readers will need support. That is, the premise itself will need arguments to back it up, and the supporting arguments should be indicated in your outline. (Some premises, though, may not need support because they are obvious or generally accepted.) As discussed in chapter 3, you can support a premise (claim) through deductive or inductive arguments with premises made up of examples, analogies, empirical evidence (such as scientific research or trustworthy observations), and authoritative judgments (such as those from reliable experts). Here's how the preceding outline might look with (fictional) supporting arguments clearly shown:

> **THESIS:** Allowing coal-burning power plants to emit more sulfur dioxide will most likely increase the incidence of respiratory illnesses.
>
> I. Excessive amounts of sulfur dioxide in the air have been linked to increases in the incidence of asthma and other respiratory illnesses.
>   A. EPA data show an association between high amounts of sulfur dioxide and increased respiratory illnesses.
>   B. Cities that monitor air pollution have noted increases in hospital admissions for asthma and other respiratory ills when sulfur dioxide emissions are high.
> II. Many areas of the country already have excessive amounts of sulfur dioxide in the air.
>   A. Scientists have reported high levels of sulfur dioxide in the air in fifteen major cities.
>   B. The EPA confirms this.

III. Most sulfur dioxide in the air comes from coal-burning power plants.

    A. Many environmental scientists assert that coal-burning power plants are the source of most sulfur dioxide.

    B. A few owners of coal-burning power plants admit that their plants emit most of the sulfur dioxide in their region.

IV. Therefore, allowing coal-burning power plants to emit more sulfur dioxide will most likely increase the incidence of respiratory illnesses.

You should expand your outline until you've indicated how you intend to provide support for each claim that requires it. This level of detail helps ensure that you will not encounter any nasty surprises in the writing phase.

Your essay should somehow address objections or criticisms that your readers are likely to raise, and your outline should indicate how you intend to do this. Answering objections can make your case stronger and lend credibility to you as the writer. Sometimes it's best to address objections where they are likely to arise—in connection with specific premises or arguments. At other times, your essay may be more effective if you deal with objections at the end of it, near the conclusion.

As you work through your outline, don't be afraid to rework your thesis statement or to make changes in arguments. Satisfy yourself that the outline is complete and that it reflects a logical progression of points.

From Outline to First Draft

If you have developed a detailed outline, then you have a path to follow as you write. And while you're writing an argumentative essay, having a path is much better than searching for one. Your outline should make the writing much easier.

No outline is a finished work, however. As you write, you may discover that your arguments are not as strong as you thought, or that other arguments would be better, or that changing a point here and there would make an argument more effective. If so, you should amend your outline and then continue writing. The act of writing is often an act of discovery, and good writers are not afraid of revisions or multiple drafts.

Start your draft with a solid opening that draws your readers into your essay and prepares the way for your arguments. Good openings are interesting, informative, and short. Grab the attention of your readers with a bold statement of your thesis, a provocative quote, a compelling story, or interesting facts. Prepare the way for your arguments by explaining why the question you're addressing is important, why you're concerned about it, or why it involves a pressing problem. Don't assume that your readers will see immediately that the issue you're dealing with is worth their time.

Include a clear statement of your thesis in your opening (in the first paragraph or very close by). In many cases, you will want to tell the reader how you plan to develop your argument or how the rest of the essay will unfold (without going into lengthy detail). In any case, by the time your audience reads through your opening, they should know exactly what you intend to prove and why.

Consider this opening for our imaginary essay on air pollution:

> Respiratory experts at the National Institutes of Health say that sulfur dioxide in the air is a poison that we should avoid. Yet the current administration wants to loosen environmental rules to allow coal-burning power plants to emit more sulfur dioxide than they already do. That's a bad idea. The latest evidence shows that letting the plants emit more of this poison will most likely increase the incidence of respiratory illnesses in hundreds of communities.

This opening gets the reader's attention by sounding the alarm about a serious health hazard. It provides enough background information to help us understand the seriousness of the problem. And the thesis statement in the last sentence announces what the essay will try to prove.

The body of your essay should fully develop the arguments for your thesis statement, or conclusion. You should devote at least one paragraph to each premise, though several paragraphs may be necessary. You may opt to deal with objections to your argument as you go along, perhaps as you put forth each premise, or at the end of the essay just before the conclusion. Each paragraph should develop and explain just one idea, which is usually expressed in a topic sentence. Each sentence in each paragraph should relate to the paragraph's main idea. Any sentence that has no clear connection to the main idea should be deleted or revised. Link paragraphs together in a logical sequence using transitional words and phrases or direct references to material in preceding paragraphs.

Here are two paragraphs that might follow the air pollution opening:

> Scientists used to wonder whether there is a connection between airborne sulfur dioxide and respiratory illness—but no more. Research has repeatedly shown a strong link between high levels of sulfur dioxide in the air and diseases that affect the lungs. For example, data from studies conducted by the Environmental Protection Agency (EPA) show that when levels of airborne sulfur dioxide in urban areas reach what the EPA calls the "high normal" range, the incidence of respiratory illnesses increases dramatically. According to several EPA surveys of air quality, many major cities (not just Los Angeles) often have high normal levels of sulfur dioxide in the air. In addition, data from health departments in large cities show that when levels of airborne sulfur dioxide are at their highest, hospital admissions for asthma and other respiratory ills also increase.
>
> These findings, however, tell only half the story. Many parts of the country have more than just occasional surges in levels of airborne sulfur dioxide. They must endure unsafe levels continuously. New studies from the National

Institutes of Health demonstrate that in at least ten major cities, the amount of sulfur dioxide in the air is excessive all the time.

In this passage, a single paragraph is devoted to each premise. Each paragraph develops a single idea, which is stated in a topic sentence. (The topic sentence for the first paragraph: "Research has repeatedly shown a strong link between high levels of sulfur dioxide in the air and diseases that affect the lungs." The second paragraph: "[Many parts of the country] must endure unsafe levels continuously.") Each sentence in each paragraph relates to the topic sentence, and the relationships among the sentences are clear. Likewise the connection between the discussion in the first paragraph and that of the second is apparent. The transitional sentence in the second paragraph ("These findings, however, tell only half the story") helps bridge the gap between the paragraphs. Both of them help support the thesis statement.

How you end your essay is often as important as how you start it. In short or simple essays, there may be no need for a conclusion. The thesis may be clear and emphatic without a conclusion. In many cases, however, an essay is strengthened by a conclusion, and sometimes a conclusion is absolutely essential. Often without an effective conclusion, an essay may seem to end pointlessly or to be incomplete. The typical conclusion reiterates or reaffirms the thesis statement without being repetitious. Or the conclusion of the essay's argument serves as the conclusion for the whole essay. In long or complex essays, the conclusion often includes a summary of the main points discussed.

Sometimes a conclusion is a call to action, an invitation to the reader to do something about a problem. Sometimes it relates a story that underscores the importance of the essay's argument. Sometimes it highlights a provocative aspect of a claim defended earlier. In all cases it serves to increase the impact of the essay.

The conclusion, however, is not the place to launch into a completely different issue, make entirely unsubstantiated claims, malign those who disagree with you, or pretend that your argument is stronger than it really is. These tacks will not strengthen your essay but weaken it.

Matters of Style and Content

1. *Write to your audience.* Almost everything you write—from college papers to love notes—is intended for a particular audience. Knowing who your audience is can make all the difference in what you say and how you say it. Unless things have gone terribly awry, you would not ordinarily address members of the town council the same way you would your one true love; nor your one true love as you would readers of the *New England Journal of Medicine*. You may wonder, then, who is the intended audience of your paper?

Your instructor, of course, may specify your audience and thus settle the issue for you. Otherwise, you should assume that your audience consists of intelligent, curious readers who are capable of understanding and appreciating clearly written, well-made papers on many subjects. Writing to your proper audience means that you will have to define unfamiliar terms, explain any points that may be misunderstood, and lay out your argument so that its structure and significance would be clear to any intelligent reader. This approach will both force you to attempt a better understanding of your subject and help you demonstrate this understanding through your writing.

2. *Do not overstate premises or conclusions.* Overstatement is the problem of exaggerating claims, of making an assertion sound stronger or more inclusive than it deserves. We are all guilty of overstatement, most often in everyday speech. We may say, "Everyone dislikes Professor Jones" or "Americans think the French are snobbish" when in fact only *some* students dislike Professor Jones and only *a few* of our American friends think that *some* French people are snobbish.

In everyday conversation, such exaggerations are often understood as such and are used innocuously for emphasis. But too often the overstatements are simply distortions, assertions that claim too much and lead us into error or prejudice. To a disconcerting degree, assertions regarding opposing views in religion, politics, and morality are overstatements.

Overstatement can arise in at least two ways. First, particular statements—including premises—can be exaggerated. You may be tempted to assert that whatever issue you are addressing in your essay is "the most important issue of our time." You might declare that a premise is certainly or undoubtedly true (when in fact it is merely probable) or forgo important qualifiers such as "some," "perhaps," and "many." You may get carried away and say, for example, that killing another human being is *always* morally wrong, even though you would admit that killing in self-defense is morally permissible.

Second, the conclusions of arguments can be overstated: They can go beyond what logical inference would permit. Because of your commitment to your conclusion, you may overstate it. The result is an invalid or weak argument.

3. *Treat opponents and opposing views fairly.* Sometimes it seems that most of what people know about arguing a position they have learned from the worst possible teachers—political debate-type television programs or social media. In these forums, the standard procedure is to attack the character and motivations of opponents, distort or misrepresent opposing views, and dismiss opponents' evidence and concerns out of hand. But in good writing, abusive or unfair tactics are out of order. They are also ineffective. When readers encounter such heavy-handedness, they are likely to be suspicious of the writer's motives, to wonder if the writer is close-minded, to question whether his or her assertions can be trusted, or to doubt the worth of arguments defended with such gratuitous zeal.

4. *Write clearly.* Being clear is a matter of ensuring that your meaning is understood by the reader. In most kinds of writing, clarity is almost always a supreme virtue.

Lack of clarity in your writing can occur in several ways. Inexperienced writers often produce some very murky papers because too often they assume that because they know what they mean, others will know too. Typically, others do *not* know. The problem is that new writers have not yet developed the knack of viewing their own writing as others might. In other words, they fail to adopt an objective stance toward their own words. Good writers are their own best critics.

Trying to view your writing as others might takes practice. A trick that often helps is to not look at your writing for a day or two then go back to it and read it cold. You may discover after you take this little break that some passages that seemed clear to you earlier are mostly gibberish. Another technique is to use peer review. Ask a friend to read your paper and pinpoint any passages that seem unclear.

Writing with clarity involves careful attention to language and how it's used. Most often this means properly defining terms, sorting out ambiguities, and eliminating excessive vagueness.

Definitions

As noted earlier, sometimes a dispute can hang on the meaning of a single term. Clarify the meaning, and the disagreement dissolves. In an argumentative essay, clarifying terms often comes down to offering precise definitions of words that are crucial to your argument.

In general, any definition you offer should decrease vagueness or ambiguity and thereby increase the effectiveness of your writing. Your definitions should also be consistent. If you provide a definition for a term in your essay, then you should stick to that definition throughout. Altering the meaning of a term in mid-essay, or using more than one term to refer to the same thing, can be confusing to the reader—and might even subvert your essay's argument.

As we saw earlier, good writers are also very much aware of another kind of meaning—the meaning that comes from a word's connotations. Connotations can be put to work as both euphemisms and dysphemisms. Consider these words: "soldier," "warrior," and "grunt." These terms have nearly the same literal meaning, but they differ in the emotions or attitudes they convey. Or what about these terms: "tavern," "saloon," "bar," "watering hole," and "dive." They refer to the same kind of establishment, but the images or emotions conveyed are diverse, ranging from the respectable and pleasant (tavern) to the lowly and odious (dive).

Ambiguity

Ambiguity can also make writing less clear. A term or statement is ambiguous if it has more than one meaning (and the context doesn't help clear things up). Some ambiguities are *semantic*; they are the result of multiple meanings of a word or phrase. Consider the sentence, "Kids make nutritious snacks." The word *make* could mean *prepare* or *constitute*. If the former, the sentence says that kids can prepare food. If the latter, the sentence means that kids are food.

Some ambiguities are *syntactic*; they are the result of the way words are combined. Read this sentence straight through without stopping: "Maria watched a bird with binoculars." Who had the binoculars, Maria or the bird? We don't know because the sentence is poorly written; words are misplaced. If we want the sentence to say that Maria was the one holding the binoculars, we might rewrite it like this: "Looking through her binoculars, Maria watched the bird."

Vagueness

Often a lack of clarity comes not from ambiguous terms but from *vague* terms—words that fail to convey one definite meaning. This failure can be the result of many kinds of sloppiness, but at the head of the list is the tendency to use words that are too *general*. General words refer to whole groups or classes of things, such as *soldiers*, *artists*, and *books*. *Specific* words, on the other hand, refer to more particular items, such as *Sgt. Morris*, *van Gogh*, and *The Sun Also Rises*. There is nothing inherently wrong with using general words; in fact, we must employ them in many circumstances. Used to excess, however, they can easily muddy a paper.

5. *Be careful what you assume.* Behind every argument there are presuppositions that need not be made explicit because they are taken for granted by all parties. They may be too obvious to mention or in no need of justification. (They are distinct from implicit premises, which are essential to an argument and should be brought out into the open.) In arguments about the rights of hospital patients, for example, there would typically be no need to explain that a hospital is not a Chevrolet truck, or that patient rights have something to do with ethics, or that such rights may be important to patients. You should, however, be careful not to presuppose a claim that may be controversial among your readers. If you wish to establish that abortion is morally permissible, you should not assume your readers will agree that women have a right to choose abortion or that a fetus is not a person.

An Annotated Sample Paper

Let's see how all this might be applied in an actual student essay.[1] The following incorporates the main elements of good argumentative papers and, as even the best essays do, exhibits both strengths and weaknesses—many of which are noted in the margins. Read the paper carefully, taking in the annotations as you go, making sure you understand each point before moving on to the next.

Free Speech on Campus

In order to meet the goals and purposes of higher education, free speech

Seem to be three arguments to discuss but this summary does not make that as clear as it should.

must remain intact. Thus, the University of Missouri should not adopt a campus hate speech code. ①The First Amendment protects all speech outside the university setting, and what happens outside of the university setting also should be allowed inside. ②Without an open forum for thought, though it may include hate speech, the university fails in its mission to provide a realistic experience for its students. By abolishing hate speech on university campuses, that open forum for discovery and knowledge is eliminated. As a result, learning and knowledge are stunted. ③Without the exchange of controversial ideas and opinions, there can be no real change in our society. Experiencing and debating is almost always better than suppressing, because censoring speech can never invoke real change.

Thesis statement

Summarizes the arguments to be made.

Provides background for first argument.

The First Amendment protects the right for every person to express opinions about the government and about each other. It actually "protects speech no matter how offensive the content" (Hate Speech on Campus, 1996). Just because something is offensive to one person does not mean it is offensive to another. Justice John M. Harlan wrote in Cohen v. California (1971), "One man's vulgarity is another's lyric" (Free Speech, 1996). In other words, just because something is offensive to one person docs not mean that it is offensive by definition.

Needs a more explicit transition to first argument.

Sources cited

Speech that is protected outside of the university setting also should be protected inside. Some would argue that hate speech hinders the abilities of minority students to learn, but part of the goal of higher education is to put students out of their comfort zone and to challenge their ways of thinking. In response to a sexual harassment policy being implemented

Responds to an objection to thesis.

at the University of Massachusetts, lawyer Harvey A. Silverglate (1995) wrote a memo to university administrators opposing the proposal.

> One of the primary purposes of a college education and experience is to challenge students, to make them question their comfortable lives and assumptions in short, to discomfort them in one way or another. (Silverglate, 1995)

Not clear how these quotations— which refer to sexual harassment— relate to hate speech.

In the same memo, Silverglate also wrote:

> If I am allowed to say something on the street corner, in a letter to the editor of a newspaper, or on a radio talk show, surely I should be allowed to say it on the campus of the University of Massachusetts.

First argument for thesis

This is equally true for the University of Missouri. What can possibly be gained by excluding an element of real life such as offensive speech from the campus experience? The university would only serve to deceive its students by shielding them from realistic situations while they are in school. This, in turn, only serves to place them into the real world with false expectations.

Alternatively, exploring and debating is almost always better than suppressing. The organization Justice on Campus (1995) contends that:

Introduces quotation

> When we hear speech or see images that offend us, nothing is more human than our urge to suppress or to destroy them. But as deeply human is our need to think and to share our thoughts with others. Censorship is the greatest evil because the censor's goal is to imprison the human spirit.

Second argument for thesis

In addition to providing a realistic picture of nonacademic life, allowing all types of speech on campus encourages an open forum for the discussion of all types of ideas. Discussion of controversial issues and different points of view are the fuel for a useful education. That is why higher education has a responsibility to ensure that all forms of speech are protected, analyzed, and addressed. "The right of free speech is indivisible. When one of us is denied this right, all of us are denied" (Hate Speech on Campus, 1996). By denying one point of view, we eliminate the open forum. A speech code on any university campus only hinders the ability of students and faculty to fully explore the market of ideas available to them. The University of Missouri is no exception to the idea that academic freedom is the bedrock of a free society.

Third argument for thesis

If we do not allow open expression, however hateful it is, then there can be no change, no growth. Racism, sexism, ageism, etc. are not going to diminish without being addressed in higher education. As noted by the ACLU (Hate Speech on Campus, 1995), "Verbal purity is not social change." Barring certain types of speech would be a seeming quick fix for issues such as racism, sexism, ageism, and homophobia, which often comprise hate speech. But racist statements are not the real problem between the races; racism is. If we bar all racially biased comments on campus, all we have done is fuel the racism. We have then given hatred the power to lurk and grow within us instead of communicating and debating about it in the open.

If hate speech is not allowed to occur openly, the problem of racism is never addressed. Like racism, hate speech itself is not the problem; hate is. As members of a society, we must communicate in order to solve problems and grow as individuals. This includes addressing hateful ideas and opinions. We can make no progress if we do not allow offensive kinds of speech to exist on campus. By barring them, we run the risk of being silenced ourselves.

Conclusion summarizes main arguments.

A hate speech code at the University of Missouri would be detrimental to everyone, from students to faculty. The First Amendment protects all kinds of speech, including the offensive. It does this in order to

Restatement of thesis

ensure that all voices are heard and that all issues can be addressed. To go through college with the idea that offensive speech does not happen is detrimental to students and to the society in which they live. The educational system is based on the idea that communication leads to learning and that learning leads to personal growth. Without the open forum for thought and the freedom to express controversial ideas, a higher education is worthless. Moreover, no one ever solved a controversial gender issue or a racial conflict in silence. There must be communication so that debate can transpire. In order for any change in our society to transpire, offensive speech must be allowed to continue. It can only be addressed and learned from if it is equally protected by the Constitution. Mike Godwin, of the Electronic Frontier Foundation, says, "when it comes to the Bill of Rights, what you don't use, you lose. The First Amendment is a terrible thing to waste" (Comments and quotes, 1995). If anyone has a responsibility to use the freedom granted by the First Amendment, higher education is at the top of the list.

References

American Civil Liberties Union. (1996). Hate speech on campus. [Online]. Available: http://www.aclu.org/library/pbp16.html

American Civil Liberties Union. (1996). Free speech. [Online]. Available: www.aclu.org/issues/freespeech/isfs.html

Justice on Campus. (1996). Comments and quotes on sexual harassment and free speech. [Student paper]

Justice on Campus. (1995). Speech codes and disciplinary charges. [Student paper]

Silverglate, H. A. (1995, November 23). Memo from Harvey Silverglate. [Student paper]

Answers to Exercises

Chapter 1
Exercise 1.1

1. Critical thinking is the systematic evaluation or formulation of beliefs, or statements, by rational standards.
4. Critical thinking operates according to rational standards in that beliefs are judged by how well they are supported by reasons.
6. The *critical* in critical thinking refers to the exercising of careful judgment and judicious evaluation.
8. A statement is an assertion that something is or is not the case.
11. An argument is a group of statements in which some of them (the premises) are intended to support another of them (the conclusion).
14. In an argument, a conclusion is a statement that premises are intended to support.
17. No.
19. Indicator words are words that frequently accompany arguments and signal that a premise or conclusion is present.
23. Look for the conclusion first.

Exercise 1.2

1. No statement.
4. No statement.
7. Statement.
10. No statement.

Exercise 1.3

1. Argument.
   Conclusion: He should avoid her.
4. No argument.
7. No argument.
11. Argument.
   Conclusion: Don't outlaw guns.

15. Argument.
Conclusion: Noisy car alarms should be banned.

Exercise 1.4

1. Argument.
Conclusion: Faster-than-light travel is not possible.
Premise: Faster-than-light travel would violate a law of nature.

4. Argument.
Conclusion: The flu epidemic on the East Coast is real.
Premise: Government health officials say so.
Premise: I personally have read at least a dozen news stories that characterize the situation as a "flu epidemic."

7. No argument.

10. No argument.

Exercise 1.5

3. Premise: Freedom of choice in all things is a basic moral right.
Premise: Abortion is no different from scraping off a few cells from one's skin, and a woman certainly has the right to do that.

6. Premise: Vaughn has admitted that he knows nothing about animals.
Premise: The Society for the Prevention of Cruelty to Animals has declared Vaughn a dummy when it comes to animals.

9. Premise: The Internet has led to the capture of more terrorists than anything else.
Premise: The US attorney general has asserted that the Internet is the best friend that antiterrorist teams have.

12. Premise: All the top TV critics agree that *Stranger Things* is the greatest series in TV history.
Premise: I have compared *Stranger Things* to all other TV series and found that the show outshines them all.

Exercise 1.6

1. Argument.
Conclusion: The Religious Right is not pro-family.
Premise: Concerned parents realize that children are curious about how their body works and need accurate, age-appropriate information about the human reproductive system.
Premise: Thanks to Religious Right pressure, many public schools have replaced sex education with fear-based "abstinence-only" programs that insult young people's intelligence and give them virtually no useful information.

3. Argument.
Conclusion: There is no archeological evidence for the [biblical] Flood.

Premise: If a universal Flood occurred between five and six thousand years ago, killing all humans except the eight on board the Ark, it would be abundantly clear in the archaeological record.

Premise: The destruction of all but eight of the world's people left no mark on the archaeology of human cultural evolution.

Chapter 2

Exercise 2.1

1. For critical thinking to be realized, the process must be systematic, it must be a true evaluation or formulation of claims, and it must be based on rational standards.
5. We take things too far when we accept claims for no reason.
7. You are most likely to let your self-interest get in the way of clear thinking when you have a significant personal stake in the conclusions you reach.
11. Group pressure can affect your attempts to think critically by allowing your need to be part of a group or your identification with a group undermine critical thinking.
14. A worldview is a set of fundamental ideas that help us make sense of a wide range of issues in life.
17. Critical thinking is concerned with objective truth claims.
21. Reasonable doubt, not certainty, is central to the acquisition of knowledge.

Exercise 2.2

1. Self-interest.
4. Group pressure (in this case, the we-are-better-than-them type).
7. Group pressure.
10. Self-interest.

Exercise 2.3

1. a. The charges are false.
   c. Important evidence that would exonerate Father Miller was not mentioned in the newspaper account.
3. a. A study from Harvard shows that women are less violent and less emotional than men.
6. No good reasons listed.

Exercise 2.4

1. Better-than-others group pressure. Possible negative consequence: failure to consider other points of view; discrimination against people who disagree with Ortega.
3. It's not entirely clear what the group's motivations are. This passage could easily be an example of better-than-others group pressure.

7. Appeal to popularity. Possible negative consequence: overlooking other factors that might be a lot more important than popularity.

Exercise 2.5

1. Face-saving. Possible negative consequences: poor academic performance due to overconfidence; embarrassment of failure after being so cocky; alienation of friends.

2. Self-interest. Possible negative consequences: wasting the taxpayer's money; being thrown out of office for misconduct.

Chapter 3

Exercise 3.1

4. Deductive.

8. Sound.

12. No.

Exercise 3.2

2. Step 1: Conclusion: She has a superior intellect.
Premises: Ethel graduated from Yale. If she graduated from Yale, she probably has a superior intellect.
Step 2: Not deductively valid.
Step 3: Inductively strong.
Step 4: Does not apply.

6. Step 1: Conclusion: Thus, every musician has a college degree.
Premises: Every musician has had special training, and everyone with special training has a college degree.
Step 2: Deductively valid.
Step 3: Does not apply.
Step 4: Does not apply.

9. Step 1: Conclusion: So some actors who sing also play a musical instrument.
Premises: Some actors sing, and some play a musical instrument.
Step 2: Not deductively valid.
Step 3: Not inductively strong.
Step 4: Intended to be deductive.

15. Step 1: Conclusion: So it's impossible for androids to have minds.
Premises: If minds are identical to brains—that is, if one's mind is nothing but a brain—androids could never have minds because they wouldn't have brains.
Clearly, a mind is nothing but a brain.
Step 2: Deductively valid.

Step 3: Does not apply.
Step 4: Does not apply.

Exercise 3.3

3. Valid.
8. Valid.
14. Invalid.
18. Valid.
23. Invalid.

Exercise 3.4

I.

1. Senator Greed was caught misusing campaign funds.
5. She's not incompetent.
9. The engine started right away.

II.

3. Sixty percent of the teenagers in several scientific surveys love rap music.
6. Assad's fingerprints are on the vase.
9. The murder rates in almost all large cities in the South are very high.

Chapter 4

Exercise 4.1

1. Valid; modus tollens.
6. Valid; modus tollens.
9. Valid; modus ponens.

Exercise 4.2

2. If Lino is telling the truth, he will admit to all charges.
Lino is telling the truth.
So he will admit to all charges.
If Lino is telling the truth, he will admit to all charges.
He will not admit to all charges.
So he is not telling the truth.

5. If religious conflict in Nigeria continues, thousands more will die.
The religious conflict in Nigeria will continue.
Therefore, thousands more will die.
If religious conflict in Nigeria continues, thousands more will die.
Thousands more will not die.
Therefore, religious conflict in Nigeria will not continue.

9. If solar power can supply six megawatts of power in San Francisco (which is certainly not the sunniest place in the world), then solar power can transform the energy systems in places like Texas and Arizona.
Solar power can supply six megawatts of power in San Francisco.
So solar power can transform the energy systems in places like Texas and Arizona.
If solar power can supply six megawatts of power in San Francisco (which is certainly not the sunniest place in the world), then solar power can transform the energy systems in places like Texas and Arizona.
But solar power cannot transform the energy systems in places like Texas and Arizona.
So solar power cannot supply six megawatts of power in San Francisco.

Exercise 4.3

1. Conclusion: The idea that God is required to be the enforcer of the moral law is not plausible.
Premises: (4) In the first place, as an empirical hypothesis about the psychology of human beings, it is questionable. (5) There is no unambiguous evidence that theists are more moral than nontheists. (6) Not only have psychological studies failed to find a significant correlation between frequency of religious worship and moral conduct, but convicted criminals are much more likely to be theists than atheists. (7) Second, the threat of divine punishment cannot impose a moral obligation. (8) Might does not make right.

Chapter 5

Exercise 5.1

1. Target group: people in the country; sample: adults in New York and San Francisco; relevant property: being "prochoice" in the abortion debate. The argument is weak because the sample is not representative.
4. Target group: students at this university; sample: first-year students at this university; relevant property: being against such a militant policy. The argument is weak because the sample is both too small and not representative.
8. Target group: dentists; sample: dentists who suggest that their patients chew gum; relevant property: recommending Brand X gum. The argument is weak because the sample is not representative.
12. Target group: Americans; sample: adults with an annual income of $48,000–$60,000; relevant property: being happy and satisfied with one's job. The argument is weak because the sample is not representative. (Middle-income workers are likely to have attitudes toward job satisfaction that are different from those of workers in other income brackets, especially lower ones.)

Exercise 5.2

1. Weak. To ensure a strong argument, randomly draw the sample from the entire US population, not just from a couple of bicoastal cities.
4. Weak. To ensure a strong argument, randomly draw a sample of several hundred students from the whole university population, not just the first-year students.
8. Weak. To ensure a strong argument, randomly draw the sample from the set of all dentists, not just the dentists who recommend gum.
12. Weak. To ensure a strong argument, randomly draw the sample from the set of all American workers, including respondents representative of all income groups.

Exercise 5.3

1. Does not offer strong support for the conclusion. The problem is nonrandom—and therefore nonrepresentative—sampling.

Exercise 5.4

1. a, c.

Exercise 5.5

2. Literary analogy.
6. Argument by analogy. Two things being compared; relevant similarity: working with numbers; conclusion: "he'll be a whiz at algebra"; weak argument.
8. Argument by analogy; three things being compared; relevant similarity: being pork; conclusion: "I will like chitlins"; weak argument.
12. Argument by analogy; two things being compared; relevant similarity: being foundations; conclusions: "no lasting reputation worthy of respect can be built on a weak character"; strong argument.

Exercise 5.6

1. Instance being compared: the personality traits of Ronald Reagan and George W. Bush; relevant similarities: staunch conservatism, strong Christian values, almost dogmatic adherence to conservative principles; diversity among cases not a significant factor; conclusion: "President Bush will likely be involved in a similar foreign policy mess for similar reasons"; weak argument (because of several unmentioned dissimilarities).

5. Instances being compared: Having terminal cancer and being threatened by an assailant; relevant similarities: being threatened with death or great pain; diversity among cases not a significant factor; conclusion: "suicide must sometimes be morally justified when it is an act of self-defense against a terminal disease that threatens death or great pain." This is a strong argument—*if* all the relevant similarities and dissimilarities have indeed been taken into account. A critic could argue, though, that killing oneself in self-defense is just not relevantly similar to killing another human in self-defense. The critic, then, would have to specify what the significant difference is.

Chapter 6

Exercise 6.1

4. We should proportion our belief to the evidence.
10. Two additional indicators are reputation among peers and professional accomplishments.
17. By making a conscious effort to consider not only information that supports what we believe but also the information that conflicts with it.

Exercise 6.2

4. Proportion belief to the evidence; the claim is not dubious enough to dismiss out of hand, and not worthy of complete acceptance. Low plausibility.
6. Reject it; it conflicts with a great deal of background information.
10. Proportion belief to the evidence; the claim is not dubious enough to dismiss out of hand, and it is not worthy of complete acceptance. Moderate plausibility.
14. Reject it; it conflicts with a great deal of background information.
17. Reject it; it conflicts with a great deal of background information.

Exercise 6.3

3. Do not agree. Persuasive evidence would include the body of an alien or the alien craft itself, both scientifically documented as being of extraterrestrial origin.
8. Do not agree. Persuasive evidence would include several double-blind, controlled trials demonstrating that meditation and controlled breathing shrink tumors.

Chapter 7

Exercise 7.1

2. Conclusion: "Research suggests that eating lots of fruits and vegetables may provide some protection against several types of cancer." Correlation. The argument is strong. The conclusion is a limited claim ("*may* provide some protection . . . "), which the stated correlation could easily support.

7. Conclusion: "Education increases people's earning power." Correlation. The argument is strong.

Exercise 7.2

2. a, d.

7. a.

Exercise 7.3

1. a.

4. b.

9. a.

Chapter 8

Exercise 8.1

4. A theoretical explanation is an explanation that serves as a theory, or hypothesis, used to explain why something is the way it is, why something is the case, or why something happened.

8. A causal explanation is a kind of theoretical explanation. Like all theoretical explanations, causal explanations are used in inference to the best explanation.

Exercise 8.2

2. The minimum requirement of consistency is the criterion that any theory worth considering must have both internal and external consistency—that is, be free of contradictions and be consistent with the data the theory is supposed to explain.

6. A theory that does not have much scope is one that explains very little—perhaps only the phenomenon it was introduced to explain and not much else.

Exercise 8.3

2. The state of affairs being explained is the endangered status of the spotted owl. The explanation is the powerful influence of the logging industry.

5. The state of affairs being explained is the incidence of robberies. The explanation is that there aren't enough gun owners.

8. The state of affairs being explained is the many times that psychics have seemed to predict the future. The explanation is that psychics really can predict the future.

Exercise 8.4

2. Theory 1: Jack's house was burglarized. Theory 2: Jack's dog went on a rampage.

6. Theory 1: Alice was not exposed to any germs.
Theory 2: Vitamin C supercharged Alice's immune system.

Exercise 8.6

2. The second theory is both simpler and more conservative.

4. The first theory is both simpler and more conservative.

7. The first theory is both simpler and more conservative.

Chapter 9

Exercise 9.1

6. (1) Identify the problem or pose a question, (2) devise a hypothesis to explain the event or phenomenon, (3) derive a test implication or prediction, (4) perform the test, (5) accept or reject the hypothesis.

9. If H, then C. Not-C. Therefore, not-H.

12. No. Hypotheses are tested together with other hypotheses. A hypothesis can always be saved from refutation by making changes in one of the accompanying hypotheses.

Exercise 9.2

2. Hypothesis: Two guys are perpetrating a Bigfoot hoax. Test implication: If the two guys are perpetrating a hoax, then monitoring their behavior day and night should yield evidence of hoaxing activity.

6. Hypothesis: Creatine dramatically increases the performance of weight trainers. Test implication: If creatine increases performance, then giving creatine to weight trainers in a controlled way (in a double-blind controlled trial) should increase various measures of performance in the trainers compared to weight trainers who get a placebo (inactive substance).

Exercise 9.3

3. Theory: Local climate changes. Competing theory: Heat from volcanic activity around the planet is melting the glaciers. Both theories are about equal in terms of testability, fruitfulness, and scope. The volcanic theory, however, is neither simple nor conservative. It's not simple because it assumes an unknown process. It's not conservative because it is not consistent with what is known about the effects of heat from volcanoes.

7. Theory: Religion fosters terrorism. Competing theory: Terrorists commit terrorist acts because they are insane. Both theories are about equal in terms of testability, fruitfulness, scope, and simplicity. The insanity theory, though, is not conservative. It conflicts with what we know about those who commit terrorist acts. In general, terrorists may be fanatical, but they do not seem to be clinically insane.

Exercise 9.4

2. Test implication: If brighter street lights decrease the crime rate, then reducing the brightness of the lights (while keeping constant all other factors, such as police patrols) should increase the crime rate. The test would likely confirm the theory.

6. Test implication: If eating foods high in fat contributes more to overweight than eating foods high in carbohydrates, then over time people should gain more body weight when they are eating X number of grams of fat per day than when they are eating the same number of grams of carbohydrates per day.

Chapter 10
Exercise 10.1

4. The fallacy of composition is arguing that what is true of the parts must be true of the whole.

10. They are fallacious because they assume that a proposition is true merely because a great number of people believe it; however, as far as the truth of a claim is concerned, what many people believe is irrelevant.

15. Yes.

19. People are often taken in by false dilemmas because they don't think beyond the alternatives laid before them.

Exercise 10.2

1. Composition.
5. Genetic fallacy.
10. Appeal to the person.
14. Equivocation.
19. Appeal to the person.
24. Stereotyping.
26. Euphemism.

Exercise 10.3

4. False dilemma.
6. Hasty generalization.
10. False dilemma.

Exercise 10.4

3. Jones says that Mrs. Anan deserves the Nobel Prize. But he's a friend of hers. Clearly then Mrs. Anan does not deserve the Nobel Prize.
6. In light of ethical considerations, the Boy Scouts of America should allow gay kids to be members. The reason is that banning gay kids from the organization would be in conflict with basic moral principles.
11. There are too many guns on the streets because our politicians are controlled by the National Rifle Association and other gun nuts. We don't want the NRA telling us what to do.

Chapter 11

Exercise 11.1

5. We cannot infer what should be or ought to be from what is.
9. Moral theories try to explain what makes an action right or what makes a person good.
13. Internal consistency—the requirement that the theories composing our worldview do not conflict.

Exercise 11.2

1. Nonmoral.
6. Moral.
9. Moral.

Exercise 11.3

4. The Indian government posed an imminent threat to Pakistan and the world. When a foreign government poses an imminent threat to Pakistan and the world, Pakistanis are justified in attacking that government. So the Pakistanis were justified in attacking Indian troops.

9. Hacking into a database containing personal information on thousands of people and invading their privacy is immoral. You hacked into a database containing personal information on thousands of people and invaded their privacy. Therefore, what you did was immoral.

Exercise 11.4

3. Killing another human being in self-defense is morally permissible. So it is not the case that in all circumstances the killing of a human being is wrong.

7. If helping someone to commit suicide would somehow save the lives of millions of people, the act would seem to be morally permissible. So it is not the case that assisted suicide is never morally justified.

Answers to Self-Assessment Quizzes

Chapter 1

1. A group of statements in which some of them (the premises) are intended to support another of them (the conclusion).
2. Premise indicators: *because, due to the fact that, inasmuch as*. Conclusion indicators: *therefore, it follows that, it must be that*.
3. **b.** Read the story and write a complete review of it.
4. **c.** Campus speakers should be allowed to speak freely without being shouted down.
5. No argument.
6. Argument. Conclusion: War can solve problems.
7. Argument: President Bush is not slashing domestic spending.
8. Conclusion.
9. Premise.
10. Conclusion.
11. Premise.
12. Conclusion.
13. Premise: DNA evidence is unreliable.
    Premise: Unreliable evidence should not be used in cases of capital murder.
14. Premise: No computer has yet been able to converse with a human being well enough to be indistinguishable from humans.
    Premise: Such a feat requires consciousness, and machines cannot even in principle produce consciousness.
15. Premise: All of Nostradamus's predictions have come true. Premise: The prediction about September 11 was unambiguous and specific.
16. 10.
17. 6, 7, 9.
18. 1, 2, 3, 5.
19. 8.
20. 4, 11.

Chapter 2

1. Systematic process, involving genuine evaluation or formulation of beliefs, gauged according to rational standards.
2. A surge of strong emotions.
3. We may ignore facts that contradict our beliefs and search out facts that support them.
4. The we-are-better pressure.
5. A philosophy of life, a set of fundamental ideas that helps us make sense of a wide range of important issues in life.
6. Reasonable doubt.
7. Failure to look for opposing evidence increases the chance of error.
8. Face-saving.
9. Face-saving.
10. Self-interested thinking.
11. Group pressure.
12. Group pressure.
13. Group pressure.
14. Self-serving.
15. Group pressure.
16. Face-saving.
17. Group pressure.
18. Subjectivist fallacy.
19. Subjectivist fallacy.
20. Social relativism.

Chapter 3

1. Deductive argument: intended to provide logically conclusive support for its conclusion. Inductive argument: intended to provide probable, not conclusive, support for its conclusion.
2. Valid argument: a deductive argument that succeeds in providing conclusive support for its conclusion. Invalid argument: a deductive argument that fails to provide conclusive support for its conclusion. Strong inductive argument: an inductive argument that succeeds in providing probable, but not conclusive, logical support for its conclusion.
3. Sound argument: a deductively valid argument that has true premises.
4. Deductive.
5. Inductive.
6. Inductive.
7. Deductive.

8. Anyone who doesn't openly criticize any military action against any Middle Eastern nation is a warmonger.

9. The most likely reason for Maria's failing her driving test three times is that she's not paying attention.

10. People who believe in astrology or tarot cards do not do well in college science courses.

11. Valid.

12. Valid.

13. Valid.

14. Valid.

15. *Conclusion*: Cole is up to no good.

16. *Conclusion*: The sitcom *Friends* is becoming really lame.

17. *Conclusion*: [Dolphins] are definitely self-conscious, intelligent, and creative.

18. *Conclusion*: The dictum to always tell the truth is not a valid moral principle.

19. *Conclusion*: I shouldn't vote for any independent candidate in the next election.

20. *Conclusion*: Creationism is an inadequate theory about the origins of life.

Chapter 4

1. If p, then q.   modus ponens
   p.
   Therefore, q.

2. If p, then q.   modus tollens
   Not q.
   Therefore, not p.

3. If p, then q.   hypothetical syllogism
   If q, then r.
   Therefore, if p, then r.

4. Either p or q.   disjunctive syllogism
   Not p.
   Therefore, q.

5. If p, then q.   affirming the consequent
   q.
   Therefore, p.

6. If p, then q.   denying the antecedent
   Not p.
   Therefore, not q.

7. p.   reductio
   If p, then q.

Not q.
Therefore, not p.

8. Either p or q.   disjunctive syllogism
   Not p.
   Therefore, q.

9. If p, then q.   modus tollens
   Not q.
   Therefore, not p.

10. antecedent. The first part of a conditional statement (If p, then q.), the component that begins with the word *if*.

11. weak argument. An inductive argument that fails to provide strong support for its conclusion.

12. valid argument. A deductive argument that succeeds in providing conclusive support for its conclusion.

13. cogent argument. A strong inductive argument with all true premises.

14. conditional statement. An "if-then" statement; it consists of the antecedent (the part introduced by the word *if*) and the consequent (the part introduced by the word *then*).

15. consequent. The part of a conditional statement (If p, then q) introduced by the word *then*.

16. deductive argument. An argument intended to provide logically conclusive support for its conclusion.

17. inductive argument. An argument in which the premises are intended to provide probable, not conclusive, support for its conclusion.

18. strong argument. An inductive argument that succeeds in providing probable—but not conclusive—support for its conclusion.

19. invalid argument. A deductive argument that fails to provide conclusive support for its conclusion.

Chapter 5

1. An inductive argument that reasons from premises about individual members of a group to conclusions about the group as a whole (from particular to general, or the part to the whole).

   X percent of the observed members of group A have property P.
   Therefore, X percent of all members of group A probably have property P.

2. The group as a whole is called the target population or target group. The observed members of the target group are called the sample members or sample. And the property we're interested in is called the relevant property or property in question.

3. The sample can be (1) too small or (2) not representative.

4. Analogical induction reasons that because two or more things are similar in several respects, they must be similar in some further respect.

   Thing A has properties P1, P2, P3 plus the property P4.

   Thing B has properties P1, P2, and P3.

   Therefore, thing B probably has property P4.

5. All the women in my yoga class are against the war. Ninety percent of the members of a national women's group (twelve thousand members) are against the war. And all my women friends are against the war. The fact is, almost all American women oppose this war. Weak. Not representative.

6. Recently there was a racially motivated murder in Texas. Two white men killed a black man. Then another murder of a black man by some racist whites occurred in Louisiana. And in Mississippi an admitted racist finally was convicted of the murder of a black man that occurred years ago. The South has more racist killers than any other part of the country. Weak. Small sample; not representative.

7. Most professors at this college are not grading as strictly as they used to. They now give B's for work to which they used to assign C's. The grading standards in American colleges are dropping. Weak. Not representative; probably small sample.

8. The first time Ariana encountered trigonometry, she couldn't understand it. And the first time she read Shakespeare, she didn't get it. She will never understand anything. Weak. Small sample; not representative.

9. Americans are quite satisfied with the administration's recent foreign policy decisions. An "instant poll" conducted yesterday on the CNN website got fifteen thousand responses from site visitors—and 95 percent of them said that American foreign policy was on the right track. Weak. Not representative.

10. Judging from what I've seen, anti-war demonstrators are just a bunch of peaceniks left over from the Vietnam War era. Weak (if "what I've seen" means personally witnessed). Small sample; not representative.

11. "Suppose that someone tells me that he has had a tooth extracted without an anesthetic, and I express my sympathy, and suppose that I am then asked, 'How do you know that it hurt him?' I might reasonably reply, 'Well, I know that it would hurt me. I have been to the dentist and know how painful it is to have a tooth stopped without an anesthetic, let alone taken out. And he has the same sort of nervous system as I have. I infer, therefore, that in these conditions he felt considerable pain, just as I should myself.'" [Alfred J. Ayer] Two things compared: experiences of tooth extraction; conclusion: that the other person was in considerable pain; strong.

12. "As for one who is choosy about what he learns . . . we shall not call him a lover of learning or a philosopher, just as we shall not say that a man who is difficult about his food is hungry or has an appetite for food. We shall not call him a lover of food but a poor eater. . . . But we shall call a philosopher the man who is easily willing to learn every kind of knowledge, gladly turns to learning things, and is insatiable in this respect." [Socrates] Two things compared: philosopher and eater; conclusion: that a philosopher is someone easily willing to learn every kind of knowledge; strong.

13. "Let us begin with a parable [showing that statements about God have no meaning]. . . . Once upon a time two explorers came upon a clearing in the jungle. In the clearing were growing many flowers and many weeds. One explorer says, 'Some gardener must tend this plot.' The other disagrees, 'There is no gardener.' So they pitch their tents and set a watch. No gardener is ever seen. 'But perhaps he is an invisible gardener.' So they set up a barbed-wire fence. They electrify it. . . . But no shrieks ever suggest that some intruder has received a shock. No movements of the wire ever betray an invisible climber. . . . Yet still the Believer is not convinced. 'But there is a gardener, invisible, intangible, insensible.'. . . At last the Sceptic despairs, 'But what remains of your original assertion? Just how does what you call an invisible, intangible, eternally elusive gardener differ from an imaginary gardener or even from no gardener at all?'" [Antony Flew] Two things compared: belief in an elusive gardener and belief in God; conclusion: that talk of an undetectable being such as God is meaningless. Weak.

14. "The moon was a ghostly galleon tossed upon cloudy seas." [Alfred Noyes] Literary analogy.

15. "Duct tape is like the force. It has a light side, a dark side, and it holds the universe together." [Carl Zwanzig] Literary analogy.

16. "Howard Hughes was able to afford the luxury of madness, like a man who not only thinks he is Napoleon but hires an army to prove it." [Ted Morgan] Literary analogy.

17. My brother was always good at arithmetic, so he'll be a whiz at algebra. Argument by analogy; one instance compared; one relevant similarity; conclusion: my brother will be a whiz at algebra; weak.

18. I like sausage, and I like ham, and I like pork chops. So I will like chitlins. Argument by analogy; three instances compared; relevant similarity: being pork; conclusion: I will like chitlins; weak.

19. "Vigorous writing is concise. A sentence should contain no unnecessary words, a paragraph no unnecessary sentences, for the same reason that a drawing should have no unnecessary lines and a machine no unnecessary parts." [E. B. White] Argument by analogy; one instance being compared; relevant similarity: economy of parts; conclusion: vigorous writing contains no unnecessary parts; strong.

20. "Character is the foundation stone upon which one must build to win respect. Just as no worthy building can be erected on a weak foundation, so no lasting reputation worthy of respect can be built on a weak character." [R. C. Samsel] Literary analogy.

Chapter 6

1. If a claim conflicts with her background information, she has good reason to doubt it.
2. It is not desirable to believe a statement when there is no good reason for doing so.
3. (1) Education and training from reputable institutions or programs in the relevant field; (2) experience in making reliable judgments in the field; (3) reputation among peers (as reflected in the opinions of others in the same field, relevant prestigious awards, and positions of authority); and (4) professional accomplishments.
4. The expert is guilty of blatant violations of the critical thinking principles or of simple factual or formal errors; the expert's claims conflict with what you have good reason to believe; the expert does not adequately support his or her assertions; the expert's writing contains logical contradictions or inconsistent statements; the expert does not treat opposing views fairly; the expert is strongly biased, emotional, or dismissive; the expert relies on information you know is out of date.
5. Impairment due to environmental factors, fatigue, and stress.
6. Reasons for doubt due to low visibility.
7. Reasons for doubt due to vague stimuli.
8. There may or may not be reasons for doubt; the main factor is the reliability of memory.
9. Almost certainly false.
10. Probably true.
11. Almost certainly false.
12. Almost certainly false.
13. Almost certainly false.
14. Almost certainly false.
15. Almost certainly false.
16. Probably false.
17. Yes. Slanted in favor of US policy in Iraq.
18. Yes. Loaded or biased language includes "Ba'ath Party murderers," "Iraqi goon squads," and "regime diehards."
19. The Pentagon.
20. The story lacks the perspective of nonadministration sources and less biased reporters. Some aspects not mentioned: details about specific criticisms of US policy, casualties among Iraqis, evidence for Rumsfeld's claims.

Chapter 7

1. School violence is caused mainly by teens playing violent video games. Incidents of violence in schools have increased as more and more teens are playing violent video games, as the video games themselves have become more graphically and realistically violent, and as the number and variety of video games have expanded dramatically.
Conclusion: School violence is caused mainly by teens playing violent video games. Weak. Overlooking relevant factors, failing to rule out coincidence.

2. Smoking and exposure to secondhand smoke among pregnant women pose a significant risk to both infants and the unborn. According to numerous studies, each year the use of tobacco causes thousands of spontaneous births, infant deaths, and deaths from SIDS. Death rates for fetuses are 35 percent higher among pregnant women who smoke than among pregnant women who don't smoke.
Conclusion: Smoking and exposure to secondhand smoke among pregnant women pose a significant risk to both infants and the unborn. Strong.

3. Why are crime rates so high, the economy so bad, and our children so prone to violence, promiscuity, and vulgarity? These social ills have arisen—as they always have—from the "moral vacuum" created when Americans turn away from religion. Our current slide into chaos started when prayer was banned from public schools and secular humanism swooped in to replace it. And as God has slowly faded from public life, we have got deeper in the hole.
Conclusion: Serious social ills occur because Americans turn away from religion. Weak. Overlooking relevant factors, failing to rule out coincidence.

4. The twelve of us went on a hike through the mountains. We all drank bottled water except Lisa, who drank from a stream. Later she got really sick. Some intestinal thing. But the rest of us were fine. We've repeated this adventure many times on other hikes, with all but one of us drinking bottled water and one drinking from a stream. Everything else was the same. Each time, the person who drank from the stream got really ill. Drinking from streams on these hikes causes intestinal illness. Don't do it.
Conclusion: Drinking from streams on these hikes causes intestinal illness. Strong.

5. Ever since I started drinking herbal tea in the morning, my energy level has improved and I'm a lot calmer during the day. That stuff works.
Conclusion: Herbal tea boosts energy and calms the nerves. Weak. Overlooking relevant factors, failing to rule out coincidence, possibly confusing cause and effect.

6. Yesterday my astrological chart—prepared by a top astrologer—said that I would meet an attractive person today, and I did. Last week, it said I'd

come into some money, and I did. (Jack paid me that hundred dollars he owed me.) Now I'm a believer. The stars really do rule.

Conclusion: The stars rule. Weak. Failing to rule out coincidence.

7. Most of the terminal cancer patients in this ward who had positive attitudes about their disease lived longer than expected. Most of the negative-attitude patients didn't live as long as expected. A positive attitude can increase the life expectancy of people with terminal cancer.

   Conclusion: A positive attitude can increase the life expectancy of people with terminal cancer. Weak. Failing to rule out other relevant factors, failing to rule out coincidence, possibly confusing cause and effect.

8. *Conclusion*: Oranges and lemons were the most effective remedies for the illness. Joint method of agreement and difference. Strong.

9. *Conclusion*: Johnny's brother was the cause of this outbreak. Method of difference. Strong.

10. *Conclusion*: The extra calcium caused the increased density. Joint method of agreement and difference. Strong.

11. *Conclusion*: The new traffic light has made quite a difference. Method of difference. Strong.

12. *Conclusion*: There's a causal connection between serum cholesterol levels and risk of atherosclerosis. Correlation. Strong.

13. *Conclusion*: Tune-ups can improve the performance of lawnmowers. Method of difference. The argument is strong.

14. *Conclusion*: The reason there have been so many terrorist attacks in Western countries in the past ten years is that the rights of Palestinians have been violated by Westerners. Method of agreement. Strong.

15. *Conclusion*: Charlie is upset because he got word that his grades weren't good enough to get into medical school. Method of difference. Weak.

16. *Conclusion*: [Implied] Having a major war somewhere in the world causes the price of oil to hit $40 a barrel. Method of agreement. The argument is strong if all relevant factors have been taken into account, which might not be the case.

17. *Conclusion*: Running a major appliance interferes with my TV reception. Method of difference. Strong.

18. *Conclusion*: Lather-Up is better at killing germs. Joint method of agreement and difference. Strong.

19. *Conclusion*: [Implied] Only five students got A's on the midterm exam because they studied the night before the exam and reviewed their notes just before walking into class to take the test. Method of agreement. The argument is strong.

20. *Conclusion*: Jackie M's criminal behavior is caused by high outdoor temperatures. Correlation. Weak.

Chapter 8

1. Inference to the best explanation:
   Phenomenon Q.
   E provides the best explanation for Q.
   Therefore, it is probable that E is true.

   Enumerative induction:

   X percent of the observed members of group A have property P.
   Therefore, X percent of all members of group A probably have property P.

   Analogical induction:

   Thing A has properties P1, P2, P3 plus the property P4.
   Thing B has properties P1, P2, and P3.
   Therefore, thing B probably has property P4.

2. A standard of internal and external consistency that a theory must meet to be eligible for further consideration.

3. Testability: Whether there is some way to determine if a theory is true.
   Fruitfulness: The number of novel predictions made.
   Scope: The amount of diverse phenomena explained.
   Simplicity: The number of assumptions made. Conservatism: How well a theory fits with existing knowledge.

4. With testable theories there is a way to determine whether they are true or false; untestable theories cannot be checked.

5. Four steps to finding the best explanation:
   Step 1. State the theory and check for consistency.
   Step 2. Assess the evidence for the theory.
   Step 3. Scrutinize alternative theories.
   Step 4. Test the theories with the criteria of adequacy.

6. The best theory is the eligible theory that meets the criteria of adequacy better than any of its competitors.

7. d

8. a, b

9. a, b

10. a

11. Phenomenon: The rise in popularity of a newly elected president. (1) The so-called honeymoon effect in which a new president enjoys popularity until he or she is involved in serious or controversial decisions.

12. Phenomenon: Your friend has been skipping class, and you haven't seen her in days. (1) She's in bed with the flu.

13. Phenomenon: Ships, boats, and planes have been disappearing off the coast of Florida for years. (1) Considering the meteorological and atmospheric conditions of the area, it's normal for some craft to be lost from time to time.

14. Phenomenon: The rapid spread of an unknown, dangerous, viral disease throughout North America. (1) The lack of awareness and defenses against a new mutated virus.
15. (1) People buy high-ticket merchandise because of subliminal advertising—their minds are being influenced by imperceptible stimuli designed by ad execs. (2) The purchase of high-ticket merchandise. (3) Normal advertising and sales ploys influence people to purchase high-ticket merchandise. (4) The alternative theory is more plausible.
16. (1) In cold fusion research, skepticism skews scientists' observations. (2) The lack of evidence for cold fusion. (3) Cold fusion does not exist. (4) The alternative theory is more plausible.
17. (1) Eleanor must have a system that enables her to pick winning numbers. (2) Eleanor's winning the state lottery twice in nine months. (3) Coincidence. (4) The coincidence theory is more plausible.
18. (1) The embezzlement was caused by the divorce of his parents when he was very young. (2) The embezzlement. (3) He embezzled because he needed the money to pay debts. (4) The alternative theory is more plausible.
19. (1) Schoolchildren do poorly in school because of the low or negative expectations of their teachers. (2) Poor performance of schoolchildren. (3) Students do poorly because teachers want them to fail. (4) The expectations theory is more plausible.
20. (1) The woman is possessed. (2) The woman's bizarre behavior, including stigmata (bleeding from the palms). (3) The woman suffers from some form of psychosis, which can manifest itself in many strange symptoms, including bleeding from the skin. (4) The alternative theory is more plausible.

Chapter 9

1. An observational consequence implied or predicted by a hypothesis.
2. No. Hypotheses often contain concepts that aren't in the data.
3. If H, then C.
   Not-C.
   Therefore, not-H.
4. If H, then C.
   C.
   Therefore, H.
5. It's always possible that we will someday find evidence that undermines or conflicts with the evidence we have now.
6. A hypothesis can always be saved from refutation by making changes in the background claims.
7. Hypothesis: Lack of sufficient lighting on Blind Man's Curve is contributing to an increase in automobile accidents. Test implication: If the hypothesis

is true, ensuring sufficient lighting on Blind Man's Curve should cause a decrease in accidents.

8. Hypothesis: Juan did the fatal stabbing. Test implication: If the hypothesis is true, at least some of the blood on his shirt is likely to belong to the victim, which a DNA test can confirm.

9. Hypothesis: The lights were coming from a meteor fireball breaking up in the atmosphere, and the claim of alien spacecraft was the result of misinterpretation caused by viewer expectation and poor viewing conditions. Test implication: If the hypothesis is true, scientists should be able to confirm that a meteor fireball did enter the atmosphere at the time the mysterious lights were said to appear.

10. (1) Maria drank contaminated water from the creek. (2) Maria ate poisonous berries. (3) The water from the creek contained toxins that can cause gastrointestinal illness, and Maria drank some; Maria ate berries that were poisonous and known to cause gastrointestinal illness. (4) Evidence that Maria drank the water and that it contained the suspected toxins would confirm the hypothesis; failure to detect the toxins would disconfirm the hypothesis.

11. (1) Students pay more attention with two teachers in the class. (2) Students get more individual attention from the teachers. (3) Students concentrate more on their studies when two teachers are in the class; when there are two teachers, they spend more time with each student. (4) Evidence that students were paying more attention would confirm the hypothesis; evidence that students did not pay more attention would disconfirm the hypothesis.

12. (1) Higher levels of air pollution cause more stress. (2) An increase in crime causes more stress. (3) Air pollution levels have increased, and they contribute to stress; crime has increased, and the amount of crime correlates with stress. (4) Evidence of pollution causing stress and of a significant increase in pollution would confirm the hypothesis; evidence showing no change in air pollution levels would disconfirm it.

13. (1) Super Cold-Stopper With Beta-Carotene prevents colds. (2) The Vaughns have been exposed less often to people with colds. (3) Taking Super Cold-Stopper With Beta-Carotene decreases the incidence of colds; the Vaughns have come in contact with fewer people with colds. (4) Evidence that the product does in fact decrease the incidence of colds would confirm the hypothesis; a failure to demonstrate this effect in well-controlled studies would disconfirm the hypothesis.

14. Esther stole the book from the library. Test implication: Esther should be seen on security cameras stealing the book. Evidence: Video from the security camera clearly showing Esther stealing the book.

15. Most people—both white and black—are economically better off now than their parents were thirty years ago. Test implication: Economic data from

the past thirty years should show significant increases in several indicators of economic well-being. Evidence: Data from several trustworthy sources showing the relevant changes in the indicators.

16. The health care system in this country is worse now than it was when Barack Obama was president. Test implication: There should be significant declines in several standard measures of the quality of a health care system, including the number of people who have access to health care, the effectiveness of medical treatments, and infant mortality rates. Evidence: Reliable data from nonpartisan sources that show the relevant declines.

17. d

18. a, b

19. a, b, c

20. Theory: Joseph is possessed. Phenomenon: Joseph's strange behavior. Alternative theory: Joseph is an epileptic. The evidence for the possession theory is almost nonexistent. Strange behavior, common among humans, is not evidence that seizures are an indication not of possession but of epilepsy and other neurological disorders. The epilepsy theory is testable; the possession theory is not. The possession theory is a failure in fruitfulness, scope, simplicity, and conservatism; the epilepsy theory does well by these criteria. The latter is the better theory.

Chapter 10

1. Straw man.
2. Appeal to ignorance.
3. Appeal to the person.
4. Appeal to the person.
5. Red herring.
6. Appeal to the person.
7. Appeal to emotion.
8. Appeal to popularity.
9. Begging the question.
10. Composition.
11. False dilemma.
12. Appeal to ignorance.
13. Appeal to the person.
14. Slippery slope.
15. False dilemma.
16. Hasty generalization.
17. Dysphemism.
18. Straw man.
19. Red herring.
20. Rhetorical definition.

Chapter 11

1. A moral statement is a statement asserting that an action is right or wrong (moral or immoral) or that something (such as a person or motive) is good or bad.

2. At least one premise is a moral statement that asserts a general moral principle or moral standard. At least one premise makes a nonmoral claim. And the conclusion is a moral statement, or judgment, about a particular case (usually a particular kind of action).

3. Consistency with our considered moral judgments; consistency with our experience of the moral life; workability in real-life situations.

4. By trying to think of counterexamples to it.

5. No.

6. Of course we should have offered protection to the Kurds. They were in grave danger and they asked for our help. *And it is our duty to offer protection to people if they are in grave danger and they request our help.*

7. The supplement manufacturers knew that the herb ephedra was dangerous. *If a company is aware that its product is dangerous, it is obligated to remove it from the market.* So they should have removed it from the market.

8. The Democrats insulted the president. *Insults to the president should never be allowed.* They should have never been allowed to do that.

9. The Smiths were consenting adults who were having sex in the privacy of their own home. *Sex between consenting adults in the privacy of their own home is morally permissible.* These actions by the Smiths are morally permissible.

10. Randi killed his neighbor, and the killing was not in self-defense. *Killing someone except in self-defense is morally wrong.* He should not have committed such an act.

11. Lying is wrong under all circumstances. *Counterexample: Lying to save the lives of a thousand people.*

12. People who commit crimes should not be punished—they should be retrained to act legally. *Counterexample: Adolf Hitler committed massive crimes against humanity. Wasn't he deserving of punishment?*

13. All humans, whatever their circumstances, have full moral rights. *Counterexample: Do insane individuals have full moral rights? murderers? people in comas?*

14. All creatures that are alive and sensitive to stimulation are equally valuable and should be accorded equal respect. *Counterexample: Is it just as wrong to kill a goldfish as it is a horse? Should we give turtles the same respect we give to children?*

15. The morally right action is the one that produces the most happiness, everyone considered. *Counterexample: Is it morally right to arbitrarily imprison and torture an innocent person if doing so will produce the most happiness for the most people?*

16. Right actions are those that are in one's own self-interest. *Counterexample: Murdering a friend could conceivably be in your own best interest—would it therefore be morally permissible?*

17. Medical experimentation on a patient without her consent. *Defense: If the experimentation could save hundreds of lives and would have no major negative consequences for the patient or for society, it would be justified.*

18. Taking food, shelter, and other resources from rich people and distributing them equally among poor people. *Defense: A more equal distribution of resources would result in greater happiness for a greater number.*

19. Any form of expression or speech that offends people of faith should not be tolerated. *Penthouse* magazine definitely offends people of faith. Ban it! *Evaluation: The first premise is dubious, for it would have us violate the autonomy of persons—by, for example, dramatically curtailing freedom of speech.*

20. Anyone who disagrees with the basic moral dictums of the prevailing culture should be censored. Dr. Tilden's graduation speech clearly was inconsistent with the prevailing moral opinions on campus. She should be reprimanded. *Evaluation: The first premise runs counter to several plausible moral principles, including respect for autonomy, freedom of speech and conscience, and tolerance.*

Notes

Chapter 2

1. W. K. Clifford, "The Ethics of Belief," in *The Rationality of Belief in God*, ed. George I. Mavrodes (Englewood Cliff, NJ: Prentice-Hall, 1970), 159–160.

2. Bertrand Russell, *Let the People Think* (London: William Clowes, 1941), 2.

3. Thomas Gilovich, *How We Know What Isn't So* (New York: The Free Press, 1991), 54.

4. For a more thorough review of various forms of relativism, see Theodore Schick and Lewis Vaughn, *How to Think About Weird Things*, 7th ed. (New York: McGraw-Hill, 2014), 68–92.

Chapter 6

1. Stephen Law, *Believing Bullshit: How Not to Get Sucked into an Intellectual Black Hole* (Amherst, NY: Prometheus Books, 2011).

2. Eugene Kiely and Lori Robertson, "How to Spot Fake News," FactCheck.org, November 18, 2016.

3. "Work Farce," *New York Post*, June 22, 2003.

4. "Soldiers Sweep Up Saddam's Hit Goons," *New York Post*, July 1, 2003.

Chapter 7

1. David G. Myers, "The Power of Coincidence," *Skeptic Magazine* 9, no. 4 (September 2002).

2. Julie Steenhuysen, *Reuters*, "U.S. Study Clears Measles Vaccine of Autism Link," September 4, 2008.

Chapter 8

1. Charles Darwin, *The Origin of Species* (New York: Collier, 1962), 476.

2. W. V. Quine and J. S. Ullman, *The Web of Belief* (New York: Random House, 1970), 43–44.

3. For the latest research and discussion on the placebo effect, see A. Hrobjartsson and P. C. Gotzsche, *New England Journal of Medicine* 344 (2001): 1594–1602; J. C. Bailar, *New England Journal of Medicine* 344 (2001): 1630–1632; and Keith Bauer, "Clinical Use of Placebo," http://www.ama-assn.org., July 2001, journal discussion.

4. See C. Hill and F. Doyan, "Review of Randomized Trials of Homeopathy," *Review of Epidemiology* 38:139–142, 1990; Report, Homoeopathic Medicine Group, Commission of the European Communities, December 1996; J. Wise, "Health Authority Stops Buying Homeopathy," *British Medical Journal* 314(1997): 1574; K. Linde et al., "Are the Clinical Effects of Homeopathy Placebo Effects?" *Lancet*, 350, no. 9081 (1997): 824.

5. "Shark Attacks Are Down for Third Year in a Row," January 29, 2004,.http://www.CNN.com.

6. "Study Examines Cancer Risk from Hair Dye," January 28, 2004, http://www.CNN.com.

Chapter 9

1.   I owe the inspiration and general outline for this section to Theodore Schick, Jr., in Theodore Schick, Jr., and Lewis Vaughn, *How to Think About Weird Things,* 7th ed. (New York: McGraw-Hill, 2014).

2.   See Stephen Barrett et al., *Consumer Health,* 6th ed. (New York: WCB/McGraw-Hill, 1993), 239–240.

3.   Thomas S. Kuhn, *The Copernican Revolution: Planetary Astronomy in the Development of Western Thought* (Cambridge, MA: Harvard University Press, 1957), 179.

4.   Section 4a of Act 590 of the Acts of Arkansas of 1981, "Balanced Treatment for Creation-Science and Evolution-Science Act."

5.   National Academy of Sciences, *Science and Creationism* (Washington, DC: National Academy Press, 1998).

6.   National Academy of Sciences, *Science and Creationism* (Washington, DC: National Academy Press, 1998).

7.   Theodosius Dobzhansky, quoted in National Academy of Sciences, *Science and Creationism,* www.nap.edu/openbook.php?record_id=6024

8.   National Academy of Sciences, "Preface," in *Science and Creationism.*

9.   Theodore Schick, Jr., in Theodore Schick, Jr., and Lewis Vaughn, *Doing Philosophy: An Introduction Through Thought Experiments* (New York: McGraw-Hill, 2010), 490, 492.

10.   Richard Wiseman, Matthew Smith, and Jeff Wiseman, "Eyewitness Testimony and the Paranormal," *Skeptical Inquirer,* November/December (1995).

11.   Tom Byrne and Matthew Normand, "The Demon-Haunted Sentence," *Skeptical Inquirer,* March/April (2000).

12.   Theodore Schick and Lewis Vaughn, *How to Think About Weird Things,* 3rd ed. (San Francisco: McGraw-Hill, 2002), 190–191.

13.   Robert T. Carroll, "Ouija Board," The Skeptic's Dictionary, October 27, 2003, http://skepdic.com.

Chapter 10

1.   The inspiration for this unconventional categorization comes primarily from Ludwig F. Schlecht, "Classifying Fallacies Logically," *Teaching Philosophy* 14, no. 1 (1991): 53–64; and Greg Bassham et al., *Critical Thinking: A Student's Introduction* (San Francisco: McGraw-Hill, 2002).

2.   W. Ross Winterowd and Geoffrey R. Winterowd, *The Critical Reader, Thinker, and Writer* (Mountain View, CA: Mayfield Publishing, 1992), 447 448.

3.   Reported in Richard Whately, *Elements of Logic* (London: Longman, Greens, and Co., 1826).

Chatper 11

1.   "Ethics," Internet Encyclopedia of Philosophy, http://www.utm.edu/research/iep.

2.   Immanuel Kant, *Groundwork of the Metaphysic of Morals,* trans., H. J. Paton (New York: Harper and Row, 1964), 88.

Chatper 12

1.   Student paper reproduced by permission of Mitchell S. McKinney, University of Missouri, http://www.missouri.edu/,commpjb/comm104/Sample_Papers/Free_ Speech/free_speech.html.

Glossary

ad hoc hypothesis: A hypothesis, or theory, that cannot be verified independently of the phenomenon it's supposed to explain. Ad hoc hypotheses always make a theory less simple—and therefore less credible.

ad hominem (appeal to the person): The fallacy of rejecting a claim by criticizing the person who makes it rather than the claim itself. *Ad hominem* means "to the man."

affirming the antecedent: *See* **modus ponens.**

affirming the consequent: An invalid argument form:

> If *p*, then *q*.
> *q*.
> Therefore, *p*.

analogical induction: *See* **argument by analogy.**

analogy: A comparison of two or more things alike in specific respects.

antecedent: The first part of a conditional statement (If *p*, then *q*.), the component that begins with the word *if*. *See* **conditional statement.**

appeal to authority, fallacious: The fallacy of relying on the opinion of someone deemed to be an expert who in fact is *not* an expert.

appeal to common practice: The fallacy of accepting or rejecting a claim based solely on what groups of people generally do or how they behave (when the action or behavior is irrelevant to the truth of the claim).

appeal to emotion: The fallacy of using emotions in place of relevant reasons as premises in an argument.

appeal to ignorance: The fallacy of arguing that a lack of evidence proves something. In one type of this fallacy, the problem arises by thinking that a claim must be true because it hasn't been shown to be false. In another type, the breakdown in logic comes when you argue that a claim must be false because it hasn't been proved to be true.

appeal to pity: The attempt to persuade people to accept a conclusion by evoking their pity, compassion, or empathy.

appeal to popularity (or to the masses): The fallacy of arguing that a claim must be true merely because a substantial number of people believe it.

appeal to the person: *See* **ad hominem.**

appeal to tradition: The fallacy of arguing that a claim must be true just because it's part of a tradition.

apple polishing: The attempt to persuade people to accept a conclusion by flattering them.

argument: A group of statements in which some of them (the premises) are intended to support another of them (the conclusion).

argument by analogy (analogical induction): An argument making use of analogy, reasoning that because two or more things are similar in several respects, they must be similar in some further respect.

background information: Background information is that huge collection of very well-supported beliefs that we all rely on to inform our actions and choices. A great deal of this lore consists of basic facts about everyday things, beliefs based on very good evidence (including our own personal observations and the statements of excellent authorities), and strongly justified claims that we would regard as "common sense" or "common knowledge." Background beliefs include obvious claims such as "The sun is hot," "The Easter bunny is not real," "Humans are mortal," "Fire burns," and "George Washington lived in the eighteenth century."

begging the question: The fallacy of attempting to establish the conclusion of an argument by using that conclusion as a premise. Also called arguing in a circle.

biased sample: A sample that does not properly represent the target group. *See* **representative sample.**

burden of proof: The weight of evidence or argument required by one side in a debate or disagreement.

causal argument: An inductive argument whose conclusion contains a causal claim.

causal claim: A statement about the causes of things.

claim: A statement; an assertion that something is or is not the case.

cogent argument: A strong inductive argument with all true premises.

composition: The fallacy of arguing that what is true of the parts must be true of the whole. The error is thinking that the characteristics of the parts are somehow transferred to the whole, something that is not always the case.

compound statement: A statement composed of at least two constituent, or simple, statements.

conclusion: In an argument, the statement that the premises are intended to support.

conditional statement: An "if-then" statement; it consists of the antecedent (the part introduced by the word *if*) and the consequent (the part introduced by the word *then*).

confidence level: In statistical theory, the probability that the sample will accurately represent the target group within the margin of error.

conjunct: One of two simple statements joined by a connective to form a compound statement.

conjunction: Two simple statements joined by a connective to form a compound statement.

consequent: The part of a conditional statement (If *p*, then *q*) introduced by the word *then*.

conservatism: A criterion of adequacy for judging the worth of theories. A conservative theory is one that fits with our established beliefs.

criteria of adequacy: The standards used to judge the worth of explanatory theories. They include *testability, fruitfulness, scope, simplicity,* and *conservatism.*

critical thinking: The systematic evaluation or formulation of beliefs, or statements, by rational standards.

decision-point fallacy: Arguing that because a line or distinction cannot be drawn at any point in a process, there are no differences or gradations in that process.

deductive argument: An argument intended to provide logically conclusive support for its conclusion.

denying the antecedent: An invalid argument form:
> If *p*, then *q*.
> Not *p*.
> Therefore, not *q*.

denying the consequent: *See* **modus tollens.**

disjunct: A simple statement that is a component of a disjunction.

disjunction: A compound statement of the form "Either p or q." A disjunction is true even if only one disjunct is true, and false only if both disjuncts are false.

disjunctive syllogism: A valid argument form:
> Either p or q.
> Not p.
> Therefore, q.

In the syllogism's second premise, either disjunct can be denied.

division: The fallacy of arguing that what is true of the whole must be true of the parts. The error is thinking that characteristics of the whole must transfer to the parts or that traits of the group must be the same as traits of individuals in the group.

dysphemism: Words used to convey negative attitudes or emotions in place of neutral or positive ones.

enumerative induction: An inductive argument pattern in which we reason from premises about individual members of a group to conclusions about the group as a whole.

equivocation: The fallacy of using a word in two different senses in an argument.

euphemism: Words used to convey positive or neutral attitudes or emotions in place of more negative ones.

expert: Someone who is more knowledgeable in a particular subject area or field than most others are.

explanation: A statement or statements intended to tell why or how something is the case.

fallacy: An argument form that is both common and defective; a recurring mistake in reasoning.

false dilemma: The fallacy of asserting that there are only two alternatives to consider when there are actually more than two.

faulty analogy: A defective argument by analogy.

fruitfulness: A criterion of adequacy for judging the worth of theories. A fruitful theory is one that makes novel predictions.

gambler's fallacy: The error of thinking that previous events can affect the probabilities in the random event at hand.

genetic fallacy: The fallacy of arguing that a claim is true or false solely because of its abstract or nonhuman origins.

hasty generalization: The fallacy of drawing a conclusion about a target group based on an inadequate sample size.

hypothetical syllogism: A valid argument made up of three hypothetical, or conditional, statements:
> If p then q.
> If q, then r.
> Therefore, if p, then r.

indicator words: Words that frequently accompany arguments and signal that a premise or conclusion is present.

inductive argument: An argument in which the premises are intended to provide probable, not conclusive, support for its conclusion.

inference: The process of reasoning from a premise or premises to a conclusion based on those premises.

inference to the best explanation: A form of inductive reasoning in which we reason from premises about a state of affairs to an explanation for that state of affairs:
> Phenomenon Q.
> E provides the best explanation for Q.
> Therefore, it is probable that E is true.

innuendo: Suggesting something denigrating about a person without explicitly stating it.

invalid argument: A deductive argument that fails to provide conclusive support for its conclusion.

logic: The study of good reasoning, or inference, and the rules that govern it.

margin of error: The variation between the values derived from a sample and the true values of the whole target group.

modus ponens (affirming the antecedent): A valid argument form:

> If p, then q.
>
> p.
>
> Therefore, q.

modus tollens (denying the consequent): A valid argument form:

> If p, then q.
>
> Not q.
>
> Therefore, not p.

moral statement: A statement asserting that an action is right or wrong (moral or immoral) or that something (such as a person or motive) is good or bad.

necessary condition: A condition for the occurrence of an event without which the event cannot occur.

peer pressure: Group pressure to accept or reject a claim based solely on what one's peers think or do.

philosophical skepticism: The view that we know much less than we think we do or nothing at all.

philosophical skeptics: Those who embrace philosophical skepticism.

post hoc, ergo propter hoc ("after that, therefore because of that"): The fallacy of reasoning that just because B followed A, A must have caused B.

premise: In an argument, a statement, or reason, given in support of the conclusion.

property in question: *See* **relevant property.**

random sample: A sample that is selected randomly from a target group in such a way as to ensure that the sample is representative. In a simple random selection, every member of the target group has an equal chance of being selected for the sample.

red herring: The fallacy of deliberately raising an irrelevant issue during an argument.

The basic pattern is to put forth a claim and then couple it with additional claims that may seem to support it but in fact are mere distractions.

relevant property (property in question): In enumerative induction, a property, or characteristic, that is of interest in the target group.

representative sample: In enumerative induction, a sample that resembles the target group in all relevant ways. *See* **biased sample.**

rhetoric: The use of nonargumentative, emotive words and phrases to persuade or influence an audience.

rhetorical definitions: Influencing someone through an emotion-charged skewed definition.

ridicule: The use of derision, sarcasm, laughter, or mockery to disparage a person or idea.

sample (sample member): In enumerative induction, the observed members of the target group.

scare tactics: The attempt to persuade people to accept a conclusion by engendering in them an unwarranted fear.

scope: A criterion of adequacy for judging the worth of theories. A theory with scope is one that explains or predicts phenomena other than that which it was introduced to explain.

simplicity: A criterion of adequacy for judging the worth of theories. A simple theory is one that makes minimal assumptions.

slippery slope: The fallacy of arguing, without good reasons, that taking a particular step will inevitably lead to further, undesirable steps.

social relativism: The view that truth is relative to societies.

sound argument: A deductively valid argument that has true premises.

statement (claim): An assertion that something is or is not the case.

stereotyping: Drawing an unwarranted conclusion or generalization about an entire group of people.

straw man: The fallacy of distorting, weakening, or oversimplifying someone's position so it can be more easily attacked or refuted.

strong argument: An inductive argument that succeeds in providing very probable—but not conclusive—support for its conclusion.

subjective relativism: The idea that truth depends on what someone believes.

subjectivist fallacy: Accepting the notion of subjective relativism or using it to try to support a claim.

sufficient condition: A condition for the occurrence of an event that guarantees that the event occurs.

syllogism: A deductive argument made up of three statements—two premises and a conclusion. *See* **modus ponens** and **modus tollens.**

target group (target population): In enumerative induction, the whole collection of individuals under study.

testability: A criterion of adequacy for judging the worth of theories. A testable theory is one in which there is some way to determine whether the theory is true or false—that is, it predicts something other than what it was introduced to explain.

TEST formula: A four-step procedure for evaluating the worth of a theory:
> Step 1. State the **T**heory and check for consistency.
> Step 2. Assess the **E**vidence for the theory.
> Step 3. **S**crutinize alternative theories.
> Step 4. **T**est the theories with the criteria of adequacy.

theoretical explanation: A theory, or hypothesis, that tries to explain why something is the way it is, why something is the case, or why something happened.

truth preserving: A characteristic of a valid deductive argument in which the logical structure guarantees the truth of the conclusion if the premises are true.

tu quoque ("you're another"): A type of ad hominem fallacy that argues that a claim must be true (or false) just because the claimant is hypocritical.

two wrongs make a right: Arguing that your doing something morally wrong is justified because someone else has done the same (or similar) thing.

valid argument: A deductive argument that succeeds in providing conclusive support for its conclusion.

weak argument: An inductive argument that fails to provide strong support for its conclusion.

worldview: A philosophy of life; a set of beliefs and theories that helps us make sense of a wide range of issues in life.

Credits

1.1 – AP Photo, File

2.1 – Photo by William Lovelace/Express/
Getty Images

2.2 – Everett Historical/Shutterstock.com

3.1 – Dilbert @2003 Scott Adams. Used
by permission of Andrews McMeel
Syndication. All rights reserved.

4.1 – Rawpixel.com/Shutterstock.com

5.1 – jannoon028/Shutterstock.com

5.2 – www.CartoonStock.com

6.1 – Reuters/Alamy Stock Photo

6.2 – heliography/Stockimo/Alamy
Stock Photo

7.1 – N/A

7.2 – N/A

7.3 – AP Photo/The Wichita Eagle, Mike
Hutmacher, File

8.1 – PCN Photography/Alamy Stock Photo

8.2 – David Alexander Liu/Shutterstock

9.1 – csp_pasiphae/Fotosearch.com

9.2 – ScienceCartoonsPlus.com

9.3 – Christopher Jones/Alamy Stock Photo

9.4 – Gaertner/Alamy Stock Photo

10.1 – Marben/Shutterstock.com

10.2 – Mimi and Eunice, September 15, 2011

11.1 – Brandon Bourdages/Shutterstock.com

Index

Note: Page references followed by a "*t*" indicate table; page references in italics indicate photographs